## "FOR THE GOOD OF THEIR SOULS"

D1600198

A VOLUME IN THE SERIES

Native Americans of the Northeast

EDITED BY

*Colin G. Calloway, Jean M. O'Brien, and Lisa T. Brooks*

# "FOR THE GOOD OF THEIR SOULS"

Performing Christianity in
Eighteenth-Century Mohawk Country

## WILLIAM B. HART

University of Massachusetts Press
*Amherst and Boston*

Copyright © 2020 by University of Massachusetts Press
All rights reserved
Printed in the United States of America

ISBN 978-1-62534-495-3 (paper); 494-6 (hardcover)

Designed by Sally Nichols
Set in Caslon Classico
Printed and bound by Maple Press, Inc.

Cover design by Frank Gutbrod
Cover art: Detail from *Classroom of a Native American School, 1786*, by James Peachey.
Courtesy of Bridgeman Images.

Library of Congress Cataloging-in-Publication Data

Names: Hart, William B., author.
Title: "For the good of their souls" : performing Christianity in
eighteenth-century Mohawk country / William B. Hart.
Other titles: Native Americans of the Northeast.
Description: Amherst : University of Massachusetts Press, [2020] | Series:
Native Americans of the Northeast | Includes bibliographical references
and index.
Identifiers: LCCN 2019044406 | ISBN 9781625344946 (hardcover) | ISBN
9781625344953 (paperback) | ISBN 9781613767405 (ebook) | ISBN
9781613767412 (ebook)
Subjects: LCSH: Mohawk Indians—New York (State)—Religion. | Missions—New
York (State)—History—18th century. | New York (State)—Church
history—18th century.
Classification: LCC E99.M8 H37 2020 | DDC 974.7004/975542--dc23
LC record available at https://lccn.loc.gov/2019044406

British Library Cataloguing-in-Publication Data
A catalog record for this book is available from the British Library.

An earlier version of chapter 4 was originally published as William B. Hart, "Mohawk School-
masters and Catechists in Mid-Eighteenth-Century Iroquoia: An Experiment in Fostering
Literacy and Religious Change," in *The Language Encounter in the Americas, 1492–1800: A
Collection of Essays*, edited by Edward G. Gray and Norman Fiering (New York: Berghahn
Books, 2000), 232–57. An earlier version of chapter 6 was originally published as William B.
Hart, "'As Formerly under Their Respective Chiefs': Factionalism and the Foundation of
Two Exile Mohawk Communities in Upper Canada, 1785–1800," in *Proceedings of the North-
eastern Native Peoples & the American Revolutionary Era, 1760–1810*, edited by David Naumec
(Mashantucket, CT: Mashantucket Pequot Museum & Research Center, 2008) 16–23.

To Ewa.

# CONTENTS

# ACKNOWLEDGMENTS

This book began initially as an interrogation and critique of the term "nominal Christian" used by many historians to describe the quality of religiosity among eighteenth-century baptized Mohawks living in the Mohawk Valley of New York. My hope is that this study has revealed the inadequacy of that term, for baptized Mohawks reflected a broad range of identification with Christianity. Historians today should not ascribe a general state, degree, or quality of Christian identification to the entire Mohawk nation of the eighteenth century, as they so often did earlier. Rather, we must look closely at individuals and their communities and assess their relationships with missionaries and their institutions.

To parse through the evidence and arrive at some interpretation of what eighteenth-century baptized Mohawks did, I have relied heavily on two scholarly strategies beyond the discipline of mere history: ethnohistory, a methodology, and performance theory. Ethnohistory is, in brief, an interdisciplinary methodology that relies on the concepts and methods of several disciplines—for example, history, anthropology, archaeology, linguistics, comparative religion—to discern the essence of a culture or society that left few written records. The vibrant and vital conversations of ethnohistorians and historians of the Native American past drew me to this field and to this exercise of unpacking the term "nominal Christian." Performance theory permits the historian to assess and frame what his or her subjects did, which in turn illuminates complexities of agency. Since my early but brief career in the professional theater, I have been intrigued by the roles that everyday people enact in their everyday lives. Moreover, I share the belief of many scholars of religion that faith is what one *does*, not necessarily what one believes.

Over the years, many smart people with deep knowledge in these scholarly and theoretical fields helped me to think and rethink and to write and to rewrite this book. I must first acknowledge the incomparable training I received from my three graduate school mentors: the late William G. McLoughlin (history, Brown University), a model scholar-activist; Shepard Krech III (anthropology, Brown), a highly disciplined and inspirational scholar; and James Merrell (history, Vassar College), the epitome of a careful, critical thinker about Native American history. Others from whom I have learned at professional conferences or during casual conversations include Colin Calloway, Jean O'Brian, Dan Richter, Dan Mandell, Ed Gray, Norm Fiering, Tiya Miles, Theda Purdue, Mike Green, Rebecca Kugel, Nancy Shoemaker, Joanne Melish, Susan Sleeper-Smith, Rachel Wheeler, James Axtell, Francis Jennings, James Brooks, Bill Paden, Melanie McAlister, Patrick Rael, Al Raboteau, Dean Snow, Scott Lyons, Karim Tiro, Harold Prinz, Jere Danielle, David Silverman, John Saillant, Louise Burkhart, Patricia Bonomi, Larry Yarborough, Andrew Cayton, Fredrika Teute, and Mary Beth Nevins. My apologies for overlooking those of you with whom I served on various academic panels and with whom I have shared research tables. I learned much from you, as well, and I am deeply grateful to all for their counsel and friendship.

I also benefited from access to several collections at world-class institutions, libraries, and archives. I began this book at Brown University and thus must thank the library staffs at the Rockefeller Library, the John Carter Brown Library, and the Hay Library. As a Ford Foundation Minority Postdoctoral Fellow and a fellow in the Center for the Study of American Religion at Princeton University, I enjoyed the fellowship of Robert Wuthnow and his friendly support staff, as well as that of the superb staff at the archives in Princeton's Firestone Library. A Thurgood Marshall Dissertation Fellowship at Dartmouth College, a Mary Catherine Mooney Fellowship at the Boston Athenaeum in Boston, a Gilder Lehrman Fellowship at the New-York Historical Society, and a

Mellon Resident Research Fellowship at the American Philosophical Society Library in Philadelphia allowed me to discover great treasures housed at each institution. I am also grateful for the support and assistance I have received over the years from the staff in Special Collections and in Inter-Library Loan at Middlebury College, from the New York State Library, and from the New York Public Library.

Several colleagues in the History Department at Middlebury College also deserve special thanks for their ongoing support and comradery: Travis Jacobs, Jim Ralph, Darien Davis, and Ian Barrow. I also want to thank the editorial team at the University of Massachusetts Press, who have kept the faith.

Finally, I want to thank my wife, Eva Garcelon-Hart, for her love and her steadfast support as I brought this book to completion. And I thank my daughter, Emily, for her love and patience while Dad devoted what must have seemed like an inordinate amount of time and life to this book.

FIGURE 1. A Map of the Country of the Five Nations, belonging to the Province of New York, Cadwallader Colden, 1747.

—*Courtesy of the John Carter Brown Library, Providence, Rhode Island. Licensed for use under CC BY-SA 4.0 (https://creativecommons.org/licenses/by-sa/4.0/).*

# "FOR THE GOOD OF THEIR SOULS"

# Mohawk Beliefs and the Needs of the Soul

William Andrews, the Church of England minister assigned in 1712 by the Society for the Propagation of the Gospel in Foreign Parts (SPG) to the Mohawks living west of present-day Albany, New York, wasted no time establishing his mission. Immediately upon his arrival in mid-November at Fort Hunter, the recently built English fort located south and east of the Schoharie Creek–Mohawk River confluence and across the river from the Mohawk village Tiononderoge, Andrews preached a sermon and baptized two Mohawk children in the fort's twenty-four-by-twenty-four-foot board-and-shingle chapel. Thereafter, he "read prayers & instructed them every Wednesday and Lordsday," using an array of texts—a large Bible, two Common Prayer Books, a book of homilies—to teach the Mohawks "the chiefe fundamentals of Religion," which included "the Doctrine of God, of the Creation, of Providence, and Man's fall and Restoration of faith, Repentance, the nature & use of the Sacraments etc." He deemed his hearers ready to receive the Gospel, perhaps because Lawrence Claessen, his Dutch interpreter, who knew Mohawk but very little English, explained that many were "already baptized, some by priests from Canada, others by Dutch ministers." Regardless, between November 1712 and September 1713, Andrews baptized forty-five Mohawks, ranging from infants to the elderly. By 1715, the number of baptized Mohawks who regularly attended his church services grew to around 100, nearly 18 percent of the total Mohawk population of about 580, two-thirds of whom lived at Tiononderoge.[1]

Within two years of his arrival, Andrews boasted that at Tiononderoge, the village where most of his initial Mohawk congregants resided, one could find "a great many very good women [who] can give a good acc[oun]t of their faith." After church on Sundays, several of them would "meet together at one of their Wigwams or houses and one or two of them that have better Memorys than the rest," Andrews noted, would "repeat over again what the[y] heard to the others." He learned that some of the women even prayed as much as "an hour together." Judging by the women's expressive behavior, Andrews had every reason to feel good about his early efforts.[2]

Because Haudenosaunee women exercised control over matters that took place in their villages—child rearing, horticulture, providing hospitality to visitors—the Mohawk women who constituted this Sunday-afternoon sodality re-created in the semiprivacy of their longhouse a village event: the church service. Through mimesis—the act of imitation—the women reviewed, deconstructed, and reenacted for themselves Andrews's liturgy. From Andrews's naive perspective, these women performed his liturgy in order to solidify their emergent faith. However, it is most likely that these women engaged in a reiterative performance of a ritual—the Sunday church service—using what Joseph Roach has called "expressive movements as mnemonic reserves, including patterned movements made and remembered by bodies, residual movements retained implicitly in images or words" in an effort to fix Andrews's service within.[3] Anthropologist Roy Rappaport defines a ritual as a set order of acts and utterances, encoded not by the performers but performed by them through their participation. In this case, the Mohawk women repeated the hymns, prayers, and homily they had sung, read, and heard only hours earlier. Anthropologist Richard Bauman characterizes such performances as "taking the role of the other" and looking reflexively at one's self in that role. These Mohawk women were doing just that: trying on, so to speak, and committing to memory Andrews's Church of England service, perhaps to share later with their children and Mohawk brethren; or perhaps to make sense of the service, which Andrews delivered in English, with which Claessen was largely unfamiliar; or perhaps to compare and contrast the Church of England service with the more familiar liturgy of the Catholic and Dutch Reformed Churches.[4]

Without their thoughts, it is difficult to discern with certainty the Mohawk women's intentions. However, one thing is clear: Claessen's observation that most of the Mohawk women were familiar with

Christianity, and thus knew how to perform it, revealed more to Andrews than he may have realized at the time. The Mohawks, the keepers of the eastern door of the Longhouse Confederacy, had long ago developed and continued to maintain transactional relationships with European priests and ministers and their religions, in the same way that they had long collaborated with European merchants in the transatlantic trade. By opening the door of the longhouse to French Jesuits, Dutch dominies, and now Anglican priests, the Mohawks calculated the benefits to be accrued by individuals, communities, and the nation through reciprocity, a tradition of mutuality and cooperation intrinsic to Native culture for fostering good, beneficent relationships.[5] As example, Haudenosaunee people of the same clan cared for the needs of visiting clanspersons of other nations. Moieties, related kinship groups, or "sides," within clans, took care of each other during times of mourning. The Mohawks expected mutuality and cooperation to inform the discourse at council meetings, trade relations with other Native Americans and with Europeans, military alliances in times of war, and with European clergy.

This is not to suggest that interactions with European clergy were necessarily rationally predetermined through a cost-benefit analysis, in which Mohawks justified forging alliances with pastors only for political or economic reasons. Although this thinking did inform some relationships, some Mohawks embraced Christianity as a new moral code for living in a changed world. Others who sought identification with priests and pastors, expressed through the imprimaturs of baptism, communion, and literacy, did not necessarily identify as true converts. Although gestures of mutuality and reciprocity with pastor-brokers earned the Mohawk nation the reputation among Haudenosaunees and non-Haudenosaunees alike as the "faithful, praying Indians," the Mohawk women who reenacted Andrews's homily were not necessarily trying to become "bona fide" Christians. As Rappaport explains, acceptance of a message is not synonymous with belief in that message. In other words, accepting Christ is not that same as believing in his divinity. In accepting Andrews's message, the Mohawk matrons endeavored to enter into an imagined community of believers embodied by the Church of England. Emile Durkheim identified the church as an imagined society in which its members share a common understanding of the relationship between the sacred and the profane. Membership in the Protestant Church required the Mohawks to augment their understanding of the sacred world; Haudenosaunee cosmology regarded the sacred and profane, or the good and the bad, not as antipodal but rather as complementary. In their willingness to adjust their thinking about the sacred world, these Mohawk women sought to enter what Benedict Anderson has termed an "imagined community," which Anderson uses to explain the creation of an America creole community during the early Republic through such shared cultural productions as newspapers, almanacs, and other print artifacts. I use "imagined faith community" to mean a multivalent society, composed of indigenes and white settlers, who through learned rituals and shared texts performed—and thus shared—aspects of a common religious worldview.[6]

The praying Mohawk women whom Andrews observed sought not to assume new identities but rather to reinforce their identities and responsibilities. One of their roles as matrons and *otiyaners,* or clan mothers, was as door openers to other nations and communities—in this case the English, in order to establish an imagined faith community—in fulfillment of the Haudenosaunee tradition of the Great League of Peace and Power, premised on domestic peace, power, harmony, reciprocity, and mutual aid "to unite all nations of the earth."[7] Kanien:keha'ka/Mohawk scholar Kahente Horn-Miller has illuminated the centrality of Haudenosaunee women in nurturing political and cultural alliances: not only did they perform the roles of interpreter, diplomat, culture broker, and provider to the "other," but *otiyaners* also maintained the political, economic, and social structure and substance of the Haudenosaunee culture. The *otiyaners* chose the male leaders, made decisions about war and peace, organized horticulture and trade, and cultivated international relations.[8] The Haudenosaunees symbolized their desire to unite the nations of the earth by asking other nations to exchange people with them, "not so much in the way of hostages for their good faith," as one Jesuit put it, but to turn outsiders into insiders in order "to begin to make only one Earth and one Nation of themselves and us."[9] Asking the priest Andrews to live among them constituted the Mohawks' initial step toward constructing a unified imagined community. However, the Mohawk women imagining themselves as Church of England Protestants was quite another matter.

Although some Mohawks may have experienced under the tutelage of French Jesuits and Dutch dominies what Durkheim called "collective effervescence"—that moment of transformation, or rebirth, or conversion attained through ritual—these women had not. During Andrews's service, they prayed to their rosary beads, genuflected, and made signs of the cross at times Andrews considered awkward, because these Catholic sensory codes served as mnemonic devices that helped them remember Andrews's Protestant service. Mohawk identification with the mission and its missionary unshackled and underpinned traditional Mohawk roles: through orality, Mohawk mothers reproduced what they understood to be Christian "behavioral patterns and arte-facts"; as keepers of the eastern door of the Longhouse Confederacy, the Mohawks—and, more specifically, a few particular individuals to be discussed—fulfilled their functions as *reciprocators* to outsiders. In the process, many Mohawks *performed*—but not yet *practiced*—the institutionalized expressions of an emergent imagined faith community.[10]

I use the concept "performance" rather than practice or *praxis* to indicate iterative behavior that conveys intentionality, purposefulness, premeditation, and reflexivity. A performance is rehearsed behavior and is intended to be observed, consumed, and judged. Richard Bauman has argued that performance "assumes responsibility to an audience," which thus requires the performer to exhibit effective communicative skills in order for the audience to find the performance credible.[11] Through rehearsed behavior, one "becomes" rather than "is." In the process, performance inscribes on the performer his or her condition of liminality, of becoming, of emerging as something or someone else. "Practice," on the other hand, I argue, carries the connotation of "is," conditioned by unthinking routine and habitualness. It is behavior that Michael McNally implies "go[es] without saying" because it does not depend on the judgment of a surveillant to affirm its credibility. However, just as the performances of Molly and Joseph Brant as diplomats and culture brokers required a degree of self-consciousness, according to Elizabeth Elbourne, so too Mohawk performances of Church of England Protestantism required deliberate, self-conscious behavior in a realm beyond what James Peacock calls the "ordinary routines of living."[12] Performances of religious translation were carried out within what Michel Foucault termed "the new economy of power," a "vast system . . . comprising the functions of surveillance, normalization, and control," in which the Church of England, its mission societies, and other reform organizations had long "carried out . . . the functions of social discipline." The intent of the Mohawk women was to appropriate, borrow, and improvise Church of England Protestantism to meet the needs of what Robert Orsi calls "particular circumstances": exercising control over the purpose of the mission at Fort Hunter—to intubate the Mohawks with what it considered proper English values, beliefs, and behavior. [13]

Mohawk performances of Protestant Christianity align with James Peacock's assertion that performances are "deliberate effort[s] to represent, to say something about something." Diana Taylor offers that the purpose of "embodied and performed acts" is to "generate, record, and transmit knowledge." As such, performances, according to anthropologist David Delgado Shorter, make knowledge and establish truths.[14] Applying these three interpretations of performance enables one to see Mohawk performances of Church of England Protestantism—for example, church attendance; singing hymns; submitting to the two sacraments, baptism and communion; reading and reciting prayers and passages from the Bible; attending the mission school; and teaching Mohawk children in Mohawk the lessons of Christ—as baptized (and some unbaptized) Mohawks *enacting* behaviors to signal to Mohawk and non-Mohawk surveillants alike their *identification* with the imagined Protestant community, in whole or in part. "Identification with" rather than "identity as" carries the condition of "becoming" through a process, of an emergent self, constructed situationally and contextually, rather than the state of "is," made so through deed or declaration.[15] Because identification is processual, it emerges from what one *does*. Thought of in this way, identification with Christianity references the claim of Ojibwe/ Dakota scholar Scott Lyons that "Indian identity is something people *do*, not what they are."[16]

The Mohawk women of Andrews's church believed that they performed what was required of them to enter the imagined community of Church of England Christians. Like many of the Native peoples in the refugee communities of the late seventeenth century in the *pays d'en haute* of the Great Lakes region, who, when in face-to-face encounters with the English, spoke and behaved in ways that they believed appealed to English sensibilities, beliefs, and values in order to maintain balance of power, the Mohawk women signaled their understanding of and identification with Church of England Protestantism, even if their performances did entail using rosaries and genuflecting.[17] Thus, their performances constituted their contestation over the power assigned to the mission *and* concomitantly expressed their agency by taking on leadership roles.

In invoking "performance" as an interpretive trope, this study does not analyze the performances of staged events or rituals, although some of the events discussed in this book were indeed choreographed. Nor does this book consider performances of quotidian acts of behavior, such as gestures or remarks that some scholars insist embody such performative categories as ethnicity, gender, and sexuality.[18] Rather, this study examines and explains the meaning of what many Mohawks *did*—and *why*—situationally in the presence of English missionaries, schoolmasters, commissioners, and their Mohawk brethren. Just as Linford Fisher encourages historians to adopt "a practice-centered interpretation" of Native Christianity, which allows the historian to see a range of responses to Christianity, this study does not try to determine if or whether baptized Mohawks were "bona fide" converts, but rather seeks to illuminate and understand the various meanings of Mohawk engagement with English Protestantism.[19]

Mohawk actors performed Protestant Christianity for different reasons. Some embraced the new faith fully as a new moral code. Others supplemented their "traditional faith" with this new, potentially powerful medicine. Like the Wampanoags on Martha's Vineyard in the seventeenth century, the Mohawks engaged in a modified version of what David Silverman calls "religious translation," which he explains as "filter[ing] Christian teachings" through indigenous "religious ideas and terminology." In the process, an indigenous Christianity emerged among the churched.[20] However, Catholic and Dutch Reformed Protestant teachings also informed Mohawk translations of Church of England Protestantism. Throughout most of the eighteenth century, the majority of Mohawk enactors of Church of England Protestantism practiced "alternation"—that is, they alternated situationally between performing Haudenosaunee faith rituals and Protestant customs. Rather than blend the two faiths syncretically, they performed them side by side—Protestantism (or Catholicism) before one set of surveillants and their traditional Haudenosaunee faith before another, depending on the exigency of the moment. Alternating faith practices situationally and contextually in order to access sacred truths conditionally empowered baptized Mohawks to live transformative lives liberated by multiple truths revealed through numerous supranatural entities.[21]

Alternation was possible because the Haudenosaunees relied on sacred truths revealed continuously. *Continuous revelation*—that is, the regular petitioning of the spirit world through ritual speech and action to learn the "truth" about, for example, the impending hunt, the brewing war, the approaching growing season, or traveling abroad—lay at the center of Haudenosaunee cosmology. By the early eighteenth century, many Mohawks, living in a world buffeted by more than fifty years of war, disease, displacement, and death, found their traditional faith practices alone insufficient. For example, many Mohawk adoptees, exposed previously to Jesuit teachings in Mohawk country and in New France, and some locally born Mohawks supplemented their traditional faith practice with some Christian traditions. At times, some found that Christianity, rooted in *discontinuous revelation*—God's truths, once revealed, now fixed immutably in the Bible—carried more certitude and reliability than Haudenosaunee sacred practices. Thus, some Mohawks strengthened their traditional sacred practices of continuous revelation with the additional medicine of Christianity and its discontinuous revelation in order to armor themselves against new calamities. Others jettisoned completely the former in favor of the latter.[22] Divining continuously sacred truths, no matter the methodology—whether through dreams, or through the prophecies of a seer, or through the Bible, or through all three means—lay at the core of Haudenosaunee sacred world. An example of this in action is revealed by Wouter (Walter), the nephew of the late-seventeenth- to early-eighteenth-century baptized biracial Mohawk-Dutch interpreter and culture broker Hilletie Van Olinda (circa 1646–1706 or 1707).

In 1679 Wouter wished purportedly to be baptized by the Protestant Dutch dominie Jasper Danckaerts, a Labadist—a Calvinistic, ascetic denomination in the Netherlands composed of the elect—and to learn from him "the Dutch language . . . and become a good Christian." Because Wouter knew, as modern-day linguists know, that the proper use of language is key when engaging the spirit world, he assumed he needed to speak Dutch to communicate effectively with his new god. The dominie described Wouter as "a full-blooded Mohawk," who dressed in Dutch clothing and had been touched by God "through her [Hilletie's] instrumentality." Hilletie, the biracial daughter of a Mohawk mother and Dutch father and married to a Dutch entrepreneur, had "instructed him [Wouter] as much as she could," teaching her nephew how and when to pray. He also learned a little about Christianity from French Jesuits, "whom Wouter had heard preach several times in his own language."[23]

So eager was Wouter to become a "true Christian" that he even "abandoned all . . . his Indian friends and relations, and live[d] with his uncle" Jacques, Hilletie's biracial brother, in Schenectady. However, Uncle Jacques discouraged Wouter from learning Dutch out of fear that he would lose him as a valuable trapper and *busloper* for his fur-trading business. While biding his time, Wouter continued to hunt. One day while hunting and growing sick of constantly eating beaver, he prayed to God to "hear him and give him other food, not so much to satisfy him, as to show that he was God and loved him." In time, "a fine deer" followed by "a young buffalo" presented themselves to Wouter, which he quickly felled. As he rushed forward to begin butchering the animals, anxiety and shame suddenly seized him. He realized that he had felt covetous because "he had not thanked God" for presenting the animals. With great humility, he fell upon his knees to ask for God's forgiveness, "thanking Him . . . for both" animals and declaring that "he was not worthy to have the second and larger" beast.[24]

Wouter's prayers to God to reveal himself through the presentation of game, followed by his prayers of thanks, conform to continuous revelation and Haudenosaunee hunting practices. In order to have a successful hunt, the hunter must supplicate the Great Spirit through a series of prayers and rituals. During the hunt, the hunter prays to the game to show itself. Once he makes the kill, the hunter must offer prayers of thanks to the indwelling spirit of the beast for allowing itself to be killed. Nurturing and acknowledging this symbiotic animal-human relationship ensured successful hunts in the future. Disrupting this delicately balanced relationship by forgetting to perform or observe one or more of the rites and taboos could bring disaster, such as starvation, upon the hunter's family or his village. Wouter beseeched God to reveal a sign that would reward his efforts at hunting and praying, in the same way he would have supplicated the Great Spirit. However, he then directed his postkill prayer of thanks to God rather than to the indwelling spirits of the deer and buffalo. Hence, Wouter covered himself situationally by drawing on both the Haudenosaunee faith tradition of continuous revelation for

game to reveal itself and the Christian tradition of giving thanks to God
for the plenty that he now enjoyed. Contrary to some historians who
characterize Wouter as a Christian neophyte, I see Wouter as a Mohawk
warrior who supplemented, and thus bolstered, his Haudenosaunee lived
faith by translating a few Christian concepts through his Mohawk sensibility in order to coexist and thrive in the increasingly hegemonic Dutch
world.[25]

Wouter's story is emblematic of many Mohawks—both born in and
adopted into Mohawk communities—whom Andrews met in 1712 who
had some familiarity with Christianity and thus were ready to welcome
a new parson. About a decade had passed since they had contact with
a Church of England pastor-patron based in Albany who met their
approval. Moreover, as early as 1690, whole Mohawk families were
baptized, including that of Tejonihokarawa, a Mohawk headman,
who asked dominie Godfridus Dellius of Albany to baptize him and
his family. Tejonihokarawa, whose name in English means "open the
door," took the Dutch name Hendrick. His kin took Dutch and English
names as well. Within a year, they would form part of a core of "praying
Mohawks" in the new community of Tiononderoge, governed in large
part by Protestant beliefs and practices.[26] Over the next forty years, many
Mohawks believed that identification with Christianity opened the door
not just to salvation but also to their multiplying white-settler neighbors.
Opening the door to white neighbors became key to survival for many
Mohawks in a rapidly changing world, as one literate baptized Mohawk
from Canajoharie testified in 1753: "We [Mohawks] are one church [with
the German Palatines] and we will not part. We . . . intend to Live our
Lifetime together as Brothers." Believing in Jesus Christ, he proclaimed,
united his brethren politically and in religious fellowship with his Palatine
neighbors.[27]

Throughout the first half of the eighteenth century, identification with
the Church of England stamped Mohawks with the coveted imprimatur of "baptized," which, like the literate baptized Wampanoag men
on seventeenth- and eighteenth-century Martha's Vineyard, accorded
them distinct status within the league as respected, virtuous, honorable
individuals with a special relationship with the English.[28] However, by
the eve of the American Revolution, most Haudenosaunees viewed
most baptized Mohawks with disdain, regarding them as self-righteous,

moralizing toadies of the English. At this time, one baptized Oneida maintained that he and his baptized brethren were once esteemed throughout Iroquoia. Now they were despised. Haudenosaunee tolerance for differences in faith gave way to intolerance out of urgency for unity and self-preservation.[29]

Self-preservation required that the Mohawks adjust continuously to their new world. One of the unintended consequences of opening the door to the English was decades of land dispossession and white in-migration. By the mid-eighteenth century, the Mohawks found themselves completely surrounded by white settlements, their path to the council fire at Onondaga virtually cut off. Appropriating Christian identification and literacy constituted a means of "survivance." Anishinaabe literature scholar Gerald Vizenor has defined Native "survivance" as presence and continuance, not merely survival. "Survival," Vizenor argues, implies "clinging at the edge of existence." Survivance entails renouncing "dominance, tragedy, and victimry" and working creatively to assert agency and persistence. The cultural work of Native stories that have persisted over time is an example of "survivance."[30] So, too, is indigenized Christianity. Many eighteenth-century Mohawks appropriated literacy and the sacraments in order to continue to live proactively as Mohawks. A pious, literate Mohawk was not oxymoronic, but rather a new way of being Mohawk.

To glean what baptized Mohawks *did* when they performed Protestantism helps us understand how they orchestrated their relationships with Church of England missionaries and their accompanying schoolmasters. Their performances reveal ways in which Mohawk tyros exercised agency over the missionizing process, especially when missionaries with preconceived expectations conditioned that contact. For example, most of the priests struggled to convince their Mohawk flocks that the chapel within Fort Hunter was *their* chapel, *their* sacred space. Not all Mohawks viewed the chapel in this way. On the one hand, some Mohawks welcomed the fort as a symbol of English friendship and protection. However, many Mohawks viewed the chapel within the fort, which they shared with English soldiers and neighbors and nearby Dutch settlers, as a symbol of English imperialism and of soldiers' bad behavior. Perhaps one explanation for why some Mohawks were ambivalent about the chapel being "their chapel" is that the mission station at Fort Hunter hardly resembled or functioned like those of the Spanish and French *reducciones*, nor was it like the mission stations of the Norse missionaries in South Africa, nor even like the mission community to the Housatonics at Stockbridge, Massachusetts. At these venues, Native "converts" took up residence and claimed some degree of ownership over the space. Rather than a self-contained community of priests, schoolmasters, and baptized Mohawk farm families, the mission chapel at Fort Hunter stood garrisoned within a military fort on Mohawk land. Hence, what Church of England missionaries may have construed as a Janus-faced embrace of Protestantism was for many baptized Mohawks a deliberate pragmatic strategy to appear "faithful" through their performances of Protestantism while extracting from the faith those rituals and conventions—most importantly, baptism, communion, and literacy—that were most meaningful and efficacious to them.

This book, then, performs an intervention in the scholarship on Mohawks and missionaries by problematizing the stereotypical label "faithful Mohawks." It seeks to complicate what it meant for those baptized Mohawks who chose—or refused to choose—to "open the door" to Church of England missionaries and schoolmasters. Most recently, historians have moved away from that unitary label of "faithful Mohawks" and are beginning to recognize complexity in the handle "Christian" and "praying" Mohawks. Historian Gail MacLeitch, for example, notes that the Mohawks "resisted complete conversion, selectively adopting aspects of Christianity that made sense to them." Timothy Shannon observes that by the 1710s, the Mohawks "practiced their own version of a Protestant creed, emphasizing baptism and communal prayers and singing." Although Eric Hinderaker interprets Wouter's and his aunt Hilletie's behavior perhaps a little too uncritically, declaring them as having "abandoned their Mohawk roots to explore its [Christian love's] potential more fully," he suggests that another baptized Mohawk family also at the end of the seventeenth century may have embraced "Christianity in a cynical or instrumental way," and thus saw surely their new identities as both Christian and Mohawk as "transformative," although ultimately "we cannot know." And although David Preston correctly notes that some baptized Mohawks at Canajoharie felt kinship with their German Palatine neighbors through worship at the same church, a deeper investigation into Canajoharie Mohawks reveals a more complicated and nuanced picture, in which most Canajohariens let their arms hang by their sides—that is, feebly embraced the Church of England priests.[31]

This book focuses predominantly on two principal Mohawk communities—Tiononderoge and Canajoharie—that experienced the most extensive contact across time with French, Dutch, and English settlers, traders, commissioners, and missionaries. Adopting a microhistorical approach—the close examination of a person, community, or event that reveals larger historical forces and deeper cultural meanings—this study embraces anthropologist William Fenton's reminder that "identification with . . . [a] faction implies a way of life which is observable in the settlement patterns" of its adherents.[32] Largely depending on their physical approximation to Fort Hunter, some baptized Mohawks performed Church of England Protestantism piously, others transactionally. Some viewed the church and school as instruments for acquiring literacy, while others viewed these institutions as symbols of English imperialism and oppression, designed, according to some modern-day Mohawks, to eviscerate Mohawk culture, language, and cognition.[33] The relationship of these Mohawks, then, to their pastors and teachers also impacted other intersecting matters, including Mohawk-English political alliance, their society under duress, and their connections to English, Dutch, and French economic spheres.

Recent studies of Haudenosaunee histories by Gail MacLeitch and David Preston have reminded us quite correctly that the eighteenth-century history of the Mohawks is not explainable as one of mere declension. The Mohawks, as MacLeitch has suggested, were neither defeated nor triumphant, but rather adaptive. Their story is one of creative modification and adjustment to externally induced changes to their worlds. In short, their story is one of survivance. However, we should not downplay the degree of stress caused by disease, war, overcrowding, dispossession, and displacement. These challenges to their ecological, material, and sacred worlds caused most Mohawks to find new ways of being and believing. [34]

The sustained scholarly focus on the history of Mohawk-English missionary relations has been surprisingly patchy. Most scholars who have addressed the history of English missionaries among the Mohawks and their Haudenosaunee brethren have folded their inquiries into larger studies on the League of the Haudenosaunee and other Iroquoian speakers living among or adjacent to English and French settlements and missions in North America. Not since 1938 has an entire book been devoted to analyzing the "praying Mohawks" and their world.[35] Hence, it is time for a reexamination.

Until the last quarter of the twentieth century, most scholarship on religious encounters between missionaries and indigenes, including Haudenosaunees, viewed missionaries as agents of civilization. Most of these studies examined European missions "from the boat" and deduced that they constituted beneficent institutions of humanitarianism and Christian uplift that brought the gifts of civilization—law, religion, education, proper subsistence—to the Mohawks and other Haudenosaunee people.[36] In the 1970s, historians and especially ethnohistorians, who utilize an interdisciplinary approach to the study of the histories of preliterate peoples that requires combining ethnological concepts with historical analysis, began to reexamine Spanish, French, and English missions "from the shore"—from the indigenes' perspective—and concluded that religious encounters between Native Americans and Europeans were contests of cultures. From the latter perspective, historians found greater complexity in Native-missionary relations and regarded missions as sites of cross-cultural communication and exchange, where Native peoples exercised some authority over their relationships with missionaries, and thus determined for themselves what was useful in these relations. Some historians found bona fide converts, others wheat-and-eel adherents. Explanations for the variety of experiences ranged from Daniel Richter's puckish claim that "a message delivered often enough and sincerely enough by a respected figure was bound, sooner or later, to win adherents" to Rachel Wheeler's and Joel Martin's insightful conclusion that some Native Americans used Christianity as a tool to revitalize, strengthen, and reaffirm communal and personal identities and power just as their unbaptized brethren used nativist movements for the same ends.[37] Sustained contact with Europeans affected most Native communities negatively and resulted in depopulation by disease, loss of land, factionalism, cultural disorientation, and psychological stress, causing many to search for a new moral code by which to live in a changed world.

More recent studies have drilled down on Native agency in indigene-missionary relations by placing Native Americans at the center of their studies. Many historians anticipated the call by Alyssa Mt. Pleasant,

Caroline Wigginton, and Kelly Wisecup to "embrace NAIS's [Native American and Indigenous Studies] materials and methods" that insist on "Native peoples' centrality and humanity" by acknowledging and incorporating their texts, expertise, perspectives, and histories into their studies.[38] Many of these studies now regard missions during the period of contact as usable spaces and institutions from which Native peoples extracted what they needed—for example, literacy, community, subsistence, personal status, a new moral code, a purpose for living as indigenes in a changed world.[39] In the process, they reveal the emergence of a Native Christianity, an observable fact that is beyond question among scholars today. The Andeans in seventeenth-century Peru assimilated and reinterpreted variously Christian terms and Catholic rituals into their new lives as they adjusted to Spanish colonization. Some retained their traditional lived faith, overlain with an expressive Catholicism, while others injected Andean faith traditions into Christianity.[40] In colonial Mesoamerica, Nahua and Maya translators and interpreters participated in the process of *reduccion*—the spatial and linguistic pacification and subordination of the local indigenes—to make Catholic texts and tenets meaningful to their brethren. As a consequence, their religious translations gave rise to local indigenous Catholicisms that some scholars argue was a syncretic faith—or at least a set of syncretic practices—while others, most notably, William Hanks, insist that indigenous Catholicism was indeed Christianity, but simply performed indigenously.[41]

For the past two centuries, the Tlingits living between northwest British Columbia and Alaska have exercised agency to incorporate and reinterpret aspects of a range of Christian church orthodoxies. Most notably among them was that of the Russian Orthodox Church, but also that of the Presbyterian Church, Jehovah's Witnesses, Mormons, even the Baha'i faith, and today precontact Tlingit traditions, to establish a Tlingit Orthodoxy to meet their faith needs in an ever-evolving world.[42] For the Ojibwes in contact with Jesuit priests in the *pays d'en haute* of the western Great Lakes region, "conversion" meant a process of crossing spatial and spiritual boundaries to engage the black robes' Christianity, which for some resulted in changed hearts—that is, true conversion—but changed identities in none, as the Ojibwes applied Native interpretations to Catholicism.[43] Even the most pious, devout Iroquoian and Algonquian speakers residing in colonial New France performed a Catholicism that they believed was that of the Jesuits, but more important was more meaningful to themselves, thanks in part to Jesuit complicity in offering religious translations to their Native auditors.[44] Likewise, many of the Algonquin speakers residing near or within the bounds of British settlers in the Northeast appropriated and translated Protestant tenets in such ways that resulted in the establishment of local Native Protestant theologies and churches over which they exercised authority and control.[45] Most indigenous peoples throughout the Americas who found useful some or most aspects of Christianity introduced to them during their contact with Europeans forged an indigenous Christianity imbued with Native symbolism, meanings, and interpretations, a processual construction that continues.

Muscogee pastor Rosemary McCombs Maxey speaks for many when she notes that today, Native Christians continue to find the Christian church useful: "We often practice parallel Christian/Traditional rituals and rites simultaneously." Like her grandfather, many Native believers embraced a particular Christian denomination because they encountered a non-Native member who was "a real good one." Although the impulse to accept Christianity as an effort to "maintain separate sovereignty . . . in the face of Western expansion" ultimately failed, the Native Christian church has provided Native peoples with a usable "indigenous expression in a Christian mode."[46] Many Native Christians in the present and the past have rejected a kind of blended religiosity, preferring to see faith traditions as one thing or the other. For example, Cayuga pastor Adrian Jacobs views syncretism, the blending and reconciliation of two faith values, as "the most dangerous response to Indian culture," for although he values good aspects of the Haudenosaunee faith tradition, such as the ten-day mourning ceremony, only God through Jesus Christ, he insists, can offer sanctification to the Native individual and his culture. Nevertheless, many Native individuals, past and present, like Laverne Jacobs, have found solace in both traditions, expressed, for example, as smoking the Pipe (calumet) in a Catholic cathedral and praying to God in a Native sweat lodge.[47]

Anthropologists, folklorists, and ethnolinguists have produced a rich literature on indigenous peoples' performances as expressions of indigenous identities in the context of contact.[48] On the other hand, historians are just beginning to apply performance theory to their understanding of Native American identification.[49] This book draws on these scholarly threads to understand how and why eighteenth-century Mohawks performed Church of England Protestantism as a way of saying something and making meaning about their identification as new Mohawks during a period of profound change.

Taking a fine-grained, microhistorical approach, this book is intended to push historians further in the direction of viewing Native performances of Protestantism as a complex intersection of social, cultural, and political survival strategies. As such, I share ethnohistorian Neal Salisbury's call for historians to become more comfortable with ambiguity and seemingly contradictory behavior among the Native subjects we study, especially those who submitted to baptism. The more recent scholarship has heeded Salisbury's caution to resist binary thinking—Christian (white) versus non-Christian (Native), the converted versus the apostate. Although many historians continue to use the handle "convert" to define praying Native Americans, most now consider the many reasons indigenes submitted to baptism—for protection, for health, for political alliance, for entering heaven, for a new moral code—without assuming an ineluctable link between baptism and convert. This perspective is not entirely new; just as one early twentieth-century scholar of religious change asserted that there is no such thing as a "standardize[d] conversion"—some are sudden and "explosive," others are gradual and embody a "process"— most twenty-first-century historians now assume that there is no standard cause and effect with baptism.[50] Nevertheless, most unbaptized Mohawks in the first half of the eighteenth century viewed their baptized brethren as turning Christian and even demanded ministers for them. Thus, the generation of Mohawks who performed Church of England Protestantism at the beginning of the eighteenth century entered into the imagined community of the English on their terms. During the post–American Revolution period of reestablishment in Upper Canada, baptized Mohawks negotiated forming imagined communities with their unbaptized Haudenosaunee brethren.

I trace the evolution of the complex relationship of Mohawks and missionaries in six chronologically and thematically linked chapters. In chapter 1, I argue that toward the end of the seventeenth century, before the Society for the Propagation of the Gospel in Foreign Parts, a religious reform organization founded in 1701 with de facto ties to the established Church of England, entered the field of Native American missionization, the Mohawk world was under great strain. Rapid depopulation from warfare, disease, poisonings, and migration to New France impelled many to form relationships with Catholic and Dutch Protestant clergymen in order to revitalize their personal and communal lives. Hence, by the time the first SPG missionary arrived in Iroquoia in 1704, many Mohawks knew something of a translated Christianity. For example, when an early-eighteenth-century Haudenosaunee elder, who had been instructed as a boy by Jesuit priests, was once asked if the unnamed woman who gave birth to the twin boys in the Haudenosaunee creation myth had a name, he replied, "Not in our language, but in that of the Europeans, she is called 'Maria.'"[51]

The project the SPG embarked on at the beginning of the eighteenth century entailed reforming the manners and habits of everyone in the colonies—Europeans, Africans, and indigenes—the subject of chapter 2. Missionizing Native Americans was merely one prong of a multitined program that called for bringing all dissenters, potential or actual, and all non-Christians into England's imagined community. The project required that ordained young Englishmen be willing to live among Native peoples and learn their language and culture. Books, and thus teaching literacy, would be central to their work. Implicit in this plan was their Eurocentric belief that Native peoples could be "civilized" by reforming their sacred worlds intellectually rather than by transforming their secular habits. Consequently, the habits, customs, and traditions of most Mohawks remained intact, albeit augmented by some Christian practices, ecclesiastical and secular.

Initial SPG methods of reforming Mohawks and instilling in them the principles of Christianity—the subject of chapter 3—met with both accommodation and resistance. William Andrews, the first SPG missionary with a specific appointment to preach to the Mohawks, communicated with his flock at cross-purposes. His vision of his role did not always congrue with the expectations of the Mohawks: he saw his task as Christianizing and "civilizing" the Mohawks, while most Mohawks viewed Andrews as a broker through whom they might realize political and material advantages through alliance with the English Crown. Where the two strategies intersected, most Mohawks read utility rather than new faith, while Andrews read resistance to his efforts to save them from themselves.

In time, some baptized Mohawk headmen participated in the missionizing enterprise by teaching literacy in Mohawk to Mohawk children, the subject of chapter 4. However, low pay and mismanagement by the local SPG minister caused some to resign, leaving the school bereft of teachers. Consequently, some Mohawk parents sent their children to an English boarding school in western Massachusetts to learn English. Nonetheless, mistreatment and mismanagement there compelled Mohawk parents to withdraw their children. Now a growing number of Mohawk parents regarded the acquisition of literacy in either Mohawk or English critical for the rising generation.

Chapter 5 explores the experiences of Mohawk children at one of several new missions in the Northeast following the Seven Years' War. With the expulsion of the French government from Canada, many Anglican priests and dissenting pastors, along with some colonial officials, believed it was time to change course in missionizing the Haudenosaunees, who, except for the Mohawks, appeared to them resistant to SPG efforts. Several pastors and laymen put forth plans to "civilize" them by Anglicizing *and* Christianizing them concomitantly. Most of the Mohawks, many of whom had already adopted European modes of living, for which other League Haudenosaunee began to scorn them, were most interested in three aspects of the new program: the acquisition of literacy, the missionaries as providers of survival goods, and baptism and communion as sufficient justification alone of faith. Their persistent agency often frustrated English reformers' plans for a new strategy.

Chapter 6, the final chapter, examines the efforts of two principal diasporic Mohawk communities to reestablish themselves in Upper Canada: Tyendinaga on the Bay of Quinte on the northeastern shore of Lake Ontario west of present-day Kingston, composed largely of the former residents of Tiononderoge; and Brantford on the Grand River reserve about seventy miles west of Fort Niagara, composed largely of former residents of Canajoharie. The leaders of these two new settlements debated little with their brethren over establishing the Anglican Church in their respective communities. Those living at Tyendinaga had lived nearest the mission at Fort Hunter and now considered themselves Christians. In time, they built their new church with their own hands. At Brantford, Joseph Brant, the titular founder of the eponymous community, foisted immediately the church upon the Native settlers. His unilateral decision, along with his decision to sell land to white Loyalist friends, engendered strain at Brantford. In time, proponents of a return to the traditional faith of their ancestors threatened the harmony of the community. However, a compromise proposed by Brant permitted the performance of both Haudenosaunee and Protestant faiths.

These six chapters present a century-long, diachronic picture of Mohawk engagement with Church of England Protestantism. Ultimately, most Mohawks performed Church of England Protestantism on their terms, the product of a process that Marshall Sahlins has termed "externally induced, yet indigenously orchestrated."[52] Throughout, I have tried to capture the story of Mohawk performances of their faith from their perspective, fully aware of the call by NAIS scholars to include indigenous documents and perspectives. Where possible, I have tried to do so. However, herein lay the challenge of doing Native American history: most evidence about Mohawks and other indigenes prior to the nineteenth century is contained in written documents left by European and American colonial clergymen, commissioners, traders, and settlers. Thus, this study draws heavily on non-Native-produced documents, which admittedly are laden with self-interested Eurocentrism. Moreover, translations of Native speeches are often approximate iterations of what was actually said. Sometimes missionaries and their catechumens, according to Joseph François Lafitau, an early-eighteenth-century Jesuit missionary in New France, communicated in an invented language of "periphrases and compounds . . . of their language." Much must have been lost in translation.[53]

Nevertheless, all is not lost. The use of documentary evidence to discern the impulses behind Mohawk performances of faith requires the historian to not only read the documents "across the grain," but also to employ a multidisciplinary approach to the study of a people of an oral-based culture. I have borrowed modes of analysis from myriad disciplines, including anthropology, archaeology, comparative religion, history, linguistics, and sociology. Whether this book is ethnohistory or simply history is less important to me than the effectiveness with which it problematizes ways in which "faithful Mohawks" engaged and performed Protestantism across the eighteenth century.

# CHAPTER I

# "Dwindl'd to Nothing Almost"

## *The Mohawks and Their World at 1700*

Men need a religion.

—Father Joseph Francois Lafitau, 1724

On the eve of King William's War (1689–97), also known as the War of the Grand Alliance and the War of the League of Augsburg—a war between New France and New England over territorial rights in the American Northeast—Tahiadoris, a Mohawk headman, pledged Haudenosaunee military support to the English against the French and their Native American allies. He vowed that he and his fellow warriors would "Pursue our Enemies the French Vigorously . . . for they are your Enemies also[;] yea if all our People should be Ruined and Cutt in Peeces, wee will never make peace with them." Tahiadoris and more than half of the Mohawk warriors and headmen would not survive the war and its collateral damage.[1]

King William's War left the Five Nations of the Haudenosaunee "in a staggering condition." After England signed a peace treaty with France in 1697, Robert Livingston, the town clerk of Albany and, since 1675, the secretary for the commissioners for Indian affairs, reported to the Lords of Trade in London, the governmental body that administered England's foreign affairs, that "our Indians are diminish'd and much shaken from their former vigour and zeal against the French." The Mohawk Nation, the easternmost of the Five Nations of the Haudenosaunee Confederacy, had "dwindl'd to nothing almost," having been "spent and wasted" by the "tedious long warr."[2]

For the commissioners at Albany, the situation had become grave: "most of our praying Indians [Mohawks] . . . whom we could most confide in," they lamented, were either dead or gone to Canada. Their destination was Kahnawake, the Jesuit-run multiethnic mission community near Montreal, organized and structured like a French village, where their relatives lived. As early as 1691, one Mohawk warrior expressed to kin at Kahnawake his distress over the loss of important warriors and headmen and the difficulty of "requickening" (mourning and replacing) them: "all those . . . who had sense are dead."[3]

Some English officials scolded the Mohawks for not doing a better job of defending and protecting their homes. In February 1692–93, Peter Schuyler, the mayor of Albany and a commissioner for Indian affairs, accused the Mohawks of being "little concerned" about the enemy, seeming to be "disposed to goe along with the Enemy as soon as they came," for already "the enemy have twice been at the Gates of their Castle Undiscovered and tied a bunch of small reeds or straws at the very door." He berated them for not sleeping "with their arms in their hands and one eye open," not understanding that the League Mohawks did not want to engage militarily their kin in Kahnawake. That month the French burned to the ground the three principal Mohawk villages.[4]

In response to these reports of suspected Mohawk apathy, if not outright complicity, New York governor Benjamin Fletcher sailed into Albany that February 1692–93 to tell the Mohawks that the recent calamities that befell them were unacceptable, as they were of their own making. He was shocked that the mighty Mohawks could be routed so easily, for he could "never suppose my brethren the Maquas would be soe supine and careless as to suffer the French and the Indians to enter their Castles without the least resistance." The Mohawks may not have taken Fletcher's outrage seriously, for he arrived at the council meeting empty-handed, with no goods with which to gift the Mohawks in show of reciprocal friendship. Instead, like a seemingly concerned patron rather than as an equal ally, he proclaimed that he would now "provide for the Maquas Nation" by offering to find a new place of residence for them, as their homes had been destroyed, presumably so that they might recover and continue fighting.[5]

Through their Mohawk-Dutch interpreter, Hilletie Van Olinda, the Mohawks conveyed several concerns to Governor Fletcher, whom they called "Brother *Cajenquiragoe,*" which means "Great Swift Arrow," a Mohawk translation of his surname, "Fletcher," "arrow maker." They wanted him to know that they were in no condition to undertake revenge killings at that moment, for they needed to condole their dead. Nevertheless, they were pleased to learn that Governor Fletcher would return in the summer to help them resume the fight. Meanwhile, they asked Fletcher why the English did not mount a fleet and destroy the French by sea.[6] They added that one of their warriors got drunk and "killed an Indian that came over from the French," for which they were "much concerned." In consequence of this event, they asked Fletcher to halt the sale of rum to them "whilst the war is soe hot, since our soldiers cannot be kept within bounds when they are drunk." Fletcher pledged that he would see to their request to prohibit the sale of rum during the war, although few rum merchants honored Fletcher's vow. Meanwhile, the Mohawks, Fletcher insisted, should "bee vigilant and carefull."[7]

The Mohawks could ill-afford to lose any more warriors and war chiefs, the war had so depleted their ranks. Census figures gathered in 1689 at the beginning of the war and again in 1698 at the official end of the war reveal that each of the five Haudenosaunee nations—the Mohawks, Oneidas, Onondagas, Cayugas, and Senecas, east to west—suffered declines to their respective warrior populations from between 33 percent and 60 percent. The Mohawks, the keepers of the eastern door of the Longhouse and the putative elders of the Five Nations, lost 110 out of 270 warriors, a casualty rate in excess of 40 percent.[8] For several years after the war, the warrior class remained so depleted throughout the Haudenosaunee Confederacy that Livingston remarked in 1701 "the long war and the great loss which they sustained in their youth hath almost dispirited" the Haudenosaunee people. English officials were deeply troubled by the dramatic reduction in the warrior population, for they viewed the Haudenosaunees as a bulwark against French incursions into Virginia and Maryland. They feared that if the Five Nations fell, Albany would tumble, followed by the "small and poor province" of New York, and then all the other colonies in succession, like dominoes, until "all America" lay prostrate before the French.[9]

Other factors in addition to mortal combat wounds also accounted for the depletion of the Mohawk population in the Mohawk Valley. The small-pox epidemic of 1689–91 that ravaged some of the English colonies and depleted Albany's Dutch population also cost ninety Mohawk and Oneida lives. Continuous out-migration to New France also drained the Mohawk population. According to one estimate in 1700, two-thirds of the League Mohawks had removed themselves to Kahnawake. Mohawk émigrés gave myriad reasons for migrating there: cheaper goods; reliable supplies of food, clothing, and shelter; and easy access to priests. The outflow of League Mohawks to Kanawake was so steady that one Albany official was sure that the Jesuits were "intent upon making a desert of their country and completely ruining their villages."[10]

A perhaps more pernicious factor also reduced the Mohawk population: the increased use of poisons. Both Haudenosaunees and Europeans regarded the use of poisons the work of sorcerers. In 1700, one Albany official warned that the "diabolical practice" of Catholic Mohawks in Canada and League Mohawks in Iroquoia "poysoning one another" had "dispatched out of the way" entire families that were "true to the English interest." Fear of being poisoned caused Aqueendera, "the Chief Sachem of the Onondaga Nation" and an ally of the English, to flee Onondaga and hide in Albany on the property of Pieter Schuyler, the first mayor of Albany, New York (1686–94), and chair of the commissioners for Indian affairs. Aqueendera's "proof" was that his son had not only been poisoned but had also been bewitched: "a sore broke out on one of his sides, out of which there [came] handfulls of hair." Resorting to the use of poisons to settle disputes indicates that the Haudenosaunees responded radically to acute stress.[11]

For some Mohawks, these cumulative deaths led to crises in faith. The war made condoling fallen headmen, warriors, and other family members difficult. Condolence ceremonies, similar to memorial services, were critical for maintaining balance and harmony in Haudenosaunee society. At the mourning service for the deceased, a leader of the clan from the reciprocal moiety spoke soothing words to the immediate family members of the deceased to quell their anguished hearts. Relatives of the deceased gave wampum belts to the next of kin to wipe away their tears. They also presented the family either with the scalp of an enemy, or a living war captive, by which means the dead person was "requickened," or replaced. The adoption of war captives was an important practice used by the Haudenosaunees to "sustain their tottering families and increase their number."[12] If important members of the Mohawk community were not condoled and requickened because of a lack of headmen available to perform the ceremony, or because of too few warriors to secure a scalp or a captive, then the world of the victim's family and community remained out of balance. Such was probably the case for some Mohawk families in 1700 when the commissioners learned that some of the "far Indians" were reluctant to come to Albany for a council meeting with the governor of New York, for fear that "some Indians, in their drinke might kill them, in revenge for their relatives lost in the warr." Their resentment over their inability to condole their dead festered and infected their diplomatic relations with England. In 1702, the Mohawk headman Onucheranorum reprimanded Governor Lord Cornbury of New York (1702–8) over the "little assistance from our Brethren during the late warr [that] forced [us, the Mohawks] to wage war alone and [we] lost many of our people but see none of our brethren either to assist us or to revenge the blood we had lost by the French." Many Mohawks now felt betrayed by the English, with whom they had forged an alliance through the Covenant Chain, an economic and political relationship of mutual interdependence and reciprocity, defined by the Haudenosaunees as *kaswentha*. The Mohawks first fashioned a chain of iron with the Dutch in the early seventeenth century and now polished a silver chain with the English. The Two Row Wampum Belt—a long belt of white wampum transected by two parallel lines of purple wampum that represent the close parallel yet autonomous worlds and lives of the Haudenosaunees and the Dutch—is a Haudenosaunee document that symbolizes *kaswentha*. Aqueendera expressed an iteration of this ideal when he declared that through the chain, "the English and we were one," meaning that they were to be codependent yet sovereign.[13] Many Mohawks now began to question this proposition.

Aqueendera's claim invoked a political solution to peace and prosperity sealed in a 1701 treaty known as the Grand Settlement that called for Haudenosaunee Francophiles—the Senecas, predominantly—to renew alliances with New France; for Anglophiles, especially the Mohawks, to rebuild alliances with New York; and for neutrals—the Onondagas, particularly, who kept the Haudenosaunee council fire—to work with Pennsylvania and other colonies, as well as ally themselves with Native nations toward the south, all in the interest of maintaining peace and harmony.[14] Because the long war had inflicted a heavy political and cultural toll on the Mohawks, they and other League Haudenosaunees welcomed

the Grand Settlement of 1701 as the beginning of a new era, which one
New York official and chronicler of New York—indigenous relations
dubbed in the mid-eighteenth century the era of "Modern Indian Politics." Historian Daniel Richter posits that by this phrase, Peter Wraxall
meant a new political balance among the Haudenosaunees, the French,
and the English, which led to relative peace and stability, with a few
exceptions, throughout Iroquoia for the ensuing five decades. However,
Richter argues further that most Haudenosaunees probably would
have regarded the Great Peace as the restoration of the Great League
of Peace—the fifteenth-century intra-League peace agreement, under
which internecine war ceased and peace and unity resumed throughout
Iroquoia—because now Haudenosaunee headmen cultivated personal
relationships among themselves and their neighboring European power
brokers, resulting in spiritual well-being returning to the Haudenosaunee
people.[15] A key element for spiritual return required that individuals
either reinvigorate their traditional faith practices or perform new ones
that met their spiritual needs.

### "Teach them Religion & Establish Traffick"

During the second half of the seventeenth century, most Mohawks who
knew anything about Christianity learned about Catholicism from Jesuit
missionaries and from baptized kin and neighbors who ventured back
and forth to Kahnawake, and about Protestantism from a small corps of
Dutch dominies. Hence, by the time the first English missionary from
the Society for the Propagation of the Gospel in Foreign Parts reached
Mohawk country in 1704, some Mohawks already performed some
aspects of what they understood to be Christian praxis, a term coined
by anthropologists to explain that individuals do—or do not do—certain
things out of obligation and interest determined within a seamless, holistic system that is at once cultural, social, political, economic, and ideolog-
ical.[16] Reverend Thomas Barclay, a Church of England priest assigned
to Albany, who baptized Mohawk children from time to time, observed
curiously that many Mohawks had been "converted to the Christian
Faith by the popish [French] missionaries and [the Dutch dominies]
Mess. Dellius, Freeman, and Lydius." However, Barclay, rigidly culture

bound, regarded their performances of Christianity "so ignorant and scandalous that they can scarce be reputed Christians." Barclay observed that Mohawks who attended the Dutch Reformed services in Albany combined Catholic and Protestant practices; Marie Tsiaonentes, for example, "recite[d] her Rosary . . . with great devotion all the time while the [Dutch Reformed] Minister preached."[17]

Mohawks who sought political and spiritual revitalization through sacred solutions fashioned a response that differed from the classic model of religious revitalization, first articulated by Anthony F. C. Wallace in the 1950s. Wallace posited that in order for a native revitalization movement to occur, several variables must synergize: a prophet brings to a community under stress a reformulation of their sacred world, which is often a recalculation of the past, seen as glorious, combined with religious principles borrowed from another culture. The stresses experienced by a society may be various, but its members generally view the sources as external to them. Individuals become aware of difficulties when their efforts to address the problem fail, while alternative strategies seem to offer satisfying answers. A prophet envisions a new strategy, and a period of preaching and making converts follows, after which the people integrate the new religious formulation into their culture. Their society then feels renewed, reborn, revitalized.[18]

Participants in religious revitalization movements, according to Wallace, self-identify with one or two of three processes of revitalization. They may strive to revive their "traditional" culture, as through "ghost dance" movements, which supplicate dead ancestors and call for their return. They may seek to appropriate aspects of an alien culture, as through "cargo cults," a disparaging term once used to describe movements that link the return of the dead with an awaited abundance of material goods. Or they may claim to do neither, but instead construct a new culture from whole cloth, that they may argue belongs neither to their ancestors nor to an alien culture. In reality, most religious revitalization movements adopt dual identifications, in the fashion of the Handsome Lake religion, the early-nineteenth-century Haudenosaunee faith, that syncretized "traditional" sacred beliefs with imported Christian beliefs and practices. Yet many of these processes and conditions were absent in Mohawk country in 1700 and thus cannot be used uncritically to explain adequately what occurred there.[19]

No prophet, like Deganawidah, the fifteenth-century Huron Peace-maker, who brought an end to the internecine warfare among the Haude-nosaunees; or Handsome Lake, whose syncretic Haudenosaunee-Quaker faith restored the spiritual life of many native peoples in the eastern Great Lakes region at the turn of the nineteenth century; or Hendrick Aupau-mut, who drew on Mahican traditions and Protestant principles to revi-talize life for many displaced Stockbridgers at the beginning of the nineteenth century, emerged among the Mohawks. Instead, several Mohawk individuals and local families banded together to perform new faith practices, or at least to augment their old faith practices with the new. In the process, they asked repeatedly the New York commissioners for Indian affairs to send them Protestant ministers "to teach them Reli-gion & Establish Traffick amongst them [so] that they might be able to purchase a Coat & not go to Church in Bear Skins." Mohawks who shared this sentiment linked Christianity with spiritual, material, and political prosperity, an articulation of the purported purpose of the Great Peace of 1701.[20] Even those who were uninterested in Christianity sup-ported the wishes of those who had begun to pray, realizing that their own souls may also reap some collateral material benefits. Like their Catholic kin, praying Protestant Mohawks sought to restore their lives by performing aspects of Christianity in whole or in part. Only a few jetti-soned completely their Haudenosaunee sacred practices. For these few, the Haudenosaunee gods, shamans, and dreams ceased to be efficacious. They strove to embrace Christianity in as complete a form as they under-stood it, supplicating the god of Christians and following the religious teachings of Christ. However, for the majority of Mohawks, shamans and dreams continued to play vital roles in their lives, even among some of those who prayed. For them, performing selectively specific Christian practices on their terms, such as taking the sacraments of baptism and communion, provided enough of a layer of spiritual well-being and pro-tection to satisfy their souls.[21]

### "One Earth and one Nation of themselves and us"

At the turn of the eighteenth century, most League Mohawks continued to find rewards and satisfaction in the ways and beliefs of their ances-tors. However, some found that a rapidly changing world rendered the old ways unsatisfactory. Dreams, feasts, shamans, supplications, singing, and dancing alone seemed to keep neither their world nor their souls as ordered, balanced, healthful, and satisfied. However, performing Christian prayers and hymns, baptism, and the symbolic ingesting of the body and blood of Christ, which stamped the baptized with the imprimatur "one of us," supplemented by or privileged over the Haudenosaunee tenet of reciprocity that opened the door to outsiders and turned them into insiders, provided many Mohawks the armor, protection, and equilibrium they needed in an evolving world.

Haudenosaunee cultural beliefs informed the actions of many of the Mohawks pulled toward Christianity. The "constitution" of the League of the Haudenosaunee, founded on the principles of reciprocity and harmony, provided for bringing "foreign nations" into the Great Peace by reason and by persuasion. According to the foundational myth, Deganawidah, a Huron prophet, brought a message of peace to the People of the Longhouse who were experiencing great pain and distress. As an outsider, he was able to grasp the problem that insiders could not see, namely, terrible internecine violence, which ravaged Haudenosaunee society. With the help of Hiawatha, an Onondaga adopted by the Mohawks, Deganawidah persuaded the warriors of the Five Nations to bury their hatchets under a Great Tree of Peace and to enter into a confederation, the Great League of Peace and Power, premised on peace, power, and mutual aid.[22] Should a foreign nation refuse to accept alliance with the Haudenosaunees, then the tenets of the Great Peace gave the Haudenosaunees permission to declare war on the resistant nation in order "to establish the Great Peace by a conquest of the rebellious nation." They gave little thought and less respect to the nation that wished to remain autonomous, as the league took a universalist, *requirmiento* approach to imparting "the Good News of Peace" to all nations in order "to unite all the nations of the earth." The Haudenosaunees symbolized this desire by asking other nations to exchange people with them, "not so much in the way of hostages for their good faith," as one Jesuit put it, but "as to begin to make only one Earth and one Nation of themselves and us."[23] Hence, the insistence of some Mohawks that the commissioners provide them with English priests.

Likewise, Mohawks may have constructed Christian identification in a similar manner, framing "conversion," represented by baptism, as symbolic of entering into league with another nation, of certifying reciprocity and mutuality. In 1667–68, for example, a year after Tionontoguen rebuilt itself from the ashes following Tracy's scorched-earth campaign across the Mohawk Valley in 1666, Mohawk headmen permitted the Jesuit missionary Fremin to establish the mission Saint Marie in their village, most likely for the benefit of the forty-five "old-time Christians"—captive Hurons who had been baptized earlier by the Jesuits. In exchange, the Mohawks handed over to Fremin twelve Algonquin prisoners. In 1672–73, at the most eastern Mohawk village, Gandaouague, the site of the French mission Saint Pierre—named after Saint Peter, identified in the book of Matthew as the rock (*petra*), or foundation, of the Christian church— nearly 8 percent of the estimated four hundred residents in Mohawk country submitted to baptism. Surely, many of those who received the sacrament were Huron and Algonquin captives, who constituted two-thirds of the population of Gandaouague. Nevertheless, the Mohawks' willingness to accept French Jesuits among them was a stark about-face from thirty years earlier, when "Father Jogues watered with his blood" the ground at Gandaouague. Although the Jesuits read the Mohawks' submission to baptism as "the force of true Christianity and the Spirit of Jesus Christ" at work, it is more likely that the Mohawks regarded their performances of Catholicism as entering into alliance with New France—joining an imagined community—premised on enacting a commonly shared faith practice. Some Mohawks may have read holy water as nourishing metaphorically the roots of the Great Tree of Peace, which would enable the branches to grow eastward and northward to shelter the Mohawks' Christian neighbors.[24]

Many baptized Mohawks regarded Christianity as a restorative mechanism not just for themselves but for all of Iroquoia as well. Ideally, missionaries, forts, and traders, whether French, Dutch, or English, would bring prosperity, protection, power, and privilege to all. Yet Christianity failed to catch on as a League-wide revitalization movement for most of the eighteenth century for three critical reasons. First, biological and fictive kinship relations—the means by which political alliances were often forged—among and between Mohawk, French, Dutch, and English societies drove the "conversion" of some Mohawks, which kept religious supplementation or replacement small and local. Second, the lack of a charismatic native religious formulator, who could have articulated the benefits of the new faith practice to his Haudenosaunee brethren, limited the reach of Protestant Christianity beyond Mohawk country. Third, most of the Haudenosaunee nations west of the Mohawks, save the Oneidas, found immediate, short-term relief from social and cultural stress through economic and diplomatic means rather than through faith-based solutions, which rendered moot the need of those Haudenosaunees in less frequent contact with Europeans to examine the efficacy of their traditional faith practice. Trade and security remained more important to the western League Haudenosaunees than worrying if prayer should replace reading dreams. For example, Dekanissore, the powerful Onondaga headman, explained to both English and French commissioners in 1701 that the Five Nations would accept the priests of whichever nation—France or England—sold them trade goods the cheapest (see chapter 2).[25] For Dekanissore and other Haudenosaunee peace chiefs, priests were ancillary to trade and diplomacy.

## A World of Balance, Harmony, and Reciprocity

Haudenosaunee religion in the seventeenth and eighteenth centuries was not relegated to a separate, compartmentalized sphere of life, but rather was a lived religion, an integrated, complex web of practices and beliefs, constituted of parables, rituals, festivals, songs, and dances. Rites and rituals defined the form of worship: sacrificial offerings of tobacco at council meetings and on the eve of warring expeditions were to ensure success, feasts of thanksgiving held at specific times throughout the year were to satisfy the Creator, the propitiation of game killed on the hunt would ensure successful subsequent hunts, and the observance of taboos, the use of talismans, and the reading of dreams would safeguard good health for all.

Antipodal pairings kept the world balanced and harmonious: day had its night, summer its winter, sky its earth. The Sky World, the home of the Creator, was very much like the Earth World, and the spirits who inhabited the Sky World were very much like real men and women on Earth. The spirits of the Sky World figured directly into the creation myth of the Haudenosaunee people.

In brief, Sky Woman, the progenitor of the Haudenosaunees, lived in the Sky World with her husband, until she fell—or was pushed—through a hole in the sky and tumbled down to Earth. Waterbirds caught her on their wings and then gently placed her on the back of a sea turtle. Muskrat, an earth diver, brought mud up from the bottom of the sea and made the land on which the Haudenosaunee people would live.

In time, Sky Woman gave birth to a daughter. When the daughter came of age, a suitor placed several arrows by her side, which impregnated her. Soon, she gave birth to twins: Teharonghyawago, the good twin, and Tawiskaron, the evil twin. The twins became bitter rivals. The evil twin, whom the grandmother (Sky Woman) favored, killed his mother. In retaliation, the good twin killed their grandmother and severed her head, which he threw up into the sky, creating the moon. Because the brothers represented irreconcilable opposites—good and evil—they fought. Eventually, the good twin defeated the evil twin and banished him to the edges of the mundane world, from where he tempted the souls of men and women. Teharonghyawago then went about making all the living things on the earth and, like Christ, teaching men and women how to live and how to keep thanksgiving festivals.[26]

This truncated version of the Haudenosaunee creation myth reveals a world of complementaries: twin siblings, good and evil, revenge killings, Sky World and Earth World. The Earth World is actually balanced above by the Sky World, which represents goodness, order, light, and life, and by the Underworld from below, where evil spirits, chaos, darkness, and death lurk.

Spirits, good and evil, were central to Haudenosaunee cosmology. All things were animated by their positive spirits, or power. One's personal *orrenna*, crudely translated as "guardian angel," guided one throughout one's life. It was more important than the Creator, for one consulted routinely one's guardian spirit—not the Creator—especially during times of difficulty, such as illness, or during times of transition, such as from childhood to adolescence. One called upon one's *orrenna* to help crush negative spirits, which were responsible for mischief, illness, and misfortune in the world. The Haudenosaunees commonly supplicated evil spirits to beg them to cease and desist fomenting misery. Nearly all missionaries mistook this form of petition as "devil worship." The underlying principle and purpose of Haudenosaunee faith practice was to increase and renew through worship and thanksgiving the positive spirit forces and to quash the negative ones.[27]

Six key thanksgiving celebrations regenerated their world. The Midwinter Festival, the most important of all the thanksgiving ceremonies, held in late January or early February and lasting usually eight or nine days, designated the transition from the old year to the new.[28] Single-day festivals included the Thanks-to-the-Maple Festival, which occurred in late February or early March when the maple sap began to run and was collected; the Corn Planting Festival in May or early June; and the Strawberry Festival in June. The Green Corn Festival lasted four days in late August or early September to celebrate the ripening of the corn crop. Afterward, the women harvested the corn, beans, and squashes and placed them in winter storage. In October, Haudenosaunee villages held a one-day harvest festival to thank the spirit forces for a successful harvest.[29]

Thanksgiving addresses, singing, dancing, and feasting marked the activities at these celebrations. The activities at the Midwinter Festival, however, were the most elaborate. The ritualistic sacrifice of a white dog in some communities and dream guessing distinguished this particular celebration from others. The Jesuit Fremin called dreams "a single Divinity" among the Haudenosaunees. The Haudenosaunees paid close attention to their dreams, for they portended the future and revealed continuously the needs of the body, the soul, and the guardian spirit. One missionary noted that if a warrior dreamed that "another gave him a Blanket, a fat Deer[,] hog[,] or anything else, nay if he dream[ed] that he lay with his wife, the other does not deny him on the thing of his Dream." To not answer the dream doomed one to "soon die," or, at the very least, meet with misfortune for the rest of his or her life. *Yakononghwarore,* or dream guessing, also known as "the telling of minds," involved a person running from lodge to lodge, dropping clues about his or her dream, which the residents in the longhouses had to piece together and guess. It is believed that the ritual was held in honor of the Creator, Taronhiaouagon, "he who holds up the sky," which is also an alternate spelling of the name of the good twin.[30]

Sometimes dreamers called on experts—shamans, also known as diviners—to interpret and reveal to them the meanings of particularly difficult or disturbing dreams. They also called on said seers when there was a need to get in touch with "the other side of the Sky"—the Sky World—and divine the future. Shamans were unique in and invaluable to Haudenosaunee society, even though they had no special training for or birthright to that position. They were ordinary people who were "more favoured by the spirits," and therefore could peer "into the depths of others' souls." They possessed special powers that permitted them to walk among spirits who revealed to them sacred truths imbedded in dreams, wielded methods for bringing forth rain to the scorched earth, and knew how to "uncover the source of evil, conjure it, turn it aside, and apply a suitable remedy to it" (for example, to cure the sick with special potions, prayers, and rituals). Their ability to harness both positive and negative spirit forces and use them for "the public good" by revealing secrets and truths separated shamans from ordinary Haudenosaunee men and women.[31]

One condition most Protestant missionaries insisted on when baptizing a native tyro was that he or she vow publicly to renounce shamans, dreams, propitiation, and rituals of thanksgiving—what most missionaries and some baptized Mohawks came to regard as "all the superstitions of the country." Although most baptized Mohawks were unable to sustain their renunciation of all the old sacred ways, several found at the moment of "rebirth" their old Haudenosaunee ways less edifying. Christian concepts, such as sin, penance, forgiveness, and a merciful, glorious, just God—principles that did not exist in the Haudenosaunee sacred tradition—inspired some baptized Mohawks either to graft a new God-centered moral code onto their traditional habits and values or to replace the latter with the former, thus giving their lives new meaning in a world permeated with misery. This new code allowed them to sort out behavior: all acts should be directed toward pleasing God; all transgressions—injuries to one's self or others—displeased God. For both religious and secular reasons, they viewed the risks of compromising or forfeiting their "traditional ways" smaller than the danger of continuing to venture down a path strewn, from their perspective, with drunkenness, witchcraft, murders, and deadly diseases.[32] Faith in Christ, they reasoned, might light a new path.

Some Mohawks and other Haudenosaunee individuals who embraced Christianity did so for the rewards, both worldly and other worldly, that they perceived to be inherent in that faith. However, some individuals based their decision to embrace Christianity or to continue with the religion of their ancestors on the choices made by family or friends. This phenomenon helps to explain why so many members of a single family, like that of Tejonihokawara's, accepted Dutch Reform Protestantism in 1690, or why large groups comprising significant portions of Mohawk clans left the Mohawk Valley and relocated at Kahnawake during the final thirty-three years of the seventeenth century to live among Catholics. For example, Kryn, a Mohawk war chief, also known as Canaqueese; also Joseph Togouiroui; also Smiths John, the Great Mohawk; also "the Flemish bastard," conducted at his baptized wife's insistence two bands containing forty family members and friends from the Mohawk Valley to Kahnawake in the mid-1670s, where he "converted" to Catholicism and became an important headman. Some of the baptized Mohawk headmen who stayed behind in the Mohawk Valley generally desired that their families join them in performing Christianity, too. Some obliged them; many did not.[33]

Reciprocity and the need to maintain social equilibrium help explain the impulses behind individuals conforming to family and clan expectations. Members of the same clan residing in other nations—for example, Mohawk Wolves and Seneca Wolves—felt responsible for each other when visiting the other's village. The first question often asked of a stranger on entering a village was "Who are your people?" Once the visitor established his or her clan, the resident women of the clan prepared immediately a meal for the stranger. The Haudenosaunees also extended reciprocity through their moieties, which were related kinship groups, or "sides," within clans that sat across the longhouse fire from each other. During times of crisis, notably when burying and condoling the dead, members of the moiety complementary to that of the deceased were obliged to conduct mourning services and to attend to the needs of the grieving family.[34]

The league also divided itself into moieties: the Mohawks, the Onondagas, and the Senecas—the elder brothers—sat on one side of the council fire, while the younger brothers—the Oneidas, the Cayugas, and sometime after 1712 the Tuscaroras—sat on the other. At Onondaga, the site of the council fire, the six nations conducted business through selected leaders and orators with a strong sense of reciprocity, of give-and-take, as sachems of the elder nations discussed matters with their younger brothers across the fire before taking their considered opinions, reached by consensus, before the body of forty-nine peace chiefs.[35]

Likewise, reciprocity and balance conditioned relations between Haudenosaunee men and women. Men and women governed their respective domains according to the customs of the matrilineal-matrilocal Haudenosaunee society: men were in charge of the "forest," the setting beyond the village where warfare, hunting, fishing, trading (although many women also conducted trade), diplomacy, and treaty making occurred; women handled the village clearing, the venue for most matters domestic: horticulture, cooking, child rearing, festivals, supplying warriors, decisions of adoption, appointing sachems, and greeting strangers, including missionaries. The structure of Haudenosaunee society accorded Haudenosaunee women great influence, authority, and responsibility in society and politics.[36]

Most baptized Mohawks carried on with their traditional roles and obligations, but some did not, adopting instead the husbandry and domesticity practiced by their Dutch and English neighbors. Many non-baptized Mohawks regarded these baptized brethren as having "abandoned the Customs of their Country." Their Haudenosaunee critics often viewed them not as real men and women, but rather as French or Dutch, or sometimes as virtually dead. When in 1671 a highly esteemed Mohawk clan mother migrated with her two children to Kahnawake, her extended family held a public meeting to strip her of her inherited rank of honor, *otiyaner,* which they then conferred upon another. Nevertheless, most baptized Mohawks continued to live and identify as Haudenosaunee, as they observed the gendered and cultural rules governing Haudenosaunee society.[37] Nevertheless, baptized and nonbaptized Mohawks coexisted for decades before the first official SPG missionary arrived in the colony of New York in 1704 to service the Mohawks. By then, quite a few Mohawks had learned about Christianity from Jesuit priests and Dutch dominies, and thus held some expectations of the role missionaries ought to play.

## Identifications, Networks, and Performances among Catholicized Mohawks

Throughout the mid-seventeenth century, when conflicts among the Mohawks, Hurons, and the French were at their peak, Jesuit missionaries ventured down from New France to save the souls of the Haudenosaunees.

One of the first priests to take on this challenge was Father Isaac Jogues. In 1642, while on his way to deliver supplies and sermons to Huronia, Mohawk warriors in New France captured and transported him to Mohawk country. Along the way and in several Mohawk villages where his captors paraded him, Jogues and his party of four Frenchmen and fewer than a dozen baptized Hurons were ritually beaten, burned, and humiliated, according to wartime customs. The Mohawks killed a few of the Huron captives, and eventually slew Rene Goupil, a *donne* (assistant) to Jogues, whom his captives suspected of practicing witchcraft. Jogues lost a thumb and several fingers, and, like several of the Huron prisoners as well as Goupil, was adopted by a Mohawk family. In time, some nearby Dutch settlers, certain that the adopting family ill-treated Jogues, sequestered the priest and negotiated his release. When he returned to France, Jogues received special dispensation from the church to excuse him from administering communion. Amazingly, three years later, with the cessation of Mohawk-Huron-French hostilities, Jogues returned to Mohawk country to complete the task of establishing a mission there—a mission the Jesuits named "the Mission of martyrs." During his absence, the Mohawks suffered blight to their crops, for which some in the community blamed Jogues. They suspected that the small chest with his belongings that he had left behind had bewitched them. Shortly after the Jesuit's return, a young warrior took revenge on Jogues and with an ax cleaved and severed his head, which he then jammed onto a pole for public display as a caution to future black robes.[38] The Mohawks were not yet ready to receive Christianity.

However, once the Haudenosaunees concluded their withering war with the Hurons in the mid-1650s, the Mohawks, although not quite ready to accept the peace themselves, agreed to listen to Jesuit ambassadors rather than harm them. In 1654, Jesuit missionary Simon Le Moyne founded a mission at Onondaga, the League council seat. Some Mohawk headmen were unhappy about being bypassed, as the Mohawks regarded themselves the elder brothers of all the Haudenosaunee nations, and therefore should have been consulted first. Kryn, who would embrace Catholicism, cleverly berated Le Moyne for unilaterally choosing Onondaga by asking "ought not one to enter a house by the door, and not by the chimney or roof of the cabin, unless he be a thief, and wish to take the inmates by surprise . . . ? [W]ill you not enter the cabin by the door . . . ? It is with us Anniehronnons [Mohawks] that you should begin."[39] Kryn intimated to Le Moyne that if he wished to pray with the Haudenosaunees, he best learn Haudenosaunee etiquette.

A dozen years later, the Mohawks hosted two Catholic missions: Saint Pierre at Gandaouague, and Saint Marie in the nearby village of Gandagaro (Canagora). The Jesuit missionary Jacques Bruyas regarded the mission at Gandaouague more important than Le Moyne's at Onondaga, calling the Saint Pierre mission "the first and principal mission that we have among the Haudenosaunee." More Haudenosaunees performed Christianity here than anywhere else in Iroquoia because captive baptized Hurons and Algonquian speakers made up two-thirds of the population of Gandaouague. Father Fremin was pleased to report that this first chapel in Mohawk country was built by the Mohawks themselves, primarily for the use of the Hurons.[40] Unchurched Mohawks recognized and accepted that some among them needed to supplement their traditional faith with Christianity, or had exchanged the former for the latter.

The missions had a dual purpose: to increase God's flock by transforming Haudenosaunee traditionalists into Catholics, and in the process bring Iroquoia into France's political and commercial orbit. After 1664, when England purloined New York from the Dutch, English officials worried over the Jesuits continuously drawing off Mohawks and other Haudenosaunees to Kanawake. English officials viewed the Haudenosaunees as the bulwark against French incursions. One New York governor called the work of Jesuits "a stalking horse to there [sic] pretence," meaning the priests used religion as a means to political ends.[41]

The priests adopted several methods to meet their ends. They often commenced their work by trying to cultivate positive relations with the male headmen of the particular village targeted for the mission. They not only believed that converted leaders would make the social and political environments of their respective villages safer for missionaries, but also insisted that the headmen would serve as positive examples for the rest of the community. The missionaries also tried to insinuate themselves into the community by discrediting and then supplanting the shamans, the native seers and diviners. The Jesuits scoffed publicly at the medicine they practiced, particularly the reading of dreams, hoping that the residents would see this exercise as superstitious. They employed "tricks" to shame the shamans, such as predicting lunar eclipses, reading and writing, and rendering compasses, clocks, and other objects of European technology mysterious. They even proclaimed religious superiority over shamans on the grounds that their own immune systems were more robust than that of shamans in combating European-imported diseases.[42]

Perhaps the stealthiest Jesuit method of undermining the prominence of shamans was to make correlations between Christian doctrines and venerated figures and Haudenosaunee sacred beliefs and spirits. For example, the Jesuits encouraged their native hearers to equate God with Taronhiaouagon, the Creator; the Virgin Mary with Sky Woman; Jesus with a warrior, who like Christ endured torture; baptism with adoption and rebirth; the symbolic powers of Christian amulets, including crucifixes, rosaries, and rings, with the spirits of Haudenosaunee talismans, such as small leather pouches containing bits of bone and hair and other objects of powerful medicine, wampum belts, and stone and wooden relics. Some catechumens accepted these equivalents, while others found them too farfetched.[43]

Two key Christian concepts that Haudenosaunee neophytes had difficulty grasping were sin and its associated commandment, forgiveness. Neither sin nor forgiveness was an axial concept in the Haudenosaunee sacred world. In Christianity, the greatest sin of all was displeasing God, for which one must ask forgiveness. In Haudenosaunee faith practice, displeasing God was unknown. However, one could commit a terrible offense by failing to propitiate the guardian spirit of a slain animal. Asking God for forgiveness for transgressions committed against him was an unfamiliar concept, for the Haudenosaunee's Creator was not all omnipotent. On the other hand, the Haudenosaunee concept of maintaining balance and harmony in ones world through reciprocity with *individuals* was foundational. Thus, harm done to an individual required redress, not forgiveness. Historian Daniel Richter has demonstrated convincingly how some Native neophytes in New England translated this concept by holding God's sixth through tenth commandments, which itemize transgressions against fellow human beings, much more dearly than the first five commandments, which define sins against God. Although some Mohawks would find forgiveness helpful in minimizing revenge killings, most neophyte and baptized Mohawks wrestled with this concept. For example, in summer of 1700, David Schuyler, an Albany-area fur trader and frequent emissary to New France, met a young baptized Mohawk living at Kahnawake. To test the mettle of his newfound Catholic faith, he asked the young man if one warrior killed another, should not it be enough to simply "go to the Priest and he shall absolve him" of his crime, although the Old Testament asserts that blood spilled will be avenged with blood? The young neophyte, well aware of the Haudenosaunee principle of small-scale mourning wars to replace the dead, answered that he doubted he could forgive the killer.[44]

Although sin and forgiveness may have been difficult for Jesuits to translate, they were largely successful in conveying the practice of singing psalms, of venerating pictures of Mary and Christ, and of participating in ceremonial services, including submitting to baptism, which most Haudenosaunees regarded as powerful medicine. The Jesuits also convinced many baptized Mohawks of the importance of taking communion, which they explained conferred on one a new identity, a new personhood. For most Haudenosaunee people, the most daunting initial hurdle to taking the plunge was baptism. If the ritual did not kill one and send one "to Heaven sooner" than one wished—Jesuits baptized regularly many mortally ill indigenes just before they died so that their souls might go to heaven—then perhaps it may act as a curative, or at least offer protection prophylactically from future calamities and diseases. Concomitantly, Jesuits often refused to baptize Native supplicants who insisted on it but appeared unready to "embrace the faith." Most priests thought of these individuals as "desir[ing] baptism solely as a means which they consider suitable for the success of some design." Often, the Native petitioner replied that he or she would then wait and, by and by, "pray to God from time to time in the Chapel" and would let the priest know when he or she was ready. Although some confusion may have materialized among the Haudenosaunees when the Jesuits made correlations between the two faiths, one modern-day sociologist suggests that Native hearers may not have had to make a great cognitive leap, for all supranatural beings of all faiths have always required worship, propitiation, and sacrifice. Consequently, the Jesuits believed they had great success in making Christianity meaningful to the Haudenosaunee. By their own count, they baptized about sixteen thousand Native peoples in the Northeast during the middle third of the seventeenth century, including scores of Mohawks who were drawn to Kahnawake and other missions in New France.[45] The story of Assendasé, an influential Mohawk headman, stands as an example of one who submitted to baptism on his terms when he was ready.

When Father Jacques Bruyas and Assendasé met around 1671, the sachem was known as "one of the most notable men of [the Mohawk] nation . . . the head of one of the leading families." Assendasé resisted repeatedly Bruyas's entreaties to learn about Catholicism, for as the priest put it the headman "derived considerable profit from the practice of superstitions," meaning that Assendasé either exalted publicly Mohawk shamans or himself practiced augury. Bruyas denounced what he viewed as Assendasé's "arrogance and his treacherous and dissembling character," for it "rendered his conversion very difficult." Perhaps Bruyas misread Assendasé's dissemblance as a "yes" that the headman meant as a "no," which the historian John Webster Grant has shown was a form of native etiquette used to not embarrass the other party during face-to-face encounters. Native peoples resorted often to this discursive weapon, which James Scott has called a "partial," or "hidden," transcript. Such behavior constitutes a performance of dissimulation that was a form of resistance that disguised and protected one's true interests, deployed most often when in contact with a more powerful broker.[46]

Bruyas complained that Assendasé's resistance to him lay in the headman's unwillingness to bear the "raillery" that he was sure to invite as a convert. Assendasé, a man in his sixties, forestalled submitting to baptism for another two years, when, according to Bruyas, the headman had an epiphany following a diplomatic visit to Canada. There, in the summer of 1673, on the eastern banks of Lake Ontario, not far from the Haudenosaunee village of Kente (Quinte), Assendasé, along with "more than sixty of the oldest and most influential of the sachims" of the Haudenosaunee Confederacy, heard the Count de Frontenac, the new governor of New France, offer a powerful inducement to the Haudenosaunees to "embrace the [Catholic] faith." Perhaps the first key incentive lay in Frontenac's venturing into Haudenosaunee country, the first governor of New France to do so. Until then, the Haudenosaunees had to travel to Montreal or to Quebec City to parlay with the French. Frontenac came to the Great Lake to ratify a treaty that his predecessor, Governor Courcelle, had negotiated that established the terms of peace and trade between the Five Nations Haudenosaunee and the Ottawas. The agreement stipulated that the Haudenosaunees were to give to the Ottawas "all the goods they required." In return, the Ottawas were to "carry to them [the Haudenosaunees] all their peltries, and the exchange was to take place on Lake Ontario."[47] However, there was one catch to this deal: the Haudenosaunees had to become Christian.

Assendasé and the other Haudenosaunee headmen appeared to be intrigued by this offer. It embodied reciprocity at its best: the Five Nations would prosper through trade and feel militarily secure while New France prospered under the protection of—and in cooperation with—a reinvigorated Ottawa nation. All that Frontenac required of Assendasé and the other headmen was to "adore the same God that I [Frontenac] adore." Frontenac explained that he called his god Jesus, who is "the Sovereign Lord of Heaven and of Earth; the absolute Master of your lives and properties; who hath created you; who preserves you; who furnishes you food and drink; who can send death among you in a moment . . . who can render you happy or miserable, as he pleaseth."[48] Evidently, Frontenac tried to translate Christ as a very powerful *orrenna*.

Frontenac concluded his offer by redefining Franco-Haudenosaunee sociopolitical relations by fashioning himself as "father" to his Haudenosaunee "children." No other French governor had used that "mark of authority," and the Haudenosaunees had never before agreed to the parent-child metaphor for defining their relationship with the French, always insisting on the term "Brother."[49] Fathers, according to Haudenosaunee tradition, were providers and protectors. However, brothers of mothers were also referred to as "fathers," which indicates that "father" did not carry the weight of patriarchy for the Haudenosaunees as Frontenac had assumed. Nevertheless, Assendasé and the other headmen appeared to accept this redefinition, perhaps to save face for Frontenac.[50]

To clinch the deal, Frontenac offered to make trade goods—"all sorts of refreshments and commodities"—plentiful and available "at the cheapest rate possible" at a newly proposed fort on Lake Ontario. To reinforce his point, the governor distributed among the sachems gifts of muskets, powder, lead, and flints; large overcoats, shirts, and stockings; packages of glass beads; and wine, brandy, and biscuits. To the women and children, he gave bread, prunes, and raisins.[51]

Assendasé and many of the other headmen thanked Frontenac for his generosity and for urging them to become Christians, which they explained diplomatically "was the greatest advantage that could ever accrue to them." They offered "that they would themselves endeavor to show them [the young men and children] the example by receiving respectfully the Instructions of the Black Gowns [Jesuits]." The headmen then immediately pressed the point about trade goods priced as cheaply as possible. What "was the price [Frontenac] would fix on the merchandise" at the new fort? Frontenac skirted the issue, claiming that he did not know, for he had not yet calculated the costs of shipping the goods to the new fort. But not to worry: he intended to treat them not "otherwise than as Frenchmen."[52]

Ostensibly, Frontenac was able to accomplish what Bruyas could not for more than two years: steer Assendasé toward a new path. According to Bruyas, Assendasé was so overcome by "divine inspiration" at this 1673 council meeting—and likely puffed with pride and exuberance over a new trade deal—that on return to his village, the headman insisted that the Jesuit instruct him in Christianity at once and baptize him. At sixty-five years of age, he submitted to baptism and took the name Peter Assendasé. On the surface, his "conversion" appears to have been motivated by the need to satisfy material and political exigencies. Now that peace between the Mohawks and the French had been restored, it was to Assendasé's benefit as a headman to seek advantageous relations with their neighbor to the north by whatever means necessary. Yet Assendasé, risking "raillery," became a model Christian, according to Bruyas, one of the most devout Catholics in all of Iroquoia, surpassing in piety the Onondaga sachem Daniel Garakontie, regarded by most Jesuits as the other model convert in Iroquoia. Peter Assendasé denounced "all the superstitions of the country" and "renounced dreams," the cornerstone of Haudenosaunee sacred practice. No more did he participate in *yakononghwarore,* or dream guessing; or tolerate *oski,* the invocations offered by shamans as part of their curing practices; or supplicate positive and negative spirits to keep the world in harmony. Rather, Peter Assendasé allegedly worshiped the same God as Frontenac. Like the bishop of Peterborough, who claimed almost a century later that the "seeds of [established] Religion . . . will be the firmest bond, the most assured pledge of . . . fielty" to nations and alliances, Assendasé affirmed that by performing Catholicism, he signaled that he would not relinquish the affection he felt for the French, even if the French made war on his Mohawk brethren. Assendasé felt so committed to his new faith that he desired that his fellow Mohawks, beginning with his family, "should receive baptism, as he had done."[53]

Assendasé's wish supports the theory that conversions tended to occur among family members. Still, Bruyas linked the baptism of Assendasé and his kin with a groundswell of interest among Mohawks in general in baptism. He administered the sacrament to eighty Mohawk individuals between 1673 and 1675, baptizing fifty alone in 1675. So many children and adults presented themselves to the Jesuit that he grew very cautious and selective over whom to baptize. Nevertheless, with the increased interest in baptism grew the wrath of some of the elders, who threatened to expel the priest from Iroquoia.[54]

Bruyas was not the only target of the elders' anger. Assendasé did indeed suffer "railleries" and other abuses from his brethren for renouncing dreams. Bruyas had predicted one cost to the headman: Assendasé was alienated from his community. When sickness struck Assendasé's lodge about February or March 1675, he refused to let shamans examine and treat him. Some headmen denounced Assendasé for bringing "misfortune upon himself by his baptism." Bruyas quipped that Assendasé's brethren were so upset with him that they almost made him the first native Christian martyr in Iroquoia. One relative actually attacked Assendasé physically, ripping the crucifix from his neck, and threatened to kill him if the headman did not renounce his new faith. Assendasé refused, wishing, according to Bruyas, to die happily "for so good a cause."[55] If we may believe Bruyas, Assendasé's faith may have run deeper than biscuits and prunes.

Nevertheless, Assendasé's performance of Catholicism reinforced his role as an important broker to form relationships with the French through their key brokers, in this case Father Bruyas and Governor Frontenac, to solidify the Haudenosaunees' commitment to enlarge their imagined community. Through baptism, Assendasé expanded his and his family's sphere of influence beyond their local village and nation. Through a new trade alliance and a peace accord with New France, he hoped to mitigate the need for war in the future. One way to accomplish this was through middle-ground accommodation, often expressed through performance of what is imagined to be the other's culture. Ultimately, performance requires an audience to edify the performer's presentations, and Assendasé found his onlookers in both his Mohawk brethren and Bruyas.

Like Assendasé, some baptized Mohawks performed their Christianity with sincere passion and enthusiasm at great personal risk. The most pious of them usually had to leave the Mohawk Valley and move to Kahnawake, as did Kateri Tekakwitha.

One historian has argued that Kateri Tekakwitha, who was orphaned at an early age, is an example of a Mohawk who relocated to Kahnawake and fully embraced Catholicism because she lacked "broad webs of kin and friends." Although Kateri may have felt isolated from her kin and clan, she nevertheless tapped into a broad web of friends, primarily baptized Huron women, who brought her over to Christianity.[56]

Kateri Tekakwitha was born in 1656 in the village of Gandaouague (Kaghnuwage), the site of the Saint Pierre mission. Adopted baptized Hurons constituted the majority of worshipers at Gandaouague. Kateri's mother, a baptized Algonquian speaker, was raised among the French at Trois-Rivières, located on the St. Lawrence River halfway between Montreal and Quebec City. Mohawk warriors captured her during their raid on the French settlement and brought her to Gandaouague, where a Mohawk family adopted her, and in time she married Kateri's Mohawk father. In 1660, smallpox killed Kateri's parents and brother and left Kateri with weakened eyes that were extremely sensitive to light. Her infirmity limited her ability to perform the chores expected of Mohawk girls and young women, such as hauling water, gathering firewood, and grinding corn. She spent most of her time secluded in the darkness of her aunt's longhouse.[57]

One of Kateri's favorite activities that brought her out of the longhouse was seeing to the needs of visiting Jesuit missionaries, a role assigned to women. In 1667 when Kateri was about twelve, Fathers Jacques Fremin, Jacques Bruyas, and Jean Pierron arrived in Gandaouague to rekindle their missionary work. They were pleased to find at Kateri's village so many of their "old Christians who had formerly been instructed in their own Huron country by our Fathers." The three men claimed that despite the fact that these Hurons "had been several years deprived of the sight of their pastors," piety remained "well rooted . . . in the souls of these poor Captives."[58] Although the Jesuits may have credited God with keeping the Hurons "faithful," a sodality of baptized Huron women at Gandaouague kept the embers of piety warm and instructed some Mohawk women in Catholicism.

One unnamed Mohawk woman badgered Fremin to instruct and baptize her. The priest put her off, finding her a pest, for he neither had instructed her nor knew her. At length, the woman explained to Fremin that "a good Huron woman" had instructed her daily in "the prayers and principal Rites of our Faith." Upon examination, the woman recited for Fremin "without error all the prayers and principal articles of the Faith." He baptized her.[59]

Baptized Huron women also played a critical role in Kateri's performance of Catholicism. Kateri participated regularly in—or observed—church services at the Saint Pierre mission, and so witnessed and listened intently to the church choir, composed largely of Huron women. The music historian Glenda Goodman suggests that Native psalmody validated the efficacy of the missionary's project. Perhaps "certified" Native mimesis of Christianity rather than validated mission work is a more useful way of thinking about indigenous performances of psalmody. The Jesuits at Gandaouague declared that the women sang "the hymns and sacred canticles . . . with much exactness and harmony," thanks to their fine ears and "a rare taste for music." Perhaps drawn by psalmody, Kateri visited the chapel for daily prayers and instruction and asked the new Jesuit priest, Jacques de Lamberville, who arrived at Gandaouague in 1675, for her own personal prayers, devotions, and penances. Lamberville obliged her, and in time Kateri proved to be such a devout woman of incomparable virtue that she refused to take a husband, choosing instead to marry herself to Christ. She was baptized on Easter Day 1676 and given the Christian name "Catherine" after Catherine of Siena, the fourteenth-century ascetic saint.[60]

Because of Kateri's celibacy, piety, and her delicate health, often compounded by injury and illness, she suffered the wrath of her father's family for being an unreliable member of the community. Some Mohawk women even withheld food from her. They decided that if she neither worked nor married a provider, she should not eat. Eventually, Kateri concluded that her only option for survival lay in migrating to Kahnawake, where she hoped to find providers and protectors.[61]

After careful, deceptive planning, Kateri arrived secretly at Kahnawake in 1677. She resided in the longhouse of Anastasia, a pious widow who lived formerly in the village of Gandagaro, the location of the Saint Marie mission. Anastasia took it upon herself to continue instructing

Kateri, and the two women formed "a most intimate friendship." They discussed mainly the sins they had most recently committed and of ways to expiate them by doing penance. Each Saturday, Kateri inflicted mortifications on her body as mea culpas for her previous week's sins.[62]

At length, Kateri seemed unable to forgive herself for the least offense. She and some of the other baptized women devised "a thousand new inventions to inflict suffering upon themselves." Some women performed culpas for the sins that they and their children had yet to commit, hoping to atone in advance for future transgressions. Some of the most pious devotees pierced their flesh with "belts lined with points of iron," "stripped themselves to the waist . . . and remained a long time exposed to the rigor of the [winter] season, on the banks of a frozen river," where they sometimes "plunged themselves in up to the neck, and remained there as long as it was necessary . . . to recite many times the ten beads of their rosary." After hearing from Anastasia that torture by fire was "a great merit with the Lord," Kateri "burned her feet and limbs with a hot brand," in the way that Native captors branded their slaves, and by this she "declared herself the slave of her Saviour." Despite the efforts of some Jesuits to have Kateri moderate her mortifications, these and other deprivations surely contributed to her early death in 1680 at the age of twenty-four.[63]

Historians have offered several "translations" to explain Kateri's "conversion" to Catholicism. David Blanchard reads the severe culpas as Haudenosaunee expressions of crossing to the other side of the Sky, where the good spirits dwelled. Blanchard offers that the Haudenosaunee word *hotouongannandi* used by some of the most pious devotees means "public penance." Its literal translation means "they are making magic." Hence, Blanchard suggests that Kateri and the sisters of her sodality engaged in *hotouongannandi* to reveal to the Jesuits their ultra-Christian piety.[64] While Blanchard's interpretation is intriguing, it does not answer the question of where in Haudenosaunee culture one may find evidence of self-mutilation.

Nancy Shoemaker offers a compelling answer to this question by reading Kateri's baptism and performances of devotion through the lens of gender. Kateri's new identity, according to Shoemaker, represents a kind of rebirth. She suggests that women "converts" at Kahnawake may have viewed baptism as a kind of requickening and regarded self-mutilation as a referent to the physical torture meted out to captives—and to Christ. Concomitant with their self-abuse, they acquired new names and thus new identities. Both baptism and requickening used "holy water"—sprinkled at baptisms, drunk at requickenings—and relied on the custom of adoptees taking on new yet existing names and identities. For Kateri Tekakwitha, baptism may have represented a form of empowerment otherwise not available to women at a male-controlled mission.[65] However, Shoemaker's argument of baptism as the equivalent of requickening for native women may not hold up in all cases, as most captives who ran the gauntlet and thus were the target of torture and pain were male warriors, although some captive women were also subjected to similar treatment.

The historian Allan Greer argues that Kateri's sodality at Kahnawake may have had its roots in early Haudenosaunee curing societies that cohered around particular shamans, similarly to Holy Family sodalities forming under the guidance of a Jesuit priest. The two "societies" shared common characteristics: the use of sacred objects, prayers and chants, and engagement of salutary work for the benefit of the community. More-over, the extreme physical mortifications they inflicted on their bodies as part of their ascetic performance, Greer suggests in agreement with Blanchard, were a means to experiencing "mystical ecstasy." Through self-inflicted pain and deprivation, Kateri and her sisters in the sodality exercised extreme control over their bodies that altered their senses and enabled them to get in touch with the divine.[66] However, the question remains, "Which divine—the Haudenosaunee or the Christian?"

Surely, many, if not most, baptized Mohawk women at Kahnawake made connections between some Catholic practices and Haudenosaunee sacred traditions. Nevertheless, I argue that it is important to acknowledge that some Mohawks who identified as pious Christians redefined their worlds through their newfound faith. Kateri and her sisters in her sodality were doing something new: taking on the sins of the world. Although the concept of sin did not exist in the unchurched Haudenosaunee worldview, it very much existed at Kahnawake. The mortifications and mea culpas that the ultrapious inflicted on themselves may have been their way of bearing the weight of the sins of the world, caused not by outside agents, like alcohol or witches, but by impious, sinful individuals themselves. The job, so to speak, of many of the baptized women as wives to Christ—as tortured surrogates—was to rebalance the world by taking on the responsibilities of the world's sins according to their reading of God's sixth through tenth commandments forbidding acts of transgression against fellow human beings. Moreover, Kateri found a network of fictive kin dedicated to the Virgin Mary. Their sodality would have attracted many Haudenosaunee women who were single, widowed, or infirm, like Kateri and Anastasia. Performing together the rites and rituals of the sodality gave these women their identification and offered them a supportive and affirming community.

Mohawks who stayed behind in Mohawk country experienced relationships with Protestant ministers very differently from their brethren in New France. In New France, Mohawk neophytes felt invited to learn Catholicism, and thus regarded themselves as equal participants in reciprocity. Those who remained in the Mohawk Valley often felt marginalized by Dutch pastors, who rarely ventured into Mohawk country. Some dominies baptized many, but only a few select Mohawks, whom the dominies deemed most pious, experienced reciprocity.

### Identifications, Networks, and Performances among Protestantized Mohawks

Dutch dominies filled the lacunae left by Jesuits, who grew increasingly scarce in Iroquoia after 1680. Seething resentment between French authorities in New France and English authorities in the colonies to the south led to growing French anti-Haudenosaunee sentiments, demonstrated by French raids into Iroquoia in the 1660s and 1680s. These feelings garnered, in turn, reciprocal anti-French feelings among many Haudenosaunees. As it became riskier for Jesuits to meet with their baptized Haudenosaunee tyros, some Mohawks called for Protestant ministers.

In May 1691, a group of "praying Indians of the three Tribes or races of the Maquas"—that is, from the three principal Mohawk villages—approached Governor Henry Sloughter at the annual council meeting in Albany and asked for ministers. These men attended the meeting not "commissionate by the Sachims of our Nation to treat of publick affairs," but rather as men of minor authority, who wanted to pray.[67]

They first explained to Sloughter what had become obvious to them: "the weake and faint setting forward of that great worke hitherto among

us"—that is, the lackluster commitment to instruct them in Christianity—
"has occasioned our Bretheren to be drawn out of our Country to the
French by their Priests." Now, they wanted Sloughter to realize that it
was their "earnest request and desire . . . that we may have ministers
to instruct us as well"—as effectively and as dependably—"as the French
send Priests to instruct their Indians . . . [for] the Great God of Heaven
has opened our eyes, that we discerne the difference betwixt Christianity
and Paganism." The unnamed Mohawk orator assured Sloughter that
his group, if not his brethren as a whole, were prepared and equipped to
receive religious instruction, for they had "partaken of that benefit to be
instructed in the (true Christian Religion, and we Desyre and Pray the
Continuation of it, that we may be Instructed in the) Religion of the Great
King of England that is the Protestant Religion, wherein we are instructed
already."[68] The orator, most likely either Hendrick or Joseph, both baptized in 1690, deployed middle-ground diplomacy by demonstrating that
they knew something about Christianity and by appealing to what they
presumed to be Sloughter's belief about alliance building through a shared
religion. They also performed concomitantly Haudenosaunee diplomacy
by punctuating each important point with a gift of either a beaver or an
otter pelt.[69]

Sloughter was surprised and pleased to learn that their "understanding in Religion [was] so farr advanced" that from his Manichaean
understanding of the world, they could not only "distinguish between
the Christian Religion and Paganism but also between the Reformed
Religion and that of the Romans." What Sloughter may not have fully
understood is that these Mohawk diplomats communicated their desire
to perform the faith of and with their Dutch neighbors in order to bring
them into the Great League of Peace.[70]

Some Mohawks may have desired Dutch ministers for reasons of
familiarity with the Dutch language, faith, and Dutch patrons. Their
relations with the Dutch reached back to the time of the Two Row Wampum Belt during the early seventeenth century. Their first encounter
with a Dutch dominie dates from the 1640s, when the minister Johannes
Megapolensis arrived in Rensselaerswyck, the settlement just east of
present-day Albany. Between 1642 and 1650, Megapolensis learned a
little of the Mohawk language and customs so that he might someday
preach to them. However, he had little success making converts, due

to Mohawk skepticism over his teachings, coupled with Megapolensis's arrogance and intolerance. He whined that the Mohawks were so "very stupid [that] I sometimes cannot make them understand what I want." Reflecting on his own limitations did not occur to him. A man of delicate sensibilities, Megapolensis also complained about what he considered their poor personal hygiene, which he described as "slovenly": "they wash neither their faces nor hands, but let all remain upon their yellow skin, and look like hogs." One can imagine the repressed dread and anxiety of the minister and his wife when one night eight Mohawk overnight guests fell asleep "at once . . . upon the floor . . . in our chambers before our beds."[71]

Although Megapolensis claimed to find the Mohawks "very friendly to us," he actually spent little time with them. The few Mohawks who came to his services often stared in wonderment that he was allowed to speak at such length "while none of the rest may speak." Sometimes they laughed when the white congregants prayed. The efficacy of hushed prayer seemed ludicrous to them when compared to the lively, audible supplications, like dancing, chanting, and singing, designed to grab the attention of Haudenosaunee spirits. Finally, when Megapolensis explained to the Haudenosaunees that he admonished Dutch settlers for stealing, for lewdness, for drunkenness, and for committing other sins—and that he would soon be by to admonish the Mohawks for the same—they replied that he "did well to teach the Christians." When asked why professed Christians do these things, Megapolensis had no answer, but explained that the Dutch had to "set a better example" for the Mohawks if the church was to reap a good harvest of Native souls.[72]

Missionary work conducted by Dutch ministers among the Mohawks fell off when Megapolensis departed for New Amsterdam in 1650. A few dominies preached off and on to the Albanians over the next three decades. However, not until the 1680s would the Dutch of Albany and their Native neighbors have access to a reliable resident Dutch minister.[73]

Godfridus Dellius, thirty years old when he arrived at the Dutch Reformed Church in Albany in 1683, answered the community's call. Very quickly, he became popular among the local Dutch residents and, in time, earned the acceptance of the Mohawks who sought his services. He began instructing the Mohawks in the autumn of 1689, a few months before he fled to New Jersey, then to Long Island, and finally to Boston to escape political persecution by Jacob Leisler during his coup (1689–91). Before departing the Albany area in 1690, Dellius baptized the Mohawk headman Tejonihokarawa—"open the door"—who took the Christian name Hendrick. Like Assendasé's family, Hendrick's family followed his example and submitted to baptism. They and a few others whom Dellius baptized represented a small corps of Mohawks who continuously lobbied New York officials to see to their reciprocal duties of sending ministers to them.[74]

Later in 1690, Dellius's congregation wrote to the classis in Amsterdam to convey its disappointment over Dellius's absence. His flight left not only his own church and all of "the neighboring churches . . . in a languishing condition," but "grieve[d]" the Mohawks, whom he had instructed "during the past year . . . at his own expense . . . out of pure love." Following Leisler's execution on May 16, 1691, Governor Sloughter asked Dellius to return to Albany. Sloughter paid Dellius sixty pounds per year to instruct the Mohawks, and within a few years housed three Mohawk pupils in his home. By the late 1690s, Dellius had "incorporated quite a number [of Mohawks], after public confession and baptism, in the church, much to the astonishment of everybody." In 1693, the New England Company, the missionary body that oversaw the catechizing of Iroquoian speakers in New England, endorsed his work among the Mohawks by contributing forty pounds per year to his salary. With the help of Hilletie Van Olinda, his assistant and provincial interpreter for New York, for which she received twenty pounds per year, Dellius learned to be sensitive to certain Mohawk customs, bringing often small gifts to his church and prayer services whenever Mohawk churchgoers came to Albany or Schenectady to conduct trade.[75]

Hilletie also helped Dellius communicate the Dutch Reformed Calvinist teachings to his Mohawk catechumens. Together, they translated "several prayers, the Ten Commandments, the [Apostle's] Creed . . . the Confession of Faith . . . before the Lord's Supper . . . and eight or ten Psalms," from Dutch into Mohawk. Dellius set psalms to music, which the Mohawks sang "with sweet melody." Largely on the strength of this evidence and that of a staunchly devout group of baptized Mohawks, the bishop of London hailed Dellius in 1700 as "the only man that understood how to converse with the Mohacks [sic] of whom he had converted several to a sincere embracing of the Christian Faith."[76] Yet it would be folly to credit Dellius solely for this success, as Hilletie carried great influence among tyros and catechumens.

As a biracial Christian daughter, wife, and mother, Hilletie inhabited for years the cultural margins of greater Albany's Dutch-Mohawk community. Early in life, she lived with her Mohawk mother, Ots-Toch, in Canajoharie, but later in life she resided in Schenectady and the world of her carpenter-mason Dutch father, Cornelis Anthonisz Van Slyck, and her merchant husband, Pieter Danielson Van Olinda, as well as her two biracial brothers, who identified as Dutch. In time, Hilletie and her mother apparently took advantage of Cornelis's and Pieter's connections, for they interacted frequently in Schenectady and Albany with Dutch traders, who also visited their Mohawk village.[77]

Through repeated contacts, Hilletie attracted the attention of some of the more pious Dutch settlers in Schenectady. After noticing that her behavior (and no doubt her physical features) bore "more resemblance to the Christians than the Indians . . . and that she was not so wild as the other [Native] children," some Dutch residents in Schenectady took an interest in instructing Hilletie in the principles of Dutch Reformed Protestantism. Ots-Toch would not hear of it. Nevertheless, the more the Dutch persisted, the more Hilletie grew to like the idea of becoming a Christian, and the more her mother and siblings criticized and abused her. Soon, Hilletie was forced to leave Ots-Toch's lodge and village and relocate to Schenectady, where she took up residence in a household as one of several servants.[78]

In addition to performing Dutch-style housework, Hilletie learned how to read and write Dutch and studied the Bible and the traditions of the Dutch Reformed Church. Meanwhile, the other maids, presumably Dutch, constantly expressed their vexation and annoyance with her, possibly because of Hilletie's deep desire to grasp the meaning of Christ rather than rejoice in the splendor of sweeping. The maids were not alone in harassing Hilletie; Dutch boys and young men bullied and badgered her, as well. In 1680, she told Jasper Danckaerts, the Labadist, that sometimes when she rebuked her tormentors for their drunkenness and use of foul, godless language, they replied, "'Well, how is this, there is a sow converted. Run boys, to the brewer's and bring some swill for a converted sow,' words which went through my heart, made me sorrowful and closed my mouth."[79] These bullies read Hilletie's "reduction" as a form of domestication; she transformed herself into the chattel of the Dutch and, thus, could be sustained as much by the slop from the distillery—swill, the waste product commonly fed to hogs—as by the teachings of Christ.[80]

Such insults and slights stiffened Hilletie's piety rather than weakened it. Danckaerts found Hilletie far more devout than the local Dutch residents and expressed surprise "to find so far in the woods . . . a person who should address me with such affection and love of God." Danckaerts testified that her husband, Pieter Danielson Van Olinda, was quite lucky to be married to Hilletie, who set him "a good example" and knew "how to direct him."[81] A combination of factors, similar to those that affected Kateri Tekakwitha, help explain why Hilletie embraced Christianity. As with Kateri, kin pushed Hilletie from her Mohawk community. Concomitantly, a few pious Dutch worshipers and dominies, rather than the community of Schenectady, pulled her into the Christian fold. Hilletie yearned from an early age to penetrate the secret religious knowledge of her father's community at a time when the Mohawks could ill-afford to lose League-born members. Moreover, the two Jesuit missions, St. Pierre and St. Marie, in two of the Mohawk communities, stood as visible signs of Mohawk alliance with the French. As such, the Mohawks in Canajoharie may have regarded Hilletie's allegiance to her Dutch father's community problematic. Nevertheless, kinship ties, like a shared faith, forged strong links of alliance in Haudenosaunee society. Initially, Hilletie's embrace of Dutch Reformed Protestantism may have been her search for a new moral code. However, in time, Hilletie also acquired the ancillary worldly reward of literacy, which accrued her the additional rewards of an income, status, and influence in the Mohawk-Dutch political and religious worlds.

## Conclusion: The Imagined Christian Community

Without the encouragement of individual Catholic priests, Dutch pastors, and colonial officials, it is doubtful that more than a few Mohawks would have been enticed to cross the cultural divide and perform their faiths. These European culture brokers promised these native neophytes rewards, some worldly, others otherworldly, if they embraced Christianity. For some, such as Assendasé, material rewards—trade goods, enhanced wealth and prestige, and military protection—were sufficient rewards to justify supplicating Jesus Christ, perhaps as a supplementary spirit, although during his few short Christian years, Assendasé appears to have tried to thwart the influences of the sacred world of unchurched Mohawks. Kateri Tekakwitha and Hilletie Van Olinda, on the other hand, sought first and foremost a new moral code by which to live. Their new faith allowed them to fit more comfortably into their new worlds orchestrated by priests and pastors than that of the old shaped by sachems, warriors, and clan matrons. Yet Hilletie's additional rewards—literacy, income, status, and privilege—earned her ostracism from some members of her Mohawk community and discrimination from Dutch settlers.

Nonetheless, through their identification with Christianity, these seventeenth-century baptized Mohawks shared other common variables. Assendasé and Kateri found some comfort in their final years in communities of baptized kin, biological and fictive. In the process, all three "opened the door" to priests and pastors, individuals with whom each formed close relations in fulfillment of their roles as culture brokers.

During the tumultuous times of King William's War, most baptized Mohawks felt compelled to choose sides—French, Dutch, English, or Haudenosaunee Protestant—in order to survive with dignity. Many of the Mohawks who aligned themselves with Europeans changed some aspects of their cultural habits: Christian rituals supplemented or replaced Haudenosaunee sacred practices, European-style subsistence farming slowly replaced Haudenosaunee horticultural practices, fabric garb augmented or replaced animal hides and furs. Some even changed their places of abode and patterns of subsistence. As early as 1684, Johannes Sanders Glen of Schenectady had contracted with a Mohawk sachem to plow the headman's fields. Although Haudenosaunee women still "commonly owned" the land and thus exercised authority over who could do what with it, Glen's contract implies that some male sachems may have claimed private ownership to some land.[82]

The Mohawks experienced the most sustained contact with Europeans among all the Haudenosaunees. They responded to the stress of contact in creative and flexible ways by typically invoking the Haudenosaunee principle of reciprocity, the engine that powered all interpersonal and international relations. In the process, they insinuated themselves into the other's faith community and sought to turn outsiders into insiders. They drew upon the convention of "covenant chains" to remind the French, the Dutch, and the English of their political, economic, and cultural obligations and responsibilities. About this same time, pious men in England responded with their own ideas on how to build an imagined Haudenosaunee-Anglo community on *their* terms using faith as the foundation on which to build the community, the subject of the next chapter.[83]

# CHAPTER 2

# "Ordering the Life and Manners of a Numerous People"

## The Ideology and Performances of the Society for the Propagation of the Gospel in Foreign Parts

Tis a sad thing to live in the wilderness like the
Wild Indians without God in the World.

—John Talbot, April 16, 1707

In June 1700, a group of Kahnawake Mohawks ventured down from their Catholic settlement near Montreal to trade "as formerly" at Albany, for there they found the goods to be "cheap and reasonable." During their stay of several weeks, the commissioners for Indian affairs approached the sachems and made a proposition. They began by forgiving the Mohawks for having "deserted [their] native country and gone over to strangers where everything is much dearer then [*sic*] here." They even hinted at taking some responsibility for the Mohawks' decision to leave: a lack of ministers to instruct them in Christianity. David Schuyler, a prominent Albany merchant and frequent emissary for New York governors and commissioners to New France, confirmed this reason when he went to Montreal that summer on a diplomatic mission. There, Schuyler asked Touyenijow, a League Mohawk living at Kahnawake, why he did not return to his home in the Mohawk Valley. The young man replied that "he had a great inclination to be a Christian and that detained him at Canada." In his report to Governor Bellomont, Schuyler contended that the Haudenosaunees desired "to be instructed in the Christian Faith . . . the want of ministers to instruct them therein being the apparent cause of their everyday going over more and more to the French, that it will be absolutely impossible to keep the said Indians firm and steady to the Covenant Chain without such ministers."[1]

The commissioners, feeling partly responsible for this situation, now wanted to make amends. They explained to the Kahnawake Mohawks visiting Albany that they hoped very shortly to have "Protestant ministers to instruct your kindred and relations in the Xtian true religion, which togeather [sic] with your love for your country hope will prevaile upon you to come and live among your kindred, your fires burning still in your castles, the same houses you left being still ready to receive you, with all the stores of plenty to make you live for ever happy." These pretty words betrayed why Touyenijow and several of his brethren had left the Mohawk Valley for Kahnawake in the first place: the theft of a great deal of their land by their Dutch dominie Dellius. He and other unscrupulous Dutch merchants, abetted by Hilletie, many Mohawks suspected, had fraudulently obtained tens of thousands of acres of Mohawk land through the consent and participation of several unwitting and gullible baptized Mohawks, including "open the door" Hendrick. The theft and Dellius's subsequent dismissal so disappointed the Mohawks that few now traveled to Albany to trade. To try to make things right, the commissioners gave the visiting headmen the necessaries for a great feast—venison, a fat hog, and a "barrill [sic] of strong beer to be merry with your friends of the 5 Nations that are here."[2] The food and brew, the commissioners hoped, symbolized their love for the Kahnawakes and their Mohawk brethren who remained in Mohawk country. They hoped that the victuals would act as emollients to soothe and benumb feelings of jealousy and resentment that had seethed among so many emigrant and remaining Mohawks.

However, the Kahnawake headmen were in no mood to forgive and forget quite so readily. Their orator, or spokesperson, Sagronwadie, explained to the commissioners that they were there to trade, "not to speak of religion." He added how strange it was that "all the while I was here before I went to Canada I never heard any thing talked of religion or the least mention made of converting us to the Xtian faith." After offering essentially a "no thank you" to the commissioners' offer to supply Protestant ministers, Sagronwadie replied with a qualified, guarded "yes": he and his brethren would be glad to listen to their offer, he said, "if at last you are so piously inclined to take some pains to instruct your Indians in the Xtian Religion."[3] Sagronwadie pressed ahead with his oblique discourse: "I wish it had been begun sooner that you had had ministers to instruct your Indians in the Xian faith; I doubt whether any of us ever had deserted our native country; but I must say I am solely beholden to the French of Canada for the light I have reced. to know there was a Saviour born for mankind, and now we are taught God is every where, and we can be instructed at Canada, Dowaganhae [Ojibwe country] or the utter most part of the earth as well as here."[4]

Rather than agree to return to Iroquoia, Sagronwadie proposed that Kahnawake Mohawks would perform Protestantism when in Albany. However, they saw no need to return permanently to their former homes to perform the faith of the English, now that they understood that God heard their prayers whether they prayed in Albany, or in Kahnawake, or in Montreal, Ottawa, Tiononderoge, or Detroit, or wherever they may find themselves. For emigrant Mohawks and other Native refugees at Kahnawake, New France had become an imagined community bound by a commonly shared faith and mutual reciprocity. Because of a long history of unanswered requests and unfulfilled promises, they did not believe that such mutuality with the English was achievable. However, they would be willing to perform Anglican Protestantism when in the colony of New York to signal their friendship with the English.

The commissioners were not alone in wanting the Kahnawake Mohawks to return physically and politically to the Mohawk Valley. Dutch citizens of Albany, concerned about trade, petitioned Governor Bellomont for "good Protestant Ministers . . . to instruct the Indians in the Christian Faith," for too many had been drawn off to Canada, which resulted in lost trade revenues. Governor Bellomont, who had already petitioned the Lords of Trade, went before the provincial assembly to ask for "Protestant ministers to instruct [the Mohawks] in the Christian religion, and a Fort [for them] to cover in" in order to "secure the Five Nations of Indians in their obedience to the Crown." The assembly took Bellomont's request one step further and in August 1700 banned "Jesuits & Popish Preists [*sic*]" from the province of New York. Violators of this legislation would be branded an "incendiary and disturber of the publick peace and Safety," and if caught would be confined to "perpetuall Imprisonm't." Robert Livingston added that forts in Iroquoia would be a "cheque and discouragement to the French emissaries" and advised that "every fort have a Chaplain in it who may likewise instruct the Indians in the Christian Religion."[5] The cross and the sword in Iroquoia, Livingston reasoned, would protect English lives and interests.

The links of the Covenant Chain that had fastened these Mohawk émigrés first to the Dutch (of iron) then to the English (of silver) had grown tarnished and brittle. The French in Canada, however, had continuously polished their chain of friendship with the Mohawks, cognizant that political alliances could be built on common religious grounds. England's Lords of Trade understood this when they debated how best to win the Haudenosaunees over to the English side: "Religion," the Lords reasoned, "has been found to be one of the strongest bonds of union." They believed that people and states who shared a common faith might also share other beliefs and values, such as the benefits of commerce and husbandry. The Lords perceived this to be the case elsewhere, as in New Spain, where the *indios* appeared to be attached to the Spanish Crown through Catholicism. The Lords supposed that Native Protestants could also bond with the English Crown through the Church of England. In the process, the Native "converts" would protect and preserve "those of the protestant religion who are in those parts"—that is, English settlers in New York, Pennsylvania, and New England.[6] However, exactly how to "convert" the Mohawks and other Haudenosaunees to Protestantism and, in the process, construct a holistic imagined religious community of mutually happy and safe people of distinctly different societies and cultures was more easily imagined than implemented.

Two major problems complicated bringing League and emigrant Mohawks over to the English side through Church of England Christianity. First, no mechanism existed in 1700 for implementing and administering such a program. One English missionary society, the Society for the Propagation of the Gospel in New England, founded in 1649 and known more popularly as the New England Company, operated largely in the New England colonies as a dissenting organization, supported by the Congregational Church rather than the Church of England. When Governor Bellomont of New York (1698–1701) asked the Lords of Trade to beseech the New England Company to support five missionaries to the Haudenosaunees, Henry Ashurst, an officer of the company, replied that the work of the company was restricted to New England, despite its having underwritten part of the salary of dominie Dellius in Albany. Shortly thereafter, the New England Company agreed to underwrite the salaries of five Anglican priests to the Haudenosaunees. However, by this time, Bellomont had changed *his* mind, believing that it was in England's best interest if conforming priests proselytized the Haudenosaunees. In 1701, lay and ecclesiastical reformers solved the problem of the lack of a mechanism to support missionaries to Iroquoia when they founded the Society for the Propagation of the Gospel in Foreign Parts.[7]

With the SPG in place, the second obstacle to bringing the Haudenosaunees over to the English Crown through faith lay in how to carry out the project. Should it use nonordained pastors in the colonies, or should all missionaries be ordained priests? Should the SPG target only indigenes, or should it also reach out to backsliding white colonists and the enslaved? Should the SPG use Native catechists or only white instructors? Should SPG missionaries simply preach the Gospel to Native catechumens on the belief that the Gospel alone will enlighten, reform, and "civilize" them, or should the missionaries "civilize" the indigenes first—that is, mold them into pious husbandmen and good wives before "converting" them to Protestants? What kind of mission did missionaries require—a flying, peripatetic mission or a fixed mission station? The SPG founders debated these questions at length before sending their first priest to Iroquoia.

Many English reformers and Anglican priests supported the "gospelize first" approach to missionizing the Haudenosaunees. Most agreed that to preach to indigenes most effectively required priests to learn the Native language and culture. However, living, sleeping, and eating in Native country seemed beyond the pale for most English priests. Governor Bellomont agreed; the only way he could entice a minister "to goe and live in that open country to the hazard of his life," he believed, was through the comfort and protection of a fort. No missionary, he believed, could be expected to live among a people, whom he regarded as "so nasty as never to wash their hands or the utensils they dress their victuals with." Furthermore, the Governor derided their food as "loathsome to the last degree; tho' they eat great stores of venison pigeons and fish, yet Bear's flesh is a great part of their diet, and when they feast themselves and their friends, a dog is esteem'd with them a princely dish."[8]

Livingston expanded Bellomont's vision: forts, he believed, could serve a dual purpose—offer priests protection and English comforts, but also provide economic benefits by housing "a good magazeen [*sic*] or store, as the French have at Montreal, ready upon all occasions" to sell a variety of goods, ranging from firearms to mittens to dried bacon. In this way, forts could meet the needs of the SPG, enrich local economies, and be self-sustaining.[9]

Because of a lack of funding and personnel to oversee the implementation of the SPG's project, building self-contained mission communities for the Haudenosaunees, like the New England Company's praying towns in Massachusetts, lay beyond its means. The New England Company gathered Native congregants into segregated reserves, where ministers worked to expunge indigenous habits, such as hunting, performing sacred rituals, and drinking. Instead, they took up farming and spinning, lived in small English-style dwellings rather than wigwams and longhouses, wore English clothing, and acquired literacy in Massachusett, an oral-based language.[10] The goal of the company was to "civilize" while Christianizing the indigenes, a program that the SPG could not afford to mount. Instead, the SPG hoped that by merely living in close proximity to English settlers, the Haudenosaunees, churched and unchurched, would become "civilized."

One strategy that the founders of the SPG believed was essential for Christianizing the Haudenosaunees was teaching them literacy. They believed that in addition to listening to sermons and learning ones catechism, one ought to have "a capacity to read" the Bible. For some English reformers, literacy was marginally important, for, as one clergyman put it, "what is constantly used"—as in heard—"will in a short time, be treasured up in the Memory." Just as modern-day folklorists know how persons in oral-based societies learn through repetition, perhaps this priest knew well how the illiterate parishioners in his parish learned: through repeated observations of and participation in performances of the faith. The church and the SPG, then, needed only an army of dedicated ministers of good "*breeding up*" who could learn and "understand the great variety of Languages of those [indigenous] Countries in order to be able to *Converse* with the Natives, and Preach the Gospel to them." With the proper books and a reasonable stipend, the willing missionary, the SPG contended, could not help but be successful at reforming the religious habits and sacred world of the Haudenosaunees.[11]

Still, questions lingered about a one-size-fits-all approach to gospelizing the unchurched, whether Native, black, or white. Bishop Burnet, who virtually claimed that God's language was English, cautioned that preaching the Gospel in the manner so well understood in Europe might not work as well among the indigenes in America. The discontinuous revelation that was the foundation of Christianity, after all, had been transmitted across time not only by way of tradition but more important through texts and manuscripts in Greek and Hebrew, as well as in other languages. Contrarily, sacred truths were revealed to Native Americans continuously through dreams and divination. Could they grasp Christianity's discontinuous truths through print? New ways of conveying the life and teachings of Christ to Native catechumens, the bishop warned, would have to be found. However, rather than offer answers or strategies for gospelizing Native peoples effectively, Burnet simply called for missionaries to use "wisdom and zeal," to be kind, and to have patience. And none should expect miracles.[12]

The objective of the SPG, then—and, by extension, the Church of England—was "ordering the Life and Manners of a numerous People Spread over exceeding large Countries," to rid the colonies of what they regarded as heathenism, atheism, and immorality. Yet the SPG fell short of its principal objective because as Laura Stevens has noted in characterizing the history of seventeenth- and eighteenth-century English missionary work, the project was one of "ambivalent benevolence," in which "words outweighed deeds and textual production exceeded conversions." The society provided neither enough ministers nor enough resources to support churches, schools, and teachers.[13] Nevertheless, its founders did not hatch in a vacuum the daunting task of reforming the religious and secular habits of everyone in the colonies. Their scheme sprang from a domestic reform movement to bring social and religious order to England.

## To Promote the Glory of God

In England in 1660, many Church of England men and women predicted that the return of the Stuart monarchy signaled halcyon days ahead for church and country. Charles II promised to restore the church to its rightful place as the nation's established church and vowed to punish those clergy who had supported the interregnum governments of Oliver Cromwell (1649–58) and his son, Richard (1658–59). During the interregnum, known as the "Puritan Revolution," the government virtually abolished the Church of England and promoted dissenting Calvinist churches, especially the Presbyterian Church. With the support of Charles II, the established church restored itself spontaneously. The Act of Uniformity (1660–62) reinstated a number of Church of England practices, including the use of the Book of Common Prayer at church services, subscription to the Thirty-Nine Articles of Faith, and the ordination of the clergy by bishops, all of which were banned during the Interregnum.[14]

Nevertheless, a sense of foreboding darkened the consciences of many members of the established Church. They believed that atheism, vice, license, permissiveness, and moral decay—all in surplus, they imagined, during the interregnum—retained a firm grip on English society during the Restoration. The great fire of London in 1666—the symbolism of the last three digits, the "number of the beast," according to the "Book of Revelations," struck fear in the hearts of many Englishmen and -women—and suspected popish plots in the early and late 1670s stood as concrete evidence for many that England remained an irreligious country. Meanwhile, in 1672 Charles II trumpeted his Declaration of Indulgence, which protected licensed dissenting denominations and permitted Catholics to worship in private. This decree created anxiety among many Church of England members and forced Charles II to withdraw the law the following year. As if condoning religious dissenters were not enough, several prominent clergymen accused the king himself of adultery and other sinful behavior.[15] In short, many Anglicans brooded that the Restoration might not signal the return of a more pure and pious England.

Perhaps more troubling to many established church members than Charles's seemingly capricious judgment were the religious views of his brother James II, the heir to the throne. When James, a Catholic, inherited the throne in 1685 upon Charles's sudden death, he immediately tried to legitimize the Catholic Church under the guise of religious liberty. He revived his brother's Act of Indulgence, which he demanded be read in all the churches and cathedrals across England. Tellingly, most pastors who presided over both established and dissenting churches, finding themselves in the awkward position of opposing royal authority, refused to comply.[16] Luckily for these opposition churches, English nobles invited William III, Prince of Orange in the Netherlands and King James II's nephew *and* son-in-law, to invade England and depose the king.

In 1689, following James's dethronement, Parliament appointed William and Mary, William's wife, first cousin, and daughter of James II, coregents of England, Scotland, and Ireland. Although William favored the Toleration Act of 1689 that protected some nonconforming Protestant churches, intolerance of Catholics and some dissenting churches continued. Moreover, King William demanded that England's bishops and clergy swear allegiance to the Crown. A half-dozen bishops and several hundred clergy refused to comply (hence, known as "nonjurors"), swearing their allegiance to James II through the divine right of succession.[17]

By the final decade of the seventeenth century, many Englishmen viewed their fellow countrymen and countrywomen as lost, wayward, immoral, and ill-mannered. To them, the only proper antidote to the stresses produced by these troubling circumstances lay in individual reform through personal piety. Scores of religious societies and societies for the reformation of manners began to appear, some as early as the 1670s. Skilled mechanics who were members of the Church of England constituted a large percentage of the membership of many of these religious societies. These organizations, which usually held weekly prayer meetings under the direction of a clergyman, collected membership dues and fines for transgressions, which were then distributed to local charities. The societies for reforming the manners of the people of England operated as watchdog groups. Their members, believing that the government had failed to enforce existing laws designed to curb immoral behavior, took it on themselves to inform on working-class neighbors and friends (rarely on elites) who swore, gambled, drank, and broke the Sabbath.[18]

During this period of social and religious anxiety, Thomas Bray (1656–1730), called by his friends the "Great Projector" because of the many projects he dreamed up to improve society, offered a solution for elevating morally the populace. In 1696, Bray, a pietistic, educated country pastor, published his well-received tome, *A Course of Lectures upon the Church Catechism in Four Volumes*. In these texts, Bray poses and answers a series of fundamental questions, including the following: What is the catechism? What is a moral life? What does it mean to be a servant of God? What is repentance? He used the proceeds from this publication to organize parish libraries. Then, in 1698, Bray proposed educating the English clergy and laity throughout the world. The principal task of the Society for the Propagation of Christian Knowledge (SPCK), a voluntary

reform organization with both lay and clerical involvement, was "to promote and encourage the erection of charity schools in all parts of England
and Wales: to disperse both at home and abroad Bibles and Tracts of
religion and in general to advocate the honor of God and the good of
mankind, by promoting Christian knowledge both at home and in the
other parts of the world by the best methods that shall offer."[19]

In time, the SPCK gained the reputation as the clearinghouse for
charity schools in England. Fulfilling the SPCK's charge abroad, however, proved to be more difficult, as Bray discovered firsthand during his
tenure as commissary to Maryland, the English colony founded in 1634
for England's Catholics. Maryland's colonial assembly was too mired in
other matters to pay for the care and support of a Church of England
priest. It thus became clear that the SPCK needed a sister organization to
meet its needs abroad, an independent body that would have the support
and backing of the English government and of the Church of England.
Such an organization was founded in 1701 as the Society for the Propagation of the Gospel in Foreign Parts.[20]

The SPG justified its existence by citing in its charter exigencies in the
colonies. The supply of clergymen to the nation's "Plantacons, Colonies,
and Factories beyond the Seas" was "very mean," a regrettable situation, it claimed, as "many of our Loveing Subjects doe want the Administration of God's Word and Sacraments, and seem to be abandoned to
Atheism and Infidelity." The charter also argued that "divers Romish
Priests and Jesuits [who were] the more incouraged to pervert and draw
over Our said Loving Subjects to Popish Superstition and Idolatry" wors-
ened the situation. Consequently, it was necessary that the SPG "promote the Glory of God, by the Instruccon of Our People in the Christian
Religion" by seeing to it "that a sufficient Mainteyance be provided for
an Orthodox Clergy to live amongst them, and that such other Provisions
be made, as may be necessary for the Propagation of the Gospell in those
Parts."[21] In other words, the SPG pledged to supplant what it deemed
to be the false beliefs of Catholics, Jews, Quakers, atheists, idolaters,
apostates, and the superstitious with what it considered the true religion:
Church of England Protestantism.

The society adopted an official seal at its second meeting on July 8,
1701, to convey an image of voluntary humanitarianism tinged with
paternalistic imperialism.

FIGURE 2. Seal of the Society for
the Propagation of the Gospel in
Foreign Parts, Joseph Downing,
1706.
*—Courtesy of the John Carter Brown
Library, Providence, Rhode Island.
Licensed for use under CC BY-SA 4.0
ps://creativecommons.org
/licenses/by-sa/4.0/).*

The seal depicts a sailing ship, traveling across the sea from right to left (east to west). An Anglican priest stands on its prow, holding a Bible in his right hand, his right arm outstretched. He is about to encounter a group of people gathered on the shore—presumably Native Americans, judging by the natural environment—who speak words in Latin printed in a banner floating above their heads: *Transients Adjure Noose*—"come over and help us"—the same text used on the seal of the dissenting colony of Massachusetts. The SPG sought to thwart accusations of imperialism by depicting the indigenes as solicitous of priests who will save their souls.[22]

One may ask to whom do the "Us" in the SPG's seal and the "Our People" in the SPG's charter actually refer? Church of England bishops tried to clarify but probably created confusion. In February 1701–2, Dr. Richard Willis delivered the first annual SPG sermon, in which he announced that the society would first "settle the State of Religion, as well as may be, among our *own* people" abroad "and then proceed in the best methods . . . towards the *Conversion* of the *Natives*." Four years later in his annual SPG sermon in 1706, Dr. J. Williams, bishop of Chichester, expanded the pool of people the society would serve by making it clear that enslavers had an obligation to Christianize their enslaved. By

1710, the SPG flipped again its priorities by maintaining that "the design of Propagating the Gospel in foreign parts, dos [*sic*] chiefly and principally relate to the Conversion of the Heathens and Infidels, and therefore the Branch of it ought to be prosecuted preferably to all others." Thus, by 1710, preaching to "heathens" and "infidels"—typically thought of as unbaptized nonwhites—became the society's primary focus, at least publicly.[23]

Not all SPG clergymen in the colonies agreed with this top-down decision making, reached by the society's officers in their comfortable London offices, to focus most of the society's resources on ministering to free and enslaved Native Americans and Africans. The handful of missionaries who preached to these populations during the first decade of the eighteenth century experienced difficult living and working conditions. Virulent diseases, unfamiliar food, defiant enslavers, and Native behavior that appeared to embody the extremes of indifference and hostility frustrated the efforts of many of the English newcomers and kept many away. Charles Smith offered that he "worried about Indian hostilities" as his reason for declining the invitation to be the first SPG missionary to the Haudenosaunees, deeming the undertaking too dangerous: "This one consideration of winning souls to God outweigheth all . . . [and reveals] my insufficiency and unworthiness. . . . [F]ear restrains me."[24] Many white clergymen and settlers shared Smith's reservations.

Stories about raids on frontier towns in western Massachusetts and eastern New York over the last quarter of the seventeenth century fueled Smith's fears. Solomon Stoddard, the Congregational minister at Northampton, Massachusetts, raged that Native Americans were beasts, depraved and hopelessly irredeemable. Let the English "Hunt the Indians with dogs," he suggested in 1703, "as they do Bears." To Stoddard, all indigenes were "thieves and murderers, they doe acts of hostility, without proclaiming war." Because they "act[ed] like wolves," Stoddard declared, they had "to be dealt withall as wolves."[25] Many white settlers shared Stoddard's racist attitude.

In addition to fears over Native depredations, concerns over the growing multiethnic and multiracial colonial population compounded white anxieties. For some, the expanding ranks of dissenters and nonbelievers constituted a dangerous sign of disorder. As early as 1687, New York governor Thomas Dongan alluded to religious and ethnic chaos in his multireligious colony: "Foreigners . . . are the most prevailing part of this Government. Here bee not many of the Church of England; few Roman Catholics; abundance of Quaker preachers[,] men and women especially; singing Quakers, Ranting Quakers; Sabbatarians; Antisabbatarians; some Anabaptists[,] some Independents; some Jews; in short[,] of all sorts of opinions there are some, and the most part of none at all."[26] Over the next twenty years, the diversity and thus seeming disorder in the vicinity of the city of New York only increased. Adam Brown taught children on the south side of Staten Island, "where there [was a] mixture of almost all Nations under heaven." John Bartow believed that the Quakers in his district of West Chester had a particularly bad influence on the few "Negroes and Indians [who] came to our Assemblies." When they did visit, they saw, he claimed, so much unchristian behavior among the white settlers that "they contentedly remain[ed] unbaptized." Reverend John Thomas called for instructing Englishmen and -women before teaching Native peoples and Africans because it would be more cost-effective. He found in his district of Hempstead "Infidels, God knows, of my own Colour, too many, upon whom I bend my whole force," who were "in a great measure sunk into paganism & Infidelity." He deemed it his duty to rescue his own people, "especially the children, who run about, for want of Letters and education, as wild, uncultivated, and unimproved as the Soyle was when their forefathers first tread it." Enslaved Africans, whom he criticized as "overgrown with almost invincible ignorance," and Native Americans, whom he denigrated as "sottish, Debauched, [and] incapable of any Instruction," lacked, Thomas alleged, the "capacity" to receive "any Christian Impression."[27]

By the turn of the eighteenth century, New York City and its surrounding communities had truly become multicultural, multiracial, multiethnic, and multilingual. One observer noted that the enslaved who had lived in the city for a while were able to converse in several European languages, most commonly English, French, and Dutch. A few enslaved indigenes added to the city's racial mix, despite legislation passed in 1679 outlawing the enslavement of Native Americans throughout the province of New York. Nevertheless, "by reason of their colour which [wa]s swarthy," they were enslaved.[28]

Shortly before the turn of the eighteenth century, a pair of reformers—a colonel and a minister—teamed up to diagnose what they considered to be the source of the disorder in New York and to offer a solution for restoring harmony and prosperity that would later inform the structure and strategies of the SPG. Colonel Caleb Heathcote, who took command of New York City's militia in 1692, found the colony to be "the most rude & Heathenish Country I ever saw in my whole Life." He observed that on Sundays, people who "called themselves Christians" engaged in "all manner of vain sports & Lewd Diversions."[29] John Miller, the chaplain at the garrison in the city from 1692 to 1694, concurred in his 1695 essay *New York Considered and Improved* that the residents seemed to exude "wickedness & irreligion." He complained that too many ministers were unqualified and that marriage was no longer a sacred institution, for many couples cohabited out of wedlock. Hence, Heathcote and Miller recommended a peculiar range of reform measures: install a bishop and a cadre of ordained priests, look for silver mines in the region using enslaved labor, exploit the "soile black & rich [that] brings forth corne . . . [and] fruits" to the north in Iroquoia, and subdue New France.[30] In addition, Heathcote called for a missionary to the Mohawks, who must be a young man "able to grapple with fatigue" and to "endure hardships," as he must "live with the Indians in their own country and according to their way and manner." Only in this way could a missionary learn the Mohawk language and communicate effectively with his Native catechumens.[31]

Throughout the eighteenth century, scores of young men accepted the challenge of undergoing ordination, then making the dangerous transatlantic trip either from the colonies to England and back or from England to the colonies. They then settled in what they considered a strange land with even stranger people, many of whom spoke a most strange language and practiced the strangest of cultures. However, in the beginning, the dean of Asaph stated pithily the situation in 1708 when he remarked that "the harvest truly is plenteous, but the laborers are few."[32]

## Wanted: "Fit Persons to Be Sent Abroad"

In 1702, the SPG printed and circulated a request for "fit persons to be sent abroad" as missionaries. The society required that all letters of application and recommendation provide a brief biographical sketch of the applicant. It wanted to know the candidate's age, his marital status, his temperament, his level of education, his habits (for example, sober or prudent, profligate or virtuous), his style of conversation (plain or learned, profane or pious), his work ethic, his affection for the state, and the degree of his devotion and conformity to the Church of England. The ideal applicant, now called an "aspirant," was English born, educated at either Oxford or Cambridge, twenty-four years of age and thus eligible for ordination, and ambitious, with great endurance and imagination. If selected, the aspirant had to pass a grueling oral examination before the bishop of London and several SPG officials.[33] The examination tested the aspirant's reading, preaching, and pronunciation skills and abilities, as well as his knowledge of Greek, Latin, church history, the Bible, the Book of Common Prayer, the Thirty-Nine Articles of Faith, and the Creeds. If he passed the exam, his status changed to "postulant," and he prepared for ordination. Upon becoming an "ordinand," he was robed and received a certificate of ordination and a license from the bishop of London. He was then given his assignment, often at the recommendation of the governor of a particular colony.[34]

The ordinand, or priest, received the current salary for Church of England priests in England: fifty pounds per year. Most missionaries in the colonies, where the cost of living was higher and the congregations too poor to augment their salaries, found their salaries inadequate. John Bartow of Westchester, for example, complained in 1706 that the SPG's fifty pounds and the fifty more promised by the white community to which he ministered were insufficient to feed and "cloathe me and my family." Two factors kept him poor. The first was nonpayment; he had not yet received thirty-four pounds owed him by the SPG. The second factor was increasing out-of-pocket expenses due to the "changeableness of our office in this Wilderness, our parishes being scattered about in the woods, so that we're often obliged to ride seven or eight miles to visit the sick, to Baptize etc., and when they come to church [they] expect some refreshment from the ministers."[35] Unforeseen out-of-pocket expenses also kept Thomas Barclay, the society's minister in Albany, poor.

Reverend Thomas Barclay, on the SPG's payroll as pastor in Albany and also to the Mohawks from 1708 to 1712, complained repeatedly that his annual salary of fifty pounds was too little to support his family. He claimed that his annual expenses for food and lodging alone came to forty-five pounds per year. Moreover, he had to pay out of his own pocket the costs for tutoring "an Indian boy put upon me by the Commissioners of the Indian Affairs," which amounted to fifteen pounds per year for the boy's "cloathing[,] diet & Schooling." After providing for the boy, whom Barclay probably used as a servant or slave, the priest probably found himself on the verge of—if not *in*—debt. He may have dipped into the ten pounds the SPG advanced missionaries to begin stocking their parish libraries if none existed, knowing that he had at least the five pounds worth of small tracts to distribute among the poor in his congregations.[36]

Newly minted SPG priests, armed with half their salary and letters of introduction for the governor of the colony and for the parish to which they were assigned, set out on a harrowing voyage across the Atlantic that lasted anywhere from five weeks to six months. Storms at sea, unpredictable winds, dwindling food and water supplies, and shipboard illness surely gave some young priests second thoughts about leaving England. Once they arrived in the colonies, the church expected them to be models of exemplary living and extend themselves to the population, like the pastor on the prow of the ship on the society's seal.[37]

At all times, the priests were to keep in mind their mission: to save the souls of men, women, and children through preaching the Gospel. They were to give no one cause to criticize them personally or the work of the SPG. This meant living a pious existence and inspiring others to lead "sober, righteous, and godly" lives. The priests were to "visit frequently their Parishioners" and to seize "any fair Opportunity of preaching to any Number of People as may be occasionally met together from remote and distant Parts, tho' it may not be on a *Sunday* or Holy day." They should reserve those days for members of their congregation. The priests were also told not to meddle in the civil affairs of the colonies. Church and state were on the same side, so any mingling in that relationship could give dissenters ammunition and sully the SPG's project. In fact, they were instructed to "endeavour to convince and *reclaim* those who dissent from, or oppose them, with a Spirit of Meekness and Gentleness only." Edward Vaughan, the SPG minister at Elizabeth Towne in East Jersey, where a large number of Quakers had settled, found that when he entered the home of a dissenting family, adopting "an affable even temper" accompanied by "the force of argument" usually worked best "to engage their affections & conformity" to the Church of England.[38]

In addition to conveying gentleness when speaking with dissenters, SPG priests were to take "special care" when catechizing "Children or other ignorant Persons," meaning indigenes and Africans, to whom they were to "explain the Catechism . . . in the most familiar Manner." When instructing non-Christians, the missionaries were to begin with "the Principles of Natural Religion"—that all things are the result of God's work—and then work their way up to "the Necessity of Revelation . . . contained in the Holy Scriptures." This work not only demanded great diligence and profound faith, but also required optimism and self-confidence in their abilities to present themselves as credible instruments of God.[39]

Once at work as a parish priest or as an itinerate missionary serving several communities, the pastor filed reports every six months with the SPG that quantified the state of piety in his district, a task that Colonel Caleb Heathcote of New York reminded the SPG in 1704 and 1705 was originally his idea. The society required each of its priests in the colonies to provide statistical information in seven categories in his biannual *Notitia Parochialis*: the total number of inhabitants; the number of inhabitants who were baptized; the number of adults baptized since the last report; the number of actual communicants of the Church of England; the number of those who professed themselves of the established church; the total number of dissenters, especially papists; and the number of heathens and infidels (Native Americans and Africans). The missionary often worked with a schoolmaster, who helped the priest tally the statistics, although in many instances the missionary was also the schoolmaster.[40]

Taking a cue from the SPCK, the SPG decided early on that parochial schools were essential for "reducing" the population in the American colonies. Hence, schoolmasters were an early component of the tripartite model of missionization: parsons, teachers, and books. Most schoolmasters were American born, although some who were born in England and underwent ministerial training held the position of deacon, curate, or clergyman, but did not shoulder the responsibilities of the priest to their particular congregation. Their principal task included "instructing and disposing Children to believe and live as Christians." To accomplish this, the schoolmaster was to "teach them to read truly and distinctly, that they may be capable of reading the Holy Scriptures, and other pious and useful Books, for informing their Understandings, and regulating their Manners." In other words, from the point of view of the SPG, before one could be a good Christian, one had to become literate. God may have spoken to some in mysterious ways, but for those Englishmen engaged in the SPG's project, he spoke most clearly through printed English. As Carla Pestana implies, biblical literacy was a critical component of English empire building. Its utility, Hilary Wyss suggests, centered on fostering order, coherence, stability, obedience, and civility.[41]

A good Christian child, the SPG claimed, was one who knew not only his or her catechism but also "how to write a plain and legible Hand, in order to the fitting them for useful Employment; with as much Arithmetick as shall be necessary to the same Purpose." Hence, schoolmasters were not only instructed to mold children into good Christians—children typically observed morning and evening prayers in the classroom and were required to attend church services—but also charged with providing the children with the knowledge and skills to be honest, virtuous, and productive workers and helpmates.[42]

Because children were thought to have a capacity more limited than adults, schoolmasters were to be gentle and loving in their instruction and with their reprimands. The society directed its teachers to teach children to be always truthful, to respect their elders, and to fear Almighty God. And because the English believed that indigenes and Africans possessed a capacity equivalent to that of children, they were to teach Native and black adults the same lessons they taught children. In 1704, the first official SPG school established in the colonies took root in New York City. Its purpose was to "catechise the Negroes and Indians and the children of the town" under the instruction of Elias Neau, a French Huguenot refugee, who spoke and wrote English tolerably well.[43] Many reformers viewed his educational project with particular urgency: while many of the city's white residents were at church on most Sunday mornings, witnesses noted "the Streets [were] full of Negroes, who dance[d] and divert[ed] themselves."[44] The society came to believe that Neau, to whom they offered the post of missionary to the Mohawks but who declined their offer, preferring to teach the enslaved in New York City, kept the model catechism school for instructing not only free and enslaved Africans but also Native Americans.[45]

All who knew Elias Neau regarded him as a "good religious man," "a worthy Person," "of exemplary Zeal and Piety," and "a person of great humility, which is the foundation of all virtue."[46] Rather than meet in the new Trinity Church, built in 1698, where most white adults, apprentices, and children met for catechetical lessons, Neau met his catechumens of color in his "town of York" home—or, more specifically, in his forty-by-twenty-two-foot attic. There, on Wednesday, Friday, and Saturday evenings, Neau catechized by candlelight between 75 and 100 adult and young catechumens, although that number could reach between 150 and 300 on a cold, dark winter's night. The many persons of color flocked to Neau because of his caring, solicitous nature; he was known to creep into "Garrets, Cellars and other nauseaous places, to exhort and pray by the poor slaves when they are sick." Many who observed Neau's efforts believed he was particularly suited to this work, having himself been enslaved for a year on a French galley ship for refusing to renounce his Protestant faith, during which time he proselytized his fellow enslaved prisoners.[47]

Neau commenced catechizing his New York City flock through trial and error, instructing his pupils initially by trying to inculcate in them "the great Truths of the Gospel and the Dutys required of them" by explaining the importance of baptism. When he realized that they had trouble following him, Neau resorted to telling his pupils stories—"the History of Creation, the flood, the giving of the Law, the birth, miracles, and Crucifixion of our Saviour." He also incorporated into his teaching lots of praying and singing of psalms, which, he claimed, his pupils enjoyed, for they appeared to derive pleasure from seeing "who shall sing best." Neau realized that his catechumens learned through orality. He hoped that through both observing and repetitive participating in his performance, his neophytes learned that "God plac'd them in the World only for his Glory; and that in praying and singing those divine Prayers, one doth in part obey his Commands."[48]

To lock these lessons into his catechumens, Neau relied on the heuristic of repetition, an important learning technique of orality. He led his students slowly, patiently, and repetitively through the recitation of a number of sacred texts, including catechetical lessons, public prayers, the Lord's Prayer, the Apostle's Creed, and several psalms. Unsure that the texts alone were self-evident to his students, Neau always gave himself "the liberty to add what I think necessary to make them understand what I say to them suitable to the[ir] Capacity." He catechized his students one at a time—three at a time if attendance was large—beginning "at one end" of the classroom and finishing "with the other." In the process, each student stood up to recite the catechism, so that by the time Neau reached the last student, the class would have heard the catechism perhaps forty or seventy-five or even a hundred times. Additionally, at the end of his discourse on the history of creation or on Christianity, Neau checked his students' grasp of the catechism and other texts by having them rise and "with their faces turn[ed] to the East, repeat the Belief or Symbol of the Apostles, after which [he] ma[d]e them repeat word for word the Church catechism as it stands in the Liturgy and all in English."[49] Neau's approach to translating Protestantism to his flock of color required both flexibility and rigor.

Despite his success in drawing folks of color to his catechetical lessons, only about two dozen of his catechumens—about 12 percent on average of those who regularly attended his classes—were baptized during his tenure between 1704 and 1722. Nevertheless, we should not see Neau's work as a failure; rather, some of the scores of people of color who stepped foot in Neau's attic—perhaps up to a quarter of New York City's enslaved and free population of color—took away from Neau several key benefits and lessons, including leisure time, a safe place to bond with others in their enslaved community, and the acquisition of literacy.[50]

To teach literacy required books, which were arguably the most important tool of the missionary's trade. Christopher Bridge, the SPG missionary at Rye, New York, found it difficult in 1710 to catechize the young people there and to persuade "the lower sort of the necessity of publick worship" without books, which he deemed "most serviceable." For him and other SPG priests, the Bible and the Book of Common Prayer were the most important texts. The former contained the revealed truths of God and the latter distinguished Church of England Protestantism from all other Protestant doctrines. Other key texts included psalters (hymnals), which enabled the churched to worship publicly and communally by singing praise to God, and shorter catechisms, which ministers and teachers used to instruct children and adults of "meaner capacity." Priests also used hornbooks and primers to teach children and adults of color. Selections from this cornucopia of documents constituted the first religious texts that Dutch and English clergymen and their interpreters translated into Mohawk.[51]

Missionaries also used published sermons, expositions, and treatises, written mainly by Anglican bishops, with which to craft their own sermons, lectures, and general conversations with catechumens and the unconverted. They discoursed on topics ranging from interpretations of the New Testament to the Thirty-Nine Articles, from biblical parables to the history of the church, and from "primitive" Christianity to Church of England festivals and fasts. A number of lay treatises on civil and religious topics also supplemented the biblical and catechetical texts that missionaries and schoolmasters used. These supplementary essays focused generally on the moral-bound duties required of good Protestant Englishmen, -women, and children, which were necessary, the society claimed, for maintaining a well-ordered society. The handbook, *The Whole Duty of Man,* probably written by Richard Allestree, lectured the reader on his or her duties and responsibilities according to his or her rank and station.[52]

Despite their privileging texts, SPG missionaries to the Mohawks would find that their Native catechumens privileged material goods, such as food, knives, buttons, buckles, blankets, shirts, stockings, hand-held gilded mirrors, rings, and toys, over excerpts from Robert Nelson's *Companion for the Festivals and Fasts of the Church of England.* By the turn of the eighteenth century, most Mohawks had redirected much of their energy and resources from hunting game for subsistence to hunting animals for the fur trade. Therefore, many were forced to rely on trade goods provided by Dutch, French, and English traders. Hence, most preferred bolts of blankets over leaves of psalters.[53]

### "Of Great Advantage to his Majesty's Plantations"

In May 1701, Robert Livingston, the secretary for the commissioners of Indian affairs in Albany, conveyed to the Lords of Trade in London as urgently yet as optimistically as he could that "the Five Nations have received such impressions of the Christian Religion that if ministers were planted amongst them to convert them to the Christian faith, it would be of great advantage to his Majesty's plantations." Livingston, whom the Haudenosaunees also regarded as their secretary—at one point, they insisted that he travel to London "to acquaint Coraghkoo [the king of England] . . . of our condition"—overstated the case in hopes of eliciting a response from the board. Although some Mohawks had some acquaintance with Christianity, gleaned through the exhortations of

French Jesuits and Dutch Reformed dominies, and through scores of adopted baptized Hurons, only a few Mohawk individuals and families, along with a handful of Oneidas and Onondagas, expressed outright hope of having clergymen among them. At the July 1701 Great Peace conference, Onucheranorum, the anglophile Mohawk orator, spoke on behalf of the few rather than the many when he asked New York's lieutenant governor Nanfan for "a good large Church made in the first or newest castle Called Ochniondage," a variant of Tiononderoge.[54]

Bellomont and other previous New York governors had promised the Haudenosaunees ministers, churches, and forts of their own. None had been forthcoming, save a few Dutch ministers whose primary responsibilities were to Dutch congregations in Albany and Schenectady. Consequently, many League Haudenosaunees and especially those Mohawks who migrated to Kahnawake questioned the sincerity of some of the English officials. Shortly after Dellius's dismissal for his participation in the land-fraud scheme, two baptized Mohawks—Tejonihokawara, baptized as Hendrick, and Joseph, both of them signatories to Dellius's fraud—beseeched Bellomont to do everything in his power to "propagate the Christian religion amongst them [Mohawks], which hath been much neglected and faintly perform'd of late years." This situation could be rectified, they believed, if Bellomont simply ordered "a minister . . . to Reside with them at their Castles for the cherishing and Comforting of the few Converts that are already in the Christian faith and for the converting the rest of their Bretheren who have good Inclinations to Embrace the said faith if they had Ministers to instruct them therein."[55] In indicating to Bellomont once again the desire of some Mohawks to embrace Church of England Protestantism, the petitioner also implied their willingness to turn their backs to the French and extend their hands to the English through the church, not only for reasons of piety but also for profit and protection. However, it would be another five years before an English priest approached the Mohawks and another eight years beyond that before the Mohawks could claim an Anglican priest for themselves.

In the meantime, Bellomont told baptized Mohawks to simply stop at the Dutch Reformed Church in Schenectady, under the ministry of dominie Bernardus Freeman (a.k.a. Freerman), whenever they traveled east, for Freeman, he was certain, would "take paines to teach you." With few options, most Mohawks preferred to continue their practice of journeying on to Albany and meeting at the house of dominie Lydius, where they held "their exercises of praying and singing, as they were accustomed to do under Rev. Dellius."[56]

The desire of the Mohawks to meet with Lydius rather than Freeman may be explained by either force of habit or out of convenience while conducting other business in Albany or because Freeman's dubious reputation preceded him. Prior to Freeman's installation at Schenectady, some members of the Dutch Reformed Church of Albany looked into hiring him as their pastor. The classis of Amsterdam in Holland, the body that governed ecclesiastical matters of the Dutch Reformed Church, including the licensing of ministers, warned the congregation to avoid "such a patch-cutter," who had tried before "to force himself as a hireling into the service of the church." Freeman was a tailor and, according to one critic, had "just come from his cutting-board and had neither learning nor ability" to preach. He had failed his exams, "even when he desired to go [to New York] only as a *Krankbesoecker* [Comforter of the Sick]." How he now passed his ministerial examination the classis had no idea.[57] In short, the body found that Freeman lacked humility and deference, was deficient in skill and temperament, and did not have the necessary qualifications to be a good Dutch Reformed pastor.

Nevertheless, the Dutch Reformed Church in Schenectady welcomed Freeman in July 1700, perhaps out of desperation for a minister, despite the classis of Amsterdam refusing to recognize him or set his salary, which it left up to the congregation to provide. That same month that Freeman preached his inaugural sermon in Schenectady, Governor Bellomont asked him to instruct the Mohawks. Despite their initial coolness to Freeman, many Mohawks warmed up to him over time, finding the unorthodox pastor less prickly than Lydius. In fact, in many respects, Freeman would become a model minister for the Mohawks. In time, he was able to make himself understood in Dutch and in Mohawk, the latter acquired, the Dutch interpreter Lawrence Claessen believed, with the help of an unnamed Mohawk assistant, probably his servant, whom he had "constantly by [him]." In fact, Freeman became proficient enough in Mohawk to create a sixteen-letter alphabet and to compile a vocabulary, by which means he "taught that Indian [servant] to read & write perfectly." The pastor also boasted that he "likewise taught . . . Interpreter [Claessen] to read and write."[58]

The Mohawks may have appreciated Freeman's latitudinarian approach to evangelizing. He felt just as much at home preaching the liturgy of the Dutch Reformed Church to Lutherans as he did reading the Church of England liturgy to Mohawks. Moreover, he liberally baptized Mohawks—113 between 1700 and 1705, almost 2 per month, on average—which most Mohawks regarded as an act of commitment enough to indicate their adherence to the faith.[59]

Freeman also jettisoned some Church of England practices in favor of Dutch Reformed Church traditions. For example, he offered the Mohawks "a form of baptism and matrimony according to the order of the Dutch Church." The Calvinist Dutch Reformed Church, guided by the principles outlined in the early-seventeenth-century Canons of Dordt, baptized infant children of the elect as well as rebaptized those reborn through a religious awakening. The Church of England, following the Westminster Confession of Faith in 1646, also believed in baptizing infants if at least one baptized parent had come to God freely, but declared baptism a once-in-a- lifetime sacrament. As for marriage, the Dutch Reformed Church used a *bann,* a public announcement of the intentions of the bride and groom, who had to be confirmed by members of the church, to publicize their wedding. The Church of England merely required Christians to marry fellow Christians. It is difficult to determine if these differences were important or even knowable to those Mohawks whom Freeman married. What does seem to be clear is that some Mohawks seemed to be drawn to his idiosyncratic "short sistem [*sic*] of Theology," which he explained as "I take notice of the Errors of the Church of Rome . . . because of the Errors the Jesuits had initiated them in." Freeman's ecumenical approach to Christianity—of combining some tenets of the Calvinist Dutch Reformed Church with some principles of the Arminian Church of England—perhaps provided a level of comfort for some baptized Mohawks, who themselves borrowed from other faith traditions.[60]

Still, the dominie, with the aid of a variety of liturgical texts that he and his assistants translated into Mohawk, did devote much of his time and energy teaching his Mohawk catechumens the principles of Church of England Protestantism. These texts included morning and evening prayers, the Creed of Athenasius, the Litany, and a number of passages from the Bible, including "the Gospel of St. Matthew from the beginning to the End," as well as several chapters and verses from Genesis, Exodus, Corinthians I and II, and Psalms. He had also translated a relation of the "Birth, Passion, resurrection, and assencion of our Saviour," a "Short Explication of the 10 Commandments," and the Apostle's Creed. Freeman believed that the Mohawks "had a great veneration for the English Liturgy," especially the call-and-response Litany, "at the Reading of which they frequently did tremble."[61] Like Neau, Freeman experimented with translating Protestantism to his Mohawk catechumens, most importantly through their language.

Yet despite the Mohawks' growing approval of Freeman, his popularity with New York governor Edward Hyde, a.k.a. Lord Cornbury (1702–8), Bellomont's successor, and with some members of the Schenectady congregation, waned. Freeman soon entertained an offer from a congregation in Breukelen (Brooklyn), at which time some of his detractors complained to Cornbury, who had to issue the requisite certificate of character so that Freeman might move from one post to another, that the pastor was a troublesome "seditious and quarrelsome person," who would "create uneasiness, discord and quarrels" in the Breukelen church. Nevertheless, Freeman transferred to Breukelen in 1705, thereby ending his mission to the Mohawks.[62]

Mohawk feelings toward Freeman's departure were ambivalent, largely because many questioned Freeman's arrangement with some of the Mohawk headmen to grant English woodsmen permission to harvest lumber on behalf of the king on Mohawk lands in perpetuity, which reminded some of the unpleasant specter of Dellius and his earlier land scheme. Moreover, the New York commissioners needed little reminding that they needed to act fast to replace Freeman with an English minister before the Mohawks turned their gaze northward to New France.[63]

### Thoroughgood Moor and a "Strange Commotion" in the Mind

In June 1701, almost a year into Freeman's tenure as pastor at Schenectady, Dekanissore, the powerful Onondaga headman, delivered a dramatic ultimatum to New York authorities. During a meeting at Onondaga, the headman bragged to Johannes Bleeker, an interpreter for the province of New York, and David Schuyler, an ambassador from Albany, how warmly and generously the authorities in Montreal had treated him during a recent visit there. The two agents from Albany, irritated by his insinuation that the English could not match the French in their love and generosity, blurted out, "Are you soe brutish and stupid[?] See how the French creep and cringe to you with beads and shirts to make friends with you."[64]

Dekanissore shot back bitterly that he and his brethren discovered in the last war that their "covenant" with England, which was supposed to hold that "he that touch'd one all the rest would resent itt," was worthless. "When the French came and destroyed our Country and the Maquase," Dekanissore lamented angrily, "we gave you seasonable warning, but gott no assistance and that makes us afraid what to doe." The two men patronized Dekanissore by insisting that he "be not affraid of the French" and challenged the Haudenosaunee warriors to "Speake like men and behave yourselves like soldiers, for which you have always been famous."[65]

Dekanissore, perhaps feeling that these white men now challenged his and his fellow warriors' manhood, explained patiently that one of the most pressing matters affecting the league was whether they should welcome Catholic priests of the French or the Protestant priests of the English. For the past nine months, since shortly after Freeman's arrival, "all the five nations [had] satt and considered" two belts of wampum: one from Governor Bellomont urging them to "take ministers into their Castles," the other belt from "Mon. Marikeur"—Paul Le Moyne de Maricourt, a well-known "go-between" between the French at Montreal and the Native converts at Kahnawake—which advised them to "take Jesuits into their Country." At this point, Dekanissore admitted, the Haudenosaunees "were much confused . . . and extremely divided." Bleeker and Schuyler cautioned the headman that because Corlaer (governor of New York) "tender'd you first a Protestant Minister," to give Jesuits access to Iroquoia "would render you ridiculous."[66]

Dekanissore now erupted with anger: "You both [English and French] have made us drunk with all your noise of praying." His frustration boiled over with their dead-wrong claim that the governor of New York was the first to provide the Haudenosaunees with Protestant ministers, surely having in mind earlier Dutch dominies. He insisted that the headmen would not be rushed into reaching consensus on this matter. Until such time, Dekanissore suggested cleverly, the Haudenosaunees would resort to what we today might call a Native game-theory approach to accepting missionaries. Modern game theory holds that cooperation and conflict, and winners and losers, define nearly all relationships, and that one enters pas de deux relationships rationally aware of this. Playing up the connection between conversion, commerce, and covenant, Dekanissore bluntly told the two agents that both the French and the English sold the Iroquois goods too dearly, which forced him to "put on a bear skin to goe to church withall a Sundays." From now until the League headmen reached a decision: whichever nation sold them "their goods cheapest[,] whether English or French, of them will wee have a Minister."[67]

Within three years, as Freeman was preparing to depart Albany, the SPG, at the strong urging of the New York commissioners for Indian affairs, replaced the departing Dutch pastor with an ordained Church of England priest. Upon his arrival in Albany on November 6, 1704, Thoroughgood Moor found a receptive Governor Cornbury, who had given a warm and laudatory character reference of Moor to the Albanians prior to his arrival. Consequently, the priest felt "very Civilly received by the People" of that town. He stayed at the home of Dominie Lydius, where over the next few weeks two Mohawk delegations greeted him. Their encounters were both cordial and concerning.[68]

On November 22, Moor received the first delegation, "a Mohock [*sic*] Indian and his Squa being in Town & hearing of me & my Design." They expressed their joy at his having arrived safely in Albany, but added that they were aggrieved over his coming "in the time of *war,* when 'tis uncertain whether you will live or dye with us."[69] This seemingly unassuming couple were clearly aware of the conflict between the English and the French; the famous raid on Deerfield, Massachusetts, carried out by about fifty French soldiers and about two hundred of their Native warrior allies, had occurred less than nine months earlier on February 29, 1704, and resulted in the deaths of almost fifty villagers and the kidnapping of more than a hundred. There was no telling where or when fighting might next erupt.

A pastor of less courage and commitment might have packed his bags right then and there and left. Although the couple's remark may have been a test of Moor's mettle, their next comment may have comforted him: Moor, they said, would be very welcomed in their Mohawk village, for "they have so long desired it."[70] Curiously, neither the prospect of violence nor the ominous reception he received from another Mohawk delegation a month later deterred Moor.

At the December 1704 gathering, a Mohawk woman, perhaps a respected clan mother, confirmed with the other men with her that they were glad that God had sent Moor to "open our Eyes which hitherto have been shut." However, she confessed that his arrival "raised a strange Commotion in her mind . . . an unaccountable mixture of Joy & fear."[71] The Mohawk woman, perhaps concerned that his presence represented England's beachhead into Mohawk country, may have subtly signaled to Moor that uncertainty awaited him at Tiononderoge. Rumors circulated that Moor would surely bring an onslaught of English forts, trading posts, and white settlers, which in all likelihood would invite unwanted surveillance.[72] Furthermore, Moor's mission in Mohawk country would surely signal to their Haudenosaunee brethren and to the French that the Mohawks were not neutral after all, but rather were the minions of England. And now, traditionalist Mohawks and Haudenosaunees had to uphold their end of the bargain and tolerate their baptized brethren receiving Christian instruction. In many ways, baptized Mohawks had found it easier to perform Christianity in Schenectady or Albany, safely out of view of their nonbaptized brethren. Now, however, the pastor assigned to instruct them was *theirs*, and Mohawk etiquette required that they—baptized and unbaptized alike—love and protect him.

Unrelenting snow prevented Moor from reaching Tiononderoge to explain "his design" until early February 1705. After crossing nearly fifty miles on foot and on sleigh, Moor received a warm welcome from the Mohawks, who fired an eight- or ten-gun salute. His Mohawk hosts lodged him in "one of their little houses . . . made very clean with a good fire," perhaps the home of a baptized patriarchal Mohawk family or a hut that Robert Livingston had requested be built for missionaries. Two hours after his arrival, a delegation of Mohawk headmen met with Moor. After fifteen minutes of silence, the sachems told Moor that they would let him know if they would accept his design after they had consulted with their brethren at the other Mohawk castle. Moor left the next day, disappointed and puzzled, knowing "little as to their willingness to accept me." He believed that they were "generally desirous nay longing for the Light of the Gospel." However, rather than question whether their equivocation was directed at him or toward their dissenting brethren,

Moor rationalized that the devil had tapped some of the Mohawks and used them as "Instruments . . . to abate their eager desires of the Gospel" and "still keep them in darkness."[73]

Within a week, the headmen gave Moor their answer: because they were unsure of how the other four nations would react to a church with a bell and a parsonage in Mohawk country, a delegate of headmen had to consult with the other Haudenosaunee nations and reach consensus, "for we are all but one house." Their upping the ante was a brilliant waffle that was neither a yes nor a no.[74]

Out of impatience, frustration, and ignorance, Moor, befuddled, committed a blunder that began to sour Mohawk enthusiasm for him. Eager to commence his work, the priest demanded a speedy reply from the orator. The orator, miffed at Moor's ignorance over the Haudenosaunee need to reach consensus through unhurried debate and discussion, replied sarcastically "that he wondered a minister should not be more deliberate; sudden answers were not their Custom." Of course, the headmen's answer was also a stall.[75]

Moor made additional mistakes the next day when he met with the headmen, beginning by addressing the Mohawk orator as "Child" rather than the customary "Brother," the latter term one of mutuality and interdependence. Furthermore, his message simply added to what the Mohawks regarded as English insincerity when he insisted that he expected daily a deployment of missionaries "for . . . every other Nation," which he qualified with "as soon as proper and willing Persons can be found." The Mohawks had heard this before; five English missionaries had been promised, one for each nation, and Moor was the first and only to arrive.[76]

Finally, Moor pointedly told the Mohawks that he would send to them a sixteen-year-old English boy, who would live among them at his expense, in order to learn their language. Again, the orator responded with a yes that was a no: *he* would agree to this, but first he had to consult his fellow headmen before giving Moor an answer.[77]

Over the next four months, Moor bided his time, unable to "get them so much as to tell [him], whether they would or no" accept him as the queen's missionary. Moor believed that his reasonable requests that "their Answer might be speedy" were met with "unreasonable delays & frivolous excuses." Finally, in June 1705, after "having some little encouragement from one of the sachems," Moor packed "some biscakes" and had them delivered by a young English boy. Not surprisingly, the Mohawks took the biscuits but refused to accept the boy.[78]

This last rebuff was too much for Moor to bear. In August, he journeyed to Schenectady to "demand their [Mohawks'] Answer which they had long delayed." The delegation told Moor that they did not know when they could let him know, maybe in twelve months, which the priest read as "a positive denial."[79]

Moor accepted minimal responsibility for his aborted mission. He admitted that he could have been more patient. However, he also believed that several other factors beyond his control doomed his mission, including that the Haudenosaunees bore "no good will, but rather an aversion" toward the English for good reason: the English in New England, at least, had been "very unchristian, particularly in taking away their land from them without a Purchase." In addition, the rude manners and behavior of the English soldiers at the garrison in Albany, with whom the Mohawks came into frequent contact, further prejudiced them against his countrymen. Moreover—and perhaps most troubling to Moor—Dutch liquor traders denounced Moor. The traders' commercial interests with the Haudenosaunees, Moor implied, compelled them to misrepresent the intentions of the English, especially with regard to forts and missionaries. Some Haudenosaunees believed Dutch claims that the English intended to impoverish and enslave them.[80] No wonder, then, Moor concluded, that they should hate him. He recommended to the SPG that it no longer support Dutch ministers or Dutch schools in the province, a sentiment shared by Lord Cornbury, who in time, ironically, became one of Moor's harshest critics. Both men believed, along with John Miller, the chaplain at the garrison in New York City in the early 1690s, that the province should be Anglicized.[81]

Although Moor blamed the Mohawks and external factors for the failure of his mission, the most plausible reason for his leaving Mohawk country was his ethnocentric desire to missionize "our own People here [who] have a more just right to our Care." In agreement with the sentiments expressed by Bishop Willis in his 1701–2 SPG sermon, Moor declared that the white settlers were a "thriving growing people" and deserved the attention of the society. The Haudenosaunees, on the other hand, Moor claimed, were "wast[ing] away & had done so since our first arrival amongst them (as they themselves say) like snow against the sun." He predicted that in another forty years, there would "scarce be an Indian seen in our America." The pastor believed that their rapid extinction was due to "God's Providence . . . [for] no cause of their Decrease [was] visible unless [one counted] their Drinking Rum with some new Distemper we have brought amongst them." In short, Moor insinuated that Native peoples lacked the physical and moral capacity and endurance to withstand God's "very wonderful"—meaning awesome—plan.[82]

In less than a year after his arrival to Mohawk country, Moor departed for Burlington, New Jersey, because he refused to "fling away my Life . . . with so little use as I must do by Living amongst them." His departure began a seven-year hiatus in SPG activity to the Mohawks. The society would learn from Moor's mistakes; subsequent SPG missionaries would try to be more sensitive to Mohawk culture, needs, and desires. Some priests and schoolmasters would even try to learn the Mohawk language rather than rely so heavily on interpreters. Still others would try to be flexible and experiment with new tactics to entice the Mohawks and other Haudenosaunees to church and to catechetical lessons. Nevertheless, most subsequent missionaries to the Mohawks would eventually agree with Moor: greater value and satisfaction were to be gained in reforming and ordering the life and manners of the numerous Europeans living in the colonies than in trying to reduce the Mohawks.[83]

## Conclusion

In his 1711 annual SPG sermon delivered at St. Mary le Bow in London, Bishop William Fleetwood, the lord bishop of St. Asoph, declared that "all Christians, both by the Nature and Reason of the Thing, as well as Christ's Command, stand obliged to . . . [bring] the whole World to the Knowledge and Faith of Christ." Bishop Fleetwood articulated the universalist, millenarian charge of the church that all the world must be converted to Christianity—and preferably Church of England Protestantism—in order to bring about the Second Coming. Spreading the "good news" was an old tradition, mandated by Christ, whose disciples, most notably Paul, became itinerant missionaries.[84]

At the turn of the eighteenth century, the Church of England had the will to bring the Mohawks and other Confederate Haudenosaunees into its socioreligious world but lacked the means. Its reform organization, the Society for the Propagation of the Gospel in Foreign Parts, ethnocentric and culture bound, exercised limited vision and imagination for how to best implement its project in Mohawk country. The Mohawks, who valued flexibility within each individual, found Moor's rigid, imperious, and impetuous personality off-putting. Moor's unwillingness to take advice from those in the know rendered him blind to the creative successful strategies used by earlier Dutch missionaries, including Freeman, and even the catechist Neau in New York City.

Nevertheless, missionization is dialogical, a conversation held along a two-way street: catechumens must be willing to receive instruction from their catechists, and catechists must be willing to read and hear their catechumens. No amount of Bibles, psalters, common prayers, or instructional tracts could have mitigated the distaste the Mohawks held toward Moor. Debate between baptized Mohawks and unbaptized Mohawks over Freeman's and Moor's ministries remained contentious. Most who were baptized—regarded as anglophiles—tried to appear united in their desire to be instructed by English priests. Most traditionalists, who, like Dekanissore, regarded themselves as neutralists at this time, resisted Moor's designs. They preferred to present themselves as nonaligned in order to maintain good relations with the Dutch, the French, and the English.

Although Moor's mission failed, the society learned several important lessons about Mohawk culture and attitudes. Missionaries could not operate the way they did in England, that is, on the authority of a few members of the consistory, as Freeman did in Schenectady. They required the consensus of the headmen and residents of a Mohawk community, sometimes that of the entire league. If that was not forthcoming—if the answer was "silence"—then the missionary ought not to read that response as a quiet affirmation, but rather as a loud and clear no. Moreover, SPG missionaries should not take Mohawk complaints over the "spiritual blindness" of their Haudenosaunee brethren as a signal to proceed full speed ahead but rather as a cautious, ambivalent opinion expressed by some baptized Mohawks wishing to connect individually with the missionary. No wonder, then, that so many missionaries, French, Dutch, and English, left Mohawk country baffled and bewildered.

The SPG learned another important lesson about proselytizing the Mohawks: that embracing the missionary and his faith was often contingent on other matters, especially the material well-being of the Haudenosaunees. The provincial government of New York understood the importance of reciprocity in building English-Haudenosaunee relations, and thus often went to great lengths to polish the Covenant Chain with gifts bestowed on Native headmen at conferences in Albany. Often, however, New York governors complained about the expense of gifting forty to fifty headmen at Albany with dozens of outfits of clothing; duffels, strouds, and blankets; kettles of all sizes; hundreds of pipes, knives, and hatchets; lead shot, flints, muskets, and barrels of powder to supply a small army; and of course the ubiquitous gallons of rum. The headmen divided these goods, Robert Livingston reported, "by a natural principle . . . of distributive justice[; even] those of them who are most in the French interest and are aiding to the debauchery of the rest, have as much as those who are firm to the English."[85]

The reciprocal exchange of goods and obligations kept the Haudenosaunee world balanced and harmonious. Initially, society missionaries read these gifts as initiating interest in the work of the SPG and not as enticements to get the Mohawks to embrace Church of England Protestantism. This sentiment would change over time as the number of devout Mohawks increased.

CHAPTER 3

# "Laying a Good and Lasting Foundation of Religion"

*Success and Failure at the Fort Hunter Mission, 1710–1719*

> The Indians are a People who must be taken . . . their own way, and Managed by
> One who understands their Language and Customs, and can lodge a Night or two upon
> the Ground with them in the Woods, when he visits them.
>
> —John Checkley to Philip Bearcroft, October 26, 1743

From the deck of his sloop sailing up the Hudson River on its approach to Albany, New York, on November 13, 1712, William Andrews, the newly minted Church of England priest assigned to the Mohawks, "saw the Indians upon the banks looking out for [his] coming." His approach to the riverbank reproduced exactly the seal of the Society for the Propagation of the Gospel in Foreign Parts, his employer. He, like the pastor on the prow of the ship, would be God's instrument, who had come over to America to "help" the Mohawks convert to the "true religion," Church of England Protestantism.[1]

Once he was onshore, the Mohawks received Andrews "with abundance of joy," he noted, "shaking me by the hand, bidding me welcome over and over." Two days later, a delegation of Mohawks, composed of five principal headmen, several "Chief Squas" (clan mothers), and numerous young warriors, met with Andrews and the commissioners for Indian affairs. Andrews expressed to the Mohawks how happy he was that it pleased God to make him an "Instrument worthy of doing any good among them for their Souls & welfare." He was particularly joyful that Queen Anne had chosen to honor their request for a pastor. As he spoke, Andrews observed that the Mohawks seemed "Extraordinarily well pleased" by his remarks. Tarachjoris, an orator from Canajoharie, the upper Mohawk village, whose role as orator was to speak publicly on behalf of his brethren, rose to say that he had been "deputed" by his community to welcome Andrews. He acknowledged that they understood that the minister had been sent at their request by the "Great Queen of Great Britaine to Instruct them in the Christian Religion for the good of their Souls." After giving the priest his hand, Tarachjoris promised that the people of Canajoharie would "give all the Protection and Encouragement unto him that shall lye in their Power."[2] This was perhaps Andrews's first lesson of Mohawk reciprocity: attention, friendship, and protection in exchange for Queen Anne's commitment and his presence.

Hendrick—Tejonihokawara, or "open the door"—the Anglophile baptized headman and orator, whom other headmen had deputized to receive Andrews on their behalf, stepped forward next to greet the priest. He welcomed the pastor as courteously as Tarachjoris, albeit a bit more coolly and curtly. After saluting Andrews as "their Minister and father," thanking "the most religious Queen Anne" for sending Andrews to them, and extending his gratitude to the late archbishop, "their ghostly Father," for his letter and set of communion plates, Hendrick set down two firm ground rules: first, no buying their land clandestinely, as had Dellius fifteen years earlier, which caused many angry Mohawks to "go over to Ottowa or farr Indians"; and second, the baptized Mohawks did not want to be tithed, like those at Kahnawake, "who are obliged [to] pay the Tenth of all to their priest." Hendrick also begged the commissioners who were present to "sell them no more Rum." Andrews agreed to all of the demands, assuring Hendrick and his brethren that he had "not come for the Lucre of their Land nor to lay Burdens upon them, but to instruct them in the True Christian Religion." Furthermore, he made them two promises: that he would do all in his power to prevent the buying of Mohawk land clandestinely and that they were not to worry about his support, for "the honorable Society had taken care to pay him."[3]

Not all Mohawk headmen supported befriending and protecting Andrews. Taquayanont, a headman from Kahnawake in New France, who relocated to Tionoderoge, so opposed Andrews that later he poisoned one of his Mohawk assistants, for which Taquayanont was banished from the major Mohawk towns. If his opposition to Andrews was based on fear of rum flooding into the nation or losing more land, then it is hard to explain why he—along with Hendrick and others—signed away six hundred acres of Mohawk land on Schoharie Creek (present-day Fulton, formerly known as Vroomansland) in 1711 to Adam Vrooman, a Dutch mill owner residing in Schenectady, in exchange for more than a hundred gallons of rum, unless he felt honor-bound by kinship ties. In 1691 Vrooman married Gretje Ryckman, the widow of Jacques Cornelise Van Slyck, the late brother of Hilletie Van Olinda, one of the colony's Mohawk interpreters.[4]

Nevertheless, because a minority of headmen voiced their opposition to his presence, Andrews believed that his mission with the Mohawks would succeed where all others had failed, despite a troublesome incident just one month earlier: Reverend Thomas Barclay, the aloof, Albany-based interim Church of England priest to the Mohawks, had scolded several "impious" Mohawks—either hunter-warriors, or their sisters, wives, or mothers, whose job was to dress game—for using the brand-new chapel built especially for the Mohawks within Fort Hunter as "a Slaughter house" to butcher their game. For the dedication of the chapel, Barclay crafted a sermon based on Matthew 21:13—"'My house shall be called a house of prayer': but you are making it a robber's den"—in which he admonished the Mohawks for their "profanation of God's house."[5] It is unclear how these individuals carrying game got access to this space located inside the fort. Furthermore, it is uncertain whether they carried out this bloody act as criticism of what lay ahead or whether the chapel may have merely provided the butchers shelter from inclement October weather. No matter, Barclay took their deed as a blasphemous act.

Regardless of whether the Mohawks considered the chapel a sacred space or merely a convenient venue, more than five dozen Mohawks flocked dutifully to the 576-square-foot wooden church in Fort Hunter on Andrews's arrival in mid-November to hear him preach. After being reminded not to tithe them, he baptized two Mohawk children during this initial service. Andrews believed that most of those who had gathered at the chapel were "very well disposed to receive [the] Christian Truths," for several had been baptized previously by French Jesuits and Dutch dominies. However, he remained skeptical that those who had been baptized understood Christianity properly, for according to

Lawrence Claessen van Volgen, Andrews's interpreter, who lived among the Mohawks as a captive when a teenager, few if any had received any formal instruction before or after baptism. Claessen claimed that some had been "brought to baptism by Threatenings and others by Presents."[6] Nevertheless, many baptized Mohawks played their parts convincingly, bringing to Andrews's church services sacred objects, including rosary beads and pictures of saints. They performed their understanding of Christian conduct, such as enthusiastic genuflecting and crossings, to show that they knew something about Christianity—albeit Catholic Christianity.[7]

Once settled at Fort Hunter, Andrews threw himself full bore into his work. He preached the "Christian Truths" every Wednesday and Sunday to ever-growing numbers of Mohawk hearers. Between November 22, 1712, and September 3, 1713, he baptized thirty-seven children, ranging from infants to teenagers, and eight adults, between the ages of twenty-two and seventy-five. By 1715, the Mohawks who attended his church services regularly numbered about 100 of the 580 Mohawks who lived in the Mohawk Valley. Many parents played active roles in their children's mission education. Within the first year of Andrews's arrival, Mohawk parents even built a schoolhouse, where John Oliver, the assistant to Claessen, taught upwards of forty Mohawk children.[8]

However, soon the novelty of the school wore off. Attendance began to fall within a few months of the school's opening in late 1713. By 1716, only about "six or seven" Mohawk children came regularly to school. A little more than a year later, Oliver was fired and the school closed. Concomitantly, by 1716 attendance at church had dropped dramatically. At that time, "about fifty Indians . . . [came] pretty constantly to the Chappel when at home, [while] a great many others . . . [were] casual hearers, & in all about 38 Communicants" took communion about once a year. However, by fall 1717, not a single League Haudenosaunee from any of the other nations and only about two dozen Mohawk worshippers—two men, the rest women, all from Tiononderoge—attended chapel regularly. It was not unusual for the few men and women who did attend to sleep through services, only to awaken to eat the food that Andrews set out to attract them. Andrews acknowledged that his mission was rapidly declining. Soon, he lost hope "of ever making them any better."[9]

Some students of Haudenosaunee history have judged the mission at

Fort Hunter a complete failure. James Axtell and Daniel Richter, among others, have argued that social strain brought on by external factors—principally the in-migration of the Tuscaroras in 1713–14, a smallpox epidemic, and rumors spread by devious Dutch rum merchants that the English were there to steal their land—led to apostasy and to a decline in interest in the SPG's project. Proof of the mission's failure includes several baptized Mohawks returning to traditional Haudenosaunee sacred practices.[10] While these factors did contribute to the mission's decline, the tensions between Andrews and the Mohawks lay rooted in the latter's expectations of the former. Their cross-purposes gave rise to a milder, mutual form of "epistemic murk," which anthropologist Michael Taussig defines as that state of confusion and terror that arose among white settlers based on irrational fears rooted in misperceptions, rumors, half-truths, and conjectures about the indigenes and their environment that the white settlers had trouble reading, which they then used to justify inflicting violence on them.[11] Strains between the Mohawks and Andrews did not quite reach that level of violence, although some Mohawk warriors did plot to kill the priest. Nevertheless, the "murk" at Tiononderoge and Fort Hunter resulted from rumors of misdeeds; misreadings of intentions, both willful and unwitting; and unrealistic expectations. In time, the Mohawks, so enthusiastic about finally getting a priest of their own, shunned Andrews, who in turn disengaged from the Mohawks.

## The Faux Kings

On his arrival to Albany, William Andrews reminded the Mohawks that he owed his presence to the four Native men who visited London in the summer of 1710. The purpose of their visit was twofold: to meet with Queen Ann and request pastors for the Haudenosaunees and to press for military support to subdue New France. The several officials and commissioners from Albany who accompanied them on the trip promoted the Native ambassadors as "kings" of the Haudenosaunees, who had been deputized by their brethren to represent the entire league. In truth, three of the men were Mohawks and the fourth Mahican. Only one, the baptized Hendrick (Tejonihokarawa), was a headman, who, in the opinion of one minister, could not "command ten men." The other three—Cenelitonoro (a.k.a. Honeyeathtonorow, a.k.a. John of Canajoharie), Tagayonauaroughton

(Brant of the Mohawks), and Etawacome (Nicholas of the River Indians, or Mahicans)—were "men of no consideration . . . neither chiefs nor deputies," who were later "disavowed by the five nations." Nevertheless, in London they received the royal treatment.[12]

Throughout their stay in London of several weeks, the four "kings"—or, more accurately, the "faux kings"—feasted at several state dinners, where, as one observer reported snidely, they did "not refuse a Glass of Brandy or strong Liquors from any hands that offer[ed] it." They also met representatives of the SPG, attended masquerade balls, observed swordsmen exhibitions, toured the city, visited Bedlam, attended cockfights and the theater, and lodged in London's developing, upscale West End at the Two Crowns and Cushions, where they slept on soft, feathered mattresses. Because the commissioners, the Crown, and the English public all treated them as Native royalty, their hosts thought it imperative that the four visitors should dress accordingly. Hence, their hosts presented them to "the Playhouse Taylor," who dressed them winkingly in what he considered proper royal garb—"like other Kings of the Theatre": "black Wastcoats, Breeches, and Stockings" in deference to England's mourning the recent death of the prince of Denmark, "with yellow Slippers [deerskin moccasins], and a loose scarlet mantle cast over them, bound with a Gold Gallon; their hair ty'd short up, and a Cap something of the Nature of a Turbant upon their heads." Curiously, the dresser did not dress them in gold crowns and ermine in impersonation of King Henry IV or Henry V or Richard III or even King Lear. Rather, the costumer presented them in the garb of fictional "exotic nobles," such as Oroonoko, the enslaved African prince featured in the eponymous 1695 play written by Thomas Southerne, based on the 1688 novel by Aphra Behn, or Montezuma in the 1664 play *The Indian Queen,* by Robert Howard and John Dryden. The costumer clothed the four Native visitors in attire that he considered appropriate to their exotic, indigenous nobility—turbans and banyans (robes or dressing gowns). The turban is the true giveaway. In the seventeenth century, elite Muslims wore turbans, a garb of Islamic origin, to signal their elite status. Seventeenth- and eighteenth-century European painters and theater costumers depicted typically elite Moors and other Muslims wearing turbans. Hence, to convey not only their exotic foreignness but also their exalted status, the London playhouse tailor bedecked the faux kings in similar garb. Johannes (John) Verelst, the Dutch-born painter (1648–1734), who

FIGURE 3a. *Tee Yee Neen Ho Ga Row [Hendrick], Emperour of the Six Nations,*
John Verelst, 1710.
—*Courtesy of the John Carter Brown Library, Providence, Rhode Island. Licensed for use
under CC BY-SA 4.0 (https://creativecommons.org/licenses/by-sa/4.0/).*

moved to London a few years before the faux kings' visit, painted their
full-length portraits revealing their exotic royal sartorial garb. Printmakers
reproduced their images for popular consumption for decades afterwards.[13]

The faux kings performed their parts well to admiring English audiences. They appeared several evenings dressed in their tailored vestments,

FIGURE 3b. *Sa Ga Yeath Qua Pieth Ton King of the Maquas*, John Verelst, 1710.
—*Courtesy of the John Carter Brown Library, Providence, Rhode Island. Licensed for use under CC BY-SA 4.0 (https://creativecommons.org/licenses/by-sa/4.0/)*

sitting in reserved box seats at the opera house and at the theater, where they received ovations. On two of those evenings, they saw, ironically, two tragedies about kings, power, jealousy, revenge, and defeat: *Hamlet* and *Macbeth*. We do not know if they nodded in recognition at Hamlet's need to exact revenge for his father's murder, a motivator for a Mohawk warrior, or if they regarded the witches' foretelling of Macbeth's fate as perfectly natural, as witches, agents of pain, suffering, and misfortune, were commonplace in Haudenosaunee life. If they understood anything of these plays, it is because Abraham Schuyler, their Dutch interpreter, interpreted the plays for them as they unfolded. Yet it is questionable if Schuyler could have kept up with plays performed rapid-fire in English.[14]

Nevertheless, Abraham Schuyler, cousin to Colonel Pieter Schuyler, translated for the Mohawk visitors when they met with the queen. Major Pigeon, an aide to Pieter Schuyler, read the two requests, scripted no doubt by the Mohawks' Dutch patrons Colonels Vetch and Schuyler and Lieutenant General Nicholson, among others, who sought to vanquish New France but needed the support of Haudenosaunee warriors to do so. The first request, constituting 362 of the roughly 520-word speech, issued a call for the military conquest of New France. The appeal presented a detailed pretext explaining the need and urgency for the action. The organizers of the trip believed that if the queen believed that the Mohawks were sincere in their wishes to have Canada subdued, then she would make amends for failing to send the fleet in 1709—a fleet assembled that year in Boston to sail up the Atlantic Coast and then up the St. Lawrence River never materialized—and now would recommit herself to this effort.[15] Following this plea, the delegation offered Queen Anne a wampum belt to symbolize and commemorate this entreaty.

The second request, 77 words in length, called halfheartedly for each of the Five Nations to have a pastor of their own: "if our *Great Queen* will be pleas'd to send over some Persons to instruct us, they shall find a most hearty Welcome." To "welcome" priests did not necessarily commit the Haudenosaunees to "convert" to Church of England Protestantism. Rather, the gambit represented an appeal to the queen to show how much she loved the Haudenosaunees. To answer the perennial requests made by a handful of baptized Mohawks would show all Haudenosaunees that England was willing finally to fulfill one of its obligations spelled out in the Great Peace of 1701. Moreover, if the queen was willing to meet the needs of a few Mohawks, she would surely not hesitate to meet the Crown's larger interests with the Haudenosaunees through trade and a military alliance. Ironically, the second plea risked being ignored or forgotten, for either Pigeon failed to honor, the Mohawks omitted, or the scribe forgot to record an important gesture following this request that would have symbolized the deep importance and sincerity of it: a string of wampum, apparently not offered.[16]

Despite lingering questions, Queen Anne did respond to both requests. To the first petition, the queen agreed to provide the necessary manpower and financial resources to invade New France. However, as with the 1709 planned invasion of New France, the 1711 invasion came to naught. The massive war fleet with about eight thousands troops left Boston in late summer, intending to rendezvous with close to a thousand forces, most of whom were Haudenosaunee warriors, near Montreal. However, fog caused ship pilots, unfamiliar with the uncharted St. Lawrence River, to lose their way and run aground, resulting in the loss of several ships and about a tenth of the troops along with many civilians. The commanding officers, embarrassed and disgraced, called off the invasion.[17]

To the second appeal, Queen Anne asked that the SPG consult with the Dutch-Mohawk delegation, after which the society agreed to address several objectives. First, it stated that its chief goal should be "the Conversion of Heathens and Infidels" and that this objective should "be prosecuted preferably to all others." The society would now put a "stop . . . to sending any more Missionaries among [white] Christians, except to such places whose Ministers are or shal [*sic*] be dead or removed." Second, the society changed the character of the mission by favoring an in-resident missionary over an itinerant priest to the Mohawks, which had been the practice in the past. Moreover, the missionaries were to be "single persons" and accompanied by "an Interpreter." Both should be paid generously—the priest 150 pounds per year, the interpreter 60 pounds, triple the standard salary for both. Both should reside at "Tynderooghe [Tiononderoge] the principal village of the Mohawks," where "a Chapel and house should be prepared . . . and an Indian fort [built] for their defense."[18] The SPG now began to take seriously its commission of proselytizing the Haudenosaunees.

The society also desired that some of the Mohawk children "be Instructed in Our Tongue," that is, in English, so that the children might later teach their brethren the true principles of Christianity, which, according to English thought, were better understood in English. For now, however, the society, deeply rooted in the imperative of literacy, insisted on providing their missionaries with texts, including "a brief History of the Bible or New Testament, a Catechism, some prayers, psalms, etc . . . translated into the Indian Language"—Mohawk—for quick apprehension. Finally, the society pledged to recommend that the governors of New England and New York pass laws "against selling Rum, Brandy and other intoxicating Liquors, to the Indians, this being the earnest request of the Sachems themselves," some of whom were known to be prodigious drinkers.[19]

After Abraham Schuyler read and explained the society's resolutions to the faux kings, the Native diplomats "promis't to take care of the ministers sent to them and that they would not admit any Jesuits or other French Priests among them." Their pledge to bar the Jesuits from Iroquoia was what the society most wanted to hear.[20]

The entire encounter between the faux kings and their London hosts was a carefully stage-managed performance, scripted by Vetch, Schuyler, and Nicholson for consumption by the Native envoys and by the English nation. One of Colonel Vetch's objectives for sending the Native men to England, besides having them appear before the queen, was to impress them with England's wealth and power in an effort to diminish the appeal of France as their ally. Most European Americans viewed Native Americans as poor, deprived, and covetous. They would be duly impressed, the commissioners believed, by England's wealth and, consequently, would wish to embrace eagerly the Crown, the church, and the English nation.[21] By the same token, Vetch and his fellow commissioners strove mightily to make the audience with the queen appear to be the sole idea of the faux kings. Of course, the Native delegation and their New York chaperones collaborated on crafting the speech event, as evidenced by Haudenosaunee forms of diplomatic protocol and patterns of orality, characterized by the repetition of key words and phrases, such as "Brothers" and "Corlaer" (governor of New York), as mnemonic devices, interlaced with the linear, nonrepetitive patterns of discourse common to written English. For the speech before Queen Anne, the orator invoked "Great Queen" but once, at the beginning of the discourse. The scribe may have deleted additional salutations for readability. Nevertheless, other features of Haudenosaunee discourse remain.[22]

The text utilizes Mohawk names for some of the New York escorts, including *Queder* for Colonel Pieter Schuyler, *Anadagajaux* for Lieutenant General Francis Nicholson, and *Anadiasia* for Colonel Samuel Vetch. Moreover, certain Haudenosaunee expressions lent the text an air of authenticity: "We hung up the *Kettle,* and took up the *Hatchet,*" the expression for "declared war," seems authentic rhetorically. "With one Consent [we] join'd our Brother *Queder*" reads as an expression of consensus. In fact, neither example of rhetoric is necessarily authentically Mohawk, but rather each is a product of bicultural collaboration, a concept, according to Hilary Wyss, most often attributed to writings by Native Americans.[23]

The more ephemeral translation of oral exchanges required skilled "linguisters" who did not provide literal word-for-word translations of the spoken word, but rather brought their knowledge of the customs, cultures, and traditions of the two or more sides they mediated to their interpreting. The most successful interpreters also knew the difference between interpreting common conversation and interpreting more formal public oratory, which required them to adjust their interpreting accordingly. Moreover, interpreters would sometimes exercise discretion when translating, and thus would alter or excise phrases or ideas they found to be too incendiary at the moment. Nevertheless, according to Yasuhide Kawashima, the highest compliment one could pay an interpreter was he or she "spoke their words and our words, and not his own."[24] The forty-seven-year-old Abraham Schuyler had lived in Seneca country for several years, but the Seneca and Mohawk languages, related linguistically, were not that closely related grammatically. Conversations between individuals of the two nations were held with some difficulty. Hence, much may have been lost in translation during the faux kings' visit to London in June 1710.

In sum, Queen Anne, representatives of the SPG, political and social elites, and all others involved in the London performance of the "four kings" behaved wittingly as both eager players and gullible audiences. They were complicit in enabling and abetting the roles and status of the four brokers as kings because they were trussed by their own preconceived ideas of propriety, power, and authority. Only heads of state met with other heads of state, unless the visitor was a most powerful client. Their middle-ground treatment of their Native guests—treating them as they believed they would have wanted to be treated, as exotic royalty—demonstrates the kind of miscommunication and misinterpretation that would soon contribute to an "epistemic murk" in Mohawk country.

The path between the promises made in London to building and dedicating a fort, a chapel, and a parsonage at Tiononderoge was anything but smooth and straight. To begin, the queen agreed to pay for all three buildings, which the society estimated would cost between 350 and 400 pounds. However, rather quickly, Pieter Schuyler, who selected the site of the fort with its chapel approximate to Tiononderoge, recalculated the added costs of local labor, supplies, and ancillary fees and adjusted the estimate upward to about 900 pounds. Once construction began late in 1711, the society knew that it would have to pay as much as 1,000 pounds (almost $215,000 today) for the structures.[25]

Additionally, while crossing the Atlantic on board the *Draggon* on their way home, the faux kings acted improperly when they signed a letter with their clan totems as if on behalf of the league. The letter, written most likely by one of the Schuylers, reminded the society to keep its promise to send ministers "with as much speed as possibility [*sic*]" so "that the Chapel may be built." The ministers and the initial chapel placed in Mohawk country, they allegedly claimed, "will undoubtedly occasion a Credit to our Six Nations of whatever we shall relate to them concerning our Great Queen's especial care of us her allies." According to Haudenosaunee diplomacy, this letter was problematic in that it sought to further legitimize the faux kings as valid diplomats authorized to conduct League affairs. Protocol required that the men first report on their journey to the principal League sachems at Onondaga, a requirement to which they alluded with the words "we shall relate to them," so that the body of leaders could reach consensus on giving the Society the go-ahead. At a meeting in August 1710, attended by several League headmen and Governor Hunter and his commissioners, Hunter asked the headmen whether they approved of the delegation that made "their application to the Great Queen to send missionaries amongst them to instruct them in the religion and worship of the son of God the saviour of the world." The Onondaga orator, Kaquendero, also known as Sadekanaktie, began his response with an ironic correction: the "four kings," he reminded Hunter, were members of the "Mohogs [Mohawks] nation." Nevertheless, Kaquendero, exercising Native etiquette, added diplomatically that each delegate might as well have been from one of the Five Nations, they, the Haudenosaunee, "being all united." Consequently, the headmen were thankful that the faux kings had an audience with the queen and were well treated throughout their visit to London. Kaquendero, appealing to Hunter's cultural and political bias, added that they welcomed the prospect of receiving instruction in Christianity, to have forts and chapels "in each of our Castles," and to even have "a Christian sachem in each Castle to take notice what is transacted there and defeat the French Intreagues." To Governor Hunter, Kaquendero's amenability must have seemed like a great victory, marred only slightly when a faction of Mohawks confronted Hunter and insisted that the queen had promised *their* delegation *two* ministers—one just for the Mohawks, whom they wished would be Freeman, by order of the queen, to live at Tiononderoge "and not at Schinnectady nor Albany."[26]

Governor Hunter ordered that construction on the fort and the chapel begin immediately. Both were completed in August 1712, but not without difficulties. From time to time, Mohawk warriors harried and chased away the five carpenters from Schenectady hired to build the structures. Rumors ricocheted throughout Iroquoia that the fort represented the first sign of the intention of the English to cut off the Haudenosaunees and that Haudenosaunee warriors were preparing to launch preemptive strikes against Schenectady and Albany, which fueled more epistemic murk. Finally, perhaps because of the expense of the Mohawk fort and chapel, the same structures promised for Onondaga would now not materialize. [27]

## Required: Zeal, Courage, and Large Presents

Between Thoroughgood Moor's departure from the region in 1705 and William Andrews's arrival in 1712, Thomas Barclay, the SPG priest at Albany and Schenectady, ministered to the Mohawks when they traveled east. To many white settlers in the region, Barclay seemed to be the ideal pastor for the Mohawks because of his experiences with diverse congregations. In April 1707 the SPG appointed him chaplain to the garrison in Albany, and in October 1709 the society expanded his duties to include those of "missionary and Schoolmaster at Albany and Schenectady." Barclay, who was able to converse in both English and Dutch, the latter the language of his Albany-born wife, taught the Church of England catechism in English to his sixty to eighty young catechumens, the majority of whom were Dutch children. However, when conducting church services to his adult congregation in Albany, he often read parts of the Church of England service in Dutch, as several Dutch families attended his services. Likewise, when he traveled each month to

Schenectady, where, he noted, a "numerous Dutch Congregation" filled
the "convenient and well-built [Dutch Reformed] church which they
[the consistory] freely gave me the use of," Barclay conducted much of
the service in Dutch. His aggregate congregation consisted of the forty
English soldiers at the garrison, sixteen English families, and about a
hundred Dutch families. From time to time, he preached to Mohawks
who ventured east to Schenectady and Albany, for he almost never
traveled to Tiononderoge, preferring to have Native proselytes come to
him.[28] Thus, Barclay seemed to engage in the religious translation of the
Gospel for a diverse constituency with creative ease and willingness.

Barclay's ecumenical latitudinarianism may have appealed to some
Mohawks. He explained to the society that he had no enemies among
dissenters, who in Albany were largely the Dutch. On the contrary, he
lived "in intire [sic] friendship with those of the Dutch Congregation" and
thanked God (with little humility) that he had "a heart enlarged towards
all mankind, my Charity not being confined to those of my own Nation
or Church only." Although Barclay believed that "unity in opinion and
worship and consent in action are most desirable qualitys," he fervently
maintained that he could not "damn all that differ from me," even
though he thought everyone should conform to the Church of England,
which he claimed, as one virtually on its payroll, was "undoubtedly the
best."[29] However, despite his strategy of trying to reach all hearers, he did
not extend his equanimity to the Mohawks. In 1710, he characterized
the thirty Native communicants, who had been without a minister since
Freeman's departure in 1705, as "so ignorant and scandalous that they
can scarce be reputed Christians."[30]

Despite his seeming religious tolerance, Barclay actually took a hard
line with Mohawks and other Haudenosaunees who sought to perform
Christianity. One Saturday in June 1711, more than fifty Mohawks
and other League Haudenosaunees, whom Barclay described as having
been "converted to the Christian faith by the popish missionaries and
by Mess. Dellius, Freeman, and Lydius," met with the pastor at the
Dutch Reformed Church in Schenectady. After examining several of
them, he found only "three fit for receiving the Sacrament," which they
received "devoutly" the following day. Barclay attributed the weak
state of Christianity among the Mohawks to a combination of religious
and social factors. The religious factors included previous instruction in

Catholicism, which most Protestants thought of as the wrong brand of Christianity, and inadequate instruction in Protestantism by the Dutch dominies. Some of the social reasons included heavy drinking "of that Nasty Liquor Rum" to the degree "that they are lost to all that's good" and, most troubling to Barclay, opposition to him from some of the residents of Albany. Among those opposed to Barclay were "some zealots of the Dutch Congregation," which included the new young Dutch minister Pieter Vandressen (Van Driessen), and his patron and brother-in-law, Major Myndert Schuyler, along with some Dutch fur and liquor traders in Albany, who "are loath that Religion get any footing among them [Mohawks]." Many among the Dutch opposition feared that social reform measures, such as prohibition, called for by some of the Mohawks themselves and supported by the society and some members of the provincial assembly, would hurt their trade. They were correct, for Barclay urged Parliament to pass legislation that would prohibit the "selling [of] strong Liquors to the [indigenous] Nations in any of her Majesty's Colonies in America." Already, the New York Assembly had passed "an Act reviving an Act against selling Rum, to the Indians."[31]

Given what he considered the deplorable state of Christianity among the Mohawks, Barclay advised the SPG to send missionaries who have great "zeal and courage," for they "will find hard work of it" in Mohawk country. Moreover, they also must have "an Honorable allowance and large presents to give, otherwise they will have but few Proselytes, and . . . their mission may prove as ineffectual as Mr. Moor's."[32]

Barclay confirmed for the society what others had often reported: that the salary of a priest in the colonies was inadequate to cover his professional and personal expenses. The SPG acknowledged this and sent William Andrews with an annual salary of 150 pounds—three times Barclay's pay—some of which he was to use to buy gifts for the Mohawk children and adults. Once Barclay learned of the level of Andrews's support, as well as his zeal, his courage, his determination, and his skill in interacting with the Mohawks, he happily relinquished his responsibilities to the Mohawks, including Claessen, to Andrews. Barclay retreated to Albany, where he dedicated himself to propagating "religion where it is not, and . . . cultivat[ing] it where it is established." There, where only twenty-six of the more than thirty-three hundred inhabitants of Albany were communicants of the Church of England, Barclay continued his work as catechist to English and Dutch children and applied himself particularly to the conversion of "the Negro and Indian Slaves" there.[33] He left it to others to propagate the Gospel in Haudenosaunee country, where he grumbled faith did not exist.

### Books, Bobbs, and Victuals: Laying the Foundations for the Church and the School

Reverend William Andrews, born in England around 1671, educated at Oxford, and ordained in 1700, arrived in North America in 1702 to preach at a parish in Virginia. Over the next ten years, he displayed all the requisite personal characteristics that the SPG valued deeply: he was single, had lived in the colonies for a decade, possessed a fine character, and allegedly knew something of a Native language. Between 1708 and 1712, more than a dozen men from the Eastern Shore of Virginia certified that Andrews had read prayers faithfully and conformably and that he was a sober and honest person, "Exemplary in his life and Conversation." With these assurances, the society sent Andrews to Albany "to perform all the office of his Sacred Function among the said Six Nations of the Indians in North America, particularly in the Country of the Mohawks," where "such of them . . . have already embraced the Christian Religion."[34]

When Andrews arrived in New York, he retrieved several gifts and furnishings for the Mohawks and their new chapel that the society had previously shipped. Some of the items, compliments of the queen, included cloths for the communion table, the altar, and the pulpit, as well as a carpet for the communion table, damask napkins, sitting cushions, a surplice of Holland linen, a large Bible, two Common Prayer Books, a book of homilies, four of her majesty's Coats of Arms (one for the church, the other three to be distributed to three Mohawk castles), and a handsome set of silver communion ware, including a large and a small salver, two large flagons, a dish, and a chalice. Also among the items were over four dozen copies of mezzotints of the portraits of each faux king, painted by Verelst two years earlier. The archbishop of Canterbury also included two tablets of the Ten Commandments and copies of the Lord's Prayer and the Creed, along with "ninety-seven prints of the Queen's Effigies, Arms, etc. to be distributed" as Andrews saw fit. The society added, through the efforts of Lieutenant General Nicholson, an ardent supporter of the SPG and

English imperialism, twelve large Bibles and copies of the society's seal to be placed in the chapel, which, like wampum, marked and punctuated the society's claim and authority over the space. The society also threw in five dozen sermons for distribution throughout New York, a not-so-subtle effort to bring white dissenters over to the Church of England.[35] Through its array of texts and ancillary items, the SPG signaled its readiness to undertake its work in Mohawk country and beyond.

Andrews commenced his work by "read[ing] prayers & instruct[ing] them [Mohawks] every Wednesday and Lordsday" at Fort Hunter, where he also preached to the fort's soldiers at separate services on Fridays and Sundays. His method was to "teach them . . . in a Catechetical Way," that is, through set questions that required rote answers. Like Neau in New York City, Andrews began by walking his catechumens "thro[ugh] briefly the chiefe fundamentals of Religion," which included "the Doctrine of God, of the Creation, of Providence, and Man's fall and Restoration of faith, Repentance, the nature & use of the Sacraments etc." No matter how familiar or dull or obtuse the Mohawks found his discourse, such as the "Exposition of the Church Catechism and . . . a practical Discourse from Text of Scripture," Haudenosaunee etiquette required that they listen politely to the lesson he had prepared.[36]

Some historians have argued that books and other printed materials were powerful instruments in the hands of missionaries, especially Jesuits. According to the historian James Axtell, books "enhanced and extended" the magic of the indigenes' world. Some Native Americans, he asserts, viewed texts, or "talking papers," as gifts of the gods. Others viewed the ability to read and write as powerful shaman-like skills, for it enabled white men to communicate unseen across vast distances, an extraordinary accomplishment, as heretofore Native peoples of oral-based societies relied on face-to-face encounters to communicate thoughts and ideas. Other scholars have cautioned us to not elevate print in Native American society to such lofty heights, for Native peoples across North America had long used graphic symbols—pictographs, graphic designs, maps, tattoos, totems—as a means to communicate nonverbal thoughts, ideas, and histories.[37] These new insights enable us to see printed texts not as fabulous items in Native country, but rather as a different form of nonverbal graphic communication, which, as Lisa Brooks has shown, Native peoples had already incorporated into their world. Hence, writing and

literacy did not necessarily reorient Native Americans' ways of conceiv-
ing of the world, as earlier anthropologists argued, but rather augmented
and complemented their perceptions of the world.[38]

The Jesuits' use of printed texts seemed to have had some success in
bringing Native peoples over to Catholicism. Axtell wonders why Protestant missionaries in the Northeast, other than John Eliot, did not try to
"cash in on literacy's preternatural power." SPG missionaries, including
Andrews, did try to cash in. Mohawk catechumens and parents conveyed
initial interest in books and texts translated into Mohawk by Freeman and
Andrews. However, in time, the neophytes lost interest in these texts, but
not for the reason Axtell offers: religious texts translated into Native languages diminished the novelty and mystery of God's words and, concomitantly, the exalted status of the ministers.[39] Just the opposite was true in
Mohawk country. Most Mohawk parents insisted that their children learn
to read and write their own language. Power, they realized, lay in acquiring
literacy in one's own language, for it allowed one to fix and disseminate
the ideas and beliefs of individuals and communities and in the process
assert and preserve the sovereignty of one's community or nation.[40] The
decline in Mohawk interest in literacy lay not in Mohawk boredom with
texts printed and written in Mohawk, but rather in a lack of people who
could explain suitably the meanings imbedded in their translated texts.

Reading and writing, especially in the context of catechism classes, are
not solitary acts, but rather are rooted in a social process. A catechist must
be on hand to explain to the catechumens what they are reading and
parse the meanings of the readings. This process at Fort Hunter required
multiple layers of translation. Andrews, who could not communicate well
in Mohawk, taught and preached from manuscripts and books rendered
in Mohawk and in English. The English schoolmaster John Oliver could
explain in Dutch to Claessen what Andrews said. However, he could
not explain to the Mohawk children what they were reading. That task
was left up to Claessen, Andrews's interpreter. Without Oliver, Claessen
could not explain to the children what they were reading. And when
Claessen was absent—and his contract stipulated that he be on hand
no more than every fortnight—then neither Oliver nor Andrews could
help the children. The difficulties inherent in this level of cross-cultural
communication contributed to the weakness of, rather than the power of,
print at the mission school at Fort Hunter.[41]

Regardless, Andrews was most eager to begin his work with children rather than with headmen of leading families, assuming that by training a generation of Christian Mohawk youths, Christianity would sweep across society and trickle down to successive generations. The best and quickest method for realizing this goal, Andrews proposed to the parents, was to teach the children literacy, for they could best absorb God's truths by reading the Bible. The major question that lay behind this proposition was in which language should they be required to acquire literacy. Mohawk parents preferred Mohawk; the SPG preferred English, but acknowledged the value of texts in Mohawk. Andrews agreed with the parents that in the beginning, teenage catechumens, at least, should learn the catechism in "their own Language" for purposes of quick apprehension as well as to shield them from the immorality of English neighbors, soldiers, rum dealers, and the three or four Mohawks who knew some English and in that language liked to "swear & use foul" words, especially when intoxicated. Besides, the mothers, who as keepers of the village were responsible for their children's education, were "not willing their Children should learn any other" language. The mothers needed to know what their children were learning. The SPG eventually agreed with Andrews and reached a compromise: all books should be printed either interlinearly, with alternating Mohawk–English lines of text, or with adjacent Mohawk and English folios, so that Andrews's young catechumens who would learn to read Mohawk may "be instructed in the English Language as a means for their better Information in the Christian Religion."[42]

Andrews also reasoned that to teach children properly, he needed a school. Thus, he convinced the Mohawk parents to build "a large School house, 30 foot Long and about 20 foot broad," to which they were "very forward to send their Children . . . upwards of 40," where John Oliver instructed them using bilingual texts.[43] Andrews had recommended to the SPG John Oliver, the English-speaking assistant to Claessen and clerk to Barclay, for schoolmaster at Fort Hunter. Barclay had approved of Oliver for the job, describing him as "a sober man" and a "Constant Communicant of the Church," who would be ideal at keeping "School for the Indians." However, one hurdle caused the SPG to question Oliver's suitability: he knew no Mohawk, and thus could not communicate directly with the Mohawk children. This meant that when Claessen was absent, which was rather frequent, the school remained shuttered, for Oliver could not communicate directly with his pupils.[44]

The SPG asked Andrews to find someone who could fill both Claessen's and Oliver's positions, someone who understood "the English as well as the Indian languages because such a Person will be more proper to answer the Purpose of the Society and yourself." While Andrews recognized the value of paying one interpreter rather than two, he rejected the society's request, noting how important the bilingual Dutch interpreter Claessen was to his enterprise. Because of the years he spent with the Mohawks at Kahnawake, Claessen understood "the Indian Languages the best of any in the province, as I am informed," Andrews explained, "& that there is not any either of the English or Dutch that can come near him, or that is able to turn a Chapter of the Bible into the Indian [language], and if they can't do that, [they] are not fit to be Interpreters." Claessen's linguistic skills were more than serviceable; as a provincial interpreter who interpreted Dutch and Mohawk, his services were sought regularly for council meetings between the Haudenosaunees and the commissioners at Albany. As he interpreted, he was what one scholar of interpretation calls "the man in the middle," whose task was to serve two sides simultaneously. However, in truth, his linguistic skills were not flawless; Andrews noted that Claessen was "at a great loss sometimes for words, for all he is lookt upon to understand the Indian Language so well, and is forced to take in the assistance of an Indian."[45] Because of the tripartite structure of interpretation and translation, much must have been lost at Fort Hunter.

Andrews had learned a little Mohawk, and so to hasten the training of a few children who in time would be "serviceable for Translating or Interpreters," Andrews housed two Mohawk boys in the spring of 1714, who may have served as servants, but whom the priest ostensibly instructed in English. Andrews hoped that if the young Mohawk catechumens "Learn[ed] their books," then they would "be the principle means of laying a good and lasting foundation of religion among them." The New England Company had used this strategy fifty years earlier in its praying towns, and several youths eventually became lay chaplains and schoolmasters.[46]

Literacy constituted the principal work the children undertook in the school. They required proper tools—books, quills, and paper—for reading and writing. When the school opened, Andrews asked the society to send about two hundred hornbooks printed in Mohawk and two or three dozen hornbooks and primers printed in English, "2 or 3 Ream of Writing Paper," and "6 Dozen of Inkhorns and as many penknives," the latter a square-handled tool with a fixed short blade—not at all like today's small pocketknife—used only to shape, scrape, and cut the nib off the feather writing instrument. Many of these books had to be newly translated, designed, and printed. For this to be accomplished, Andrews assembled bits and pieces from various manuscripts that included passages from the Bible, morning and evening family prayers, and the catechism, many of which Claessen and Freeman had translated and Barclay had used. In addition, Andrews transcribed passages from existing published texts, such as Nelson's 1703 catechism, *Companion for the Festivals and Fasts of the Church of England, with Collects and Prayers for Each Solemnity,* an inventory of saints, prayers, and homilies for fasts and festivals used by priests when writing sermons for holy days. He sent the entire manuscript package to the society for its approval and to New York for printing.[47] The imminent invasion of the book would have long-term consequences for Mohawk life and culture.

This was an exciting time for Andrews. While several of his catechumens had begun "to read pretty well," one young Mohawk boy stood out. He was lame, "haveing [*sic*] one legg shorter than the other, and therefore incapable to hunt and so is most of his time in the house." Like Kateri Tekakwitha, he devoted himself to his studies, making "a good proficiency" in his skills of writing and reading, the latter of which he could do "extrodinary [*sic*] well," and decipher "any of the Sermons and prayers wee have in Indian."[48] At last, Andrews felt vindicated.

The lame boy's inability to hunt and, thus, be a good provider is a plausible reason for why he continued to come to school after many of his friends and relatives began to skip. Within a few months of the school's opening, just about the time that many boys prepared to go into the woods for the winter hunt and girls learned lessons at their mothers' and aunts' sides, some of the children absented themselves. They had grown "weary of learning and left off coming," Andrews noted, "their Parents not obliging them who are generally so over fond of their children and having but little value for [classroom] learning." Their absence was most noticeable whenever Andrews, Claessen, and Oliver returned from a visit to another Mohawk town, where they preached and baptized children. Andrews, a stickler for commitments, accused the Mohawk children of preferring to "be at their play than their books," not realizing that the hunting games the boys "played" and the domestic lessons girls learned were teaching moments of survival skills. As Kateri learned, these acquired skills defined ones future value as a Mohawk adult.[49]

Andrews sensed difficulties ahead. He entreated the fewer than two dozen remaining pupils to stay at their books by "giving them Victuals and other things or else wee should have but very few [students]." Although Andrews shared Claessen's abhorrence of Jesuits who brought some of their catechumens to baptism "by threatenings and others by presents," Andrews was forced to change and comply with this practice. The gift of literacy was not by itself reward enough to an oral-based society that had other pressing needs, such as adequate food and clothing. To Andrews, the Mohawks were "very poor and fare hard[,] especially all the Summer haveing nothing to Eat but a sort of root they digg out of the ground[,] Indian corn[,] and a little dryed fish." His students appeared so hungry for the food he set out that he swore that if he had "100 or 200 [pounds] a year to feed the Children I should have Schollars Enough[!]" Instead, he and John Oliver gave them "what Encouragement" they could and enticed them with a little food and more books.[50] Little changed.

When food and books ceased to attract Mohawk pupils to Oliver's school, the schoolmaster and the priest added "toys" to their bag of enticements. The English considered these items—assorted large beads, mainly green, black, red, and amber; assorted knives, large and small, some with painted handles, others with bone handles, some spring loaded; large scissors; pictures in gilded frames; assorted buttons; assorted rings; mirrors in leather gilt cases; buttons; buckles; large-tooth combs; "bobbs for the eares"; and "gartering stuff"—mere trifles, while the Mohawk children and their parents saw them as not only useful tools but also signs of reciprocity that symbolized how much Andrews and Oliver loved them. The children were also discriminating in their taste; Andrews notified the society not to send any more small beads (too close to wampum?), small scissors (too awkward for big fingers to operate?), forks (too awkward to master?), or mirrors in plain frames (not pretty enough?).[51]

By the spring of 1716, however, neither food not "trifles" could entice Mohawk children or their parents. Only five to seven children bothered to come to school for their lessons. Andrews admonished the parents for not taking better care of their children's education by explaining to them "the Great Advantages of Learning." They should all take full advantage of the benevolence of the "Good Society," he beseeched them. To sweeten the pot and capture their interest, Andrews made a promise: if he could get ten to twelve students to constantly come to school, he would write to the society and ask for "Blankets, Shirts, and Stockings." At first glance, the Mohawks viewed this promise as customary; they expected such tokens of friendship from the Jesuits at Kahnawake, where "Blanckets and Sheets were given every year." It was "upon the same score," Andrews realized, that the Mohawk parents "were so forward at first to have their children taught to read and not out of any love they have for learning." By the fall of 1717, Andrews dismissed Oliver for lack of students. A year later, Andrews gifted the lame lad and each of the four remaining girls—"all that can read"—"the Books that were printed in their own Language," with the hope that someday they "may make a good Use of them." But Andrews was pessimistic, sharing Claessen's belief that they would "soon forget all."[52]

Cultural misunderstanding and miscommunication led Mohawk parents and Andrews to work at cross-purposes, as though each side performed different scripts. The parents viewed their relationship with Andrews as defined by mutuality: they protected him while he passed along to their children "survival goods," which ranged from food to tools to literacy. For Andrews, the children and their parents were indifferent to learning; reading and writing did not constitute the foundation of the mission school for the Mohawks, but rather victuals and gifts did. They tolerated literacy, he believed, in order to benefit materially.

As at the school, attendance at the church, high initially because of the food Andrews laid out to recruit hearers, now began to wane, most noticeably when he withdrew victuals and small presents. Soon, he discovered somewhat to his dismay that only a small corps of mostly elderly, pious Mohawk women remained.

## Gender, the Sacraments, and Resistance at the Mission Church

Andrews should not have been surprised to find from the very beginning that women constituted the foundation of his mission church. As he noted himself, in this matrilineal, matrilocal society, women were the keepers of all things within the village, while men monitored affairs beyond the village proper. One of the duties that befell women was overseeing the education of their young daughters and sons. Hence, Mohawk mothers would naturally be interested in monitoring the activities at the SPG's church and school. In fact, Andrews noted that Mohawk mothers and grandmothers, most likely baptized, insisted that their children say their morning and evening prayers, the catechism, and their letters.[53]

Mohawk mothers and grandmothers not only surveilled their children and grandchildren but also observed Andrews and church activities. The priest was indeed pleased that within two years of his arrival, several pious Mohawk women attended Sunday services regularly and then prayed together afterward in one of their longhouses. Still, he lamented that "very few of the men" were "so good," and those few who did attend Sunday services, he observed, were often intoxicated by the afternoon.[54] Over time, Andrews blocked such men from receiving communion.

The "feminization" of the mission church concerned Andrews. He expressed disquiet in his letters to the society that "the men of this Castle where we are [Tiononderoge] are but little better now Excepting four or five or there about and Many of [the] women." He acknowledged women here almost as an afterthought, in the same way that he often took church attendance, noting men first and women second. Most Englishmen at this time, steeped deeply in patriarchy, presumed that the health of the church and society rested on the leadership of pious, virtuous men. However, Andrews failed to consider fully the sociocultural structure of Haudenosaunee village life. At Tiononderoge, then, as elsewhere in some white frontier communities and at some Native missions, notably Kahnawake, where the church operated as an extension of the domestic sphere, women sustained the church.[55]

Native women's experiences with churches in the seventeenth and eighteenth centuries were highly varied, depending on the social organization of their community and the nature of contact with white settlers and missionaries. For example, Susan Sleeper-Smith has demonstrated how Native women in the western Great Lakes region used the Catholic Church and schools to sustain their communities and their roles as culture brokers. Many indigenous women in southern New England and Upper Canada, who came to understand the limitations of their lives compared to male warriors, may have used the church as did Kateri Tekakwitha to reinvent themselves by creating "a (post) colonial identity out of cultural bricolage." At Kahnawake, the Catholic Church permitted Kateri to play the role that she believed God had chosen for her.[56] A similar argument may be made about other Mohawk women in Mohawk country who were single, widowed, elderly, or infirm, and thus were incapable of fulfilling their gendered roles as wives, mothers, and matrons.

Andrews noted that each year, several Mohawk "widows & aged" women journeyed to Canada to obtain food and clothing and some to live there. He did what he could to provide alimentary relief for these women by "taking home halfe a dozen of them at a time every Sabath day from Church to Dinner." However, he could not afford to clothe them on his salary. His pay was already stretched to the limit providing for those from the other Haudenosaunee nations who "passed by this way once or twice a year to Albany to sell their pelts & fur." He "oblige[d]" them by giving them "victuals & drink & pipes & tobacco," their items of choice.[57] Nevertheless, the elderly women who attended church regularly may have viewed Andrews and the church as conduits for both physical and spiritual nourishment.

Many Mohawk mothers embraced the Church of England out of the belief that the ritual of baptism protected their infants and children prophylactically from disease and misfortune in this world and made them "fit for Heaven" in the next. So important did they regard this rite that when Andrews turned them away, they traveled all the way to Albany just to have the pastors Thomas Barclay or Pieter Van Driessen baptize their babies. Just as some Catholic Mohawk mothers performed culpas prophylactically for sins that they and their children had yet to commit, so some League mothers believed that baptism protected their infants from unforeseen calamities yet to be known.[58]

Some Mohawks believed firmly in the curative property of baptism, viewing the ritual as powerful enough to wipe out all current faults and illnesses, thereby ensuring not only a long life on earth but also guaranteeing a good and healthy life in the hereafter. One Mohawk man, who had become ill and feared that he might die, grew "troubled that he had not yet been baptized and therefore earnestly desired" that Andrews baptize him. The priest balked at the idea initially, for he and the entire community at Tiononderoge knew the man to be "a very wicked Indian, and never had made the least notion [wish] to me that way." Naturally,

Andrews doubted the man's sincerity. However, some in the community beseeched Andrews to baptize him anyway. The sick man also made "good promises . . . of breaking off from all his wicked courses, [and] if it pleased God to restore him again to his health[,] to come to me to be further instructed and keep constantly to Church." Andrews, skeptical and ambivalent, quickly instructed the man and prepared him for baptism. Shortly after administering the sacrament, the man "recovered but forgot all his promises of amending his life [by] coming to me or the Church and became as wicked as ever he was." A short time later, when some residents of Albany complained to other Tiononderoge residents about this man's rebellious behavior, the man said to his brethren, "Let us fall to scalping of them [Albanians]." No one other than Andrews expected the warrior to reform himself and become a humble, pious Christian. Rather, for this warrior and his supportive brethren, baptism worked just as it was intended: as a powerful medicine to cure illness.[59]

Like many of the older generation, some Haudenosaunees regarded baptism as a powerful, unstable medicine that could kill. In the spring of 1714, Andrews ventured to Oneida country, where he baptized several persons, mainly children, each of whom had at least one parent who had been baptized, which conformed to the Church of England's edict. After Andrews's departure, a few of the children died. Consequently, several of the parents were ready to murder Andrews, whom they accused of poisoning their children, a craft practiced by malicious witches. Interestingly, some Mohawks, no doubt well experienced with the range of responses their brethren directed at missionaries when baptisms seemed to go badly, simply "laugh[ed]" off this situation. The Oneidas, however, were not amused. It would be another two years before Andrews would return to Oneida country to clear his name.[60]

Andrews also had difficulty with Mohawks who demanded that he admit them to the other sacrament, communion, because their social standing in the community depended on their admittance to this ritual. However, Andrews maintained a strict policy of barring from this sacrament those individuals whom he deemed "unworthy," typically because of their drinking. In the late summer of 1717, the priest learned a hard lesson: not everyone respected his policy. That summer, a gun-toting Sakamaker (sachem), an eminent headman, burst into Andrews's house and threatened to kill the priest for denying "him and his wife the

Sacrament." In informing the SPG of this incident, Andrews offered lurid, biased details about the sachem and his wife: both were "great drunkard[s] guilty of sabbath breaking and Cruelty in biting of[f] a prisoner[']s nails . . . and making offerings and consulting the Devil." The devil, Andrews learned, had told the Sakamaker that "an Indian widow woman and her two Daughters" had bewitched the sister of his wife, and now he was intent on killing the old widowed woman. Andrews thwarted the headman's plan by advising the old widowed woman to leave town.[61]

In the meantime, this sachem took it as a "great affront to be kept from the sacrament being one of their great men or sachem." The headman, baptized at one point, regarded communion as confirmation of his identification as a "friend" and ally to Andrews and thus the English, but also as a Mohawk headman of special standing and responsibility. The headman reasoned that perhaps both Christ and the Great Spirit—a sign of his practicing alternation—would smile on him for eliminating the witch, a source of calamity and misery. Another way of reading this encounter is that he and his wife demanded forgiveness from Andrews as they were about to commit an act that Christ would have considered a sin but that Haudenosaunee spirits would have considered a justified act. Andrews found him and his wife rather typical of "elite" Mohawks—sachems and clan matrons—who tended to perform Christianity more willingly than others as a means of strengthening social, economic, and political ties with neighboring Europeans without jettisoning completely their faith in Haudenosaunee sacred practices. Eventually, this sachem apologized to Andrews for his aggressive behavior, "laying the blame upon the rum," and promising to try to "not drink so much any more." Andrews explained to the SPG that blaming their behavior on liquor "is their way when they do any Mischiefe in their drunkenness."[62]

Andrews made no mention of whether he forgave the man and his wife for their behavior. The Haudenosaunees regarded offering forgiveness, along with administering the sacraments, one of the principal duties of a priest. Some Mohawks complained to Claessen when Andrews refused to "pardon their sins," noting that the Jesuits in New France did so routinely. At Kahnawake, they could get "drunk, theeve, Whore it, or do any thing they could," Claessen claimed to have been told, and then "pay their Minister, and they would pardon them." Andrews, who did not forgive easily, was convinced that Native peoples were drawn chiefly to

Catholicism by the tradition of buying indulgences, which he considered equivalent to selling salvation and paying bribes for easy absolution.[63]

In addition, the Mohawks expected Andrews to play another important role: praying for the sick and the desperate. Andrews agreed. He believed, in fact, that the Mohawks really needed him only "four or five times in a year" to "Baptize their Children, and read a prayer by them when they are Sick for their Recovery." He learned just how adamant some Mohawks could be about his praying for them when a man "seized with great horrow [*sic*] of mind" confronted him: "the Devil was coming to fetch him away and that he always saw him where ever he was and could have no rest." This man asked Andrews to "pray for him," to which Andrews agreed, as the man had been baptized earlier in life by a Dutch dominie. For the next few weeks, the ailing man was terrified of Andrews leaving his side. After many prayers and much "advice," the man eventually recovered, after which he "behaved himself very well and came often to Church." Andrews hoped of "having a great Convert in him." However, like the ailing Tiononderoge Mohawk who insisted on being baptized and then backslid, this man also dashed Andrews's hopes when he returned to his "wicked" former ways that were "of such a Savage nature and a Canibal that people were afraid to meet him in the woods alone." Eventually, the man went on a three-day drinking binge and, "by the heat of the liquor within and of the sun without[,] scorched to death."[64]

Clearly, the ailing man viewed Andrews and his prayers in Haudenosaunee terms: Andrews was a surrogate shaman, and his prayers were the incantations similar to those offered by shamans. Perhaps this man had been to a shaman, who was unable to heal him. Or perhaps because he was baptized, his shaman had to be a priest. Whatever the man's motive, Andrews's prayers cured him, as far as he was concerned. Once cured, the Mohawk continued for a short time in the way of the Christian to appease Andrews, compatible with middle-ground discourse, as one would in taking a full course of medicine. However, once he was certain his illness would not return, he reverted to his former habits, although to excess, and eventually succumbed.

Andrews blamed excessive drinking, the one vice his Mohawk hosts were "most guilty of," for ruining many a good Christian. From Andrews's perspective, rum turned Mohawk men into "ungovernable and . . . mad distracted Creatures"; some threatened to burn "their houses, others for killing their wives and Children." When wives found their husbands in this state, they "hid their gunns and hatchets from them for their own Security." Sometimes that was not enough to avoid abuse, and wives and children had to "get out of the way themselves" until their husbands and fathers sobered up. When such men were asked why they drank so much, they replied, "Why do you Xns sell us so much Rum?"[65] Many Mohawk reformers, aware of the profound stress and anxiety within these men caused by a changing world, shared their concern and asked repeatedly the New York commissioners to cut off the supply of liquor to Mohawk country.

Andrews blamed the Dutch traders from Schenectady and Albany not only for keeping Mohawk men and women in a seemingly near-perpetual state of inebriation, but also for sowing "divisions and factions among them to make them dislike my being among them." He accused the traders, whom he called "a Sordid base sort of People," of spreading lies about him, including that his presence was a way for the English to get their land; that he preached a "Popish Religion"; and that Dutch dominies were more fit to instruct the Mohawks than English priests. These skillfully planted doubts only thickened the epistemic murk in Mohawk country. Andrews learned that few of the Dutch *"handlers"* "liked of a minister settling among them [the Mohawks], Except one of their own way, for their Trading should be interrupted or their gains lessened." The rum merchants, not the Haudenosaunees, Andrews believed, ran Thoroughgood Moor out of town in 1705. With an English missionary nearby, the traders could not carry on with their trade as they had formerly, especially conduct business with the Mohawks on Sundays.[66]

For a time, Andrews's campaign to place a moratorium on the sale of rum to the Mohawks paid off. The provincial government, at the behest of some of the baptized headmen who sought moral reform, passed a short-term act soon after Andrews's arrival that briefly outlawed the selling of "strong liquors" to the Haudenosaunees. During this time of prohibition, the flow of rum into Iroquoia decreased. So desperate were some Mohawks now for the "walking stick," as some European observers called rum in Native hands, that once when Andrews visited Canajoharie, where only about a half-dozen worshippers ever attended church services, several Mohawk warriors approached him and Claessen and vowed that "if we would give them . . . a dram of Rum[,] they would come to prayers." When the provincial law expired, the *handlers* flooded Iroquoia with rum again, which they sold to the Haudenosaunees at wholesale in order to lubricate trade relations.[67]

Anti-English Dutch rum traders were not the only faction that turned some of the Mohawks against Andrews. A new, sixth, nation of the Iroquois Confederacy—the Tuscaroras—were unfriendly to Andrews as well. In 1713, about fifteen hundred Iroquois-speaking Tuscaroras removed themselves from South Carolina to escape the devastation of the Tuscarora War and journeyed north to settle among the Five Nations. Andrews blamed the Tuscaroras' "implacable hatred against Xtians" for the rise in hard feelings among some of the Mohawks and other Haudenosaunees toward him. Sometime after the Tuscaroras arrived, some of the Mohawk headmen at Canajoharie told Andrews and Claessen that they "need not trouble [them]selves to come to them any more." Nevertheless, the two men defied this order in the spring of 1717. While Andrews conducted services there, someone "ordered a little drum which they had to be beat upon [*sic*] and down the Castle" in an effort to drown out his service.[68]

At the chapel at Fort Hunter, the story was similar: when some of the Haudenosaunees from the other four nations to the west—Oneida, Onondaga, Cayuga, and Seneca—tarried at Tiononderoge for "two or three days" as they made their way to Albany to sell furs, they poked their heads through the chapel door, "look in upon us," and, to Andrews's annoyance, "go away laughing." He was sure that the attitudes of the Tuscaroras rubbed off on most of the headmen of the other four nations to such a degree that whenever the governor of New York brought up at council meetings in Albany the subject of the existing SPG mission, the delegation of headmen cut him off and did "not [let] him say any thing of Religion to them."[69]

To add to Andrews's woes, a smallpox epidemic struck the Mohawks during the summer of 1716, resulting in many deaths, and spread westward to the other nations. Some of the Mohawks resorted to traditional healing practices and consulted shamans, read dreams, retreated to sweat lodges, and made sacrifices to the spirit Andrews deemed the devil as a way of coping with and seeking relief from the disease.[70] To Andrews, the Mohawks seemed to retreat toward their old ways.

In the spring of 1718, Andrews concluded that there was nothing more to be done for the Mohawks. He observed sadly that most of them did not "much concern them selves [*sic*] about Religious [Christian] matters at their homes." He also noted with sarcasm that "they have so much respect for the Sabbath that when out of sight they can do anything on that day," including go "a hunting" so that "they may miss Church." The few who came to church, Andrews noted, slept through most of his service, only to awaken to get dinner afterward. It was not for want of trying, Andrews concluded. He conveyed to the SPG that he had "to the utmost of my power faithfully discharged" his duty, "while they gave me any incouragment." Despite the dangers to his life, Andrews asserted that he undertook his mission work "with abundance of pleasure and satisfaction." The small number of Mohawks most devoted to the mission church—for example, Hendrick and his family and the sodality of the elderly Mohawk women—would have supported Andrews's claims. They believed that Andrews had laid a *suitable* foundation of Protestant Christianity among them, for he enabled them to deepen their Christian faith and begin to identify as "Christian Mohawks."[71]

However, most Mohawks would have disagreed with Andrews and Hendrick. They criticized him for being away from Fort Hunter too often. Moreover, he and Claessen, they claimed, did not know what they were doing in producing their various Mohawk–English texts and botched the Mohawk language. These circumstances caused many Mohawks to pull back from Andrews, who in turn retreated from them. He could not understand why these Mohawks had "a Considerable time Plentifull of instruction line upon line and precept upon precept, the scripture constantly read and all the points of Religion fully explained to them together with the Practice of a holy life . . . all to as little purpose as what formerly has been done."[72] Their resistance was more than Andrews could bear.

In 1718, Andrews requested to leave his Mohawk flock, which he denigrated as "vile Wretches." They dissimulated piety in order to receive "bodily conveniences," he railed, and not out of concern "for the welfare of their souls." He claimed, blindly and unfairly, that he could not recall one among his Mohawk parishioners who ever showed penitence, "or any thing like it by any outward signs as by any affectionat [*sic*] Expressions, prayer, acknowledgment of sins and sorrow for them, sighs or tears or so much as lifting up of a hand or Eye, but seemed to be in a very stupid hardened condition." Andrews's ethnocentrism compelled him to brutally denigrate his Native flock by calling them "a sordid mercenary, beggerly people," who lived "filthy brutish lives" *because* of their "sottishness[,] sloth and laziness." Claessen tried to soften Andrews's disgust and disappointment by explaining to him that all of the previous Dutch ministers "had no better success[,] that they always begun well but end ill." Andrews was not persuaded: "Heathens they were, and heathens they will still be," he declared, adding that they "returned to their former ill lives, like the dog . . . to his vomit."[73]

## Conclusion

William Andrews left the Fort Hunter mission in 1719 and returned to Virginia, where he died in 1721. He, the governor of New York, and the SPG all considered the Fort Hunter mission an utter failure.[74] Although a majority of the Mohawks were now baptized, wholesale conversion to Church of England Protestantism did not materialize. Deleterious external factors, including rum, disease, and the arrival of the Tuscaroras, contributed to undermining Andrews's efforts. However, more significant were the internal factors of linguistic and cultural miscommunication. The Mohawks' expectations of Andrews as a multipurpose priest—a provider of survival goods, a healer through baptism and prayers, and the conferrer of approval—clashed with Andrews's view of his primary role as an instrument of God put there to impart God's truths. Soon, however, he adjusted and conformed partially to Mohawk expectations of him. In return, he expected his Mohawk hearers to be truthfully desirous of Christian instruction. Most Mohawks tolerated Andrews's presence, participated transactionally and selectively in his missionizing project, and performed deliberately a Christianity according to their understanding and needs. They took away from the mission much-needed food, clothing, a little literacy, and some knowledge of Church of England Protestantism.

Besides these tangible commodities, the Mohawks also looked to Andrews to provide essential services, including curing the sick with prayer and forgiving transgressions. They regarded admittance to communion as an important stamp of approval on their character and submission to baptism as confirmation of their identification with—although not necessarily their belief in—Christianity.[75] In short, most League Mohawks expected Andrews to perform the same role and provide the same services as the Jesuits at the mission at Kahnawake, with two key differences: they did not want Andrews to resort to corporal punishment to correct, teach, and punish their children, and they did not want him to tithe them. In some cases, Andrews conformed to *their* expectations; even when he withheld baptism or communion from those he deemed unworthy, he often later relented. In return, Andrews demanded that baptized Mohawks behave outwardly like sober, pious, churchgoing Protestant Christians. On this matter, many Mohawks prevaricated; they saw no contradiction in praying with Andrews on Sunday—and perhaps having a drink or two after church—and then consulting a shaman on Monday to read their dreams. In fact, most believed that baptism was sufficient for Christian identification. To them, instruction and church attendance should be optional.[76]

In addition to problems resulting from communication at cross-purposes, linguistic obstacles limited in part Andrews's success. The priest discovered over time what Governor Hunter often complained about: "What we say in one short word costs them [Haudenosaunees] a long sentence which causes the mistake of writing down words of yards length in all translations." Andrews found "much Confusion" in the Mohawk language, with "no certainty of rule to goe by." To him, the language seemed like "sev[era]l words Tumbled up together, person, verb, noun." Consequently, Andrews's sermons, advice, and teachings, through which he imparted alien terms and concepts, had to penetrate multiple layers of interpretation, from English to Dutch and from Dutch to Mohawk. Claessen, Andrews's Dutch-speaking "linguister," who was semiliterate and unchurched when the priest arrived in Mohawk country in 1712, confirmed the difficulty of mastering the Mohawk language: it was "almost impossible for any to learn . . . perfectly except [those who] begin with it when children."[77] In fact, Claessen had to turn to Mohawk speakers himself from time to time for help with difficult Christian concepts and vocabulary. Thus, the need for multiple interpreters at church and at school meant that some instructions were lost in translation. The Dutch and the Mohawks solved partially the problem of communication by speaking to each other in a simplistic, clipped Mohawk trade language that was "Enough for their Trade . . . but little more." Most likely, their trade language would have had difficulty conveying such alien Christian concepts as redemption; reverence for the Holy Ghost, as dictated by the "Apostle's Creed"; and forgiving trespassers according to the Lord's Prayer. In 1716, Governor Hunter offered a solution to this communication problem: he suggested that the SPG reverse course and teach the Mohawks "our Language and Religion at the same time," believing that "our Religion in their Language sounds odly [sic] to them, the Idioms of the two being so widely Different."[78] Rightly, the SPG remained skeptical of Hunter's suggestion, for in time Mohawk families regained confidence in sending their children to the SPG school when Mohawk teachers and catechists instructed them in their own language.

# CHAPTER 4

# Mohawk Schoolmasters and Catechists

## Literacy, Authority, and Empowerment at Midcentury

> He . . . took pains night & day to repeat & inculcate upon the
> minds of the Indians the truths I taught them daily.
>
> —David Brainerd on his Lenape interpreter,
> Tashawaylennahan (Moses Tattami), 1745

In 1740, Henry Barclay, son of Thomas Barclay, the SPG's minister at
Albany and at Fort Hunter prior to William Andrews's arrival in 1712,
made a bold proposal to the society: appoint from among the "several
Indians well qualified" a "Schoolmaster to Instruct their Indian youth
(upon whom the greatest hopes are to be built) to read their own Language." The SPG had not yet put a Mohawk on its payroll to teach, read
prayers, or catechize Native neophytes. The Jesuits in New France and
the Puritan clergy in Massachusetts seemed to understand the value of
this practice. The Jesuits employed routinely Native *dogiques,* or "prayer
captains," to read prayers, to catechize children, to occasionally baptize
other indigenes, and, in general, to put a familiar face on Christianity.
Even the seventeenth-century Puritans welcomed Native schoolmasters,
exhorters, and pastors, some of whom even baptized local whites. For the
SPG to follow their examples would set a precedent—and perhaps raise
a paradox: Could indigenous catechists with questionable adherences to
Church of England Protestantism be entrusted to "reduce" unchurched
Mohawks, heretofore the job of white Christians?[1]

Henry Barclay knew of what he spoke. Before he began his assignment
as the SPG's official catechist at Fort Hunter in 1735, he witnessed his predecessor, Reverend John Miln, struggle with reaching Mohawk hearers.

On September 15, 1727, Miln was assigned pastor to Albany's St. Peter's Church, a small stone structure built in 1717, the first Anglican church north of New York City, the post Henry's father, Thomas, held between 1708 and 1726. In December, Miln journeyed to Fort Hunter to preach to the Mohawks. During his first visit, the priest baptized six Native children and administered communion to "4 English and 13 of them [Mohawks]," whom he found had been "sufficiently instructed in the assential [*sic*] ground of Christianity" by "Mr. Andrews late Missionary to the Society," whose loss, Miln claimed, several of the baptized Mohawks "very much regret[ted]." Miln vowed to visit Fort Hunter "three or four times a year" to preach to the English soldiers and to the Tiononderoge Mohawks. For the ensuing six years, Miln had his hands too full ministering to his English and Dutch congregation in Albany, as well as seeing to the needs of innumerable "Black Slaves who have never been baptized nor Instructed in Christianity," to travel much the forty-plus miles west and back. The pace of the work must have been grueling, for the unrelenting responsibilities that perhaps exacerbated Barclay's mental illness laid Miln profoundly low, forcing him to resign his position and return to England in 1734. At this time, he recommended Henry Barclay as his successor once the young man was ordained. Miln cited Henry's solid credentials: "the son of a Distress't [insane] Brother . . . Rev. Mr. [Thomas] Barclay late Missionary from the Hon[orable] Society at Albany . . . [and] 4 years at the College at New Haven [Yale] . . ." Most important, Henry was "Desirous off acquiring their [Mohawks'] Language." In 1733, Henry, an acolyte at this time, began spending "some time amongst the Mohawks and attained some of their Language." He took "all opportunities to Instruct them in the Christian Religion," performing "divine Service in their Language Every Lord's Day." Some observers noted that Henry also spent "some time in teaching their [Mohawk] Children to write & Read," which the children seemed to appreciate, for they purportedly "constantly attend[ed] School and ma[de] vast progress" in their studies. The Mohawks, some observers contended, held "great Love and Regard for him and [were] very much Reformed since his coming among them." Miln, who was certain that Henry would become "an ornament to the Church," urged the society to hire him so that he may carry on the work begun by William Andrews, for only "a proper person Instructed in their tongue" could do that work suitably.[2]

Those formerly in the SPG's employ as missionary, catechist, or school-master knew how difficult it was to master the Mohawk dialect. Like Andrews, Miln, too, found their language too cacophonous and chaotic for communicating clearly Christian thought. He explained to the society that "Ideas can be but Imperfectly Convey'd to them by the means of an Ignorant interpreter, whose Immorall life Contributes to Lessen the Impression of the Dictates." Miln may have had Claessen in mind, or an imaginary unskilled, unenculturated interpreter as an example of someone who was "not qualified in any Respect" and thus unhelpful to him. Nevertheless, Miln found that when his linguister read prayers and interpreted his sermons into Mohawk, his roughly fifty "constant hearers" "behave[d] themselves decently and devoutly," a rather obtuse assessment of their behavior that may say as much about Mohawk etiquette as piety.[3]

By the SPG's standards, Henry Barclay, now fairly fluent in Mohawk, having heard it since childhood in Albany and more recently studied it, appeared to be that proper person to instruct the Mohawks in their language. Yet now, more than twenty years after the SPG had fired John Oliver, Barclay asked the society to revive the mission school, this time with a baptized Native-born speaker to instruct Mohawk children in the principles of Protestant Christianity and to teach them how to read and write in Mohawk. Cultural and language barriers, the inconsistent presence of a religious figure, and growing Mohawk cries for a greater pastoral presence made obvious—at least to Henry—the need for Native assistance at the Fort Hunter mission. [4]

Moreover, the use of Native exhorters to read prayers during the long and frequent absences of the missionaries might ease a phenomenon about which many missionaries complained: finding what they saw as chronic apostasy among their flocks whenever they returned to Mohawk country following their absence or a hiatus in SPG activity. Following Andrews's departure in 1719 until 1750, the Mohawks were without an SPG priest assigned specifically to them. If they needed the services of a pastor, they had to either await Reverend Miln's quarterly visits or journey the forty-plus miles to Albany to attend his service at St. Peter's Church or that of Dominie Petrus van Driessen at the Dutch Reformed Church there. Beginning in 1723, some journeyed to Schoharie to attend the services of Reverend John Jacob Oel [Ehle], a German Lutheran

pastor ordained by the Church of England in 1722. The region of Schoharie, often termed the "middle castle" of the three major Mohawk
villages, was increasingly populated by immigrant Palatine families.
They and Mohawk families from Canajoharie looked to Oel to perform
weddings, baptisms, and funerals.[5]

However, without a permanent Church of England priest devoted
exclusively to them, many pious Mohawks complained about backsliding
in their communities, not to mention the lack of demonstrated affection
toward them by the English Crown. Most pastors in the area, regardless
of denomination, serviced their own white and enslaved members of
their respective communities at Albany, Schenectady, and Schoharie first
and the Mohawks at Fort Hunter when they had the time to devote a
few weeks out of the year. In 1761, following the departure of two successive SPG missionaries, Little Abraham, a pious Mohawk, diagnosed the
long-standing problem:

> [W]e are now like a lost people, having no person to instruct either us,
> or our Children, who are like the wild Creatures in the woods, having no
> knowledge of the great Spirit above. . . . [O]ur grown people have become
> so addicted to liquor that unless some stop be put thereto, we shall be a
> ruined people, and as the only method of reclaiming them must be by the
> help of a Minister [who will] remain constantly amongst us, and not act as
> the former, which was as soon as they had acquired a little of our language
> to abandon us. . . . [This] is the only means we have left to render us
> happy in this, and the next World.[6]

Little Abraham called for the SPG to sustain its commitment to the
Mohawks by providing full-time resident missionaries and teachers.
Henry Barclay saw warning signs of social strain precipitated by absentee
priests and schoolteachers twenty years earlier and sought to remedy the
situation by placing Mohawks from the community in charge of their
religious and secular educations.

The society agreed with Henry that "an Indian Schoolmaster with a
Salary not Exceeding 15 [pounds] per annum"—about three-quarters
of John Oliver's school teacher salary in the 1710s—"be appointed by
Mr. Barclay with the approbation of the Lieutenant Governor of New
York and the Commissioners for Indian Affairs."[7] By the fall of 1742,
two Mohawk schoolmasters—Cornelius at Tiononderoge and Daniel
at Canajoharie—were plying their trade, each at an annual salary of ten

pounds, New York currency, five pounds less than the SPG's own recommendation. Barclay described Cornelius as "very faithful and diligent and vastly successful." Barclay, now ordained (1738) and resident pastor at St. Peter's Church, had yet to visit Canajoharie, but he had heard that Daniel was also instructing conscientiously Mohawk children and adults there. The following May, in 1743, Barclay boasted that many of the Tiononderoge Mohawks "attend the School very Steadily, and make a great Proficiency under the Schoolmaster [Cornelius], who is very diligent, and takes great pains to Teach them." By November, the two Mohawk schools flourished under the two Mohawk schoolmasters, who, according to Barclay, "carried on with great Diligence and no less Success."[8]

Thus, the hiring of Cornelius and Daniel set in motion the short-lived experiment of employing a handful of Mohawk headmen as schoolmasters, readers, and catechists at an average annual salary of between five and fifteen pounds per year.[9] Their role was to propagate English knowledge, including Church of England Protestantism, during Barclay's frequent absences, during which time he could be found in the more comfortable confines of Albany, Schenectady, or New York City. Their catechumens had some familiarity with the faith these Native teachers were asked to keep alive, but communicating its tenets and rituals, encoded in their language, remained a challenge. Their employer, the SPG, expected these men to compel their brethren to reimagine their secular and sacred worlds, to employ a new discourse that displaced a complex web of sacred beings, objects, and rituals, and place at the center of that web a new belief system headed by a single omniscient God, whose sacred truths were once revealed but were now immutable. The new belief system would allegedly relieve the Mohawks of their distress by promising salvation and life everlasting, Christian concepts that were vaguely correlative to such Haudenosaunee concepts as the Great Spirit, the ritual of divination, the concept of the soul or spirit, and belief in life after death. Other concepts, such as sin and repentance, were literally otherworldly.

In order to properly teach English knowledge and the principles of Protestantism, these Mohawk teachers had to translate English Christian discourse—those words, symbols, metaphors, and stories that expressed the religion's sacredness—that made sense to them before they could convey Christian doctrines to their Mohawk catechumens accustomed to Haudenosaunee sacred discourse, constituted by myths, stories, rituals, festivals, songs, and dance.[10] The sacred, immutable truths of Christianity lay fixed in "the Word"; the opening sentence in the Book of John of the Bible begins, "In the beginning was the Word." Orality governed the transmission of Haudenosaunee sacred truths, which rendered them flexible and mutable. Were Cornelius and Daniel literate and pious enough to interpret "the Word" to young catechumens? The evidence suggests that the Native catechists may have engaged in what David Silverman calls "religious translation"—indigenizing Christian principles by substituting Mohawk words, symbols, metaphors, and tenets for Christian ones. This strategy required the catechist and the catechumen to read and recite texts translated into the local vernacular, which in theory invested translatable powers in the scriptures.[11] Moreover, in the process, the teacher-catechists themselves underwent symbolic change. As headmen of some standing, they performed the familiar roles of authority figure and keeper of the peace. As schoolmasters, they performed similar roles with similar authority; in imparting a new moral code, they performed as prophets in the tradition of Deganawidah, the Huron prophet, who, in the fifteenth century, formulated the Great League of Peace and Power, which ended long-term internecine fighting and brought the five disparate Haudenosaunee nations together in alliance. However, the teacher-catechists also usurped the unfamiliar roles of educator and socializer, responsibilities hitherto assigned to women. Mothers taught their prepubescent children, both girls and boys, basic life skills, the ways of the world, and proper behavior. Nevertheless, the SPG placed no women on its payroll, not even to interpret, as Hilletie Van Olinda had done for the Dutch and English fifty years earlier. These pious Mohawk men performed both the familiar and the unfamiliar as they placed Christian precepts beside Haudenosaunee concepts and meanings.[12]

Native culture brokers, who often served as interpreters, translators, guides, diplomats, traders, civil servants, teachers, and catechists, have offered scholars of Native intermediaries and go-betweens a unique perspective on cultural change and continuity within indigenous societies and present a particular peek at aspects of identity construction. Many lived "between worlds," a term coined by Frances Karttunen to characterize those who occupied spaces at the margins of society. Hilletie Van

Olinda fits this model. However, as other scholars have argued, not all brokers lived liminal lives. Historian James Merrell has shown that many, if not most, brokers—especially those inhabiting or working in colonial Pennsylvania's backcountry—lived deeply rooted on one side or the other of the cultural divide, but were able to negotiate and maneuver between two or more cultural worlds. The Mohawks hired as schoolmaster-catechists were firmly planted in Mohawk society. Their first names indicate that they were probably baptized, but their actions and habits suggest that they practiced alternation in their faith and culture.[13]

## The Mohawk Discourse Brokers

Who were these Mohawk discourse brokers, and why did they agree to broker Christianity? Daniel, Cornelius, Old Abraham, Paulus, and Little Abraham, the five Mohawk headmen hired by the SPG in the middle decades of the eighteenth century to be schoolmasters and catechists, were men of influence and of local elite status. Most were war captains who became sachems. War chiefs earned their titles, such as Pine Tree Chief, through personal charisma and accomplishment. Their greatest sphere of influence was local, although according to one historian, they often pooled support and resources from beyond their village to exercise greater authority. War chiefs conferred regularly with their warrior brethren on matters of import to their communities, most notably war, peace, trade, land, and alliances.[14]

The chief job of a sachem, or Peace Chief, or League sachem, was to keep the peace nationally and internationally. Peace Chief was an inherited title at the confederated League level; fifty Peace Chiefs from the five Haudenosaunee nations met regularly in council in Onondaga to discuss and arrive at a consensus on ways to preserve the peace, which meant not merely the absence of war but rather the presence of good and kind thoughts in each man, woman, and child. Leading clan mothers identified and selected the sachems and looked for certain personal qualities in the candidates when they were children or adolescents, qualities that included selflessness, even temperedness, patience, goodwill, and eloquent oratory skills.[15] Effective speaking skills were essential, for sachems officiated routinely at condolence ceremonies for the dead. The surviving kin of the deceased valued the sachem's abilities to speak soothing words that wiped away their tears and calmed their raging hearts. An early historian of the Haudenosaunees noted that "the People of the *Five nations* are much given to *Speech-making,*" for "where no single Person has a Power to compel, the Arts of Persuasion alone must prevail." An effective sachem spoke powerfully and eloquently in order to persuade his brethren to see a matter from his perspective. In each village, headmen, whether war captains or sachems, met collectively almost daily to discuss matters of the day, especially war and peace. They reached decisions by consensus, but always in consultation with clan matrons, who carried enormous influence in Haudenosaunee society. Yet, as historian Daniel Richter has noted, coercing others did not always work. As Europeans encroached increasingly on Haudenosaunee land and lives across the eighteenth century, many sachems lost their ability to win warriors over to their side, often resulting in young warriors embarking unilaterally on unsanctioned raids against Europeans and Americans and other Native peoples, which threatened the peace.[16] Consequently, the question of who were the real influencers among the Mohawks was an increasingly contested one. Henry Barclay selected those headmen whom he thought carried authority and ability.

The essential quality the SPG desired in its Native teachers was eloquent, gentle, and loving powers of persuasion. However, three other criteria were just as important: the candidates had to be pious, sober, and baptized. The five Mohawk headmen employed by the SPG had been baptized and instructed by either an English priest or a Dutch or German pastor, and thus bridged Mohawk and European worlds. They met all of the above criteria, including sobriety, piety, and in some cases literacy.[17]

Although the documentary evidence on the five Mohawk teachers and readers is scant, what is extant reveals a general pattern: most, but not all, were baptized as youths, most were sponsored by either Dutch or Mohawk congregants, and they all took Christian first names. The Mohawk schoolmaster Daniel Asharego (probably Wolf clan) of Canajoharie, born sometime around the turn of the eighteenth century, was baptized in January 1707, possibly by Thomas Barclay in Albany. His sponsors were Jacob and Jacomina. In addition to his Christian name, Daniel, Asharego also answered to his nickname, "Cutlass." On April 30, 1710, Daniel married Elizabeth, who was baptized on April 30, 1710. Her sponsors were Rebecca Sr. and Kanastasi Jr., two baptized Mohawks.[18]

Cornelius Kryn (clan unknown), the Mohawk schoolmaster of and at Tiononderoge, was born shortly after the turn of the eighteenth century and baptized on June 21, 1712, most likely by the new Dutch dominie, Peter Van Driessen, on the day he arrived in Albany. Griete and Adam Vrooman, a wealthy trader in Schenectady, who acquired a great deal of Mohawk land in 1711 through a dubious deal with Hendrick and other Mohawk headmen, sponsored Cornelius.[19]

Old Abraham Canostens, a.k.a. Abraham Peters (Bear) of Canajoharie, was born around 1690 and was baptized as an adult in April 1731 along with his wife, Gesina, by dominie Van Driessen. Old Abraham's younger brother, Theyanoguin Peters Tiyanoga (Bear), who took the Christian name Hendrick when baptized, was born in 1692 and bore the formal clan name Sayenquerachta or Soiengarahta, the name of the chief sachem of Canajoharie. Theyanoguin, or Hendrick, Peters Tiyanoga (Bear) inherited his name and title from Brant Thowariage, one of the "faux kings" who journeyed to London in 1710, on the latter's death. In turn, Old Abraham inherited the name and title of Sayenquerachta on Theyanoguin's death during the Seven Years' War. The SPG hired Old Abraham as a catechist and perhaps a reader, for which he earned five pounds a year to catechize neophytes during the absences of the SPG missionary.[20]

Paulus Peters Saghsanowana Anahario (Turtle) of Canajoharie, the son of Hendrick Theyanoguin Peters Tiyanoga, was baptized in May 1714, either by Andrews or by Van Driessen. The SPG valued highly Paulus's role as schoolmaster at Canajoharie, for he was literate in Mohawk and English.[21]

Little Abraham Teyorhansere (Wolf), of Tiononderoge—not Old Abraham's son—was baptized sometime before getting married in 1743. By the time of his appointment as SPG catechist, Little Abraham was a clan war chief. However, in the late 1750s, he would be promoted to sachem, one of the two peace chiefs at Tiononderge. Through kinship ties, Little Abraham and his extended family, like the Peters family, would become deeply connected politically to Sir William Johnson, the powerful future superintendent of Indian affairs for the northern colonies.[22]

These five men also possessed desirable talents and qualities beyond piety and sobriety. Some were "readers," meaning that they were not just literate but also knowledgeable enough to assist the priest with the church service. To "read prayers" was to lead and instruct the Native congregants in the recitation of prayers. Cornelius possessed this skill. Henry Barclay informed the SPG that the Mohawk schoolmaster diligently "Instructs severall [*sic*] young Men and Women, and is much beloved of his brethren, and *Reads* Prayers to them in [my] Absence."[23] Additionally, readers often helped prepare communion and sometimes even preached a little. In all probability, Cornelius and other Mohawk readers served as interpreter for the priest as well.

The SPG also regarded teaching experience, like that of a reader, invaluable. Old Abraham Canostens (or Caunauhstansey) of Canajoharie had instructed children and adults at several of the Mohawk castles "in the fundamentals of religion" for three years prior to Governor Clinton's recommendation in 1749 that the society hire the older headman for the position of "catechist." Old Abraham's catechumens, like those of Cornelius, were said to be "more desirous than ever of his praying to them."[24] Even during the Seven Years' War, Old Abraham carried on with his duties. At the battle of Lake George in 1755, for example, William Johnson described cryptically the work of this pious catechist: "Good Old Abraham performed Divine Services every morning and evening."[25] He well fitted the model of a respected sachem who used his authority, eloquence, and piety to spread the Gospel as an itinerant catechist, traveling from village to village, expanding his sphere of influence beyond his village. As a result of his being "always among them [the Mohawks], while in one Castle, and then in another," Old Abraham, according to Sir William Johnson, was "much liked by them all." He was so committed to teaching the Gospel that, in the opinion of John Ogilvie, the SPG priest who will replace Henry Barclay, Old Abraham "intirely neglected his hunting in order to instruct his Brethren in the principles of Religion." Moreover, while presiding at condolence ceremonies and at council meetings, Old Abraham often chastised New York officials, including William Johnson, the governor of New York, and the commissioners of Indian affairs, for neglecting the spiritual, educational, and material needs of the Mohawk people.[26] During his tenure at Stockbridge, Massachusetts, in the late 1740s and early 1750s, Jonathan Edwards met Old Abraham, whom he characterized as "a remarkable man; a man of great solidity, prudence, devotion, and strict conversation; and acts very much as a person endowed with simplicity, humanity, self-denial and zeal of a true Christian."[27] The SPG could not have asked for a better harvester of souls, or one who worked as cheaply.

Another skill the SPG valued highly was literacy. The society treasured the ability of its Mohawk schoolmasters to read and write and to teach others the same. Cornelius, the schoolmaster at Tiononderoge, was literate, and so may have used the same texts with which he learned to read and write—Bible verses, sermons, and the church catechism—that William Andrews and his interpreter, Lawrence Claessen, translated into Mohawk and left behind at Tiononderoge and at Fort Hunter. However, neither Cornelius nor Daniel possessed the necessary teaching supplies with which to properly instruct the pupils. They needed workbooks, which they set about creating themselves. In November 1742, Henry Barclay informed the society that part of a fifteen-pound advance that he had received went to furnish the two Mohawk schoolmasters, "Cornelius a Sachem at the Lower [Tiononderoge] and . . . Daniel att [*sic*] the Upper Town [Canajoharie] . . . with paper [and] Ink." Barclay noted that Cornelius had to "take great pains" in teaching his students, for he was obliged "to write manuscript to Instruct them by having no Books printed in the Indian Tongue proper for that Purpose." Hence, Cornelius had to write out his own texts and his own writing exercises.[28]

Paulus at Canajoharie was literate in both Mohawk and English. In 1755, five years after the SPG hired him as schoolmaster at an annual salary of seven pounds, ten shillings—about three-quarters of what Cornelius and Daniel received—the missionary John Ogilvie reported that several of the more than "40 Children" that Paulus taught "every day . . . begin to read, & some to write" in Mohawk. In the 1760s, Paulus switched to teaching literacy in English at the request of the society, although William Johnson, one of the Mohawks' benefactors, insisted that Mohawk catechumens continue to learn in their own language. Johnson feared that to Anglicize the Mohawks would make them soft, would cause them to lose their warrior's virility, and thus would make the English frontier communities vulnerable to attack from the north and west.[29]

Increasingly, the more deeply involved the Mohawks became with the SPG, the more important they regarded the acquisition of literacy, initially in their own language and eventually in English. The ability to read not only enabled them to decipher the Bible and other Christian texts but also empowered them to verify the contents of deeds and to check the terms of treaties negotiated at council meetings. Mohawks insisted on keeping copies of such documents, whether the headmen could read them or not, as an insurance policy that documented agreements. As the historian Nancy Shoemaker has suggested, Native negotiators rarely forgot the contents of such agreements because both they and the British used a variety of mnemonic devices, including wampum belts, calumets, dances, eagle feathers and wings, and now parchment, throughout negotiations to mark and fix terms of agreement.[30] As such, oral and written texts coexisted. However, writing symbolized white English power and identity, which also empowered Mohawks as they appropriated it. As a result, literacy in Mohawk and eventually in English excited local ambitions and gave individuals and communities new and powerful ways of engaging their world.[31] In brief, many eighteenth-century Mohawks anticipated what Claude Lévi-Strauss claimed two hundred years later: the intent of writing (and presumably reading) was for one people to enslave another. Perhaps understanding this, several Mohawks believed it imperative to contest the hegemony of the SPG by encoding meaning from one graphic system—English writing—to one intelligible to them— writing in Mohawk. To begin teaching literacy, Mohawk catechists used English-Mohawk primers.[32]

To support the teaching of literacy required several texts in Mohawk. In essence, the early-eighteenth-century Church of England allied itself with the thinking of the Renaissance humanist Desiderius Erasmus (d. 1536), who called for the mysteries of Christ to be "published as openly as possible."[33] In publishing Christian texts in the local vernacular, the SPG replicated the long tradition of translating the scriptures into local languages. When the local vernacular carries the Word of God—the ultimate authority of the universe, according to teachers of Christianity— which then becomes accessible to individuals who are able to commune with God through their own language, then their language takes on a power hitherto not accorded it. As several students of orality and literacy have argued, missionaries who sponsored vernacular translations of Christian texts unwittingly conferred on the local languages an indisputable authority. Putting the Mohawk language in print in the form of passages from the scriptures, the catechism, rudimentary dictionaries, psalms, prayers, and hornbooks elevated the power of the language to that of English. To use the Mohawk words *Niyoh* for God and *Raniha* for

FIGURE 4. *A Primer for the Use of the Mohawk Children*, James Peachy, 1786.
—*Courtesy of the John Carter Brown Library, Providence, Rhode Island. Licensed for use under CC BY-SA 4.0 (https://creativecommons.org/licenses/by-sa/4.0/).*

Father, for example, invited a unique indigenous translation of these two concepts, which English Christians easily conflated cognitively. Thus, this translation project stamped unwittingly the Mohawk language with a seal of approval.[34]

Local ambition and autonomy could not have arisen, I argue, had it not been for Native schoolmasters and catechists who helped to translate Church of England Protestantism. The SPG viewed these pious hired headmen as men *with* God, and their literacy skills further enhanced their status by conferring a degree of power upon them. When literacy is introduced into oral-based societies, argues one authority on the subject, the elders, traditionally keepers and teachers of knowledge, are typically bypassed. Books and other printed materials carry and fix knowledge that only elders could heretofore convey and recall. This consequence of literacy—of making elders redundant—did not occur among the Mohawks because only a small number of Mohawks became literate in either English or Mohawk throughout the eighteenth century and because literacy in Mohawk country did not replace headmen but rather enhanced their status, power, and influence.[35]

It is difficult to determine exactly how Old Abraham, Cornelius, and Daniel communicated Church of England Protestantism to their cate-chumens, and even how they themselves understood and performed their new faith. They left no direct accounts of how or what they taught. However, because the Mohawk teachers were in the employ of the SPG, we may assume that their pedagogy fell in line with at least some SPG practices. Instruction by Church of England priests, catechists, schoolmasters, and readers was heavily text based. Hence, they relied heavily on religious books and instruction manuals. One such book, used by Barclay and Ogilvie in Mohawk country, was a treatise penned in 1740 by Thomas Wilson, the bishop of London in the 1730s and '40s, titled *An Essay towards an Instruction for the Indians*. His treatise is an extended essay in the form of an imaginary dialogue, in the tradition of John Eliot's *Indian Dialogues*, between a missionary of great tolerance, wisdom, and patience and an extremely articulate, yet skeptical, Native catechumen. Unlike some of his contemporaries, Wilson did not question whether Native Americans were "capable of receiving . . . Christian Knowledge." He believed that Native peoples "can reason as well as Christians." Moreover, in his monotheistic world, "we [humankind]," he argued, "are the Creatures of one and the same God." Wilson rea-soned that all men and women, regardless of birth or station, or language or culture, were capable of grasping God's truths.[36] Therefore, Wilson's missionary persuades the reluctant Native catechumen to cast off his life lived in darkness and to choose the lighted path of Christianity. Wilson's book became very popular among missionaries throughout the colonies, who regarded it as a kind of training manual, especially when catechiz-ing white, Native, and African children. Henry Barclay asked for and received several copies of the book so that he might have it translated into Mohawk, presumably so that he, Cornelius, Daniel, Paulus, and their Mohawk catechumens could learn from it.[37]

Perhaps the most fundamental truth that Native Christians were required to grasp, according to Wilson, was the tenet that God was incomparable and omnipotent. Some Mohawk catechumens may have found this "truth" difficult to understand, for according to Haudenos-aunee sacred practices, no single entity held such supreme power and authority. The Great Creator, or Great Spirit, existed, but he was one of many gods and spirits that animated the world. All things, in fact, possessed an indwelling power, or spirit. Each individual had his or her own guardian spirit, who guided him or her through life, and thus was far more important than the Great Creator. To endow a single deity with total omnipotence ran counter to Haudenosaunee belief, which held that multiple forces operate in the world.[38]

Perhaps Wilson recognized that Native peoples believed that multiple forces were at play, for he cautioned missionaries about a particularly troubling aspect of Native thought and behavior, as he saw it: indigenes, he claimed, had a strong and natural inclination toward evil. Neophytes especially, but also all Native peoples, Wilson warned, had to be constantly vigilant of this tendency, for "evil Spirits [were] always ready to take Possession" of them.[39] Interestingly, Wilson unwittingly pointed to an aspect of Haudenosaunee religion with which baptized and unbaptized Mohawks would have agreed: evil spirits *did* exist, and, depending on one's universe of discourse, one either supplicated them or asked for God's intervention.

To convince Mohawk tyros to acknowledge God and to cast off their former ways and beliefs, Mohawk catechists began by first teaching their Native hearers the church's catechism, which embodied the foundational myths of Church of England Protestantism. Its lessons consisted of a series of questions posed orally by the catechist to the catechumen, who was compelled to respond with rote answers. The drill was designed to impel the student to believe sincerely in the Articles of the Christian Faith and to become a devout person by worshipping God and following his holy commandments. In reciting the first few lines of the Articles of Faith, which establish God as incomparable and supranatural, and Jesus Christ as the Lord in human form—"I Believe in God the Father Almighty, maker of heaven and earth: And in Jesus Christ his only Son our Lord"—a Mohawk catechumen would have spoken: *"Tewakightaghkouh Niyohtseragouh ne Raniha ne agwegouh tihhaeshatste, raonissouh ne Karonia, neoni Oghwhentsya Neonoi Jesus Christ-tseragouh raonha-a Rahawak Songwayaner."*[40]

In this passage, certain key Mohawk words—*Niyoh* for "God," *Raniha* for "Father," *Karonia* for "heaven"—carry images, translations, and meanings that are specific to the Haudenosaunee creation story: *Niyoh*, most likely understood as Teharonghyawago, the Good Twin and giver of life, rather than the Great Spirit; *Karonia*, the primordial Sky World; *Raniha*, "Father," who could be a biological father or uncle, or Jesus Christ.

In addition to teaching their catechumens to memorize the Articles of Faith, the Mohawk schoolmasters and catechists would have also explained to their catechumens the importance of their daily duty to praise God through prayer and psalms. Their pupils would have had to commit to memory a number of prayers, including the *Te Deum laudamus*—"Thee, God, we praise," a prayer of thanksgiving to God—recited at morning prayers on Sundays, Wednesdays, Fridays, and on other holy days. The catechumens may have translated these prayers as the equivalent of Haudenosaunee thanksgiving songs. The first three lines of this prayer reinforced the first of God's Ten Commandments, that is, singular devotion to God alone:

> We praise thee, O God: we acknowledge thee to be the Lord.
> *O Niyoh wakwaneandon; kwayenderist-ha Sayaner.*
> All the earth doth worship thee: the Father everlasting.
> *Oghwhentsiagwegouh, yesenideghtasisk: Ne Raniha tsiniyeheawe.*
> To thee all angels cry aloud: the heavens, and all the powers
>     therein.
> *Karonghiyageghronontseragwegouh, neoni Kaeshatsteghtitserhogouh,*
>     *Karonghiyagehogouh yederon.*[41]

Perhaps the frequency of reciting the *Te Deum*, whether led by Native teachers or by Barclay or Ogilvie, reinforced the idea that God was more omnipotent than the Great Spirit. Moreover, the constant recitation of the Lord's Prayer at morning and evening prayers, at catechetical lessons, at communion, and at church services was designed to reinforce the catechumen's view of God as incomparable and sovereign and remind the proselyte of his or her responsibility to God:

> Our Father which art in Heaven,
> *Songwaniha Karonghyage tighsideron;*
> Hallowed be thy Name;
> *Wafaghseanadogeaghtine.*
> Thy kingdom come;
> *Sayanertsera sewe,*
> Thy will de done in earth, as it is in Heaven.
> *Tagserre eghniawanea tsiniyought Karonghyagouh, oni*
>     *Oghwentsiage.*[42]

Non-Mohawk speakers, including this author, should heed the request of Mohawk memoirist Tom Porter (Sakokwenionkwas), a Bear clan elder, who asks us to refrain from speaking the language if we do not know it: "Don't just say *konnoronhkwa*, if you don't know what it means. Because if you do that, you cheapen the word." Porter goes on to explain that the word *konnoronhkwa* means "love," but not "love" the way non-Native Americans tend to use it. "It means [love] not just now, and not just today," which is how most Americans use the term, Porter contends, but for all time: "the next day, the next day, the next year, all the way until I'm not gonna breathe any more breath of life. . . . If something comes that's gonna hurt you or injure you, I'm gonna stand right in front because *konnoronhkwa*." Perhaps Porter was signaling that the meaning of *konnoronhkwa* was close to "agape," brotherly love.[43] I have chosen not to include an English vernacular translation of the Mohawk. However, perhaps we can discern something from Mohawk scholar Scott Stevens, who has provided a translation of the initial stanzas of the Lord's Prayer from another Mohawk dialect:

> Father that in heaven [Sky World] you live; you should be
>   praised,
> You should be respected, you should be obeyed on the earth,
> Like in heaven, where you are obeyed.[44]

Should we assume that "Father" is God or the Creator, or Teharon-ghyawago, the Good Twin, the bringer of life? What did Mohawk hearers hear in the words "praise," "respect," and "obey"? When they supplicated spirits, whether good and evil, they asked them to intervene by revealing truths, not rest passively on the laurels of past revealed truths. As Stevens points out, SPG missionaries and their Native interpreters and translators surely encountered the difficulties Tom Porter flagged: how to translate the Gospel into Mohawk that made sense to Mohawk catechumens but did not sacrifice the meanings of the Gospel.

A critical place to begin translating Christian concepts into Mohawk is at the beginning: the book of Genesis. The Christian creation myth begins with the world as a black void, to which over the course of seven days God brings light and creates all living things, including Adam and Eve, the progenitors of human life, with Eve fashioned out of Adam's rib. The Haudenosaunee myth is just as fantastic, but differs in its gendered roots and in what constitutes the supranatural. Pre-humanlike spirits exist in a preexistent primordial world. After Sky Woman tumbles through a void, and preexistent animals create the earth for her, she gives birth to a daughter, who in turn conceives immaculately twins. Teharonghyawago, the Good Twin, is the bringer of Haudenosaunee life.

Although the prologues of the Haudenosaunee creation and the Christian creation stories differ, one may find corollaries between the former and the foundational myths of Christianity. John Norton, an early-nineteenth-century Scot-Cherokee writer who identified ethnically as Mohawk, recalled that many Haudenosaunees throughout southern Canada who identified as Christian believed that in the language of the Europeans, Sky Woman's daughter "is called Maria." Some Mohawk catechumens may have translated her immaculate conception as similar the Virgin Mary's conception of Christ. They also may have read the twins, Teharonghyawago (good) and Tawiskaron (evil), as stand-ins for Cain and Abel, the twin sons of Adam and Eve. Cain, the farmer, murdered his brother, Abel, the shepherd, and was then banished by God to the Land of Nod, similarly to how Teharonghyawago, the bringer of life, banished Tawiskaron, his evil twin brother, to the "edges of the world."[45] Nevertheless, most Christian missionaries, regardless of church or denomination, insisted that their Native tyros abandon their traditional creation myths and embrace theirs. Many baptized Mohawks viewed this requirement unnecessary, and thus often held on to both concepts of the sacred world.

To stress the supremacy of Christian identity, SPG missionaries placed great emphasis on the two sacraments—baptism and communion—to signify one's contract with God as well as with the imagined community of people of the shared faith. The two sacraments symbolized that one had been received into the holy church of Christ. Although the Church of England practiced infant baptism, adult and adolescent Mohawks who had not been previously baptized and who demonstrated a grasp of Protestant tenets through the recitation of the church catechism as well as manifested outward signs of pious behavior were also permitted to enter into covenant with Christ and the church through baptism. Concomitant with the blessing of baptism, the new "convert" took a Christian name, often that of a saint, sometimes that of the sponsor, which further symbolized rebirth.

Because the scriptures written in Mohawk carried images and meanings particular to Haudenosaunee thought, unintended consequences may have resulted when Mohawk neophytes did not fully grasp the tenets of Protestantism as their English missionaries intended. For example, many Mohawks who sought baptism or grace—*n'eadatnekoserhouh*—may have viewed the sacrament as an indulgence. The French Jesuits crossed their foreheads with holy water routinely. Why not Church of England priests? SPG missionaries tried to explain to the Mohawks that baptism constituted the literal washing away of *original* sin with sanctified water—*Snegadogeaghtist ne keagaye ne akanohharete ne Karighwanerea*—not to forgive a momentary indiscretion. Thus, while most English missionaries understood baptism and the taking of communion as marking one's spiritual rebirth, most Mohawks viewed both sacraments as constituting Christian identification, which signified alliance with England through church membership. Furthermore, as Allen Greer has suggested, some baptized Mohawks may have viewed accepting the name of a deceased saint as reenacting the Haudenosaunee requickening ceremony in which the name of the deceased was passed on to the living. Nothing further was required—no compensatory attendance at church, no outward signs of constant sobriety, and no putting away of old customs and practices.[46]

Once baptized and admitted to communion, the Mohawk catechumen may have understood that God, through his angels, now offered him or her protection for life similarly to his or her personal guardian spirit. The SPG missionaries and Mohawk schoolmasters learned from Bishop Wilson that God "will give his holy Angels charge concerning you, to guard you against the Power and Malice of evil Spirits.—And this All-powerful Spirit will guide and assist you in the Way you should go."[47] Perhaps baptized Mohawks translated *Karonghiyagaghronouh* (holy angels or spirits) in *Karonghyage* (heaven or Sky World) as Haudenosaunee spirit guardians.

Texts written in the local vernacular and explained by local leaders must have generated local excitement in that they enabled Mohawk catechumens to communicate with God on their terms. A feeling of empowerment must have arisen, as some Mohawks would eventually realize that they did not need the services of a white SPG schoolmaster or perhaps even a missionary. In fact, in 1764, the Mohawks at Canajoharie refused politely the services of seventy-five-year-old Jacob Oel, the

German minister to Palatine German families on the German Flatts just west of Canajoharie since the 1720s. For forty years, Oel had occasionally visited the Upper Castle to read prayers, catechize the youths, and baptize both white and Mohawk children and infants.[48] Now, however, Oel could not "excite any desire in his Indians in the upper castle for public worship, or the use of the sacraments." In reality, the Mohawks, who had been without the services of Paulus Sahonwadi for a few years, preferred to work with Philip Jonathan, a young Mohawk from Canajoharie, who had received an English-style education. Already, he had two star pupils who were "pretty fur [*sic*] advanced in their Learning" and for whom Jonathan sought from Brother Waronghyage (Sir William Johnson) "two of our printed Books."[49]

While literacy in Mohawk conferred power on the Mohawk language, teachers, and pupils, in time several of the Mohawk schoolmasters found literacy in Mohawk alone limiting. Many desired to learn English. However, in the early 1750s, the only active Mohawk catechist was Old Abraham, a strong proponent of literacy in English. Thus, he and others convinced several Mohawk families to remove their children from their homes in Mohawk country and enroll them at a dissenting mission school in Stockbridge, Massachusetts.

Stockbridge, surveyed in 1736, was incorporated in 1739 as a six-square-mile mission town for local Housatonics and Mahicans living in western Massachusetts. Several entities, including the New England Company; the Hollis fund, established by a London clergyman-philanthropist; and the Massachusetts General Court, the political body in Massachusetts that authorized the establishment of towns and set their boundaries but also regulated Native behavior in mission towns, all supported the new mission town financially. In 1734, the New England Company hired Yale College graduate John Sergeant as missionary to the Housatonics and Mahicans. Sergeant in turn hired as schoolmaster Timothy Woodbridge, who descended from a long line of pastors, including his great-grandfather John Eliot, the orchestrator of Native praying towns in seventeenth-century Massachusetts. Several English families, including that of Ephraim Williams, also settled within Stockbridge to stand as models of right English living. The goal of the mission school was to "change the Indians habits," to make them virtuous, pious, and industrious—in an English word, to "civilize" them. Above all, English had to replace their "imperfect and barbarous dialect." Martin Kellogg, a sixty-year-old army captain, who knew Mohawk, having lived as a captive among them on two separate occasions, joined Sergeant's team as teacher just before the missionary's death in 1749 at age thirty-nine.[50]

In October 1751, Old Abraham, his brother Hendrick, and eleven other Mohawk headmen, perhaps at the invitation of Kellogg, who promised them clothing, led a delegation of ninety-two Mohawks, including nearly three dozen children, to Stockbridge, where they informed the Congregational minister Jonathan Edwards, the mission's new pastor, that they wanted their children to "learn the English language and to read the Bible." Some of the delegates, who were not interested at all in literacy and Christian instruction but rather had come along with the expectation of receiving survival goods as they had at Kahnawake, left in disgust when they learned that only those children and their families attached to the school would receive clothing.[51] According to Edwards, those Mohawk parents who remained committed to the school considered the ability to read and write in English "a great attainment." They especially held in high esteem anyone who could "read and understand the Bible" and, to that end, were particularly "fond of their children learning the English tongue."[52] These parents found learning English from whomever was willing to teach them critically important, for once again an SPG missionary of their own had become an unreliable prospect, as Henry Barclay left them several years before and John Ogilvie had yet to prove himself. Their end game was self-reliance: their children would acquire literacy in English and teach the members of their community. Acquiring literacy in English in order to become better acquainted with the principles of Christianity was one thing. However, the ability to read English laws was becoming more and more critical to Mohawk survival. Over the previous sixty years, the Mohawks had lost much of their land to Dutch, English, and German pastors, speculators, and traders through transactions allegedly legitimized in dubious "written talks." Now, the younger generation needed to become truly bicultural in order to protect and sustain Mohawk life.[53]

The SPG seemed slow to react to Mohawk needs. Henry Barclay had quit the Mohawk mission in 1746 to accept the rectorship (parish priest) at Trinity Church in New York City. Reverend John Ogilvie, a portly man in his midtwenties, a native of New York City, a graduate of Yale, and ordained in London in 1749, did not arrive in Albany until 1750 to replace Barclay as rector at St. Peter's Church and to hold the chaplaincy at Fort Hunter. Nearly all SPG activity in Mohawk country had ceased during this four-year gap; Cornelius at Tiononderoge and Daniel at Canajoharie had quit their posts abruptly in 1746 following a dispute with Barclay over unspent funds. They discovered that Barclay had a reserve of credit from the SPG that was to go to the instruction of the Mohawks. However, neither Daniel nor Cornelius received any portion of that money and in anger resigned. Barclay later claimed that he had forgotten about the credit. Moreover, this kerfuffle occurred during King George's War (1744–48), the extension of the War of the Austrian Succession into North America. During the war, rumors circulated that the English intended to "cut off" the Haudenosaunees. While a Dutch trader was probably the source of these rumors, several Mohawks blamed Henry Barclay, claiming that his books were the source of the problem because the devil had written them.[54]

By the time Ogilvie arrived in Albany, Old Abraham was virtually the only Native schoolmaster in the entire Mohawk Valley. When the new priest journeyed to Canajoharie, he made a surprising discovery: drinking had been "greatly prevented by a very pious Indian whose name is [Old] Abraham." Old Abraham, a man in his sixties, no longer hunted, perhaps because he was too infirm, but rather spent most of his time "instruct[ing] his Brethren in the principles of Religion." His continuous performance as pious catechist-headman appeared to Ogilvie to have had some sobering effect on the community. However, at Tiononderoge, the Mohawk village nearest the chapel in Fort Hunter, no one read prayers or instructed the children or adults between 1746 and 1750. Hence, Ogilvie found the residents there "intirely given up to Drunkenness." It is tempting to read this behavior at Tiononderoge as a return to their former ways following a four-year absence of an SPG presence. However, another reading of the circumstance there contends that the public display of inebriation was a public protest against the SPG. Ogilvie would learn that the Mohawks engaged in selective temperance, and thus would wear the mask of piety and sobriety in his presence in order to meet his expectations of devoutness and virtue, a clear expression of middle-ground behavior. However, as soon as he returned to Albany, "they f[e]ll to drinking to such Excess, as to cease any good Impressions [of Christianity] they have received."

Their situational sobriety may have also represented a sign of support for Old Abraham in order to not embarrass him.[55]

Nevertheless, some Mohawks, especially Old Abraham, believed it was time to signal their displeasure with the inadequate efforts of the SPG, hence his strong advocacy for moving to Stockbridge. Jonathan Edwards, the pastor at Stockbridge, called Old Abraham his "informant" on Haudenosaunee matters. According to Edwards, the old headman urged his brethren to go to the dissenting mission in order to receive religious instruction, for they lived in darkness at Canajoharie. He promised them that at Stockbridge they would find light. Moreover, Old Abraham claimed self-deprecatingly that he knew little and, therefore, could teach them little. Because of his piety and embrace of the dissenting church, Old Abraham suffered "a sort of persecution" among some Mohawks, perhaps by warriors who increasingly questioned his role as catechist-headman, for he did not quite exercise the authority of Peace Chief yet, and by other baptized Mohawks, who wished to remain faithful to the Church of England. However, from Old Abraham's ecumenical perspective, it mattered little which pastor from which denomination instructed members of his community in Christianity and in English literacy, for the times, he believed, were desperate.[56]

Little surprise, then, that John Ogilvie should oppose the removal of the Mohawks to Stockbridge for two reasons, one secular, the other ecclesiastical. First, he feared that their removal would "divert the Trade from us [Albany] & leave our Frontiers naked & defenceless." Second, he believed that it was unwise to expose the Mohawks to "the unhappy Divisions subsisting among Protestants," for to do so "may so prejudice their minds as to render them a more easy Prey to the craft of Popish Missionaries." Ogilvie worried needlessly about Mohawk knowledge of the "unhappy divisions" among Christians; the Mohawks had long been evangelized by French Jesuits and Dutch dominies and thus were well aware of doctrinal differences. Sixty years earlier, a group of Mohawks, some baptized by French Jesuits, others by Dutch dominies, explained to New York governor Sloughter that they understood the difference "betwixt Christianity and Paganism," and presumably Catholicism and Protestantism, for they wished to be instructed in the "Religion of the Great King of England . . . the Protestant Religion." Ironically, because he viewed the Mohawks as both a bulwark against attacks and as a magnet for wealth, Ogilvie concurred partially with Old Abraham when he declared that the Mohawks should stay in place and be rendered "faithful" by changing "their present Habits of thinking and acting, and instill the Principles of Virtue and Piety, into their minds in such a Way as may make the most lasting Impressions, and withal introduce the English Language among them, instead of their present barbarous Dialect."[57] In other words, turn them into Englishmen and -women.

Ogilvie got his wish; after a three-year boycott of Ogilvie, the Mohawks who had relocated to Stockbridge began to trickle back to the Mohawk Valley. Incompetence, poor facilities, and infighting between factions at Stockbridge repulsed the Mohawk parents. Edwards charged Kellogg with unfitness; the captain supplied his students with few learning materials, provisions, or even safe living quarters. Moreover, Kellogg absented himself frequently to pursue other business. When Edwards hired schoolmaster Gideon Hawley to teach Kellogg's students, bitter quarreling erupted between Kellogg and his supporters and Edwards and his supporters, which left the Mohawk children unsupervised, untaught, and unloved. By 1754, all the Mohawks had come home.[58] Ogilvie could now embark on his plan for the great transformation.

However, Ogilvie would confront obstacles to implementing his vision. Empowered by literacy in their own language as well as in English for some, many Mohawks felt compelled to become fully self-reliant by turning to literate members of their own community to once again teach them the principles of Christian doctrine as well as literacy in English and in Mohawk. In a rapidly changing, uncertain world, characterized by slow land dispossession by degrees and empty promises for and by priests, it was becoming increasingly important to most Mohawks to acquire bicultural skills on their own terms.

## Conclusion

In 1771, Sir William Johnson, the superintendent for Indian affairs in the northern colonies, wrote to Arthur Lee, the Virginia physician who at this time served as a colonial correspondent in London, to explain that "the customs and manners of the Indians are in several cases liable to changes, which have not been thoroughly considered by authors and therefore the description of them (as is usual) at any one particular period must be insufficient."[59] Through this astute observation, Johnson acknowledged that cultures—and in particular eighteenth-century Haudenosaunee culture—were dynamic and in constant flux. One particular change to the Mohawks' culture resulted when many supplemented—or, for some, replaced—their Haudenosaunee faith practices with Protestant Christian practices, part of which entailed acquiring literacy. Literacy did not replace orality but rather complemented it as a means of communication, negotiation, and understanding. Most important, it empowered Mohawks to contest the colonizing powers of England's people and institutions, like the SPG and the Church of England.

By the middle of the eighteenth century, demographic, social, and material changes had become quite visible in Mohawk country. Many Mohawks now wore European-style clothing, lived in European-style houses, organized their families nuclearly rather than communally, had their fields plowed European style, collected rents from tenants, and worshiped God at either a Dutch Reformed or an Anglican church. In fact, many Mohawks lived much better materially than their white Christian neighbors. Tiononderoge was now virtually surrounded by white settlers and physically cut off from the other five nations, which helps explain why Johnson concluded that the Mohawks seemed to have "less Intercourse with the Indians & more with us [the English]," which had led them to blend some "of their Ancient usages . . . with Customs amongst ourselves." Nevertheless, these cultural changes did not make the Mohawks less Haudenosaunee, but rather signaled their adaptation to real-world circumstances that enabled them to survive and continue as Mohawk. In fact, most citizens of the other Haudenosaunee nations still regarded the Mohawks as "the head of our Confederacy." However, many also began to denounce them publicly as "Colonel Johnson's counselors" and, worse, servants to the English.[60]

So many Mohawk parents at Canajoharie had come to greatly value the instruction offered by Native catechists and schoolmasters that when Paulus Sahonwadi disappeared from time to time to hunt, they complained to John Ogilvie that the schoolmaster neglected their children's education.[61] Additionally, when Ogilvie left Fort Hunter in 1760 for a three-year assignment in Montreal, and with Paulus on furlough, several baptized Mohawks repeatedly asked Sir William Johnson for prayer books, as well as "Indian Almanack[s]," sometimes "daily enquiring for them." Their requests suggest that the parents were ready to either turn to others in their community who were literate or expected their children to continue their reading lessons themselves.[62] Finally, baptized Mohawks at Canajoharie were so fed up with having to make the twenty-odd-mile journey to Fort Hunter and the two- to three-day trip to Albany to attend church services that they raised enough money among themselves to someday "Build a Church at Cannojohery," with the all-important steeple bell. The Canajohariens' desire for a church of their own constituted a complete turnabout from sixty-five years earlier when they prevented Thoroughgood Moor from even entertaining the idea of an Anglican chapel anywhere on Mohawk soil.[63]

In 1755, John Ogilvie reminded the SPG of how to make the Mohawks "firm friends": unite them to us "by the sacred ties of Christianity." Baptized Mohawks at Kahnawake also voiced this perspective on alliance through a shared faith. That same year, they informed Sir William Johnson that they could not join him in battle against the French because "by Religion and Treaties, they were so united, [that] they must obey their orders."[64] For more than one hundred years, Mohawks, keepers of the eastern door of the Longhouse, opened their door first to the Dutch, then the French, and now the English by entering into various covenants with them and by performing their faiths. This strategy of building alliances through a shared faith would be put to the test during the American Revolution.

The SPG engaged in alliance building through its experiment of using Mohawk schoolmasters and catechists to teach literacy and Church of England Protestantism. The catechizing headmen performed their duties well. However, when Old Abraham died in 1757, and with Cornelius and Daniel gone from their posts since 1746, the society replaced the Mohawk teachers with several white Protestant schoolmasters. Mohawk hospitality and mutuality toward them were cool, at best.[65]

At the conclusion of the Seven Years' War, the Mohawks experienced great strain. Alcoholism, fueled by an intractable rum trade, had become a major problem, as men and women medicated themselves against stress. Some died as the result of accidents; others tried to commit brutal acts. One inebriated warrior killed the "wife of a sachem, who officiate[d] as a Reader in the Church during . . . Ogilvie's absence," most likely the wife of either Paulus or Old Abraham. To exacerbate the problem, warfare and disease had eroded the population and vitiated the culture by carrying off important leaders. In 1757, Johnson condoled several "chiefs" who were "snatched away lately by the Small Pox & other Sicknesses." Several key headmen also lost their lives during the Seven Years' War, most notably Hendrick, the brother of Old Abraham and a fair-weather friend of the Church of England. This was not the first time that the Mohawks experienced a sudden vacuum among their leaders and carriers of the culture. Such loss was felt acutely during King William's War at the end of the seventeenth century, when "all those . . . who had sense" died. At that time, a small group of Christian Mohawks confronted Governor Sloughter and pointed out what had become obvious: that "the weake and faint setting forward of that greate worke hitherto among us"—that is, instructing them in Christianity—"ha[d] occasioned our Bretheren to be drawn out of our Country to the French by their Priests." [66]

Now, as in former times, several Mohawk leaders stepped forward to ask the governor of New York and the Church of England to supply them with Protestant pastors who might assist them in revitalizing Mohawk society.

# CHAPTER 5

# "A Single Mission in the Old, Beaten Way Makes No Noise"

*New Strategies for Capturing Mohawk Bodies and Souls,*
*1760–1775*

We have no examples of even one of those Aborigines
having from choice become Europeans.
—J. Hector St. John de Crevecoeur, 1782

Sitting in a pew in a Congregational church in Lebanon, Connecticut, on the last day of June 1763, Joseph Brant, a twenty-year-old Mohawk from Canajoharie, found himself the subject of a sermon preached by Reverend Nathanial Whitaker, the pastor at the Congregational church in Norwich, Connecticut. Whitaker, a benefactor of the Congregational minister and educator Reverend Eleazar Wheelock, was giving Joseph, a boarding student since August 1, 1761, at Wheelock's Moor's Charity School in Lebanon, a hearty send-off back to Canajoharie. There he would help Charles Smith, his white tutor, establish a mission. Brant listened silently as Whitaker first addressed Smith and described the threatening environment that awaited him in the Mohawk Valley: "You are going, *Dear Brother* [Smith], into the howling wilderness, to carry the golden treasure of gospel-grace to those who sit in the region and shadow of death, and who are more ungovernable than the wild beasts of the desart [*sic*]. . . . You must dwell among a people of a hard language; and therefore, will be under great disadvantage of discerning their plots, if they should form any against you."[1] How Joseph reacted to the pastor describing his home as a "howling wilderness," his relatives as "wild beasts" who customarily plot to kill missionaries, and the Mohawk language as "hard" is unknown. During the same service, Wheelock, the headmaster of the school, cited Romans 7:9 to pile on another image of indigenes as beast-like: "Indians," he declared, "must learn that without Christ, they were 'altogether filthy'."[2]

After addressing Smith, Whitaker turned to Brant and delivered Joseph's daunting charge: "Dear Son Joseph, the eyes of us all are on you, as the medium or channel by which the knowledge of our *Lord* is to be communicated to your brethren the *Indians*. Much depends on you: You must, therefore, study to be faithful, and to deliver yourself from guilt: You must make them understand the words you hear, and speak to them with that earnestness, which such great things require."[3] Here, Whitaker defined Joseph's instrumentality: he was to be Smith's pious, careful, discerning, humble interpreter. Smith's success depended on Brant's skills at translating and making meaningful Protestantism to his brethren.

Wheelock added a final word of caution to Smith. He warned him that the diseases of the Mohawks were "spiritual and moral," which could "be cured only by spiritual and moral remedies," that is, giving "their hearts to Christ." Wheelock advised him that should he fall ill, he should not rely on the shamans or other Native individuals to cure him, for they had "neither will, nor skill, to minister suitably for your relief; you may . . . safely repose confidence in the great Physician"—God.[4] Despite these dire warnings, Smith proceeded anyway with Joseph to Canajoharie.

Brant and Smith reached Mohawk country in mid-July 1763, just as Pontiac's uprising was gathering steam. It was an inopportune time to set up a mission among the Mohawks, especially one not endorsed by the Church of England. That autumn, Delaware warriors raided farmsteads in nearby Albany and Ulster Counties. Smith panicked and returned to Connecticut. Brant remained at home in Canajoharie. Sir William Johnson, the superintendent of Indian affairs and Joseph's brother-in-law—Molly Brant, Joseph's sister, was Johnson's common-law wife—took note of a change in Joseph's behavior: he seemed "very zealously and devoutly inclined." Still, despite these changes in his demeanor, Brant was hardly equipped or qualified to take Smith's place. Nevertheless, during the decade before he made a name for himself as a Tory warrior during the American Revolution, Brant played a key role in the larger project of gospelizing the Haudenosaunees, acting as an occasional interpreter for John

Stuart, the last SPG missionary at Fort Hunter (1770–81), and taking on the role of translator on the project directed by Sir William Johnson to publish biblical passages and other Christian tracts in Mohawk.[5]

Perhaps the most consequential lesson that Brant learned at Wheelock's school was that of literacy in English. Wheelock reported to Johnson that after less than a year of instruction, Brant could "read handsomely in the Bible." He also learned to write rather fluidly in English, as his extant correspondence testifies. Not all prominent whites agreed with Wheelock's assessment; John Stuart thought Brant read "indifferently" from the Bible and that his poor grammar reflected weak writing skills.[6] Stuart's judgment mattered little to the SPG, for the society had long awaited a young Mohawk man who had acquired literacy skills competent enough to help it advance its project.

Between the 1740s and 1760s, missionaries, educators, and benefactors offered a variety of models for "converting" Native Americans to Christianity as the "more *effectual Method*" for "*instilling* in their Minds and Hearts . . . the *Principles of Virtue* and *Piety*," as they defined these two qualities. Each model shared a common theme: that Christianizing *and* "civilizing" had to go hand in hand, that mere gospelizing had proved to be not enough. Still, Henry Barclay, the SPG missionary to the Mohawks in the late 1730s and early '40s, believed that the Mohawks could be "civilized" through becoming Christian, but only through Mohawk-language texts, taught by Mohawk catechists. Reverend John Ogilvie, Barclay's successor, shared his predecessor's perspective, but believed that literacy in English would make the Mohawks genuine Christians, as God spoke to his believers in English. John Sergeant, the young Congregational minister stationed at "Indian town" (Stockbridge), believed that the best way to transform Native peoples was to place mission communities in or near Native country, but with white residents nearby to pass their culture onto the Native residents, somewhat reminiscent of Eliot's Praying Towns in seventeenth-century Massachusetts. Sergeant thought this strategy "very obvious": God had ordered that "charitably disposed Persons . . . *root out* their [indigenous] vicious Habits, and . . . change their Whole Way of Living." He saw "*no Party-View*" in this undertaking, but rather regarded the task as doing something "for the Glory of our common MAKER . . . and for the Honour of our common SAVIOUR."[7]

The proprietorial Eleazar Wheelock, an enthusiastic "New Light"

Congregational minister, proposed a more radical version of Sergeant's plan: remove Native peoples from their homelands entirely and place them in exclusively white environments, thereby separating them from their countrymen and what he considered their base habits. Wheelock preached that God had ordained reducing the "savage temper [of indigenes] . . . by the gospel, and [changing] their manner of subsisting . . . by a Christian education." However, God was now displeased, he insisted, that white Christians had permitted "the Savages to be such a sore Scourge to our Land." It was now incumbent on white Christians, he argued, to get right with God and save the souls of a benighted people. After 150 years of occupying the Eastern Seaboard of the present-day United States, and with the defeat of France in the Seven Years' War, many whites in the colonies believed that they were destined to inherit all of the territory of eastern North America and, like Wheelock, call it "our land." However, unless they helped that situation along by "making Indians into men," God might forever use the Native peoples, Wheelock warned, as "pricks in our eyes, and thorns in our sides . . . to vex us in the land wherein we dwell."[8] A good place to begin doing God's work, Wheelock maintained, was sending Brant and Smith to Canajoharie, now largely surrounded by white settlers, where they would open the eyes of the Mohawks, establish a version of his dissenting mission school, and send promising Native prospects his way.

Church of England reformers offered an alternative plan to Wheelock. Charles Inglis, born in Ireland in 1734 and ordained in 1758, who would become the first bishop of the Anglican Church in Canada, declared that the "single mission in the old, beaten way" was impractical and unsustainable. He called for a network of missions and academies across Iroquoia and into Pennsylvania, where priests and schoolmasters would reduce hundreds of Native peoples. Like Wheelock, Inglis viewed the charge of converting indigenes as a "general Obligation that Christians [are] under to communicate the Light of the Gospel to Heathens," although he admitted that that particular reason would "probably have no great Weight with many in Authority." Hence, he proposed three other reasons for converting Native peoples. The first two seemed to him self-evident: conforming Protestant missionaries should counter the alarming successes enjoyed by Jesuits, and settlers in the colonies should uphold their respective colonies' charters that called for "the Conversion of the Savages." The third reason was one not often promoted publicly by pastors but was certainly entertained by laymen, such as Sir William Johnson: "The Conversion of the Indians would be an Advantage to Commerce; as they would thereby become sober, would multiply, & be more attentive to Business."[9] Inglis proposed what might appear to be a transactional approach to proselytizing the Haudenosaunees. However, as a defender of the interests of the British Empire, Inglis was also defending the interests of the state church. His real goal, it appears, was to place a string of SPG mission stations across Iroquoia in order to keep the Haudenosaunees within the British political orbit through a shared faith and economic necessity. This strategy, he believed, would also remove them from the sphere of dissenters, such as Wheelock. Rising political tensions in the guise of tax revolts, consumer boycotts, regulator movements, and mob actions threatened the existing social, economic, and political order between England and its mainland colonies, which English officials feared might trickle down to Native allies and threaten Haudenosaunee-British relations.

In the years between the Seven Years' War and the American Revolution, then, a contest between mission projects emerged: dissenters, like Wheelock and other American clergy, promoted single proprietary schools for Native pupils in white communities and some in Native communities, while Loyalists, like Inglis and other Anglican clergy, pushed for placing multiple SPG mission schools throughout Haudenosaunee country and beyond. In essence, the two camps offered the Mohawks two visions from which to choose: either the British or the Americans'. After the Seven Years' War, the French government was no longer a factor, now that England controlled politically most of European-settled North America. Therefore, English officials believed, naively, that they no longer had to accommodate Native Americans in the ways they had before the Seven Years' War. Their attitude confirms Richard White's argument that when one side believes that it has established hegemony over the other, the middle ground—the need for both sides to appeal to the other based on preconceptions about the other—collapses.[10] Promoters of the SPG's project now felt free to promote their strategies for proselytizing the Haudenosaunees and, in essence, insisted that the Mohawks choose their side. In reality, most Mohawks had already chosen a side—their own—which tended to align more closely with the British. However, at base, they sought greater autonomy over performing Christianity.

If Anglicization of the Mohawks was one of the pressing goals of the SPG—to get the Mohawks to live more like Englishmen and women as farmers, spinners, mechanics, and consumers, and thereby relinquish much of their unneeded land—it was a bit late to the party. More than a hundred years of direct contact with European settlers, commissioners, traders, storekeepers, military leaders, missionaries, and teachers had altered Mohawk lives materially and somewhat culturally. Many Mohawks had transformed their habits of living as they became "intermixed" with their Christian neighbors. They worshiped at the same church as nearby English, Dutch, Irish, and German Palatine settlers and shopped at the same stores for the same items. Between the late 1760s and the 1770s, Mohawk shoppers at Jelles Fonda's store bought a number of fine items, including teapots and teacups, punch bowls, pewter dishes, linens, knives and forks, closet locks, padlocks, and window catches. Personal items purchased there reflected a desire to mix and match the familiar with the new: "britch clouts," Indian shoes, pipes, "tommyhawks," blankets, kettles, and steel traps, with handkerchiefs, women's stockings, gartering, ribbons, woolen hats, thread, pepper, white sugar, baked bread, snuff boxes, knee buckles, shirts, mittens, cravats, horse whips, paint, mirrors, and nightcaps. The new items were not so much luxury items as they were necessities to replace those things the Mohawks once made for themselves. These items stocked their dwellings, described as well-furnished and well-built single-family "cottages" with hewn boards, similar in architecture to their European neighbors. In fact, when Colonel Gansevoort of the Continental army led his troops into Tiononderoge in 1779, several of the local whites who had lost their homes commented on how much better materially the Mohawks lived than they. They asked Gansevoort to not destroy the Mohawk homes so that they might live in them, to which the colonel agreed. In brief, by the mid-eighteenth century, ethnic European settlements virtually encircled the principal Mohawk villages of Tiononderoge, Canajoharie, and Schoharie. Hence, planting crops in large, extensive fields removed from the villages was becoming increasingly impractical. Mohawk men still went out on the hunt each winter, but because so many white people had moved into the area, hunting took them farther away from their villages for two months longer or more. The SPG missionary John Ogilvie often complained about not being able to preach to his flock when most of the men were away hunting for so long.[11]

Because hunting had become increasingly difficult, more Mohawks found themselves drawn more deeply into the English commercial economy. For example, many Mohawks had become landlords, treating their land as an income-producing commodity, leasing portions of it around Canajoharie to white farmers. They even reserved the right to lease to whites for farming land around Lake George northeast of Mohawk country that they claimed as their hunting grounds. In December 1764 or early January 1765, a band of Mohawk hunters returning from these hunting grounds were shocked to find "a great Number of new Settlements on their Lands in that Quarter[,] a considerable number of Men from different parts"—squatters—"cutting down, and Carrying away Sawloggs, and the best of Timber from off their [Mohawk] lands to their great Surprise, and detriment." The unexpected thinning of the forests by apparent squatters meant that game would move elsewhere. It also represented the loss of potential income for the Mohawks.[12]

In addition, many Mohawks turned to wage labor to supplement their farming and hunting. Daniel and Silver Heels worked as boatmen. A few men from Canajoharie helped to drive cattle to Oswego. Others portaged heavy loads around waterfalls and rapids. Still other Mohawk men offered their services as guides, couriers, slave catchers, schoolteachers, butlers, and gardeners. Mohawk women also participated in the wage economy when they harvested ginseng for the short-lived export market in the early 1750s.[13] Changes in patterns of subsistence indicated that the world of the Mohawks had changed and for some appeared precariously unbalanced.

William Johnson allegedly lamented this shift in Mohawk subsistence, brought on by their loss of lands. However, Johnson was more than disingenuous in his anguish, for despite his claims that *he* restricted *his* purchases of land to land already patented—that is, to land previously purchased by "White Inhabitants who had purchased it of the Indians"—Johnson played a key role in the divestiture of Mohawk lands. In 1760, for example, the Mohawks of Canajoharie bequeathed him 80,000 acres of riverfront property, practically the last they owned there. One historian has read this gift as a wedding present to Johnson and his new common-law wife, Molly Brant. However, it is more reasonable to view the gift as a gesture of reciprocity, an effort to protect what little land they had left by placing it under Johnson's protection. The headmen who offered the gift defined it gloomily as "proof of our friendship, which we fear, will not be long, as our White Brethren are getting all our Lands from us." If Johnson's marriage to Molly Brant bound the Canajoharies to the Johnson family through kinship, the gift of 80,000 acres hermetically sealed their reciprocal relationship in perpetuity. In 1766, Johnson acquired another tract of land in Mohawk country measuring 20,600 acres for an Episcopate for the Church of England. He bought the more than 20,000 acres for 100 pounds (a little over $18,000 today), a gross undervaluation of the land, this time purchased from white patentees, who had bought it earlier from the Mohawks.[14]

If the loss of land forced some Mohawks to adjust their patterns of subsistence, the loss of key culture brokers forced them to adjust culturally. The Seven Years' War resulted in the swift and devastating elimination of formidable and wise Mohawk leaders and counselors. At the battle of Lake George in early September 1755, one of the first major skirmishes between French forces and their Native Allies and British forces and their mainly Haudenosaunee allies, "twelve principal men . . . fell in action," six of whom were "constant Communicants of the Church," including Hendrick, Old Abraham's brother. Reverend John Ogilvie escaped their fate; when the Mohawks asked him to accompany them into battle at Lake George as their minister, he declined, citing feebly the lack of "provisions for that purpose."[15] Old Abraham stood in his stead.

Disease also cut wide swaths through the general population. Smallpox and a "malignant fever," referred to by Johnson as "yellow fever," but identified by one scholar as typhoid fever, ravaged the Mohawk Valley between the mid-1750s and early 1760s. In fact, several Mohawk warriors and headmen were "snatched away" by smallpox at the battle of Lake George. The disease did not restrict itself to the Haudenosaunees; John Ogilvie buried his two young children within three weeks of each other in March 1757, victims of the disease. In early February 1759, Ogilvie noted in his diary, "I . . . found the Indians [Mohawks] in great Grief for yr. [their] Friends: Great Numbers having died of a malignant Fever that has raged amongst [them] for some Time." A year later, he informed the society that his "Indian Congregation is very much decreased by the late Mortality that prevailed amongst the Mohawks." Old Seth of Schoharie died in 1757, but it took until 1764 to requicken him—that is, mourn, memorialize, and symbolically restore him—so few headmen, according to one Mohawk informant, remained worthy enough to replace him.[16]

Finally, by the 1750s, many Mohawks—perhaps most—had grown weary of the "shocking effects of strong Drink" upon their communities. The perennial problem of excessive drinking, engaged in to relieve the pain and trauma brought on by disease, warfare, loss of land, and the encroachment of white settlements, caused too many Mohawks to commit "barbarous actions." Too many "attempt[ed] to burn yr [their] own little hutts, threaten the lives of yr Wives & children, [and] abuse yr Neighbours." While many believed that the only remedy lay in preventing their brethren from acquiring alcohol at all, the Mohawk headmen actually agreed to a compromise: keep liquor out of Iroquoia, but do not ban entirely the consumption of it. At the Albany conference in 1754, a Haudenosaunee orator made it clear that while his brethren feared that rum "may cause Murder on both sides," they did not want its outright prohibition. He proposed that rum not "be forbid[den] to be Sold us in Albany, but that none may be brought to our Castiles." The Cayugas spoke for themselves when they announced that they would "not allow any Rum to be brought up their River, and those who do must take the Consequences." The Mohawks of the Upper and Lower Castles jointly asked that their white neighbors "may not be Suffered to sell our People Rum; it keeps them all poor, makes them Idle and Wicked, and . . . destroys Virtue and the progress of Religion amongst us."[17] This plea fell largely silent on deaf ears.

Ultimately, the Mohawk elders, many of whom were baptized, reached an uneasy compromise with those who needed their daily dram of rum: temperance rather than prohibition. They permitted drinking outside the villages and on the road to and from Albany, about a two-day journey away. However, the villages themselves were off-limits to alcohol. To designate the villages as "dry" was a noble gesture, but difficult to enforce, despite the efforts of some powerful white patrons to support the ban. In 1755, after the Schoharie headman Old Seth (d. 1757) lodged "heavy complaints" with him about the "ill Consequences" of selling rum in his village, William Johnson wrote to Governor Delancey requesting that he use his influence to pass a measure in the assembly that Johnson had proposed almost ten years earlier: "to forbid all persons whatsoever to Buy or Exchange any Arms, Ammunition, Clothing, etc.

from any Indians of the Five Nations, or from any Indian in Alliance with them, or sell them any Rum or other Spiritous Liquors to the East of Oneida Lake, under pain of Suffering a Year and a Days Imprisonment, and a fine besides of thirty pounds." As far as Johnson was concerned, an unarmed, intoxicated warrior did not a good fighter make. Still, the rum continued to flow.[18]

Reverend John Ogilvie and some of his flock had another reason for wanting to stop the flow of liquor into Mohawk villages: strong liquors were proving to be "the most fatal obstruction to the Progress of the glorious Gospel of Christ among that unhappy People."[19] Many baptized Mohawks shared Ogilvie's concern and, like their ancestors two to three generations earlier, called for new measures to check what they perceived as a downward social and cultural spiral. Many concurred with Little Abraham of Tiononderoge, who in 1761 pleaded for a "Minister [who will] remain constantly amongst us." Only through the presence of a resident full-time pastor, he reasoned, could they reclaim their brethren "addicted to liquor." Itinerant ministers could not keep a close, watchful eye on their flocks, as Ogilvie learned, which allowed the illicit flow of liquor into Mohawk country to persist. Moreover, like past missionaries assigned to Fort Hunter, Ogilvie appeared to spend more time away from his post than with the Mohawks. His friend Gideon Hawley observed that Ogilvie "resided . . . in Albany" and therefore spent "very little of his time with his Indians," preaching instead to his white and black congregants in Albany. Ogilvie's diary shows that for the first few years of his ministry, he traveled to the Mohawks about four or five times a year and stayed at Fort Hunter for an average of two to three weeks per visit. In fact, in June 1760, Ogilvie left Fort Hunter and Albany altogether for a three-year stint in Montreal, where he ministered to the English troops, thereby leaving Fort Hunter bereft of an Anglican priest.[20]

The new measures that some Mohawks called for to revitalize their lives through Christianity did not necessarily match those called for by reformers Inglis and Wheelock. In order to understand the tensions between the visions of the reformers and baptized Mohawks, we must examine the responses of the Mohawks to them—that is, pay attention to what they enacted actively and passively, how they positioned themselves within the larger league, and how they performed their roles as schoolmasters, catechists, catechumens, readers, interpreters, translators, and students of literacy. In this way, a complex picture emerges of Mohawk agency as they sought to exercise autonomy over the missionizing process during the interwar years.

## "The Great Design": Eleazar Wheelock and Moor's Charity School

Community elders, men and women, along with powerful white male patrons, identified certain Mohawk individuals to acquire literacy in English, to learn the lessons of the Bible, and to model sober, upright behavior to their Haudenosaunee brethren. All young Mohawk men and women who attended a mission school to acquire these skills, knowledge, and habits were expected to bring them back to their communities. It is reasonable to conclude that more and more Mohawks viewed increasingly these attributes as critically important to their nation's survival as well as survivance as they were drawn further into more frequent contact with whites. Mohawk individuals educated in the ways of the white world would not only facilitate relations with their white neighbors, but also revitalize Mohawk society not by "chang[ing] their whole Habit of thinking and acting" and becoming "a civil industrious and polish'd People," as John Sergeant had hoped, but rather by enhancing their lives through literacy and a new moral code in order to remain Mohawk.[21] Sir William Johnson arranged to enroll several Mohawk children in Moor's Charity School in Lebanon, Connecticut, operated by the dissenting entrepreneurial minister, Eleazar Wheelock, the future founder of Dartmouth College.

Wheelock, a 1733 graduate of Yale College, a centrist Congregational institution, became a New Light evangelist in the early 1740s when the religious fervor of the First Great Awakening swept across Connecticut. In spreading the "good news" throughout the colony, he neglected from time to time the needs of his congregation at the Second Congregational Church in Lebanon. As a result of his actions, the Connecticut Assembly, dominated by Old Lights, terminated his salary in 1743. His redundancy forced him to board and tutor in his home college-bound white boys. However, not all of Wheelock's students were destined for college, nor were they all white. Samson Occom, a Mohegan from New London, who wanted to improve his English, made his way to the pastor's home.

Wheelock soon recognized the financial advantages of educating young Native men and women; private donors and the provincial government were eager to "reduce" Native Americans, to change their habits and ways, to teach them how to behave like Englishmen and -women in order to make their own world safer and more prosperous. In time, Wheelock received financial support from a number of sources, including the Society in Scotland for Propagating Christian Knowledge (SSPCK); the New England Company; the assemblies of Massachusetts and New Hampshire; Joshua Moor (a.k.a. More), who donated the land and buildings for Moor's Indian Charity School; and countless individuals throughout Connecticut and Europe.[22]

Wheelock patterned his school for Native youths largely after John Sergeant's mission school at Stockbridge. Although he shared Sergeant's vision of a world of Native yeomen farmers, he differed somewhat on the late missionary's strategy on how to educate Native students. Sergeant believed in bringing Native American students and their families within the orbit of a mission station, planted within or near Native communities, which also stood close enough to—or was also the home of—white farmers and mechanics who could act as role models. Wheelock, on the other hand, believed that Native peoples needed to be separated completely from what he regarded as the evil temptations of their "wilderness" environment and be totally immersed in an exclusively white milieu. Hence, Algonquian-speaking youths from all across New England and Haudenosaunee boys and girls from eastern Iroquoia came to Lebanon, Connecticut, to live and study "among Strangers of another Language, and quite another Manner of Living."[23]

Wheelock enrolled initially Native boys only, but eventually admitted Native girls. He educated the boys to be ushers—that is, church greeters and pastors' assistants—and ministers to Native communities. He also endeavored to train them in a trade, such as blacksmithing and farming. He taught girls reading and writing, but also apprenticed them to nearby English homes, where they worked as servants and learned the arts of sewing, weaving, spinning, and other skills of housewifery, skills so necessary, he believed, for their future roles as helpmates to their Native acolyte husbands. Like Sergeant, Wheelock believed that Christianizing and "civilizing" Native peoples should go hand in hand. The two ends would be beneficial not only for them, as their transformation would prevent them from "wast[ing] away," but also for white farmers: "If they [Native peoples] receive the gospel," Wheelock concluded, "they will soon betake themselves to agriculture for their support, and so will need but a very small part, comparatively, of the lands which they now claim." Hence, white farmers would naturally benefit from the unused surplus land. Wheelock offered this argument in 1773, five years after the 1768 Treaty of Fort Stanwix, negotiated largely by Sir William Johnson on behalf of the Board of Trade, which moved the 1763 Proclamation Line farther west, so that much of western Pennsylvania and virtually all of present-day West Virginia and Kentucky switched from Native control to now British ownership.[24]

The curriculum at Moor's Charity School sought to exemplify the integration of pious yeoman farm life with Christian existence. While most girls performed domestic duties at the school or were deployed to nearby homes, most boys prayed, studied, and undertook farm chores at the school. A typical school day for the boys entailed learning and reciting morning, afternoon, and evening prayers; eating an English breakfast, dinner (lunch), and supper; and receiving a classical education, which included instruction in English, Hebrew, Greek, Latin, and some of the English arts and sciences. When John Smith, a Boston merchant and an underwriter of Moor's Charity School, visited the school in 1764, he was charmed to find

> Indian Youths of Different Tribes & Languages in pure English reading the Word of God & speaking with the Exactness & accuracy on points (either chosen by themselves or given out to them) in Severall arts & Sciences, And especially to see this done with at Least a seeming Mixture of Obedience to God; a filial Love & Reverence to Mr. Wheelock, & yet with great Ambition to Excell each other And indeed in this Morning Exerci[s]es I saw a Youth Degraded one lower in the Class who before the Exercises were finished not only recovered his own place but was advanced two Higher.[25]

Wheelock could not have asked his students to stage a better performance for his donor.

Several Mohawk boys constituted the "youths of different tribes." The SSPCK had provided funding to support three Haudenosaunee youths, about which Wheelock sought Sir William Johnson's advice, as well as counsel on other matters, including expanding his operations into Iroquoia.

When Wheelock first broached the subject to Johnson in 1761 of educating Haudenosaunee children at his school in Connecticut, Johnson, a man indifferent to religion, supported the minister's "great design." Johnson agreed that "the Indian Children will not improve in their Studys near so much from the method of Erecting Schools in their Nations, as they would do according to your plan of Education, whereby they are kept out of the way of & uninfluenced by bad Example." Johnson's position may not have been a strong endorsement of Wheelock's philosophy on educating Native youths, but rather a simple declaration that Wheelock needed to keep his school in Connecticut or at least out of the sphere of *his* influence. However, as for opening a mission school in or near Iroquoia, Johnson advised Wheelock to drop his plans for opening a school on the Susquehanna River, an idea toward which Johnson's Native clients allegedly declared "their great aversion." The superintendent claimed that they were "greatly disgusted at the great Thirst which we all seem to shew for their Lands." In 1763, Little Abraham informed Johnson that the Six Nations were particularly disturbed over the intention of people from Connecticut emigrating to this region, referred to as Skahandowana (Schohandawana), or Wyoming Valley, in northeastern Pennsylvania. Moreover, when Wheelock's son showed Johnson a proposal to extend operations to the Cherokees, Creeks, Choctaws, and other nations to the south, Johnson endorsed the idea initially, but reiterated that a seminary for the Six Nations was impractical, as the Haudenosaunees lived "much more scattered and remote from any Quarter where a School can be established." Moreover, the Haudenosaunees, he argued, were "less inclinable to the design." Adopting the Native form of etiquette in which he did not offer an outright no, Johnson dissembled because in fact he wished to establish his own seminaries at some point throughout Iroquoia.[26]

Nevertheless, Johnson supported the enrollment of the first three Mohawk students: eighteen-year-old Joseph Brant, Center, and Negyes, who arrived at Wheelock's school in Connecticut on August 1, 1761. They were not the picture of health and prosperity. Center (a.k.a. Sander) and Negyes were skimpily dressed, although Joseph, whom Wheelock understood was a member "of a family of Distinction . . . was considerably cloathed, *Indian*-fashion, and could speak a few words of *English*." One of the first things Wheelock did was to "*cleanse* and cloath" them in European-style garb, symbolic of rebirth, a new beginning. Within a few months, however, two of the boys—Center, who arrived at Lebanon terminally ill, and Negyes—were sent home. Brant and Samuel Kirkland, a graduate of the College of New Jersey (Princeton) and a Presbyterian minister, who taught at Wheelock's school and would later proselytize the Oneidas and Tuscaroras, recruited two other Mohawk youths, Johannes and Moses, to fill the spots vacated by Center, who later died, and Negyes. Brant and the two replacement Mohawk lads developed the reputation as "studious and diligent" in pursuit of their studies. The following year, three more Mohawk boys joined the nearly twenty Native boys and girls at the school.[27]

Despite the appearances of success, Wheelock found instructing the Native youths frustrating. He complained to fellow evangelist George Whitefield of myriad problems, including how immature and "unpolished & uncultivated" they seemed "within as without," that his Native students gorged themselves on his food to the point of doing themselves harm (and no doubt harm to Wheelock's budget), that they preferred what he called their own "Sordid Manner of Dress" to European-style clothing. Moreover, they did not know how to sit on European-style furniture, preferring to sit on the ground like "our Children"; they rejected his standard of personal hygiene; and they were unable to speak English fluently, making communicating with them maddening. Nevertheless, Wheelock, an optimistic religious man, remained convinced that "God's Mercy [was] now near at Hand" in bringing about their transformation.[28]

As far as Wheelock was concerned, God's hand had indeed touched Joseph Brant. The headmaster conveyed to Sir William Johnson that his decision to send Joseph to him was a good one, for he deemed the lad "an excellent youth," a young man of a "Sprightly Genius, of a manly and genteel Deportment, and of a Modest courteous and benevolent Temper," who had "beg[u]n truly to love our Lord Jesus Christ." Wheelock was so impressed with Joseph's progress that he planned to send him back early to Mohawk country with Charles Smith as Smith's usher and interpreter. However, before Wheelock could set his plans in motion, Molly Brant, Joseph's sister, wrote to Joseph and ordered him to come home immediately, not as Smith's assistant but rather as a Mohawk warrior assuming his rightful role in Mohawk society.[29]

Molly's letter, written in Mohawk, caught Wheelock off guard. Joseph explained to the headmaster that his sister had "ordered [him] to come directly home; that the Indians [were] displeased with his being here at School, that they don't like the People etc." Joseph was particularly agitated over the prospects of "gaining the Displeasure of his Friends" if he did not return home, fearing ostracism by those who believed that he was losing his Mohawk identity and becoming too English. Several factors— some related to the school, others not—offer plausible explanations for Molly's action. The Native uprising inspired by Pontiac in 1763 was gaining momentum and moving closer to Mohawk country. Brant, a young warrior of a "distinguished family," had more pressing responsibilities at home, especially as he was being groomed to take on a leadership role. He had already experienced his first military campaign at Lake Champlain in 1758 at the age of fifteen under the command of William Johnson.[30]

Two other factors surely fed Molly and her brethren's antipathy toward Wheelock's "great design." Molly and others undoubtedly shared what one Oneida orator made clear to David Avery, one of Wheelock's white missionaries, in 1772 while the young pastor assisted Kirkland in Oneida country. The Oneida explained to Avery that "we [converts] are dispised by our brethren, on account of our christian profession." There was a time, he acknowledged, "when we were esteemed as honorable & important in the confederacy: but now we are looked upon as small things; or rather nothing at all." As tensions between Americans and the British increased, some Mohawks and Haudenosaunees grew increasingly aware that even the appearance of aligning oneself too closely with white ministers, especially American pastors, conveyed the message that one must be in league with white American Christians rather than with their Haudenosaunee brethren or the English Crown. Moreover, many Haudenosaunees now viewed Wheelock's style of education highly undesirable. "*English* schools," the Oneida added, "we do not approve of here as serviceable to our spiritual interests: & almost all those who have been instructed in English are a reproach to us." Furthermore, at a council meeting at Onondaga, the Haudenosaunee headmen expressed their strong distaste for Wheelock's school to the minister's arrogant son Ralph, whom his father had sent there to recruit students for the new grammar school at Dartmouth College in New Hampshire. At that meeting, one orator berated Ralph for the uncharitable, unchristian, and uncompassionate environment at the charity school in Connecticut:

Do you think we are altogether ignorant of your methods of instruction?
Why, brother, you are deceiving yourself! We understand not only your
speech, but your *manner* of teaching Indian[s]. . . . Take care brother!
. . . Learn yourself to understand the word of God, before you undertake
to teach & govern others: for when you have come to understand it yourself, perhaps some of our children will like to make trial of your instructions. . . . Brother, you must learn of the French ministers if you would
understand, & know how to treat Indians. They don't speak roughly; nor
do they for every little mistake take up a club & flog them. It seems to us
that they teach the word of God—they are very charitable—& can't see
those they instruct *naked* or *hungry*.[31]

These fighting words echo the enduring Haudenosaunee critique of
American Christians as unchristian. The headman drew knowledgeably
on the Christian doctrines of charity and love to elevate, if not celebrate
(but also overstate), the kind treatment the Jesuits extended to Haudenosaunee kin. They complained that humility, charity, mutuality, and
Christian love were absent at Moor's Charity School, for Wheelock failed
to sufficiently teach, clothe, and feed their children, the highest expressions of Christian charity and duty from their perspective.

Other Native parents had also complained of Wheelock's mistreatment and neglect of their children. One literate Narragansett father
complained in a letter to the headmaster that he had sent his son to him
"not to learn . . . how to Farm . . . but to advance in Christian
Knowledge." A student questioned Wheelock over why they should do
manual labor on his farm when he had charity money to support them.
When Hezekiah Calvin, a Delaware certified as a schoolteacher, left
Wheelock's school in 1765 to teach school at Fort Hunter, he publicly
criticized Wheelock for treating some of the female students like slaves,
exploiting them as domestics rather than teaching them as pupils. In fact,
Wheelock reportedly withheld from some of his Native students food
and clothing provided for them by the SSPCK, which he justified by
declaring brazenly that the supplies "twas too good for Indians." Other
parents were distressed that some of their children had learned little more
"than to Read, & Write." They did not believe that their children were
becoming "*wise in all* things by [Wheelock's] instruction" and demanded
that their children be "treated as *children* at [his] house, & not *servants!*"[32]
In short, many Mohawk and other Haudenosaunee parents and children
believed that the Wheelocks misrepresented entirely their enterprise in
order to benefit from their children's labor.

William Johnson expressed his qualified support for Wheelock publicly, but privately he spoke critically of the pastor's "great design." Six weeks before Joseph received Molly's letter, Johnson wrote in a draft of a letter to Henry Barclay, now the rector at Trinity Church in New York City, that Wheelock's grand plan disgusted him. He complained that dissenting New Light evangelical ministers resembled "the most bigotted Puritans," who coerced "the Country people" of their congregations to sing psalms all day long and "neglect their Hunting & most Worldly affairs." In short, dissenters, Johnson argued, were "very Worthless members of Society." Johnson deleted these passages, perhaps considering them impolitic. Nevertheless, he believed that Native Americans who gravitated toward Presbyterianism, one of the leading denominations of the First Great Awakening, were among "the most troublesome & discontented Exchanging their Morality for a Sett of Gloomy Ideas, which always renders them worse Subjects but never better Men."[33] Protestant evangelicals, he maintained, not only emasculated Native warriors by encouraging prayer over hunting, but also made Native peoples too independent minded, as one of the tenets that fueled the First Great Awakening was questioning the authority of the Church of England. To risk losing the Haudenosaunees as allies of the Crown was a mission too far.

The ten Mohawk and five Oneida youths, boys and girls, who enrolled in Wheelock's school between 1763 (when Joseph Brant returned to Canajoharie) and 1768 represented the whole of League Haudenosaunee students at the charity school. Despite Johnson's reservations about the institution, he valued the discipline that Wheelock instilled in his pupils, for Johnson kept his "troublesome" biracial son, William, whose "temper" was "know[n] to be very warm," at Wheelock's school for two years before he was dismissed in 1766. Still, he recognized that the single mission at Fort Hunter was limited and ineffective at sustaining the Haudenosaunees. This concern over how and where to educate Native children consumed a considerable amount of Johnson's time, energy, and resources during the final eight years of his life (d. 1774).[34]

## "A Single Mission . . . Makes No Noise"

Although Johnson once claimed to have "repeatedly contributed to sev'l places of Worship for all Denominations of protestants," he plainly told the SPG when it granted him membership in the society in 1766 exactly

how he and the Haudenosaunees, for whom he presumed to speak, felt
about the Stockbridge and Lebanon mission stations. His words were
clearly what the society wanted to hear: "these Schemes" were "calculated with a View to forming Settlements . . . obnoxious to the Indians
who have repeatedly declared their aversion" to them. Joseph Johnson, a Mohegan student at Wheelock's school who became a catechist
among the Oneidas, exemplified precisely for Johnson and presumably
the Haudenosaunees the kind of self-pitying, self-loathing, gloomy,
emasculated New Light warrior that repulsed him: the young Mohegan
lad referred to himself as a "good for nothing not quite Old Indian" and
"your [Wheelock's] Ignorant Pupil and good for nothing Black Indian."[35]
Joseph Johnson probably did not use "Black" as a racial designation but
rather as a metaphor for his sinful soul.

The task for Sir William Johnson was finding the best way to educate
the Haudenosaunees—that is, to teach the young men literacy and
the principles of Christianity—without emasculating them as warriors
and hunters, skills that he believed were essential for keeping them as
"usefull Members of Society." To Johnson, the model Native Christians
were praying Mohawks at Kahnawake, who, despite their attachment to
Catholicism, "were made Christians but not Civilized." They "were as
orderly a people as any of our Lower Class are," he claimed, proof that
"a Civilized Member of Society & an Indian Hunter are not incompat-
ible Characters." Johnson meant his odd remarks to be complimentary.
After Ogilvie moved to Montreal in 1760, several baptized Mohawk
parents, not worried that knowledge of Christianity and being literate would cause their young men to lose their warrior skills, expressed
repeatedly to Johnson that "they now want[ed] them [prayer books in
Mohawk] much," as well as "Indian Almanack[s]." They would teach
themselves.[36] Because texts translated into Mohawk always seemed to
be in short supply, Johnson in November 1763, concerned about the
backlash from "the ignorant imprudent at New York" over sending
Haudenosaunee youths to Wheelock but wishing to accede to the wishes
of Mohawk parents to teach their children literacy, sent Joseph Brant
"with three other Lads from Canajoharee to *Mr. Bennet*," the society's
schoolteacher at Fort Hunter, which housed several previously translated
texts. Either the physical circumstances were not ideal there, or Bennett's
racism conditioned his response, or the political climate and anxiety over

Native uprisings generated unease in him: he complained that he had no space in which to teach the pupils, despite the fact that an outbreak of smallpox left Bennett's school empty.[37]

While Wheelock benefitted briefly from Bennett's rejection of Brant, Johnson refused to cooperate with Wheelock after 1768 and ceased to send him any more Haudenosaunee youths. Their relationship was officially severed during the negotiations for a treaty talk held at Fort Stanwix between October 24 and November 6, 1768. Three thousand Native Americans attended the negotiations, at which they agreed to move the territorial boundary line established by the Proclamation of 1763 westward to the Ohio River. Representatives from several Native nations—from the Kahnawakes near Montreal to the Mingoes on the Ohio River—agreed to sell millions of acres of hunting land in parts of New York, Pennsylvania, Virginia, Kentucky, and Tennessee, for 10,465 pounds, 7 shillings, and 3 pence sterling in cash and goods (a little more than $1 million today), clearly another swindle. Land south and east of the Ohio River now became available for white settlement; land to the north and west of the river remained ostensibly in Native hands. Wheelock, worried that opening the land to white settlers would hamper his plans to open a seminary in Oneida country, sent two representatives—the young white pastor David Avery and Jacob Johnson, the rather peculiar pastor at the Congregational Church in Groton, Connecticut—to the treaty meeting to speak on his behalf. Avery and Jacob Johnson lobbied hard the Oneidas not to accept the terms of the agreement, which called for the annexation of nearly all Haudenosaunee land east of Onondaga. Their effort to undermine Sir William Johnson's carefully plotted plan, which had required him to get the support of so many Native nations to agree to have the Proclamation Line of 1763 moved westward, infuriated him. Reverend Jacob Johnson in particular annoyed Johnson when the reverend capitalized on the recent events surrounding the 1765 Stamp Act and the 1767 Townshend Acts. Reverend Johnson said that he willingly drank to the king's health when he governed his subjects, both British and American, according to the English constitution. However, should his majesty govern contrary to "the rights & privileges" accorded Englishmen, and "Govern us with a Rod of Iron . . . and refuse to hear or consider our Humble prayers"—that is, the colonists' repeated futile attempts at redress—then he was all for joining his "Countrymen in Forming a New Empire in America . . . independent of the British Empire." Jacob fully alienated Johnson, a staunch Loyalist, when the young minister berated the elder Johnson "to be serious," for Jacob, who also claimed to be a "seer," like John the Baptist, had some knowledge of "some things [which] Your Excellency [Sir William] possibly may not." Wheelock apologized profusely to Sir William Johnson for the arrogant behavior of his two emissaries, especially that of Jacob Johnson, but his apologies did not win Sir William's heart or pardon. Thereafter, Johnson remained civil toward Wheelock, but no longer trusted him, viewing the spectacle at Fort Stanwix as an attempt by Wheelock to undermine him and reclaim "their old pretensions to the Susquehanna Lands."[38]

Meanwhile, the Mohawks continued to cause Sir William unease as they "repeatedly complained . . . and lamented that they [were] so far Neglected" by the SPG. The Canajoharies, who had several "amongst them well Qualified to read prayers," but always had to travel more than twenty miles to Tiononderoge to attend church services at the fort or have their children baptized, were "desirous of having a Church, where they might occasionally have divine service." They had put aside 100 pounds, saved communally from "the produce of their hunting" for the commercial market. They asked Johnson to raise the necessary funds to go forward with the project, which was completed in 1770 at a total cost of 459 pounds (about $89,000 today), most of which came from Johnson's own pocket. Now all that most Canajoharie Mohawks—as well as Tiononderoge Mohawks—desired was a resident minister. Meanwhile, Johnson sought to refine the SPG's missionizing strategy.[39]

One of Johnson's first recommended changes, approved heartily by the Mohawks, was separating Albany from Fort Hunter, thereby designating the latter an autonomous mission. Except during William Andrews's tenure in the 1710s, the society expected the SPG minister at Albany to also preach at Fort Hunter. Now, a number of people, beginning with John Ogilvie, suggested that the two missions be separated. To have a full-time resident minister at Fort Hunter would be not just for the benefit of the Mohawks, Ogilvie and Johnson reasoned, for he could also serve the burgeoning white population. Thence forward, Johnson, realizing that SPG funds and personnel were limited, schemed to have his own growing white community springing up around Johnson Hall, located about a dozen miles northwest of Fort Hunter, serviced without alienating the Mohawks.[40]

Johnson lobbied the SPG through a series of communications with several high-profile Anglican priests in the colonies, including Reverend Samuel Auchmuty, who succeeded Henry Barclay as rector of Trinity Church on Barclay's death in 1764; Reverend Thomas Barton, the pastor at the frontier parish, St. John's Church in Carlisle, Pennsylvania; and Reverend Samuel Johnson, the founder and president of King's College (Columbia University) in New York City. William Johnson made a compelling case for separating Fort Hunter from Albany and combining Albany and Schenectady into a single mission assignment: the society needed to manage more effectively the mission school at Fort Hunter, which hiving it off from Albany would accomplish; Fort Hunter now housed "a Good Stone Church built for the Indians & . . . a Good House & Farm . . . for the service of a Residentiary Minister," which required no future investment there by the SPG; Fort Hunter was "at a Convenient distance" for all of the Six Nations, for the Haudenosaunees had become "a people Jealous even of any proposal to draw their Youth to any distance"; and, finally, the society should use the Mohawks, who were "ready to imbibe our manners & would be a religious orderly people if taken proper care of," to reach the rest of the Haudenosaunees, as well as "the more distant Tribes now Strangers to all Religion." To bolster his vision of British hegemony, Johnson added that the society also ought to consider establishing schools at Fort Pitt and in Ohio country for the more westerly nations.[41]

Meanwhile, the society, Johnson insisted, should also assign a priest to the church in his own white community of Johnstown, which had grown rapidly over the past decade. He counted 40 families in 1760. This number would grow to 240 families in 1773. Around 1766, Johnson built in Johnstown "a Very neat Stone Church" to "Serve the Town & Neighborhood," composed largely of German tenant farmers. Native neighbors would also benefit from a pastor at Johnstown, he maintained, for "it [was] a place where . . . Sev'l Indians constantly [gathered] & many hundreds Occasionally," being only "11 miles from Fort Hunter." He had only "want of a good Clergyman to render [his] plan compleat"—a dubious prospect up to that point, as so few Anglican priests wished to live that far removed from Albany.[42]

Johnson's ideas attracted both critics and supporters, both of whom wished to counter the effectiveness of Wheelock's academy. Reverend

Samuel Auchmuty of New York, for example, wondered if Wheelock did not have it right. Would not educating Native peoples "among their own Countrymen" encourage them to "imbibe too much of their Savage Disposition, & Irregular way of Living?" he asked. Johnson answered that Native parents did not like to send their children abroad. [43]

The Anglican priest William Smith, the provost of the College at Philadelphia (University of Pennsylvania), called for "a very different Manner from any Thing yet attempted by us." He proposed a two-part plan: First, the indigenes needed to be "civilized" before Christianized—"or at least . . . accompany, the Teaching of Christianity." The Christianity taught them, he argued, must be that of the conforming service kept simple, "leaving out every Thing of a deep and disputable Nature," taught and preached by those who had governmental approval. The second part of his program called for following the model of the Jesuit missions in Paraguay, called "*reducciones*," or "reductions." Spanish reductions were autonomous, self-supporting church-operated resettlements where Guarani families and individuals gathered to live. In these isolated communities run by *caciques* (Guarani administrators) but governed by Jesuit priests, the Guaranis not only worshiped Christ but also labored collectively for the mission station. Through this method, the Catholic Church sought not only to protect their Native residents from enslavement, but also to "reduce" the Guarani into reliable skilled and unskilled Catholic workers. Some scholars have called these missions social utopias, as the inhabitants shared the wealth they produced. Provost Smith probably regarded the *reducciones* as model plantations capable of producing untapped wealth for the Church of England. He proposed that the SPG establish two mission stations along similar lines as the *reducciones*—one in the colony of New York, the other in Ohio country—located on vast one-hundred-thousand-acre estates. These utopian communities would be multiethnic, with both white and Native yeomen farmers working small, inalienable farms. Everyone would shop in public stores. Most important, the children would receive religious, manual, and mechanical instruction. [44]

Johnson agreed with everything Smith proposed—except the part about transforming the indigenes into farmers before Christianizing them. Here, Johnson again argued that warriors were of more use to the English as hunters and thus fighters, to which Smith subsequently agreed, although he continued to insist that "the Children, the Women

& Elderly Men might still be employed in civil Arts, Agriculture, etc." Clearly, an important sticking point was what to do with the male population of fighting age: turn warriors into yeomen farmers, or encourage them to continue as hunters? Both propositions presented a dilemma for many whites living within Mohawk country: either way, they saw the problem as privileging an uncivilized, uncultured, unpredictable people living in their midst on uncultivated and misused yet fertile lands. They preferred that enterprising white yeoman farmers put that land to good use.[45]

Charles Inglis, the assistant curate at Trinity Church in New York City who would succeed Auchmuty as rector in 1777 on the latter's death, liked both Smith's and Johnson's plans and offered a scheme of his own, which privileged the efficacy of the church as a "reducing" agent. Inglis expressed concern that the Church of England and the SPG were failing to fulfill their mandate to "promote the Glory of God, by the Instruccon of Our People in the Christian Religion" by providing "for an Orthodox Clergy to live amongst them." One event that particularly galled Inglis was that Parliament had recently approved the appointment of a Jesuit missionary to a nation of Native Americans in Nova Scotia, at the indigenes' firm insistence. He reasoned that because Nova Scotia was now firmly under British control, the Native people there were English subjects. Therefore, the government should have assigned them an SPG missionary, not a Jesuit priest. From Inglis's perspective, it was bad enough that Wheelock and other dissenters had made inroads into Haudenosaunee country. The priest now called for unprecedented action: governmental intervention, by which Parliament would take control of the missionizing program, relieving the cash-strapped SPG of its responsibility of placing Anglican priests in Native communities. In short, Inglis found the SPG's current strategy of establishing a single mission in Mohawk country "in the old, beaten Way" had proved ineffective in converting the mass of Haudenosaunees, as it "ma[de] no Noise"— that is, this strategy was neither robust nor ambitious enough to capture the attention of the Haudenosaunees nor the SPG's benefactors.[46]

Inglis, like Johnson, disagreed with those who insisted that "in order to make [indigenes] *Christians,* they must first be made *Men.*" However, as an Anglican priest, Inglis believed that the Church "forms moral habits, corrects irregularities, and disposes the mind to submit to the restraints of government and laws," and thereby manifestly transforms Native peoples into "men." "Manners [were] the result of principles," Inglis insisted. Change the principles of a society, and you change its people's manners and behavior. For those who needed more proof, Inglis offered a utilitarian argument: Christianized indigenes would benefit—and would benefit from—English commerce, for their sobriety would make them more dependable trading partners.[47]

Inglis, whose only exposure to the Haudenosaunees occurred during a visit to Johnson Hall in 1770, at which time he stood as godfather to a young Mohawk boy at his baptism, pronounced obsequiously that the Mohawks were an example of a Native nation "civilized" by Christianity. Surely, Inglis sought to appease the Mohawks and their host, Johnson, with these sweet words, for the assistant curate defined the "civilized state" as one that promoted "industry, and the increase of mankind" and in turn suppressed inclinations toward "indolence, idleness, and intemperance." By this definition, the Mohawks were the equivalent of their rowdy, bawdy, procreating European neighbors. Johnson pointed out to the rector that many Mohawks, in addition to hunting, now "cultivated land, several of them [had] learned trades; all [had] fixed habitations; they also [raised] cattle of various kinds, [and possessed] many of the conveniences of polished life." Inglis concurred that the Mohawks were "alert in hunting" and that this alone did not disqualify them from joining the ranks of the "civilized," for "the English," Inglis added, also "apply themselves to hunting." However, he believed there was room for introducing the English arts—farming, mechanics, spinning—to more Mohawks and to the rest of the Haudenosaunees. He dropped his idea when Johnson objected.[48]

Nevertheless, Inglis offered a six-point plan for educating, reforming, and Christianizing indigenes in which the Mohawks and the Oneidas figured centrally. He based his plan on the theory that all nations evinced "a great Similarity . . . whilst in an uncivilized State." History had revealed to Inglis that people and nations had to be brought to a civilized state slowly, to which end "Christianizing & Civilizing [indigenes] should go Hand in Hand." The first point of his plan called for two missions, one at Canajoharie, the other at Oneida Town. Fort Hunter did not figure into Inglis's plan; he may have assumed that the existing Fort Hunter mission would take care of Tiononderogans, while a missionary at Canajoharie could see to the needs of the white residents in and near Johnstown, which lay a bit closer to Canajoharie than to Tiononderoge. The second point called for schoolmasters at each of the principal Haudenosaunee villages. The teachers would teach the Haudenosaunees to read and write in English *and* in their Native dialects. In the beginning, missionaries and schoolmasters, all English, would use Protestant tracts translated into the various Haudenosaunee dialects of their catechumens to speed up their instruction as they shifted over to English-language texts. Point three offered a strategy that many felt was long overdue: placing blacksmiths in "the most convenient Indian Villages." All of the League nations had called for this service for decades, and a smith lived intermittently at Onondaga, where he repaired their weapons, but only irregularly. Inglis believed that if the men learned this trade, women could be enticed to "learn Spinning, Sewing, and other Branches of female Industry." Points four and five augmented existing policy: missionaries and teachers, who had been and would continue to be certified by the SPG, would now also have to be approved by Sir William Johnson, whom most believed knew more about the Haudenosaunees than any white person in the colonies. Additionally, Johnson would approve the rules regulating the duties of the missionaries and schoolmasters, whose "Diligence in their Station, Gentleness, Condescension, and a disinterested Regard to the Welfare of the Indians, should . . . sedulously inculcate Principles of Loyalty among their Hearers, Converts and Pupils." The final point of Inglis's plan called for a "College or Seminary in the old Oneida Town," most likely to counter the influence of Wheelock and his missionary student Samuel Kirkland, both dissenters. Here Inglis voiced Johnson's position on the objections of Haudenosaunee parents sending their children great distances from them; they, like most parents, liked to "frequently see their Children." In any event, the effort to educate and "civilize" Haudenosaunees at the college, Inglis cautioned, ought to be "gradually effected."[49]

Inglis believed that conditions were favorable for implementing his plan immediately. Relative calm reigned in 1770, which meant that nearly all warriors were home, save for those on hunting expeditions. New France had been subdued, which allowed Anglican priests to now assume those missions formerly under the control of French Jesuits. The assistant curate reasoned that white settlers moving into territories occupied or formerly occupied by Haudenosaunee families would require religious instruction by the established church, not a dissenting church. Thus, Inglis hoped that these white farm families could help "civilize" their Native neighbors by their example. Ultimately, the most important sign that the time was right to Christianize the Haudenosaunees—or at least, the Mohawks—was the frequent requests made by Mohawks "that Missionaries might be sent to instruct them in the Principles of Christianity."[50]

## The Mohawk Response

What did the Mohawks mean and want by their persistent requests for ministers? Why were so many still eager to imbibe and perform Church of England Protestantism when the SPG disappointed them continuously through delays in replacing absent missionaries? Why did the baptized Mohawks risk being further alienated, like the baptized Oneidas, from their Haudenosaunee brethren? Two plausible, practical reasons appear to explain their intentions. First, the Mohawks wanted the SPG—and by extension, the English Crown—to acknowledge its long-standing relationship with them, symbolized by the Covenant Chain, and to honor that relationship based on mutuality and reciprocity. As a result, the unbaptized Mohawks and their Haudenosaunee brethren tolerated those who identified as Christian having a priest to meet their needs. To outsiders, factionalism seemed to explain the divide between baptized and unbaptized Mohawks. However, for most Mohawks, regardless of their religious identity, consensus and toleration, expressed as social etiquette, superseded plays for prerogative. Second, most Mohawk parents wanted their children to receive instruction in literacy from a Mohawk schoolmaster, who could make Christian dogma meaningful to Mohawk pupils. The best interpreters were those who could explain context as well as content, who could offer translations of equivalents and analogies, and not just translate vocabulary. Tellingly, the parents asked that literacy instruction be carried out primarily in Mohawk, not in English, by Mohawks. The German pastor Jacob Oel, a curate (assistant) to Reverend Ogilvie, learned of this desire toward the end of his career as catechist to the Mohawks.

Oel was seventy-one years old when Ogilvie left Fort Hunter in 1760. Since the 1720s, Oel had lived on the German Flatts (near present-day Herkimer), located west of Canajoharie, where he officiated as the Anglican presbyter (priest) to the Palatine Germans, who had lived in the region since the 1710s. Their poverty-stricken ancestors of the Palatines left Palatinate in the Middle Rhine region of Europe during the first decade of the eighteenth century in search of economic opportunities. After living for a brief time in England, many families migrated to New York to harvest naval stores—hemp, pitch, tar—in the Hudson Valley for the British navy. In the 1720s, many of these families moved to the Mohawk Valley, where they leased farmland from the Mohawks. The clan mothers, who controlled access to the land, saw three benefits in leasing to the Palatines: this population would be brought under the Great Tree of Peace and, as allies, would shore up the flagging Mohawk nation; as lessees, the Palatines would keep Mohawk lands out of the greedy hands of English speculators; and finally, through rents and trade with them, the Mohawks stood to augment their subsistence. When Oel was not preaching to the Palatines, he visited the Mohawks at Canajoharie, a short distance to the east. There, he read prayers, catechized the youths, and baptized both white and Mohawk children and infants.[51]

By 1770, however, the Mohawks at Canajoharie had grown tired of Oel. They preferred a younger, more energetic man of their own nation to teach their children. That year, Oel informed the society that he could not generate any excitement among the Canajohariens. When he sent his interpreter to inquire what was going on, the Canajohariens gave him politely "no manner of answer, but they remained as mute as fishes." Oel continued with his "English congregation" at the church at Canajoharie, but the Mohawks clearly did not wish to embarrass him by telling him to cease his preaching to them. It took Oel several years to catch on: the Canajoharie Mohawks, who had been used to having Paulus Sahonwadi as their teacher, had given their approval in 1764 to Philip Jonathan, a young Mohawk from Canajoharie, to become their next teacher. Jonathan does not appear on Wheelock's student roster, but he received an English-style education, perhaps at Fort Hunter. He registered his concern with "Brother Waronghyage" (Sir William Johnson) over his own style of teaching when he worried that some of the parents of his pupils may not "approve of having their children chastised if they do Ill." In addition to soliciting Johnson's advice on this matter, Jonathan asked for "two of our printed Books"—"our" meaning in Mohawk—to give to "two of my Scholars that are pretty fur [*sic*] advanced in their Learning." Jonathan and his two pupils reveal just how much the Mohawks valued increasingly the teaching of literacy in Mohawk by a literate, learned Mohawk educator.[52]

In December 1770, the SPG met the Mohawks' demand for a pastor: the Reverend John Stuart arrived to be their sole resident Anglican priest, the first step in implementing a larger, grander yet still vague project to proselytize all the Haudenosaunees. On Christmas Day, Stuart preached a sermon at Canajoharie and administered "the Holy Communion to twenty indian Communicants." Two months earlier, "scarcely more than 2 or 3 of the old Indians" revealed themselves to Oel as having "any concern for religion." Perhaps the larger turnout for Stuart indicated increased Mohawk hope for, and thus reciprocity toward, the SPG. At Fort Hunter, Stuart preached two sermons every Sunday: the first in the morning in Mohawk, whenever he could find an interpreter, and the second in the afternoon in English to "a Congregation of two hundred Persons," most of whom, according to Stuart, were "low Dutch." As formerly, the Mohawks were forced to share their parson with white Christians, although now some felt as though the Mohawk chapel belonged to them.[53]

Stuart came to a chapel at Fort Hunter long neglected and in deep disrepair. The Tiononderoge Mohawks took responsibility for the chapel and "allowed a sum of money to repair" it. The church had "neither windows, Reading Desk, nor Communion Table, & only a Pulpit of Rough Boards— the Books belonging to it [were] all lost, except the Bible." The small fund, augmented by a more generous gift from Sir William Johnson, paid for those repairs, as well as for the all-critical new "Cupola with a Bell."[54]

The chapel was not the only thing that Stuart found in disrepair. He confronted what he considered disorders of various kinds afflicting the Mohawks. He first encountered a "custom so injurious to their temporal as well as spiritual welfare"—one so heinous that he dared not name it— that he got some of the "Sachems, or head men" there to support him in "suppress[ing]" it. The disorder that Stuart dare not name was probably the perennial problem of alcoholism. He found at both Tiononderoge and Canajoharie "immoderate use of spiritous Liquors . . . often attended with horrid Consequences." How could Native people understand the Word of God, Stuart ruminated, if they existed in a state of sin? So as not to bring "a scandal on Religion, and offend the sober Part of their Brethren," Stuart barred from communion those whom he considered "notorious Drunkards" and "vicious in their Behaviour." Barring those individuals from communion, which many baptized Mohawks regarded as an imprimatur of approval, reduced them to "a kind of Dispair" and generated great rage toward Stuart. As a precaution, Paulus Sahonwadi read prayers at Canajoharie for a while, a task assigned to him irregularly since the 1750s. Following a lapse in his service, the society rehired him as an official reader there and paid him five pounds a year.[55]

Like so many SPG missionaries who came and went before him, Stuart found the Mohawk language difficult. After one year, he still had not grasped the rudiments of the language and thus had seldom been able to "give them [Mohawks] a Discourse in Church" in their language. He eventually hired a "young man of their Nation (who underst[ood] English) to reside with [him] as a private Tutor, & public Interpreter," on whom he had relied to assist him with his Sunday services. Stuart worried how long he could keep him, as he could not afford him a "sufficient Maintenance to induce him to neglect Hunting & reside constantly" at his home.[56] Like the catechist-headmen Cornelius and Daniel, this young interpreter placed what he considered a fair monetary value on his services as interpreter. Translating the Word of God cost money, but it also exacted a potentially high cost on the young man's reputation as good provider and skilled warrior. In time, the young man quit.

Stuart quickly noted another serious shortcoming at the mission: the lack of "Books proper for them, more especially Common Prayer Books, the want of which is a considerable obstacle in their way" to becoming bona fide Christians. Stuart informed the society early in 1774 that "the Indians frequently complain of the want of Books in their own Language." They desired particularly translations of the New Testament, an appeal to their priest that they saw themselves as he wished to see them—as new Protestant Christians. Following Johnson's death in July 1774, Stuart assumed full control over the project of translating the scriptures and other texts into Mohawk. To help him prepare a translation of the book of Saint Mark, along with "a large & plain Exposition of the Church Catechism & a compendious History of the Bible, all in the Mohawk Tongue," Stuart procured the aid "of an Indian who underst[ood] English," Joseph Brant.[57]

Literacy also proved crucial beyond just reading the Bible, as demonstrated in 1776 by a young literate Mohawk warrior named Ian. In May of that year, General Philip Schuyler, a general in the Continental army in charge of the Northern Department, and Volkert Douw, a Dutch merchant and former mayor of Albany, led American troops into Mohawk country, a Loyalist region, on the pretense of pursuing the enemy. At Little Abraham's house at Tiononderoge, the American detail met Ian (a.k.a. Jan). Ian railed against Douw and Schuyler for invading Mohawk country with seemingly hostile intent. Douw asked the lad to calm down and assured him that they were merely exercising the agreement that the Mohawks and the commissioners for Indian affairs had agreed on the previous year in Albany—that the road through Mohawk country would remain open. After all, Douw declared, he, like Little Abraham, was a man of peace, and his only business was "to attend on good news." The headman Little Abraham seconded Douw, explaining that "we the sachems, like Mr. Douw, are only to take [on matters] of good news." Ian said that Mohawk warriors would always do what their sachems ordered—a declaration that contradicted recent practice. He stunned the room, however, when he declared that he had in his possession a letter written by Samuel Kirkland, Wheelock's missionary to the Oneidas, and his interpreter, James Dean, a white man raised and adopted by the Oneidas and a 1773 graduate of Dartmouth College, that he found deeply troubling. Douw, taken aback by the revelation, asked Ian to produce the original and bring it to Johnson Hall, where the entire matter would be straightened out. Ian retorted with an accusation that Douw and his troops were indeed heading to Johnson Hall to arrest John Johnson, the son of the late Sir William Johnson. Ian and other Mohawk warriors present pledged to defend the Johnsons and their entire estate. In the meantime, Ian read the incriminating evidence: a copy in English of Kirkland and Dean's letter, addressed to General Schuyler, and a translation of it in Mohawk. The letter had been purloined from an Oneida courier on his way to Albany, who "got drunk and while he was so, the letters were taken from him copyed & translated into Indian [Mohawk], and the originals put up again in the Indian's bag without his knowing of it." With the truth disclosed about Douw's mission, Colonel Dayton stepped forward and confessed, claiming that he "reserved the right of pursuing our enemies of the white people amongst you." He added that if any blood were spilled, the Mohawks would be held responsible, a strategy used by individuals in power who hold others responsible for bad consequences resulting from their actions. The Spanish in New Spain called this principal *requiremiento,* a more modern version of *imperium,* which held Native people responsible for their own destruction at the hands of conquerors.[58]

No hard evidence exists to indicate how or where Ian acquired his literacy in English and Mohawk. He was too young to have studied at Stockbridge; all Mohawk parents had withdrawn their children from Sergeant's school by 1754, discouraged over the internal politics that interfered with the children's learning. Additionally, there is no mention of him at the Moor's Charity School. The scribe at the May 1776 meeting at Little Abraham's house, however, noted that Ian "live[d] near the Rev. Mr. Stuart." Colin McLeod, the schoolmaster at Fort Hunter in the 1760s and 1770s, may have tutored Ian.

Nevertheless, literacy empowered Ian with the authority to question the actions and authority of white men. His rant against their disregard for Mohawk sovereignty delayed the Douw party long enough for John Johnson, who had been forewarned of their coming, to escape. In this case, the power of literacy extended beyond Ian's ability to gain knowledge through the Bible; it enabled him to challenge in a revolutionary way the rights and privileges of white men.

Ian recognized that he and his generation now inhabited a world different from that of his ancestors. His literacy skills and Christian education were just two factors that opened an entire world to him unavailable to most of his elders. The world of the Mohawks had changed dramatically over the previous seventy-five years. Internecine conflict between Englishmen was now replacing persistent hostilities between the English and the French. A Haudenosaunee warrior had to be clear about implicating which side he was on in choosing his own side, especially when reaching out to white pastors and churches. Others in choosing their own side tried to remain neutral, like Little Abraham, and support only those who allegedly brought "good news." Life had become more complex materially and culturally through the amalgamation of Haudenosaunee, Algonquian, Dutch, English, and black peoples into Mohawk society through conquest, adoption, and intermarriage. "We are called Mohawks," Ian announced proudly to the assembled men at Little Abraham's house. "Our Ancestors have been so before us in whose stead we are." But in 1776, we are no longer "real Mohawks," he declared, but carried "only the name yet still the heart of the Mohawks [beats within]." Ian echoed Sir William Johnson's assertion that cultures change over time, yet identity continues through survivance. The escalating violence of the American Revolution in Mohawk country would not only end grand plans of the SPG to enlarge its missionizing project but would also result in a Mohawk diaspora that tested the strength, heart, and durability of their society and their faith and forced many to reexamine what it meant to be Mohawk in their souls.[59]

## Conclusion

Charles Inglis, the assistant curate at Trinity Church, noted that "Culture, with other external Circumstances, constitute the principal Difference between the various Parts of Mankind." By "culture," Inglis meant the cultivation or development of the mind, manners, and faculties through education and training. This definition of culture, which prevailed in the eighteenth century, contains an element of learned behavior and received values, to which many anthropologists subscribe today.[60] Inglis implied that educating indigenes in the religion, arts, and industries of the English—it never occurred to most Englishmen and women to embrace Native culture—would render them familiar and begin to close the cultural gap between the two worlds. Replacing what the English considered their "guttural language" with their own "harmonious language," he and other English reformers believed, would impel Native Americans to think and behave like Englishmen.

Following the Seven Years' War, several white reform-minded individuals contended that indigenes, like the Mohawks, who remained in areas where the aggregate complexion of settlements grew increasingly whiter almost daily needed to be reformed culturally and socially at once. Loyalists believed that converting them to Anglican Protestantism through the old way of preaching by part-time missionaries was no longer effective. Too many baptized Mohawks continued to hunt on what white settlers considered prime real estate for farming and logging. American dissenters believed that the best way of freeing up Haudenosaunee land was to remove some to white settlements and, after educating them, return them home to proselytize and "reduce" their brethren. This strategy also offered dissenters the ancillary benefit of making inroads into Loyalist regions. Hardly any of the white reformers could agree on the most effective strategy.

Many of the Mohawks who did alter their patterns of subsistence did so not because they believed English ways were superior but rather because necessity required them to adjust in order to survive as Mohawks. They determined the changes to their subsistence practices that they thought were best. Likewise, they performed Christianity according to their needs. Most Mohawks now found most English priests and schoolmasters too strict, too inflexible, too dull, too unhelpful, and in some cases too dishonest. As keepers of the eastern door to the Longhouse Confederacy, the Mohawks were now paying the price of turning outsiders into insiders: too often, the English failed to reciprocate by neglecting or refusing to trade goods at a good penny's worth, to provide military assistance, and to supply the Mohawks with priests and books.

Nevertheless, one English aspect of reciprocity that the Mohawks valued and insisted on receiving was literacy. Ironically, English and American reformers viewed this benefit differently than the Mohawks. White reformers regarded literacy as a necessary means for becoming a good Christian. It was simply one step on the way to becoming a God-fearing farmer or wife and mother. On the other hand, most Mohawks viewed literacy as a skill that contained newfound power. The ability to read and write enabled them to not only decipher the Bible but also discern for themselves meanings embedded in a range of texts in Mohawk and in English, whether deeds, treaties, secret missives, or the Book of Common Prayer. Literacy also empowered them to communicate their knowledge of and responses to those texts. Hence, the Mohawks were uninterested in becoming honorary Englishmen and -women through literacy. Rather, they were committed to literacy because of the power with which it endowed them to make decisions literally over life and death, as Ian discovered, to ensure survivance.[61]

CHAPTER 6

# "As Formerly under Their Respective Chiefs"

## The Mohawk Diaspora into Upper Canada, 1784–1810

We wish to get rid of all the whites.

—Sagoyewatha (Red Jacket), Seneca, 1819

The American Revolution inflicted indisputable harm on most Native American nations east of the Mississippi River. The war destroyed entire Indian towns, eradicated warrior populations, and displaced whole families. In the process, it gave birth to refugee communities that were largely multiethnic, multilingual, multiracial, and multicultural, but with reaffirmed national identities.[1] These varied consequences were no less true for the Mohawks. The war set in motion physical dislocation and economic, political, and cultural transformation. Most fundamentally, the war finalized land dispossession, a process initiated at the end of the seventeenth century by both friends and foes of the Mohawks. Reestablishing themselves in new communities brought challenges to their systems of subsistence, education, and of the sacred. Consequently, many Mohawks reformulated the needs of their souls as they performed familiar, new, or reinvigorated faiths, as they carved out new lives for themselves drawing on traditional, recently acquired, and alien patterns of living.

Despite warrior forces in support of the British during the war, most Mohawks tried to get out of the way of the fighting that disrupted "their quiet & peaceful Habitations" in the Mohawk Valley, where by 1770 they lived completely surrounded by white American and European settlers, and thus physically cut off from their Haudenosaunee brethren.[2]

More than two hundred Mohawks left their homes in the Mohawk Valley in May 1775, one month after the battles at Lexington and Concord. Following General Burgoyne's defeat at Saratoga Springs, New York, in 1777, most Mohawks knew that they would never again reside in their valley. Now entire extended families fled either north to Canada or west to Fort Niagara, abandoning their homes, their farms, their kin, their "rich tract of Country left them and possessed by their Ancestors from Time immemorial," forsaking "the Graves of their deceased Relatives & friends to be demolished by their Enemies."[3]

Of course, not all Mohawks left the area. A few, including Little Abraham (Tigoransera or Tyorhansere) and his followers, remained behind, hoping that the Americans would honor their neutrality. In 1775, the headman explained to some New York Whigs that he and his Mohawk brethren at Tiononderoge wished "not to take any part" in the war, for they viewed the conflict as a "family affair" between the Americans and the Britons, and so had chosen to "sit still and see you fight it out." He and his brethren chose to remain nonaligned, for they bore "as much affection for the King of England's subjects, upon the other side of the water as we do for you, born upon this island."[4] Moreover, neutral Mohawks believed that the 1768 Treaty of Fort Stanwix guaranteed what Sir John Johnson, the Loyalist son of Sir William, confirmed near the end of the war: that the treaty guaranteed that "the right of Soil" in Mohawk country belonged to them as sole proprietors, which had been "Agreed upon and Established in the most Solemn and public manner and in the presence and with the Consent of the Governors and Commissioners Deputed by the Different Colonies for that purpose." An American virtually confirmed the same at the beginning of the war: "We have no right or pretention to it [Mohawk lands] until after your removal or extinction as a nation."[5] Little Abraham and the other Mohawks who remained behind took it on faith that they had little to fear, as powerful white men had endorsed their sovereignty.

However, both white Patriots and Loyalists, uneasy about Haudenosaunees in their midst, distrusted Mohawks who claimed neutrality. The historian Caitlin Fitz suggests that this distrust may have been rooted in Haudenosaunee and Euro-American differences in defining "neutrality." Fitz argues that Little Abraham defined neutrality as "non-combatant pacifism" that did not necessarily preclude working politically with one side or the other in order to protect one's self interest and community. The historian Jon Parmenter has shown that Haudenosaunee neutrality does not have to mean passivity, but rather can entail limited active engagement. However, neither the Americans nor the Britons saw it that way. They regarded neutrality as "passive non-involvement of any kind," and read any gesture that hinted at favoring one side or the other—for example, forestalling one side's march through one's country, ferrying messages for one side, seeking agreements and assurances from one side or the other—as a betrayal of neutrality. Fitz maintains that in an effort to remain neutral, Little Abraham forged "a limited partnership with the Americans," which certainly gave the appearance of aiding and abetting the Americans. It is useful to view Little Abraham's actions as those of a Pine Tree Chief, selected as such for his brokering abilities. The headman, in his role as mediator, forced to live as harmoniously as possible with his Indian-hating white American neighbors, sought to walk as neutral a line as his neighbors would allow, in an effort to safeguard his homeland.[6] Little Abraham would pay the ultimate price for his brand of neutrality.

The majority of Mohawks threw their fate on the side of the British, despite the Six Nations' ratification of an agreement in 1775 with the United States pledging to remain neutral. They believed that remaining loyal to the Crown was in their best interest, for most Mohawks placed their trust in the century-old Covenant Chain that dictated their loyalty to their "great father," currently King George III, and, by extension, to his ardent supporters, most notably the Loyalist family of the late Sir William Johnson. Quite consciously, Johnson had established kinship relations with—and thereby political fealty from—the Canajoharie Mohawks through his common-law marriage to Molly Brant, Joseph Brant's sister.

Initially, most of the refugee Mohawks resettled temporarily in several venues along the Canadian-U.S. border between Montreal and Fort Niagara.[7] Despite pleas at war's end by some Haudenosaunee headmen and Canadian officials that the Mohawks consolidate themselves into a single community, the residents of the two principal Mohawk communities—Tiononderoge and Canajoharie (Schoharie was the third major village)—reestablished themselves in separate regions in Upper Canada in order to live, according Sir John Johnson of the Indian Department, "as formerly under their respective Chiefs," rather than live consolidated geographically under a single headman.[8] The former residents of Tiononderoge, the Lower Village near Fort Hunter, resettled on the Bay of Quinte (Kenty), some fifty miles west of Cataraqui on the north side of Lake Ontario. Most of the former residents of Canajoharie, the Upper Mohawk castle, resettled along the Grand River between Lakes Ontario and Erie in a town later named Brantford about forty miles north of Niagara. General Haldimand, a British general and later the governor-in-chief of Canada (1778–86), characterized these regions as "a fertile and happy Retreat for them [Mohawks]." However, the general's abiding concern was propping up Canada's sagging economy; he bragged that the Mohawks would defend "the Upper Country and the Fur Trade."[9] The de facto war-chief leaders of the two principal Mohawk villages—Deserontyon of Tiononderoge and thus on the Bay of Quinte, and Joseph Brant of Canajoharie, and thus on the Grand River—shaped the founding, character, and rebirth of their respective communities, which differed, by imposing on them their visions for Mohawk revitalization and sovereignty.

Deserontyon defined sovereignty in traditional Mohawk terms: autonomy within an interdependent Haudenosaunee empire. He wanted to recast the Bay of Quinte Mohawks in the customary role as "the heads of the Six Nations Confederacy."[10] As keepers of the eastern door of the Longhouse Confederacy since the formation of the league in the fifteenth century, the Tiononderogans had welcomed French, Dutch, English, and American missionaries and had hosted many international council meetings. Naturally, in Deserontyon's view, these responsibilities would remain with his community at the Bay of Quinte. Yet in the wake of the revolution, Deserontyon feared further displacement by whites and, thus, rejected direct white involvement in Mohawk life at Tyendinaga on the Bay of Quinte. As such, Deserontyon encouraged self-reliance, neo-nativism, and neo-nationalism. However, Deserontyon's brand of nationalism was not that of the Delaware prophet Neolin nor that of the Shawanese prophets Tenkswatawa and his brother Tecumseh, who in the 1760s and 1790s respectively called for Native Americans to reject all things Euro-American—habits, customs, beliefs, and material objects of life—and return to their traditional ways of being in order to restore balance to their worlds. Rather, Deserontyon drew on Euro-American institutions, but without Euro-Americans, to revitalize Mohawk life.[11]

At the other end of Lake Ontario, Joseph Brant, the ersatz headman at Canajoharie, embraced more fully the Eurocentric worldview to which he had become assimilated. He strove to appropriate the European principle of sovereignty—self-determination, articulated most clearly as dominion over the land. To Brant, sovereignty meant enjoying political and economic control over resources, with the power, ability, and authority to alienate or lease the land in order to enrich the community—and in the process enrich himself. He was not the nationalist Deserontyon was. However, in exchange for accommodating white neighbors, Brant demanded that Parliament recognize his community's sovereignty. He was not above manipulating white fears of a Native-warrior uprising in order to negotiate terms favorable to him and to the Grand River settlement. Ultimately, Brant was unsuccessful, which earned him the wrath of some of his Haudenosaunee brethren, as well as some modern-day Native and non-Native citizens and scholars.

Nevertheless, to a certain degree, both Deserontyon and Brant and their respective communities had become assimilated to Euro-American life and institutions. With the help of Canadian public funds, they established grammar schools, sawmills, gristmills, blacksmith shops, and so on in their respective communities. Most tellingly, both communities established rather quickly the Protestant Church of England. In both communities, the Mohawk Church of England occupied prime spaces. At the Grand River settlement, both transplanted white Loyalists and Mohawks attended the Anglican Church, built in 1785, the first built in either refugee community. However, both communities experienced inter- and intravillage strife and disputes over controlling and sharing natural resources, privileging cultural practices, and performing faiths that tested the will of community members and the integrity of their respective leaders.[12]

Most historians who have examined postrevolution diasporic Mohawk life have focused largely on the political dimensions of the struggles among Mohawk headmen, warriors, and Canadian officials over land, resources, political power, and attempts at reconfederation. With a few exceptions, the cultural impulses to reformulate Mohawk life in Upper Canada have been somewhat overlooked.[13] In these new diasporic communities, determining what was best for their souls lay arguably at the core of their struggle to remain Mohawk. A number of individuals, both Mohawk and Canadian, raised questions about Mohawk beliefs, values, subsistence, and their impact on the quotidian elements of life. What faith to perform lay at the heart of their rebuilding efforts.

Historian John Webster Grant argues that in the second quarter of the nineteenth century indigenes in Upper Canada benefited greatly from their conversion to Christianity. He contends, in short, that missionaries and their new Christian belief system rescued some Native peoples from sure extinction. One might argue that Grant overstates his well-intended interpretation, especially because he follows up this conclusion with the assessment that many Native peoples in communities in Upper Canada withdrew from the novelty of missions by midcentury and returned to their ancestors' faith. Such a quick turnaround in faith practices seems questionable, given that so many Mohawks identified as Methodist by the mid-nineteenth century.[14]

Still, we can learn from Grant by asking if the Mohawks benefited from missionaries during the *first* decade of the nineteenth century during the period of reestablishment. The answer, like so many answers to historical questions, is "it's complicated." At the turn of the nineteenth century, despite some exiled Mohawks along the Grand River feeling the tug of their traditional Haudenosaunee faith practices, most Mohawks believed that the Church of England represented their best hope for rebuilding. Having been removed from their ancestral land, many believed that the old supplications and sacred festivals performed to reveal sacred truths had lost their efficacy. Now immutable sacred Christian truths, revealed through decipherable printed texts and taught and explained by Mohawk catechists, provided new answers to new questions in their new world. Community, now composed of more than just League Mohawks, could cohere around the Church of England, which represented one cog in the total apparatus of their new society. The church embodied an imagined community comprising the king of England abroad and, at home, their white neighbors, clients, and patrons, many of whom worked in the Canadian Indian Department, which, after all, paid a portion of the salaries of native schoolmasters and interpreters. Furthermore, many Mohawk mothers continued to view baptism as offering protection against future calamities as well as ensuring salvation. For still others, communion conferred a certain social status within and without their communities. For these reasons, many Mohawks petitioned local Canadian officials to send them Anglican priests and schoolmasters.

## War, Displacement, and the Mohawk Diaspora

In May 1775, at the first whiff of war, Guy Johnson, the hail-fellow-well-met nephew and son-in-law of the late Sir William Johnson, led a retinue of 90 Mohawks, including Joseph Brant and 120 white Loyalists, out of the Mohawk Valley and headed to Canada. Some settled with Deserontyon, a headman from Tiononderoge, at Lachine on the St. Lawrence River near Montreal and others with their Catholic cousins at Kahnawake, where they awaited fighting orders. The rest followed Johnson and Joseph Brant to Fort Niagara. Thus, Lachine and Fort Niagara initially constituted the two principal diasporic communities for Mohawk refugees and other displaced Haudenosaunees. These communities reflected the future regional resettlement patterns of the diasporic Mohawk communities.[15]

Unable to secure the support of Governor Sir Guy Carleton for raising Native warriors to retake the Mohawk Valley, Guy Johnson, Daniel Claus (Guy's cousin by marriage and an agent in the British Indian Department), Joseph Brant, and John Hill (Oteronyente), a member of a distinguished Mohawk family from Brant's hometown, Canajoharie, sailed for London in the fall of 1775. After reaching London in January 1776, these men met with several key government officials, including Lord George Germaine, the secretary of state for the American Department under Lord North's prime ministry, and even King George III. The Britons feted Brant similarly to his ancestors more than sixty-five years earlier: Brant mingled with London's elite; was inducted into an elite Order of Masons; was showered with gifts, including fine shirts, a silver watch, and a pistol and a musket; and attended masque balls. Allegedly, at one ball, an English guest tried to pull off Brant's mask, which was his actual face adorned with war paint. When the guest tweaked his nose, Brant let out a war whoop and whipped from his belt a tomahawk, which he waved menacingly over his head. The guests, especially the women, recoiled purportedly in horror, until Brant explained that he was only joking. The quartet left London with halfhearted support, designed to not further enrage the Americans: Guy Johnson officially replaced his uncle as superintendent of Indian affairs in the northern colonies only, Claus was placed in charge of Native refugees in Canada, and Brant and Hill were told that the English government would provide for them and their communities after the war.[16]

Once back in Iroquoia, Brant had difficulty convincing Haudenosaunee warriors throughout the confederacy to gather themselves under his leadership. Most Seneca headmen accused Brant of arrogance and criticized him for acting above his station of mere war chief to please the English while his own people suffered. In fact, most Haudenosaunees viewed the Mohawks as quislings, which Hendrick, Old Abraham's brother, confirmed two decades earlier: "We are looked upon by the other Nations," he told delegates at the 1754 Albany Congress, "as Coll. [Sir William] Johnson's councellors." Perhaps in an effort to strike a stance of independence before the Native delegates in attendance, Hendrick added unconvincingly, "which is not the case."[17] With the Americans now in control of much of the Mohawk Valley following the withdrawal of so many white and Mohawk residents, Brant took up residence at Onoquaga (Oquaga), an Oneida community that had become multiethnic and multiracial with Lenapes, some Tuscaroras, Mohawks exiled there after the 1768 Treaty of Fort Stanwix, and white Loyalists all living side by side. At Oquaga, where he also benefited from kinship ties through his marriage to his late Oneida wife, Brant recruited enough warriors and soldiers between the spring and summer of 1777 to assemble a small personal army, referred to as "Brant's Volunteers," composed of about a hundred men. More than 75 percent of his recruits were white Loyalist farmers living in the upper Susquehanna and Delaware River valleys, willing to place their fate in a Native warrior's hands. Mohawk warriors constituted roughly the remaining 25 percent. Unpaid, Brant's Volunteers, a multiracial, multiethnic band of self-styled warriors, transgressed customary racial lines and sumptuary laws and subsisted in the same way that black maroon communities survived: through raiding, begging, and scavenging.[18] Historians have asked why these white men, most of them of the lower sorts, followed Brant, an unlikely scenario in the eighteenth century. Isabel Kelsay has offered disparagingly that the white Loyalists were "wild and undisciplined" scoundrels. They were too individualistic, she maintains, to be commanded by white officers. However, the more compelling reason is that these men found common cause with Brant in "playing Indian" because their interests and experiences—leading hardscrabble lives, marrying Haudenosaunee women, resenting the turmoil caused by settlers who identified as Patriots—aligned with the interests of the Mohawks.[19]

Brant did not have to wait long to put his military skills and charismatic leadership abilities to the test. In August 1777, a civil war between Oneidas, most of whom pledged fealty to the Americans, and Mohawks, most of whom were Loyalists, commenced with the battle of Oriskany, so named after the creek where the bloody action took place, near the Oneida town of Oriske. A nearly fifteen-hundred-man force of British regulars, white Loyalists, and mainly Mohawk and some Seneca warriors overran the Patriot force of about half as many, composed of Americans and Oneidas, which was on its way to provide relief at Fort Stanwix, the outpost run by Americans. The American forces suffered heavy casualties, while the Loyalist forces suffered moderately. Furthermore, Joseph Brant added insult to injury by destroying the Oneida town of Oriske. In retaliation, the Oneidas sacked Tiononderoge and Canajoharie, during which Molly Brant lost most of her possessions. However, the Mohawk-British victory at Oriskany was bittersweet for the Loyalist forces, as the battle was part of the larger Saratoga campaign, which resulted in a humiliating defeat for the British army.[20]

Eight months later in July 1778, in retaliation for the loss at Saratoga, the Loyalist John Butler of Butler's Rangers and the Seneca warrior Sayenqueraghta ("Disappearing Smoke") led an expedition into the American settlement of Wyoming in northeastern Pennsylvania on the Susquehanna River. They destroyed the community and took prisoners, some of whom they killed. The Americans quickly blamed these atrocities on Joseph Brant, who was not in Wyoming, but rather in Onoquaga. Three months later, in retaliation, American forces torched Onoquaga, destroying homes, cattle, and farm fields and even killing Native children cowering in the fields. The next month, white Loyalist, Mohawk, and Seneca forces sought revenge by sacking American farms in the Cherry Valley region of New York, between present-day Cooperstown and Cobleskill. Walter Butler, the inexperienced, arrogant son of John Butler, wedged his way into leading all forces, even the Native warriors, who preferred to be led by Brant or Sayenqueraghta. Here, reckless Seneca warriors committed brutal depredations and atrocities, for which the Americans once again blamed Brant. However, eyewitnesses reported that Brant kept his forces restrained and in check.[21]

The following year, in September 1779, Colonel Peter Gansevoort, a member of the American Sullivan-Clinton expedition, which a month earlier had burned down forty Seneca villages in the Finger Lakes and Genesee Valley regions and destroyed an estimated 160,000 bushels of corn, marched his company eastward to Fort Hunter with orders to arrest the few Mohawks who remained in Tiononderoge and to burn down the village. Gansevoort avoided Canajoharie, the Upper Castle, now occupied by Oriska Oneidas, their allies. At Tiononderoge, Gansevoort found all but four houses abandoned, occupied no doubt by Little Abraham and his followers, who had stayed, for they regarded remaining physically at home both as an expression of their neutrality—the Americans would surely have taken their fleeing with their refugee brethren to Fort Niagara as a sign of alignment with the British—and as the best means of safeguarding their property and community. As noted earlier, just as Gansevoort prepared to torch the homes, several Americans living in the area beseeched the colonel to leave the houses standing for them. They pointed out that the structures abounded "with every Necessary so that it is remarked that the Indians live much better than most of the Mohawk River farmers their Houses very well furnished with all necessary Household utensils, great plenty of Grain, several horses, cows, and wagons." He disobeyed his orders and permitted some of the nearby white settlers who had been burned out of their homes to occupy the confiscated Mohawk dwellings.[22] While Mohawk bodies constituted an affront to American sensibilities, their material possessions were quite the enticement.

Not surprisingly, the Americans living in the Mohawk Valley panicked in October and November 1780, when British troops, led by Sir John Johnson and Joseph Brant, virtually destroyed everything from Fort Hunter to Stone Arabia. Most critically, they obliterated the American grain crops that were to be harvested and sent to the Continental army: "Six hundred Thousand Bushells of different kinds," according to Sir John Johnson, and about 150,000 bushels of wheat, according to Governor Clinton, who also estimated that two hundred dwellings had been destroyed.[23] The Johnson-Brant expedition on the Mohawk Valley was far more devastating than the earlier Sullivan-Clinton expedition. The next year, Governor Clinton complained to Congress:

> We are now arrived at the year 1781, deprived of a great Portion of our most valuable and well inhabited Territory, numbers of our Citizens have been barbarously butchered by [the] ruthless Hand of the Savages, many are carried away into Captivity, vast numbers entirely ruined, and these

their Families become a heavy Burthen to the distressed Remainder; the frequent Calls on the Militia has capitally diminished our Agriculture in every Part of the State. . . . We are not in a Condition to raise Troops for the Defence of our Frontier, and if we were, our Exertions for the common cause have so effectually drained and exhausted us, that we should not have it in our Power to pay and subsist them. In short, Sir, without correspondent Exertions in other States and without Aid from those for whom we have not hesitated to sacrifice all, we shall soon approach to the Verge of Ruin.[24]

Clinton's alarm was familiar to Congress, which confronted throughout the war shortages of supplies, food, weaponry, and men. However, the governor's call was acutely disquieting, because if New York fell, then little could stop the mighty British army from descending from Canada and ransacking the newly independent nation.

While Clinton feared the collapse of the Patriot cause without a greater commitment from other states, the Mohawks worried about losing their lives, their villages, and their land. In the spring of 1779, some Mohawks informed Daniel Claus and General Haldimand that they wanted guarantees that their homes and land would be returned to them. General Haldimand promised to restore the Mohawks "at the Expence of Government, to the state they were in before" the war.[25] The general did not elaborate on the means of restoration or where. Captain Matthews, Haldimand's secretary, tried to further assuage their fears by having Major Ross, a British army regular, explain to the Mohawks that they could "rest assured that they will never be forgotten. The King will always consider and reward them as his faithful Children who have Manfully supported His and their own Rights."[26] Of course, Matthews could guarantee nothing. His assurance to the Mohawks was a matter of saving British face.

In an effort to secure peace and protect their claims to their homeland in the Mohawk Valley, the neutralist Little Abraham and three other Haudenosaunee headmen—Skenandon, Joseph Brant's former father-in-law, from Oneida; Agorondajats, or Good Peter, also an Oneida; and the Tiononderoge Mohawk Johannes Kryn Aneqwendahonji (a.k.a. Hance Kryn, White Hans, and John Guagua [Quaqua])—journeyed to Fort Niagara in February 1780 as emissaries of the American major general Philip Schuyler, a commissioner to indigenes in the United States and in the western territories.[27] Little Abraham tried to persuade John

Johnson and Haudenosaunee war chiefs at Niagara to let the eastern Haudenosaunees return home and live in peace, "to save themselves from Ruin," according to peace terms offered allegedly by the Continental Congress.[28] However, because their former castles were "in the Heart of [white American] settlements," and because white Americans had caused such depredations to their homes and kin, many of the refugee sachems dreaded returning to the Mohawk Valley and living under conditions of poverty and oppression. Suspecting that the group of four aided and abetted the Americans, and fearing duplicity if they let the sachems return home, the British authorities, on the cloaked advice of Joseph Brant, who had no love for the pious Little Abraham, incarcerated the four sachems in "the black hole," a series of cold, damp, underground stone vaults, where Little Abraham eventually died from exposure.[29]

Little Abraham's neutrality was for naught. As the war drew to a close, Great Britain and the United States confirmed the fears of the displaced Mohawks: no postwar provisions would be made for the Six Nations. Neither the Preliminary Articles of Peace, drafted November 30, 1782, nor the final peace treaty of 1783 made mention of the Haudenosaunees. Rather, England, according to the U.S. government, "asked for Peace, and gave up the Indian lands as part of the price." Great Britain agreed to cede all land in its former colonies as far west as the Mississippi River to the United States without any acknowledgment or recognition of Native sovereignty over these lands. Loyalist Mohawks would now have to find new permanent homes.[30]

The treaty outraged the Haudenosaunees. Captain Aaron Hill (a.k.a. Kanonraron), a Mohawk Loyalist who worked in partnership with Joseph Brant, spoke on behalf of the Haudenosaunees when he scolded British general Allan MacLean at Fort Niagara: "[The Haudenosaunees] were a free People subject to no Power upon Earth," Hill declared. "They were the faithful allies of the King of England, but not his subjects." Ergo, the king "had no right Whatever to grant away to the States of America, their Rights or properties without a manifest breach of all justice and Equity, and they would not submit to it." Besides, in days past, Hill argued, the Haudenosaunees had given the French and the British the *use* of the forts in their territory "for the Convenience of *Trade Only* without granting One Inch of Land, but What these forts stood upon." Moreover, what was the Treaty of 1768 for, he wondered? It established a permanent boundary between whites and indigenes. That England had given to the Americans land that belonged to the Haudenosaunees "Without their Consent, or Consulting them," Hill contended, "was an act of Cruelty and injustice that Christians *only* were capable of doing, that the Indians were incapable of acting so, to friends and Allies."[31] Hill did not mince words in letting the British commander know the depth of his disgust at Britain's betrayal. *They* were unchristian, evil, selfish, and uncivilized, not the Haudenosaunees. The Haudenosaunees could never be so corrupt, he implied. Hill also reminded MacLean that even the land on which the War Department built its forts belonged to the Haudenosaunees, who extended to the English government usufruct rights only to the soil beneath their foundations. The English mistook structures built on Native lands as improving it, which made the War Department de facto owners of the land in fee simple.

The English army officers and administrators in the Canadian Indian Department were entirely chagrined. They could not deny their government's negligence toward their Native allies. Even some Oneidas, who had remained loyal to the Americans and journeyed to Niagara in search of relatives, gleefully shamed the English officers when they informed them in front of the Mohawks that General Schuyler and the Americans intended to "Destroy the Six Nations, together with the Delawares, Hurons, and Shawanese, and also all the White People that served with the Indians, particularly Sir John Johnson and Colonel Butler." On hearing this, these officers may have conjured up images of another expensive war, especially after Joseph Brant threatened that the Haudenosaunees "will by & by perhaps . . . do something very outrageous, in order to retaliate [for England's] conduct to them."[32]

Governor Haldimand seemed sincere in his concern and guilt over the situation, for he confessed that he "Pit[ied] these People [Haudenosaunees], and should they Commit Outrages at giving up these Posts, it would by no means surprise me." General MacLean grew so fearful of the Haudenosaunees' wrath—especially that of Joseph Brant—that he asked Haldimand to detain Brant in Canada for as long as possible. Haldimand also feared that the warrior, "much better informed and instructed than any other Indians," would contact his Native allies and thereby "do [a] great deal of Mischief here at this Time." Yet Haldimand neither imprisoned nor detained Brant but, ironically, traveled with the warrior to the Bay of Quinte in search of land for the Mohawk refugees. After all, keeping one's enemy close is the best strategy for keeping the peace.[33]

Others in the Canadian Indian Department believed that they understood where the fault lay in the Britain-Haudenosaunee rift. Daniel Claus blamed the English Peace of Paris negotiating team for not informing their chief negotiator, Richard Oswald, an elderly statesman, of the new boundary line established by the 1768 Treaty of Fort Stanwix. Had communication been better, Claus contended, Oswald could have easily declared the territory west of that boundary line Native country and thus off-limits to white speculators and squatters, as it lay beyond England's control and authority.[34] However, Claus's contention seems more hopeful than realistic, for, as the historian Barbara Graymont has pointed out, conflicting cultural concepts over private property and sovereignty over the land led to a breakdown in understanding between Native Americans and the British. The British (and the Americans) recognized Native chattel property, but they were reluctant to acknowledge indigenous ownership of real estate, insisting instead that Native Americans residing among whites held the right of occupancy only to their property. Ironically, the Haudenosaunees held the same view of European and American occupants.[35] Alan Maclean, superintendent of Indian affairs at Niagara, reminded Haldimand that generations ago, the Haudenosaunees believed they had merely granted usufruct rights to the French and the British to build forts on their land for the purposes of trade only.[36] Although the Canajoharie Mohawks had conveyed tens of thousands of acres of their land to Sir William Johnson on his marriage to Molly Brant, they viewed Johnson as their trustee, not the new owner of their land.[37] And although many white New Yorkers had bought land from the Mohawks under shady circumstances over the years, Haudenosaunee tradition regarded their land as not alienable, not a salable commodity—at least not by a few individual Haudenosaunees. Land sales required the unanimous consent of a nation and sometimes the entire confederacy.[38]

As of the Proclamation of 1763 and the 1768 Treaty of Fort Stanwix, most whites viewed the Haudenosaunees as residing *in* the colony of New York but not *of* it. They no longer regarded the Haudenosaunees as owners of their own land with the right to sell it. The only lawful buying customer,

per the Proclamation of 1763, was the British Crown, which could then sell
it as it saw fit. Moreover, once indigenes sold their land to the Crown, they
forfeited their right of occupancy. Therefore, when Britain surrendered to
the United States in 1783, it relinquished all of its territory in the colonies,
including that part of New York that extended all the way up to and across
present-day upstate New York, the territory of the Haudenosaunee Confederacy. Britain never told the Haudenosaunees that it "owned" their land
in this way, and the Haudenosaunees, who had always viewed themselves
as independent of England and its expanding empire—the League nations
saw themselves as England's allies, not its dependents—never suspected
that a foreign nation would ever lay claim to the land they had occupied
for hundreds of years. The same relationship applied to the infant United
States. Article 9 of the Articles of Confederation authorized Congress to
negotiate treaties with sovereign indigenous nations "not members of any
state." However, a month before its formal gathering at Fort Stanwix in
October 1784, Congress abdicated its exclusive right to negotiate with the
Six Nations Haudenosaunee by deferring to the state of New York as the
preferred negotiator. In the process, New York sought to normalize peace
and trade relations with the Haudenosaunees but more significantly strove
to elicit land concessions as punishment. The Haudenosaunee delegation,
led by Joseph Brant, refused to cede its land to New York. However, weeks
later, Congress, despite exercising "temperance" toward New York's sense
of entitlement, demanded that the Six Nations give up all of its territory in
New York, save for a small amount of land to be awarded to their Oneida
and Tuscarora allies during the revolution, and cede all claims to land in
the Ohio country as well. This demand left the Haudenosaunees thun-
derstruck, for sixteen years earlier Sir John Johnson explained to them
at the Treaty of Fort Stanwix, "the right of Soil" belonged to them "as
sole proprietors," as agreed to by all the representatives from the various
colonies in attendance at the treaty.[39] From the postwar perspective of the
Haudenosaunees, then, the new Janus-faced nation revealed itself in the
same way that Captain Hill had painted the English: as corrupt Christians.

## "This Rude and Distant Quarter"

Hurt, embarrassed, and outraged, Joseph Brant, Isaac Hill, and others
knew that moving back to the Mohawk Valley would be impossible,

given the American victory and their now openly racist hostilities toward Native peoples. Many white Americans living in Tryone County would surely have approved of the Fourth of July 1779 toast made during the Sullivan Campaign: "Civilization, or death to all Savages!" Most Haudenosaunees were convinced that the Americans were bent on genocide, as the historian Jeffrey Ostler suggests, and as such wished to, as U.S. commissioners expressed at Fort Pitt in 1778, "extirpate the Indians" from the earth and lay claim to their lands.[40] Given this perception, Brant negotiated with Canadian officials, including Governor Haldimand and Sir John Johnson, for land for the Mohawks in Canada. After declining land in the Genesee Valley offered by the Senecas, Brant indicated to Haldimand and to Johnson that he and his fellow country persons would be willing to settle either in the region of the St. Lawrence River or in the area around the Grand River west of Lake Ontario.[41]

On the recommendation of Daniel Claus, the Mohawks as a nation initially accepted the Canadian government's offer of a tract of land about fifty miles west of Cataraqui (renamed Kingston in 1788) on the Bay of Quinte on the north side of Lake Ontario that would become known as Tyendinaga. There, they proposed to first build a "saw mill to facilitate making their Hutts in the Manner . . . at home"—probably log dwellings initially—and to plow the ground the following spring (1784), with the clear intention of practicing horticulture. This land, however, belonged to the Mississaugas. Therefore, the Canadian government first had to secure their permission to let the Mohawks settle there permanently.[42]

The Senecas, fearing that the confederacy would be stretched too thin geographically for mutual defense, asked the Mohawks not to remove themselves so far away. Brant acquiesced to their request, perhaps to avoid conflict with John Deserontyon and his followers, former residents of Tiononderoge, but also to appease his sister and powerful matron, Molly Brant, and others of Canajoharie, who resided in Lachine during the war and now lived at Tyendinaga. Brant asked Haldimand to find land closer to the western Haudenosaunees, pointing out that the land along the Grand River, also "commonly called *Ours* [Ouse]," located between Lakes Ontario and Erie, seemed like an attractive spot. He knew the area well; the Mohawks and other Haudenosaunees had hunted there in years past. The Grand River and other creeks teemed with fish, and the region boasted of well-drained farmland and a rich supply of timber. Moreover, Brant found the isolation of "this rude and distant quarter" appealing and, thus, ideal for their new homes. Haldimand concurred. He confided in a letter to Daniel Claus that he had always considered "the Mohawks as the first Nation deserving the attention of Government" and that he had been "particularly interested for their welfare and reestablishment."[43] The governor was able to convince the Mississaugas, the proprietors of this territory also, to sell almost three million acres of this land for less than a mere 1,200 pounds—a little more than $190,000 today—"to the King our Father, for the use of His people, and our Brethren the Six Nations."[44] The Mohawks and other Haudenosaunee émigrés were to occupy somewhere between five hundred thousand and almost one million acres of land extending "Six Miles deep from each Side of the [Grand] River beginning at Lake Erie, and extending in that Proportion to the Head of the said River, which them & their Posterity are to enjoy for ever."[45]

Not all Mohawks, however, wanted to live along the Grand River. John Deserontyon and his followers felt safer on the ninety-two thousand acres at Tyendinaga on the Bay of Quinte.[46] The location was close enough to a white Loyalist community for trade and protection but far enough away to not feel pinched by meddling whites. However, over time, white Loyalist settlements would encroach on Tyendinaga as the Canadian government repossessed more and more of the ninety-two thousand acres. The whittling away of their land commenced in 1792 with the Gun Shot Treaty, by which the Tyendinagans began the process of surrendering their land bit by bit for the use of white Loyalists "from the East," who were "very poor and hungry and some of them . . . starving." The Canadian government gave its "Royal word" but no deed to leave in perpetuity to the Tyendinagans land that stretched from the shore of Lake Ontario back "as far as you can hear a shot gun" and land a few feet back from the shores of all lakes, rivers, and creeks, at the mouths of said waterways, and the nearby islands in Lake Ontario for the purposes of hunting and fishing. In exchange, the government promised to give the Tyendinagans "supplies of Clothing, blankets, etc." for "as long as the Sun lasts and Rivers flow and as long as the grass grows." Most often, the Tyendinagans received nothing in exchange for these "very sweet" requests for more and more land.[47]

Despite the steady dispossession of land, most Mohawks at Tyendinaga preferred living there, as it kept them apart from those Mohawks by whom Deserontyon felt betrayed during the war, most notably Brant and his followers. Deserontyon informed Sir John Johnson that they "could not depend on our Friends (I meant Capt. Brants party) and you see how they have acted so shamefull a part in giving up or sacrificing their Country."[48] One's residence at either of the two new Mohawk settlements would soon stand for one's political allegiance to either Brant (Grand River) or Deserontyon (Tyendinaga), as well as nudge one's faith performance in a particular direction.

Additionally, some Mohawk families refused to abandon the Mohawk Valley altogether. A few families returning from Kahnawake, along with remnants of Oneidas and Tuscaroras, built hastily a few small, drafty, makeshift longhouses on the outskirts of Schenectady. During a visit to this village in December 1780, the Marquis de Chastellux described their dwellings as

> an assemblage of miserable huts in the woods . . . like our barracks in time of war, or like those built in vineyards or orchards, when the fruit is ripe and has to be watched at night. The framework . . . is covered with a matted roof, but is well lined within by a quantity of bark. . . . [I]n the middle of the hut is the fireplace, from which the smoke ascends by an opening in the roof. On each side of the fire are raised two platforms, which run the length of the hut and serve as beds; these are covered with skins and bark.[49]

Sadly, those Mohawks who opted to return to the Mohawk Valley could not—or chose not to—live in their former abodes, some of them framed houses, which white families now occupied. Instead, they were forced to hastily build miserable, porous longhouses without the aid of white carpenters. Although several white residents in Schenectady expressed their shock and pity to Philip Schuyler over the Mohawks' terrible living conditions, fearing that the Native families could not "pass the winter" in their huts, New York officials offered the Mohawks little assistance, hoping, no doubt, that they would simply leave and join their brethren in Canada.[50]

Thus, following the American Revolution, the Mohawks found themselves scattered from the Mohawk Valley to the north shore of Lake Ontario to the Grand River region between Lake Ontario and Lake Erie. The largest area of settlement at the Grand River contained more land than Brant believed the Mohawks were capable of improving by themselves. Although the settlement was for Native residents only, Brant asked Governor Haldimand to permit white Loyalists, which included some of Brant's friends in the Indian Department, some soldiers in his militia, and former white neighbors, some now "kin" through "marriage" to Mohawk women and fathering biracial children, to settle nearby in order to act, according to Brant, as good examples to the Mohawks and other Haudenosaunees living in the vicinity. More important, obligations of mutuality and reciprocity could now be realized in this new multiracial imagined community. The Mohawks would not only subsist on their traditional means of hunting, fishing, and planting, but also live on the rental income from white neighbors who would lease land from them and thus allow the Mohawks to participate in the new market economy. Brant foresaw that over time, the growing number of white neighbors would cause the game in the area to melt away, which would force his community to practically give up their former subsistence economy and rely increasingly on income from land sales and rentals. Actually, Brant sought to become a large landlord, like his white patron, Sir William Johnson, which the headman believed would benefit him as well as his community. His critics, both Mohawks and whites, called his plan self-interested, greedy, and covetous. While Brant did strive to live richly like his patron, arguably he also was concerned over the future welfare of the Grand River community, not just monetarily but politically as well. His larger goal was to establish personal and communal ownership over the land on which the remnants of the Haudenosaunee Confederacy could gather and restore their sovereignty as equals to the British Crown—with him as the titular leader, of course. Exercising dominion over the land, Brant reasoned, would validate Haudenosaunee independence from and equivalency to Britain. His efforts sparked outrage among many Mohawks across the diaspora and erupted into full-blown confrontations between him, his Mohawk brethren, Native allies to the west, and Canadian officials to the east. At stake stood the future of land, sovereignty, authority, race, and faith in the new Mohawk communities.[51]

## "To Have Some White People Settlers amongst Us"

After the American Revolution, many white Americans believed that the "problem" with Native peoples was that they lived in a harsh, wild environment that needed to be tamed. Hence, they lacked a full appreciation for the value of improved private property. Genesis 1:28 guided the lives of many God-fearing Americans: "Be fruitful, and multiply, and replenish the earth and subdue it: and have dominion over . . . everything that moveth upon the earth." Native peoples did not control the resources of the earth, such Americans complained, but rather merely existed in it. One English commentator declared that Native peoples had to be infused with "a just notion of Property, of morality, of Religion, and of the happiness they and their Families would derive from fixed Residence, and the pursuits of Agriculture and arts." Intermarrying whites would also help, some reasoned. Thomas Jefferson found biracial Native-white children "fine mixtures." In 1808, he told an audience of Native emissaries representing several nations, "You will mix with us by marriage, your blood will run in our veins, and will spread with us over this great island."[52] For Jefferson, intermarriage would achieve a desired end—the quiet extirpation of Native Americans. "Indian problem" solved. Curiously but explicably, Jefferson did not feel the same way about blacks as a racial group, which he characterized as immutably ignorant, unattractive, and inferior, and thus undesirable candidates for intermarriage. Moreover, through black-white intermarriages, white planters risked losing their enslaved laborers and thus their wealth, hence the need to justify the purity of white womanhood to demonize black male suitors.[53]

Brant felt similarly about Native uplift through private property and Native-white relations. He purportedly once told Aaron Burr at dinner in Philadelphia that the best route to improving indigenes was through "intermarriage and amalgamation." One may surely read Brant's statement as self-loathing and anti-Native American. On the other hand, Brant's real purpose, arguably, may have been to protect Native peoples from further evisceration and *not* have them slowly disappear through intermarriage but rather to ensure survivance as new indigenes. Although some of his nieces, Molly's biracial daughters, did cross the racial divide and marry white men, Brant viewed marriage as accruing certain benefits through kinship ties. He watched Molly extend and amplify her influence across Iroquoia and throughout parts of Anglo-America through her relationship with Sir William Johnson. One's phenotype did not need to erase one's racial identity or identification. Thus, in Brant's view, kinship

ties to white America need not destroy Native peoples' lives and identities but rather would enrich them. Furthermore, Brant conveyed to
Reverend Samuel Kirkland, one of his instructors at Wheelock's charity
school and the Oneidas' preacher, his belief in equality before God: "The
same supreme power created both them [indigenes] and the white people, but perhaps for different purposes," which he left unexplained. He
added that, regrettably, Native peoples viewed white people as "aim[ing]
at their destruction." As such, Brant believed that indigenes desperately
needed to adjust in order to survive, but that "they must first be convinced that a Change will not place them in a worse situation."[54]

Brant tried to avoid a worse situation by implementing his own vision
for revitalizing, stabilizing, and improving life at the Grand River. His
program entailed introducing or reestablishing English institutions, such
as the Anglican Church, an English grammar school, an order of Masons,
slavery, and tenancy. He reasoned that these institutions, enjoyed by
Britons and Americans of the middling and upper ranks, would encourage self-sufficiency and personal prosperity. Most important to realizing
self-reliance was having sovereignty over the more than six hundred
thousand acres of land in and around the Grand River. The Mohawks
and other Haudenosaunees living there would trade in part of their subsistence economy—hunting—and live on annuities from leases and sales
of their land to white Loyalists. Meanwhile, all Native persons living
there should become literate Anglicans.

Brant learned from his late brother-in-law and patron Sir William
Johnson that the good life entailed profiting from the labor of others. Like
Johnson, Brant liked living large as lord of the manor. By 1800, Brant
owned at least two nicely furnished two-story homes, attended by a retinue of enslaved workers, who served guests tea in the afternoons on fine
china and poured the rum, brandy, and port and Madeira wines at dinner. In 1792, one guest at Brant's home in Brantford observed that "the
servants dressed in their best apparel. Two slaves attended the table, the
one in scarlet, the other in coloured clothes, with silver buckles in their
shoes and ruffles, and every other part of their apparel in proportion."
After "drinking pretty freely at dinner," the guests retired to a nearby
lodge to dance war dances and "Scotch reels." Shortly before dawn, they
retired to comfortable beds with fine linen and English blankets.[55] Proceeds from some land sales and a pension from the Crown for his services

in the war permitted Brant to maintain this lavish standard of living. From Brant's perspective, his prosperity only benefited the community because mutuality, reciprocity, and hospitality required him as a head-man to share his wealth.[56] Canadian officials and some Native headmen thought otherwise; a "real Mohawk," they seemed to think, did not behave like an independent, free Anglo-Irish lord of a manor.

Canadian officials opposed Brant's plan to make the Mohawks land-lords, for they regarded them as their dependents, not their equals, and certainly not their betters. Brant reminded Haldimand that the Mohawk nation was sovereign and explained that he and his brethren considered the Grand River land grant only *partial* compensation for losses incurred "by the Rebellion." In addition to the land, they expected to be com-pensated for the loss of property in an "amount to near Sixteen thousand Pounds, New York Currency" (about $2.5 million today). Their losses were so deep and their consequent impoverishment so broad, Brant claimed, that they expected not to make a new start "unless assisted by Government." Haldimand agreed with Brant in principle, including set-ting aside land for white Loyalists, or for "any future Purpose," recom-mending "to His Majesty in the strongest Terms that Indemnification be made for their Losses."[57]

However, Brant and Haldimand disagreed on the principal substance of governmental assistance. To Haldimand, support meant providing the displaced Haudenosaunees with tools and any other essential mate-rial support "for the speedy and happy re-establishment of such of the Six Nations as have been driven from their former Habitation."[58] For Brant, governmental support meant an outright land grant, over which the Mohawks claimed sovereignty, with the legal right and authority to retain or dispose of said land as they saw fit. William Claus, the new dep-uty superintendent and son of Brant's old friend Daniel Claus, rejected outright Brant's proposal to divide the land into small private Mohawk-owned farms, calling the idea "a thing not possible," for indigenes held land traditionally "in common." By the mid-1790s, Brant complained to Canadian authorities that the Mohawks could no longer get a living from farming and hunting because the men were not interested in that pursuit, the land was not that fertile, and game had declined, making hunting difficult. Consequently, the Grand River Mohawks preferred to receive moneys from the rent or sale of lands. If this would not be permitted, he

warned, his brethren would grow poor and, consequently, were prepared
to return to the United States, where they were promised an annuity for
damages suffered in the war.[59]

Canadian officials argued that the Grand River settlement agreement
held no provision for "the Indians to lease their lands," which Governor Simcoe called "highly injurious to their Interests" and "illegal in
respect to the Customs and Laws of Great Britain."[60] Daniel Claus of
the Indian Department confirmed Simcoe's position when he told Brant
that according to the Proclamation of 1763, Native peoples could not
dispose of land to private individuals. In an effort to curtail fraudulent
purchases of Native lands in the future, Parliament inserted in its 1763
proclamation, "We do . . . require, that no private Person do presume
to make any Purchase from the said Indians of any Lands reserved to the
said Indians . . . but that, if at any Time any of the said Indians should
be inclined to dispose of the said Lands, the same shall be Purchased only
for Us [Crown and Parliament] in our Name, at some publick Meeting
or Assembly of the said Indians." In other words, Simcoe and Claus
explained to Brant that the Mohawks could not "possibly have Kings
subjects to be [their] Tennants." However, if the Six Nations surrendered
their title to the land as occupiers, not owners, then "his Majesty would
grant *to such persons as they [Mohawks] would recommend* such Tracts
as they were desirous of conveying."[61] To Simcoe and Claus, it did not
matter that the Proclamation of 1763 pertained to Native lands in the
original thirteen colonies, not land west of the 1768 Fort Stanwix line in
Canada.

Rather than follow up on this with Brant, Governor Simcoe left for
England, leaving Peter Russell, the new administrator, or president, of
Upper Canada (1796–99), in charge to deal with Brant. Russell suspected that Brant wanted to install tenants unfriendly to Canada and
Britain, and thus was immediately skeptical about permitting "considerable Bodies of Aliens (of whose fidelity I have every reason to be
suspicious) to obtain so large a Property in the very Heart of it, by which
they may throw open a Wide Door by the Mouth of that River for the
Introduction of their Countrymen whenever they shall form the Design
of wresting the Country from us."[62] Mindful of England's burgeoning
conflict with France, Russell not only feared that republicans would
overrun Canada, which would be detrimental to a region that respected

English law, Parliamentary government, the king, and his empire, but also worried about exposing Canada to "an Indian & perhaps an American War to which your Excellency too well knows our present strength & Resources are very inadequate."[63]

When Russell and other Canadian officials rejected repeatedly his claims of sovereignty over the Grand River reserve, Brant journeyed to Philadelphia, the new republic's capital, to register his complaint with Robert Liston, the British foreign minister. There, in January 1797, Brant pressured Liston by offering the services of the Haudenosaunees to the French "if he [Brant] did not obtain redress." Brant went so far as to dine with the French minister Pierre August Ader in Philadelphia and offered the diplomat his services. Liston saw Brant "so determined, so able, and so artful" in delivering his "earnest Complaints" that the British foreign minister, fearful of "the possible Event of an Insurrection in the Province . . . thought it right, even at the risk of appearing Officious," to "*not* appear to reject the part he [Brant] wished me to play."[64]

Once Liston learned that Brant had also stopped in Albany to meet with New York's Indian commissioners, from whom he and Deserontyon accepted $1,600 (about $32,000 today) in exchange for land claims there, he believed that he had no choice but to recommend to Russell that he gratify Brant. Russell took umbrage at "Captn. Brants Temerity in charging the Executive part of this Government with being *in a Combination from Selfish Motives to prevent him obtaining Justice.*" Russell objected personally to Brant's pressure, for, as he informed a colleague, "with respect to Indians in General, I have ever treated them with Humanity and Attention."[65]

According to one memoirist, Brant, assured by Liston of Russell's cooperation, took three hundred warriors to York (Toronto), now the capital of Upper Canada, and "extorted from the Council a Declaration that they would confirm the past [land] Sales, and urge His Majesty's assent to their future disposition of the Lands." Russell believed, according to the writer, "that the Council drove him to the Wall, and compelled his assent," which was the wrong thing to do, Russell worried, as the Haudenosaunees now knew "that the King's Government, unprotected by regular troops," could be "bullied into such measures, as they think proper to propose."[66]

Russell and the Canadian government acquiesced and sanctioned some Mohawk land transfers along the Grand River, but only through three Loyalists appointed as trustees for the Mohawks. Brant agreed to have David Smith, the surveyor general; Alexander Stewart, Brant's attorney who married a granddaughter of Sir William Johnson; and the Indian Department's William Claus.[67]

Just as Russell predicted, these few early land sales opened the gates to a flood of white settlers, especially from the States, causing Canadian officials to contemplate at one point requiring non-Canadian purchasers to take loyalty oaths. The Canadian government soon refused to permit any future sales. Brant agreed to sell all future lands to the Crown first, which would then resell it to white British settlers, although Brant did not always comply with this agreement. Tragically, but perhaps not surprisingly, only a small amount of the proceeds from the initial sales trickled down into Mohawk and other Haudenosaunee hands. Most moneys—thousands of pounds—were siphoned off by William Claus and others or wound up in English coffers, especially that of bankers. Meanwhile, many Mohawks and other Haudenosaunees objected vigorously to the presence of white settlers in the Grand River region. John Deserontyon and his followers at the Bay of Quinte felt betrayed by Brant and denounced him for acting so shamefully in "sacrificing their Country." At an 1800 council meeting at Tyendinaga, Deserontyon recounted the pique that he and his Mohawk brethren had long felt toward Brant: about a dozen years earlier, two Grand River Mohawk warriors, Captain Isaac Hill and his son, Captain Aaron, former compatriots of Brant, had become so upset with Brant's wheeling and dealing that they intended to kill him. However, before carrying out their murderous act in 1788, they complained to Sir Guy Carleton, a.k.a. Lord Dorchester, the governor-in-chief of British North America (1786–96). In turn, Carleton accused the Hill family of being troublemakers. The Hills maintained that Brant was responsible for their dispute, which was "in consequence of Capt. Brant bringing white People to settle on their lands." Carleton promised to fix that: he would simply "order all the white people off the Lands." Not surprisingly, Carleton did not or could not follow through on his promise.[68]

The Mohawks on the Bay of Quinte, distrusting white Americans in the wake of the war, bitterly opposed Brant's plan to encourage white Loyalists to live among their relatives. However, they were not opposed to white institutions in their midst; they had quickly reestablished the Anglican Church with little dissent, yet wished to have limited contact with white people. This self-imposed isolation would not last; in time, the congregation at Tyendinaga would become multiracial. In 1791, John Stuart, the SPG's missionary to the Mohawks at Fort Hunter, preached from time to time at Tyendinaga "to a numerous audience of whites & Indians."[69]

As the product of a Christian education, Brant also endorsed what he saw as the benefits provided by the Anglican Church, which he described as "highly promotive of morality and the Christian Virtues among [the Mohawk] people." To organize a church to his advantage, Brant often recommended to the SPG his friends to preach the Gospel at Brantford, whom the society rejected, declaring them unfit to fill the post and Brant, as a Mohawk, unqualified to make such recommendations. The refusal of English authorities to see Brant as an equal may have led the headman to stress the importance of literacy, acquired most efficiently through the church. For example, when Brant negotiated land deals with William Claus and asked him for written copies of his speeches, Claus denied his requests, claiming that orality was good enough for the Mohawks. Claus thought it best to keep the Haudenosaunees in a state of ignorant dependency as long as possible. Brant, desperate to break the shackles of illiteracy, believed literacy would enable his brethren to identify and prevent fraud committed by Claus and other Canadian officials. As the historian Alan Taylor implies, Brant believed that a pious, literate Mohawk population was the best defense against unscrupulous white land speculators and colonial officials.[70]

The acquisition of literacy appears to have been a central reason for establishing churches in the two Mohawk diaspora communities. Proponents of literacy taught through religious instruction by Mohawk-born speakers—or if not Mohawk by birth, then by adoption—trusted that such schoolmasters and catechists would more likely acquiesce to the inclinations of the parents. Thus, they hoped that reading and writing taught by their brethren would not only promote goodness, harmony, and stability in their new communities, but also arm them with the power to foster change and ensure survivance.

**"A Measure Necessary for the Promotion of Virtue and Order": Performing Christianity at the Bay of Quinte**

Writing in 1781 from Montreal about the impact of the American Revolution on his ministry, John Stuart, the last SPG-appointed missionary to Fort Hunter, reflected on the utter confusion created by the war. He remarked that for more than a year after the Declaration of Independence, he continued to perform divine services at Fort Hunter "without omitting the prayers for the King, as prescribed in the Litany." As a consequence, he "incurred the Penalty of High-Treason, by the new Laws," which local Committees of Safety had passed that compelled Church of England ministers to either take an oath of allegiance to the new independent nation or forswear praying for King George. Yet, a bit later in his letter, he laments, "I have not preached a sermon since the Declaration of Independence." This seeming contradiction over *when* he preached after July 4, 1776, may be rooted in the *where*—at Fort Hunter or at St. Peter's Episcopal Church in Albany. Regardless, the white Americans living in Tryone County regarded Stuart as "particularly obnoxious" because of his "connexion with the Johnson family"—he frequently preached, baptized children, married adults, and buried the dead at Johnstown—"and his relations to the Indians." Consequently, local law officials placed Stuart under house arrest in Schenectady for more than three years, during which time local whites ransacked his home and plundered his church at Fort Hunter by putting it to various uses, including as "a Tavern," with "the Barrel of Rum placed in [*sic*] the Reading Desk." At another time, it was a stable, and still later it served as a Fort "to protect," according to Stuart, "a Set of as great villains [Patriots] as ever disgraced Humanity."[71]

Stuart had to pay his jailers the exorbitant bail of about 400 pounds (more than two years' salary, almost $75,000 today) to be allowed to leave Schenectady for Montreal, taking his several slaves with him. There, the former residents of Tiononderoge living at Lachine petitioned Stuart to live among them as formerly. He declined their offer, citing his own family's needs, which could be met more easily in Kingston. Moreover, he felt compelled to take the job of chaplain to the British troops. Nevertheless, Stuart was able to preach to the Mohawks living at Tyendinaga "occasionally," about "once a month."[72]

During Stuart's long absences, Paulus Peters Saghsanowana Anahario, the former literate schoolmaster at Canajoharie, taught the Mohawk children at Tyendinaga. Thomas, a pious Tiononderoge Mohawk, who had once served as Stuart's clerk (and may have been the one who lived in Stuart's house for a time), assisted Paulus. Together, they taught the children the Mohawk alphabet from scraps of paper, until Daniel Claus, who oversaw matters in the village, provided them with primers and prayer books that he had translated into Mohawk. Many Mohawks and whites believed that Claus was the only person, "White or Indian," with the "competent knowledge of both languages" to have accomplished this task. Not even Joseph Brant could match Claus's translation and interpretation skills. Aaron Hill thanked Claus for sending to the refugee community at Niagara, largely consisting of the former residents of Canajoharie, copies of the primers and prayer books. They would keep the spirit of Christianity alive there, Hill assured him, where the Protestant faith was "upheld among us." There on some Sundays, Thomas read prayers in a log house that Brant had arranged to have "built for them to meet in for the purpose of Divine Worship."[73]

While Deserontyon and other Mohawks at the Bay of Quinte wished not to live with whites, they desired to live within trading distance of Cataraqui, the white Loyalist community about fifty miles to the east, roughly the same distance as Tiononderoge from Albany, where they could have occasional access to "a missionary, Schoolmaster, and Church." Although they built several houses between May and July 1784 in their new village, the Tyendinagans had trouble finishing by themselves their schoolhouse, even though they were ready to receive their schoolmaster, Paulus, and his scholars. Additionally, they also had trouble completing construction on "a small wooden Church" for want of glass and nails. Deserontyon and his brethren were too proud to solicit the skills of white carpenters. Thus, Mohawk mothers at Tyendinaga besieged the Reverend John Stuart whenever he visited their village and insisted that he baptize their children. When bad weather or ill health delayed Stuart, or if the mothers could not wait, they took their children to Stuart in Cataraqui. During the early summer months of 1784, Stuart baptized 107 Mohawks at Tyendinaga.[74] Like the women in Kateri Tekakwitha's sodality at Kahnawake in the 1670s, the adults and adolescents at Tyendinaga who were unmistakably marked with the imprimatur of "Christian" may have felt reborn in receiving the sacraments in their reincarnated, consecrated community in a new land.

In addition to administering the sacrament of baptism, Reverend John Stuart made teaching literacy at Tyendinaga a high priority. He recommended to the SPG that it install "Lewis Vincent, a young Lorette Indian," as schoolmaster and catechist there, for which he would be paid seventeen pounds, ten shillings per year, about half the going salary for white SPG schoolmasters. Stuart avowed that Vincent was a good candidate for the job; he had assisted him at his school, most likely in Montreal, for several months, which enabled the priest to form a "favourable opinion of his morals and capacity." Furthermore, Vincent "underst[oo]d their language, and . . . had a tolerable education, and a competent knowledge of the French and English languages." Stuart overstated this claim, for the young teacher was not fluent in Mohawk. Vincent hailed from Lorette, a multiethnic Haudenosaunee refugee community near Quebec dominated historically by Catholic Hurons. Although his Native language was Iroquoian, he grappled with Mohawk because of the linguistic distances among the various Iroquoian dialects. Nevertheless, Vincent appeared to have a gift for languages; over the next three years, he, according to Stuart, made "amazing progress in acquiring the [Mohawk] language," during which time he and Stuart carried on the translation project begun by Joseph Brant, beginning with a translation of "St. Matthew's Gospel." Stuart believed that the young Vincent would provide exceptional service "among his brethren in making translations, and otherwise promoting an increase of knowledge among them."[75]

In noting that "Mr. Vincent is very diligent" in carrying out his duties, Stuart implied that the young acolyte helped him baptize the 107 Native communicants between May and July 1784, just as the Mohawks at Tyendinaga were laying the foundation of their community. Nevertheless, in 1788, four years after Vincent commenced teaching, Sir John Johnson of the Indian Department decided to withhold the schoolmaster's salary. Neither Johnson nor Stuart offered an explanation as to why. Perhaps Vincent had already stopped teaching because of his low salary; Stuart explained to Johnson that it would be difficult to replace Vincent, for "no person will undertake the charge, unless the Indian Department will add something to the Society's bounty."[76]

In 1789, a year after Vincent's departure, Stuart found at Tyendinaga "some confusion," his euphemism for apostasy. The priest was so unhappy with the state of affairs there that he "did not administer the

Lord's Supper as usual" during one visit.[77] Stuart blamed the backsliding there on Vincent's absence. However, a more likely explanation is Tyendinagan protest toward Stuart's frequent absences and his new hire to replace Vincent, "Indian schoolmaster" Peter. Stuart regarded Peter as "tolerably qualified," despite one problem that surely the Tyendinagans frowned upon: he drank too much "to give regular attendance" to his teaching.[78]

Because the Tyendinagans were adamant about having a Native schoolmaster, Stuart hired in 1791 an individual whom he thought would be satisfactory to them: John Norton, a Cherokee-Scot, who identified as Mohawk and whom the Mohawks adopted. Joseph Brant was both Norton's patron and his "uncle." However, after teaching for a few weeks, Norton grew bored and frustrated and left his post to fish and hunt, the first of many such self-granted sabbaticals. In a short time, Norton resigned, citing a feeling of confinement and low pay as the reasons for quitting. Stuart elaborated a little more on why Norton may have resigned: "the Indians expect that a Schoolmaster should be more under their direction than most men are willing to submit to." Stuart's comment suggests that the Tyendinagans seized control of the educational project in their community and sought to instruct Norton on how and what to teach their children, to which he took umbrage.[79]

As Tyendinaga continued to reestablish itself as a community that privileged self-reliance, self-determination, racial isolation, and piety, Native and non-Native in-migration from the Mohawk Valley brought the unintended consequence of racial heterogeneity to the Bay of Quinte. In the fall of 1790, Tyendinaga received an influx of seventy Mohawk individuals, led by two headmen, from Tiononderoge, whom Stuart calculated represented the remains of his Fort Hunter congregation. He counted ten communicants among the seventy. As more whites moved into the region, Stuart found himself preaching to a growing multiracial congregation. In the late fall of 1791, he baptized "17 [white?] children" and "administered the Sacrament to 11 Indian Communicants & married 1 couple."[80]

Between 1788 and 1791, the Tyendinagans made slow but steady progress on their small chapel "of framed timbers & boarded," erected by themselves "without any assistance from the Public." In 1791, the building was "covered, glazed, & floored," but still had "neither pulpit nor pews." Thus, Stuart hired white carpenters to build "the pulpit, reading-desk, communion-table, etc.," and arranged "to erect a cupola for the Bell on the roof." However, the Tyonderogans rebuffed him on his offer of a cupola, choosing "to wait a little longer & have a steeple raised at the end of the Church . . . at their own expense, or rather with their own hands."[81] The baptized Mohawks at Tyendinaga, well informed about building designs and plans, took charge of their own church in ways that left Stuart mildly peeved.

Nevertheless, Deserontyon's snub of Stuart does not mean that the headman was too proud to accept government assistance, especially in the form of reparations. Before leaving Lachine, the governor of Canada awarded the Tiononderoge Mohawks 6,430 pounds (over $1 million today) and roughly 800 pounds (over $125,000 today) to Deserontyon alone for losses suffered in the late war. Moreover, in 1797, Deserontyon accompanied Brant to Albany to cede their land in the Mohawk Valley to the state of New York. The two men returned to Canada with peltry and other goods worth about $1,000 (over $20,000 today) to be distributed among their respective followers, plus $600 (over $12,000 today) to cover their personal travel expenses. Scandal erupted when the Kahnawage Mohawks near Montreal accused Brant of pocketing their proceeds and charged Deserontyon with neglecting to disclose his travel money. Some Mohawks were further outraged that Deserontyon, after itemizing his expenses, distributed only $200 ($4,000 today) worth of goods rather than $500 worth—half of what they received in Albany—among the scores of families on the Bay of Quinte.[82]

Deserontyon's apparent secrecy over money compounded tensions among some Tyendinagans over the increasing racial heterogeneity of their community. With so many white Loyalists now setting up residence in the area and attending chapel at Tyendinaga, Stuart hired Mr. Bininger to replace Norton and teach both white and Native children in English at thirty pounds per year. Bininger was the first of many white schoolmasters to share teaching responsibilities with Native teachers there throughout the 1790s. Stuart described Bininger as "a sober industrious man, & sufficiently attentive to this duty," who gave "general satisfaction." However, the white teacher also seemed uninspired and uninspiring. Clearly clueless about Haudenosaunee etiquette and parenting, Bininger complained "loudly of their [Mohawk parents'] indolence & neglect," adding "that they cannot be prevailed upon to send their children regularly to school." The white teacher found the situation so discouraging that he entertained "serious thoughts of leaving them." With Bininger's complaints in hand, Stuart "called a Council of their Chief men & compromised the dissension between them & the [school]Master, & they have promised to fulfill their engagements more punctually for the future, & to send their children more constantly to school."[83] The parents answered Stuart with a yes that was a no, for they never quite warmed to the white outsider, Bininger, to make him an insider. In addition to his race as well as distractions caused by the exigencies of personal resentments over Deserontyon's leadership and the stresses caused by white in-migration, the physical layout of Tyendinaga may also explain why so few parents sent their children to his school. The community's residential pattern consisted of "one continuous row of houses fronting the Bay for the distance of 4 or 5 miles." Separated by great distances, Bininger's Native pupils could not attend regularly his school, which was not a boarding school.[84] Regardless, Bininger could do little to excite Mohawk parents or children.

Persistent illness may have been another factor that explains the decline in participation in Bininger's school as well as at the Mohawk Anglican Church. In the late summer of 1793, Stuart found the Tyendinaga community "very sickly & so circumstanced in other respects that he could not as usual administer the Sacrament." New white residents may have been the vectors of unshakable illness at Tyendinaga that affected so many. By the mid-1790s, both Native and white residents suffered from of an "epidemical complaint," described as an "intermittent & dangerous fever" that "prevailed almost over the whole Province," which caused the "Mohawks, like the other Indian Tribes, [to diminish] very fast."[85] In the spring of 1795, only seven Mohawks remained firmly in the church as communicants out of at least a score to whom Stuart administered communion five years earlier. Furthermore, as the number of Mohawk scholars continued to shrink, Bininger offered to resign. Either Stuart sought to save face for his mistake in hiring Bininger, or Bininger sought more profitable employment, for Stuart claimed that the schoolmaster's dissatisfaction with the Tyendinaga Mohawks lay not so much with him or the Mohawks as with his "partiality to the Methodists," whose needs Stuart believed Bininger now sought to meet.[86]

Now out of desperation, Stuart hired ill-advisedly two white school-master to replace Bininger—Robert Tait, "a native of Edinburgh," whom Stuart described as "a man of competent abilities & good moral character," who took one look at Tyendinaga and beat it back to Montreal, and William Bell, who knew no Mohawk and from whom the Tyendinagans kept their distance.[87] Stuart felt great pressure to reengage the Tyendinagans. Yet he did not understand the degree to which the Mohawks were suffering from trauma and thus needed to disengage from white society in order to recuperate. Tyendinaga could be described as a liminal community, one that existed culturally between nativism and inclusion. They welcomed white priests conditionally, but had no need for white schoolmasters. Like many indigenes in southeastern New England in the mid-eighteenth century, the Tyendinagans dictated their relationship to the church and the school, which they used as instruments for self-actualization, spiritual and ideational sustenance, and survival as well as survivance.[88]

For some Mohawks, Tyendinaga did not provide satisfactory strategies for living in their new world. Hence, some began to shift their attention to Brant's Grand River settlement, where they believed sharing the profits of the emergent economy might better sustain them. Reverend Stuart reported that many Tyendinagans had been "principally induced by the share they expect of the annual income arising from the sale of Lands granted by the Government to the Mohawks at the close of the American war." In 1797, Brant projected that the sale of lands and the interest generated by the revenue to be about 5,000 pounds annually (over $650,000 today), which many found far more compelling than rebuilding a Christian community by their own hands on the Bay of Quinte.[89]

## Mammon and Faith on the Grand River

During his first few years in Canada, Reverend Stuart commuted between the Bay of Quinte and the Niagara—Grand River region, a roughly four-hundred-mile round-trip. In 1784, during one of his initial visits to Fort Niagara to service the Canajoharie Mohawks living at that time nine miles from Niagara, Stuart baptized seventy-eight Native infants and five adults, "the latter having been previously instructed by his Indian clerk," Thomas. Many Mohawk hearers may have been seduced by Stuart's sermon, probably preached in the log chapel that Brant insisted be built for them in 1781, which focused "on the nature and design of Baptism." Although his words are lost to us and the thoughts of the Mohawks are unknown, Stuart claimed that his message "was very affecting"; even "the windows" of the chapel "were crowded with those, who could not find room within the walls." Before ending his stay with the displaced Canajohariens, Stuart baptized at different times "24 [additional] children, and married 6 couple[s]."[90] Perhaps we should read Mohawk mothers and parents submitting themselves and their children to baptism not only as expressions of spiritual and personal rebirth and renewal, but also as gestures of reciprocity that affirmed their relationship with Stuart and the British empire.

At the Grand River in early June 1788, an eager Native audience awaited Stuart. There he preached and administered communion to 16 communicants, 4 of whom were new, baptized 65 out of 399 persons— almost 17 percent of the population—and married 3 couples in a fine "church about 60 feet in length & 45 in breadth—built with squared logs and boarded on the outside and painted—with a handsome steeple & bell, a pulpit, reading-desk & Communion table, with convenient pews." Proudly, Stuart called attention to the splendid church, which the Mohawks "on their first settling there . . . expressly stipulated with General Haldimand, that the Government should build" as well as "furnish them with a Minister and Schoolmaster. They have a Schoolmaster," Stuart noted—Thomas—"already who is paid by Sir John Johnson."[91] Brant's adept political maneuvering had begun to pay dividends for the Native residents at the Grand River.

In addition to the church, visitors to Brantford in the early 1790s would have encountered a prosperous-looking, racially and ethnically mixed community, composed of small, local alternating Native and white villages all along the Grand River. Some of the homes of Mohawks were American-style wood-frame houses with deal (wide-planked) floors, glass windows, kitchens, and stoves. Still, corn hung suspended from the ceilings of most homes, casting the community through its multivalent domesticity and built environment as a hybrid village. A commodious schoolhouse, a sawmill, and a gristmill added to the village's picture of abundance. One visitor from Britain noted that most Native families in Brantford lived better than poor white farm families in England.[92] It is no wonder, then, that so many Tyendinagans were attracted to the apparent order and wealth of Brantford.

Stuart brought to Brantford "the [communion] plate & furniture which formerly belonged to their Church at Fort-Hunter," gifts from Queen Anne in 1712. Moreover, "a small organ was employed in the [church] service." Before the war, the former residents of Canajoharie tended to keep SPG missionaries at arm's length and sought them out for special needs, such as baptism and communion. Therefore, it is curious that Stuart placed the set of communion ware at Brantford rather than Tyendinaga, whose majority of residents lived across the river from Fort Hunter and, because of their proximity to the fort's chapel, appeared to be the most churched among the Mohawks. Now, just the reverse seemed true. However, the degree of adherence to the Mohawk Anglican Church among those living at Brantford probably had less to do with why Stuart brought the communion ware there and more to do with Stuart's strained relationship with Native residents on the Bay of Quinte. Brant's followers seemed to treat Stuart with greater hospitality. When Stuart left Brantford, for example, more than a dozen Mohawks, including Brant, accompanied him all the way to Fort Niagara—an exercise in hospitality and mutuality—a journey of about seventy miles to the southeast.[93] In performing mutuality and reciprocity, Brant and his followers certainly knew how to make a representative of the church and Crown feel welcomed, despite Brant's need to exercise control over their church.

One reason Stuart undertook the trip from Tyendinaga to Brantford from time to time was to check on the translation project he had begun with Joseph Brant before the war. At Brantford, the two men worked on the Act of the Apostles, while Vincent at Tyendinaga worked on other books of the Bible.[94] However, by 1791, Stuart wanted to free himself from his obligations at Brantford, as the 400-mile round-trip was proving increasingly difficult. Some Mohawks, disappointed that their familiar would visit them no more, petitioned Reverend Robert Addison, the newly appointed missionary at Fort Niagara, who arrived in July 1792 to be their minister. Despite complaining of the distance to Brantford—nearly 150 miles round-trip—and citing the delicate state of his health, Addison ventured west to Brantford during the summer of 1793, where he "was much pleased with their [Mohawks] regular & devout attention." Although he baptized only twelve individuals, a number far lower than what Stuart usually baptized, he "was joined in celebrating the Lord's Supper by 12 women & 2 men." Joseph Brant interpreted for him, as Addison knew no Mohawk. During his visit, several Mohawks asked politely according to Mohawk etiquette that Addison visit Brantford often, to which he demurred that to do so was difficult for a man "of very small income." Brant, perhaps aware of some grumblings beneath the surface at Brantford voiced by some traditionalists, or trying to minimize his community's expectations, told the priest that he need not visit Brantford but "3 or 4" times a year. After this, the SPG granted Addison an additional twenty pounds per year to cover the traveling expenses incurred on those occasional trips to the Grand River reserve rather than hire a separate resident minister for the Native community.[95]

Stuart, not that long removed from Brantford, suspected that the real reason behind Brant's petition to Addison for only a few visits per year rather than demanding a resident priest was that some Mohawks were "afraid of the restraint which the continual residence of a Clergyman would necessarily lay them under." Stuart experienced firsthand the consequences of an absentee itinerate priest, whose "occasional visits are to be considered more as matters of form than productive of any lasting good effect."[96] Stuart drew a distinction between *performing* Christianity and *practicing* it. By the former, the congregants enacted Protestant rituals in the presence of the surveilling pastor according to what they believed the pastor wanted to see, according to middle-ground expectations. The latter embodied a bona fide faith.

Brant's actual reason for not committing to a residential SPG pastor is that he wanted to have the power to appoint the pastor himself. In 1797, Brant told Sir John Johnson that his community had "long been desirous of having a Clergyman to reside constantly with us—this we apprehend would be highly promotive of morality and the Christian Virtues among our people." In December of that year, Brant recommended to the bishop of Quebec the unordained dissenting New Hampshire minister, Davenport Phelps, grandson of Eleazar Wheelock. Brant probably knew that the bishop of Quebec and Peter Russell, the military governor of Upper Canada, would object vigorously, finding Phelps unqualified because of his dissenting views. Moreover, the home secretary in London reinforced their denial by declaring that Native communicants never "have been, nor ever will be, consulted" on the selection of their priests.

Brant took umbrage and threatened to invite a Catholic priest in Phelps's stead. He further protested church officials by sending his sons to the Native grammar school attached to Dartmouth College, the dissenting institution now run by the sons of the late Eleazar Wheelock, rather than ship them off to England to attend school.[97]

Not all Mohawks at Brantford were happy with Brant's grand plan to be the sole arbiter over economic, social, and religious development at the reserve. His land-sale schemes upset many Native residents, despite the fact that some thirty-five headmen reportedly gave him full power of attorney to negotiate the sale of lands. Nevertheless, a sizable number of Mohawk men grew to distrust Brant so much that they tried to halt the land transfers by claiming that clan mothers had to give their consent, a custom with which Canadian officials claimed unfamiliarity, noting that the practice had not been consistently observed in the past.[98] William Claus and other officials in the Indian Department also worried that Brant sought to establish himself as the principal headman over all Mohawks, and thereby consolidate his power. Sir John Johnson noted that Brant may have had "the principal lead Among the Upper Mohawks or Canajoharie Indians," but the Lower Mohawks, formerly of Tiononderoge, now residing at Tyendinaga, always considered themselves "as the heads of the Six Nations Confederacy." Claus, Johnson, and others believed it best that the Mohawks continue to live in separate communities under their respective headmen rather than combine themselves into one large community, lest factions arise and unrest erupted.[99]

Displacement, disease, and the failure of economic enrichment through land sales—in addition to Canadian officials skimming money, white speculators and investors had trouble meeting payments—gave rise to anxiety and uncertainty at Brantford. Brant took advantage of this anomie to bypass the traditional political order and usurp the authority of sachems, war chiefs, and clan matrons to make urgent decisions unilaterally about what he deemed best for the community. Consequently, discomfiture caused some to look backward for answers. In 1798, one young Mohawk warrior gave hope to some traditionalists when he described a vision: the Upholder of the Skies had appeared before him and declared that the Haudenosaunees, save the Senecas, had disrespected him by neglecting to hold the white-dog ceremony since the 1760s. For Haudenosaunee traditionalists, the ceremony was one of the most sacred of rituals, once performed during the midwinter festival in February. It involved strangling a white, unblemished dog—sometimes three—festooned with ribbons, which was then hung from a pole and eventually burned with tobacco in sacrifice to the Upholder of the Skies. This done, the world would then be restored to health and balance. Sometimes warriors performed the ceremony before going to war, as symbolic torture of enemy prisoners. Yet to enculturated baptized Mohawks, the white-dog ceremony represented an insulting reminder of their past, "unimproved" selves. When some Mohawks at Brantford raised the sacrificial pole to perform the ceremony, Brant had the pole dismantled. Ultimately, however, as the de facto arbiter of community standards whose agenda was to "Anglicize" his brethren, Brant sought to keep the peace by permitting the ritual to be performed but *only* after desanctifying it: he moved its performance in the calendar from February to May and insisted that its participants *not* regard it as "setting aside the Christian religion." The ritual appears to have disappeared completely by the early nineteenth century, for the anthropologist Elizabeth Tooker has found no evidence of it then.[100] Anglican Protestantism prevailed, Brant's ultimate goal for Brantford.

## Conclusion

Years ago, the anthropologist William Fenton reminded us that in order to understand how Native peoples aligned themselves with particular groups or factions, we need to observe closely their "way of life," which he argued is "observable in the[ir] settlement patterns."[101] General Haldimand did not understand this about Mohawk life; in 1784, he told John Chew of the Indian Department, "I speak of the Mohawk nation, for I never will entertain an Idea of any distinction between their Villages."[102] Yet the Mohawks always considered their communities as distinct and sovereign yet interdependent. Those at Canajoharie/Brantford considered the Mohawks at Tiononderoge/Tyendinaga as a "distinct party," who performed functions specific to their position within the Mohawk society and the larger Haudenosaunee Confederation. In turn, philosophical and socioeconomic-political differences on sovereignty and revitalization informed the founding and evolution of the two principal Mohawk exile communities in Upper Canada. Joseph Brant at Brantford and Deserontyon at Tyendinaga, the de facto leaders of each respective community, sought to foist on their communities their vision of what they thought was most needed by their brethren in their emergent new world. At Brantford, this meant enculturation to and assimilation with white culture by embracing white institutions of faith and learning, adopting news ways of living in the new subsistence economy, and living willingly with white newcomers to the region. However, having learned not to trust whites, Deserontyon sought to turn Tyendinaga into a self-reliant, self-sufficient community with white institutions but without whites. He was only partially successful at that.

By 1800, unintended consequences caused the two exile communities to resemble each other racially, religiously, and materially. In both communities, Mohawks built themselves—or had built—churches, schools, and mills. They lived and worshiped with white neighbors, much as they had in the Mohawk Valley. Traditional subsistence patterns declined as more and more whites crowded into the two regions, forcing Mohawks to rely increasingly on revenues from white renters and government annuities. Nevertheless, the prospects of greater prosperity at Brantford piqued the envy of many Tyendinagans, who eventually relocated to the Grand River in search of relief and comfort. However, Mohawk individuals moving in and out of Mohawk communities in search of greater prosperity intensified jealousies, envy, and factionalism. For example, Captain Isaac Hill and his son Captain Aaron Hill upset over Brant's authoritarian ways, fled to Tyendinaga, where Deserontyon, who did not trust Brant, welcomed them warmly. Soon, however, the bonhomie among them wore off; the Hills quarreled with Deserontyon, and in 1800 they killed Deserontyon's brother-in-law Lawrence and Lawrence's son.[103] Factional strife defined these two exile communities during the early years of reestablishment in ways that it had not at Tiononderoge and Canajoharie.

Factionalism around establishing the church appeared different in each community. At Tyendinaga, the church had become integral to the lives of many, as they lived nearest the Church of England missionaries at Fort Hunter. Most Tyendinagans accepted the church concomitant to the reestablishment of their new village. However, they also sought control over all matters with the church, from construction to instruction. By now, many Tyendinagans identified as "Christian Mohawks." However, at Brantford, the acceptance of the church was less certain. Brant exploited their new circumstances by demanding that the government pay restitution, which included building their church and forcing unsuccessfully the Canadian and English governments to recognize Mohawk sovereignty over the land. Yet not all Mohawks shared Brant's belief that living like their white Christian neighbors would rebalance their world. Fearing cultural evisceration, some sought to return to their former ways, including observing traditional rituals. The resistance movement was short-lived, however, as Brant accommodated these few traditionalists on the condition that the Mohawk Church of England remain.

The Church of England took root in these two communities as a means of survivance, of carrying on, of persisting as Mohawks, albeit largely as Christian Mohawks. The historian John Webster Grant has argued that two critical circumstances must prevail in order for Native identification with the church to occur: that Christianity cannot truly take root in a community "until it has fused with its culture sufficiently to make possible its appropriation in distinctively indigenous ways" and that Native resistance "was less often to Christianity itself than to the cultural genocide that seemed inseparable from it."[104] In other words, in order for the Mohawks, whether at Brantford or at Tyendinaga, to perform Mohawk Protestantism, they had to make sense of it epistemically not as an instrument of annihilation but rather as a tool of survivance on their terms. As Brant explained to Kirkland, Native peoples were able to change, adjust, and adapt, so long as the change did not have a deleterious effect on their lives and make their lives worse. Most Mohawks who performed Protestantism in the eighteenth and early nineteenth centuries did so for the good of their Mohawks souls.

CONCLUSION

John Webster Grant has identified a range of responses that First Nations people of Canada manifested historically toward missionaries: supplementation (alternation), revolution (full adoption), and passive resistance—a yes that is a no (dissemblance). Each response, he argues, is particular to a specific encounter at a particular time and place.[1] Likewise, this study has shown that the range of responses of the Mohawks to pastors and priests varied not only across time but also among Mohawks themselves. Depending on their gender, status, place of residence, historical moment, and relationships with encroaching Euro-Americans, Mohawks often responded differently to the same SPG missionary. Daniel Richter contends that students of Haudenosaunee mission history cannot discern clean patterns of conversion by noting status alone. Yet it appears that some patterns in response are discernible. Old men and women, young girls and handicapped boys and girls, and prominent headmen and their family members—people who did not venture far from their villages, who were often marginal socially or physically in some way, and influential male leaders and their families, who stood to benefit from embracing priests and pastors—appear to have been more willing than others to open the door to missionaries across the eighteenth century.[2]

Nevertheless, no single experience or response captures definitively the performance of Protestantism by baptized Mohawks. By the 1750s, most Mohawks could boast of having been baptized. Yet a good many, even some of the seemingly most pious, continued to supplement their traditional faith practice with specific aspects of Christianity, most notably singing, praying, and submitting to baptism. However, injurious circumstance

226

due to warfare, disease, and out-migration resulted in declines in the number of keepers of the faith, which often hampered their ability to conduct traditional Haudenosaunee rites and rituals, including thanksgiving festivals, condolence and requickening ceremonies, and dream guessing. Just before the turn of the nineteenth century, one young seer at the Grand River chastised the Mohawks for neglecting their traditional faith, which resulted in an attempt by some to restore Mohawk culture and society by performing a traditional sacred ritual that had become moribund. This exercise of revitalization by looking backward was short-lived, because Brant forbade it, but also because most Mohawks at the Grand River had signaled their identification with the Mohawk Church of England. This does not mean that they had become bona fide converts to Anglicanism. Rather, many practiced "alternation," practicing aspects of Protestantism situationally (reading prayers, deciphering through literacy a biblical text) and Haudenosaunee faith practices conditionally (supplicating the spirits of dead game, reading dreams, treating baptism as a powerful prophylactic, and regarding a priest's prayers as curative medicine). For most, defining their relationship to the church and its missionaries was most important. Shaping and controlling their participation in the missionizing process—from engaging the right schoolmaster to designing the contours of their church, from its design elements to who preached and taught what—were paramount. As one scholar of contemporary Chinese conversions has noted, "It is not necessary to become a believer in a 'world religion' to be a convert."[3]

However, some Mohawks—especially generations of a single family—self-identified as "bona fide" Christians. From the decades on either side of 1700 to reestablishment in Upper Canada, some baptized Mohawks and their families clamored continuously for Protestant ministers for the good of their souls. Their spiritual world was in disarray, and they sought new measures for revitalizing their communities. Some began with individual reform, striving to be good, sober models of Christian behavior. Others began by agreeing to perform Protestantism as a gesture toward polishing the Covenant Chain. Once influential individuals were armed with a new moral code, family often followed. Some did not. More significantly, no prophet stepped forward to articulate a new religious vision through Protestantism, which Anthony Wallace noted has been customary within revitalization movements.[4] Instead, noncharismatic individuals and families stood at the forefront of performing Protestant-ism. They prayed, they renounced their "heathenish ways," and they embraced fully their newfound faith. Still, because few eighteenth-century Mohawks left written records, we cannot be completely certain about the degree to which they embraced Protestantism.

Nevertheless, more than not, baptized Mohawks dictated to SPG missionaries the terms of the missionizing process—when they would come together in worship, what their children should learn and from whom, who should baptize their babies, and who and when they should receive the sacraments. The important insight to glean here is that the missionizing process, as Kenneth Morrison has noted, constituted a cross-cultural dialogue, albeit one that often resulted in miscommunication, confusion, and misunderstandings. The layers of translation with which SPG missionaries and their Mohawk tyros had to contend, conditioned by their differing world views, often led to an epistemic murk not of overt violence but of confusion and resentment that caused some Mohawks to withdraw from the process and let their arms hang by their sides and others to try to indigenize Christian concepts and teach a Mohawk Chris-tianity to young catechumens.[5]

Although most baptized Mohawks considered baptism and communion essential for their identification with and participation in the larger imag-ined Church of England community, many regarded the acquisition of lit-eracy as the most important aspect of the missionizing process. In a world becoming increasingly dependent on talking papers, to which English officials limited Mohawk access, knowing how to read and write became a tool of survivance for the Mohawks, which enabled them to carry on in a changed world as Mohawk people. Providing their children with the means for acquiring literacy in Mohawk and English was one of the key reasons Mohawk parents agreed to send their children to the SPG school at Fort Hunter as well as to dissenting schools in neighboring colonies. In time, because of growing suspicion toward and distrust of white schoolmasters, who too often abused their children and clandestinely dispossessed them of their land, many Mohawk parents and children preferred that their own brethren instruct them. Knowledge through literacy empowered Mohawks. They became increasingly aware of unfair treaties, of bad trade and land deals, and of secret American and British efforts to disfranchise them. English-language religious texts translated into Mohawk not only established the legitimacy of their indigenous language but also made cultural and political change seem possible. Mohawks were now more than just a nation of the Haudenosaunee League; they now felt that they were the true equivalent of the English, the French, and the Dutch.

However, Euro-Americans never viewed the Mohawks as their equal. It did not matter that baptized Mohawks viewed their performances as entering into fellowship with their imagined religious community. It did not matter that several had become literate and had translated religious texts for their brethren. Most Euro-Americans viewed the Mohawks, as well as most Native Americans, as simply deficient and incapable: incapable of farming the land properly, incapable of making ecclesiastical choices for themselves, incapable of knowing God without their aid and assistance. Despite assurances from both Americans and the English during the American Revolution that they would be remembered and protected, the Mohawks were not. Because they were on their own side, which did not look like neutrality to the Americans or the English, the Mohawks paid a heavy price. They recognized the burgeoning white racism toward Native peoples. Deserontyon, for example, promoted Mohawk self-reliance at Tyendinaga on the Bay of Quinte in order to limit entanglements with whites.

Removal from their homeland, from the burial grounds of their dead ancestors, and from other sacred places required many Mohawks to reconstitute themselves as a new people, as a people reborn as Native Christians. Many tried to leave behind the old practices, including witchcraft, reading dreams, supplicating sacrificial white dogs, and abusing alcohol. Because of irrepressible white in-migration, neither diasporic community in Upper Canada was immune to forces within and without that gave rise to social strain and threatened to undermine their restoration. John Norton, the Cherokee-Scot who identified as Mohawk, observed at Brantford that "the use of spiritous liquors had become very common" there and that many Mohawk men "drank to excess." When husbands "come home drunk," he recounted, "their wives tie their hands behind their backs and throw them down on their beds, where they leave them 'til they sober up." That way, the men cannot "boast of their prowess & about deeds they had done & and what val[ient] Exertions they intended."[6] The stress felt most acutely by young warriors as they reconciled themselves to a new way of life in a new place with a new identity was profound.

Compounding the stress at Brantford and perhaps also at Tyendenaga were non-Mohawk Haudenosaunee critics who harshly criticized Mohawk efforts to align themselves with the imagined Anglican community. Sagoyewatha, a.k.a. Red Jacket, for example, the powerful nationalist Seneca headman, who resided not far from Brantford on the Seneca Alleghany reservation, denounced bitterly all Haudenosaunees who mingled with whites. Like Neolin and Tecumseh before him, he called on all Native peoples to divorce themselves from all things white: institutions, beliefs, and most of all, people. In 1819, Red Jacket famously chastised David Ogden, a representative of the Ogden Company, a Massachusetts land-development firm, whose gaze had been fixed on western New York for some time: "We will not part with any of our reservation. . . . It is my wish, and the wish of all of us, to remove every white man. We can educate our children. . . . The [white] Schoolmaster and the Preacher must withdraw. . . . We wish to get rid of all the whites. Those who are now among us make disturbances. We wish our reservation clear of them."[7] Two years later, Red Jacket surely directed his biting remarks to Brant, Deserontyon, and all baptized Mohawks when he complained hyperbolically to federal agent Jasper Parrish, who was assigned to safeguard Native lands, "What has been the result of those numerous tribes who had received missionaries among them? They are extinct; they are forever gone, so that the name even is no more remembered."[8] These nativist warnings from Sagoyewatha may have caused some Mohawks at Brantford and Tyendenaga to question their relationship with their Mohawk Anglican churches, as participation declined and the exploration of American Protestant churches rose.

However, the War of 1812 caused many Mohawks to reject the Americans and resume for a brief time their support of the Anglican Church out of loyalty to the British. Nevertheless, after the war, American and Canadian Methodists expanded their sphere of influence during the Second Great Awakening and reinserted themselves at Tyendenaga and Brantford. The Anglican Church stagnated, but occasionally some priests visited Brantford until about 1830, when the church renewed its work there in earnest. However, by this time, the Methodist Church had become the preferred church for many Mohawks.[9] During the early decades of the nineteenth century, then, most churched Mohawks reached out to the church that showed them the greatest love, regardless of denomination or loyalty, for they viewed baptism, communion, singing, and praying good for their souls.

# NOTES

## ABBREVIATIONS

| | |
|---|---|
| ANTMPP | Andover Newton Miscellaneous Personal Papers Collection, Yale University |
| DHNY | *Documentary History of the State of New York,* ed. E. B. O'Callaghan, 4 vols. (Albany, NY: Weed, Parsons, 1851) |
| DRCHNY | *Documents Relative to the Colonial History of the State of New York,* ed. E. B. O'Callaghan, 15 vols. (Albany, NY: Weed, Parsons, 1853–87) |
| ERSNY | *Ecclesiastical Records, State of New York,* ed. Hugh Hastings, 6 vols. (Albany: Lyon, 1901) |
| Johnson Papers | *The Papers of Sir William Johnson,* ed. James Sullivan, Alexander C. Flick, and Milton Hamilton, 14 vols. (Albany: University of the State of New York, 1921–62) |
| JR | *Jesuit Relations,* ed. Reuben Gold Thwaites, 73 vols. (Cleveland: Burrows, 1896–1901) |
| NAC | National Archives of Canada (Ottawa) |
| NYPL | New York Public Library |
| SPG Journals | Records of the Society for the Propagation of the Gospel in Foreign Parts: Journals, 1701–1870, 50 vols. with Appendices A–D (London: Micro Methods, 1964) |
| SPG Letters A | Records of the Society for the Propagation of the Gospel in Foreign Parts, Letter Books, Series A, 1702–37 (microfilm), 26 vols. (London: Micro Methods, 1964) |
| SPG Letters B | Records of the Society for the Propagation of the Gospel in Foreign Parts, Letter Books, Series B, 1701–86 (microfilm), 25 vols. (London, 1964) |
| Wheelock's Indians | *Letters of Eleazar Wheelock's Indians,* ed. James Dow McCallum (Hanover, NH: Dartmouth College, 1932) |
| *WMQ* | *William and Mary Quarterly* |

INTRODUCTION: MOHAWK BELIEFS AND THE NEEDS OF THE SOUL

1. Andrews to Rev. Sharp, November 25, 1712, Records of the Society for the Propagation of the Gospel in Foreign Parts, Letter Books, Series A, 1702–37, 26 vols. (hereafter SPG Letters A), 8:no. 23, 251; Minutes of SPG Meeting, December 5, 1712, Records of the Society for the Propagation of the Gospel in Foreign Parts: Journals 1701–1870, 50 vols. with Appendices A–D (hereafter SPG Journals), 2:257; Minutes of SPG Meeting, February 27, 1712–13, SPG Journals, 2:273; Andrews to Secretary, March 9, 1712–13, SPG Letters A, 8:no. 24, 145; List of . . . Mohawk Indians Baptised, November 22 to March 9, 1713, and March 8, 1712–13, to September 3, 1713, SPG Letters A, 8:no. 27, 257, 8:no. 43, 304; Andrews to Secretary, October 17, 1715, SPG Letters A, 1:269; Minutes of SPG Meeting, February 12, 1713–14, SPG Journals 2:351; John Wolfe Lydekker, *The Faithful Mohawks* (New York: Macmillan, 1938), 34–38. Nine out of eleven mothers and six of the eleven fathers of the twelve children baptized between November 1712 and March 1712–13 already bore Christian given names, suggesting that Mohawk mothers may have been more inclined to submit to baptism.

2. Andrews to Secretary, October 17, 1714, SPG Letters A, 10:no. 1, 155. Andrews lamented that some of the Mohawk men who attended Sunday-morning services would occasionally "be drunk in the afternoon on the Sabbath day, if they can get Liquor." Andrews to Secretary, September 26, 1717, SPG Letters A, 12:338.

3. Richard Schechner, *Between Theatre and Anthropology* (Philadelphia: University of Pennsylvania Press, 1985), 36; Diane Taylor, *The Archive and the Repertoire: Performing Cultural Memory in the Americas* (Durham, NC: Duke University Press, 2003), 2–3; Joseph Roach, *Cities of the Dead: Circum-Atlantic Performance* (New York: Columbia University Press, 1996), 26.

4. Michael Taussig, *Mimesis and Alterity: A Particular History of the Senses* (New York and London: Routledge, 1993), 129–30; Roy A. Rappaport, "Ritual," in *Folklore, Cultural Performances, and Popular Entertainments: A Communications-Centered Handbook*, ed. Richard Bauman (New York: Oxford University Press, 1992), 252; Richard Bauman, "Performance," in *Folklore, Cultural Performances*, 48. The problem of mistranslation would be remedied somewhat when a pastor in Albany sent John Oliver, a schoolteacher, who knew English and Dutch, to Fort Hunter to assist Andrews. See Lydekker, *The Faithful Mohawks*, 34.

5. I use the term "dominie" to identify Dutch Reformed pastors, although the term did not gain general currency in the United States until the nineteenth century. Before the 1820s, Dutch ministers were generally called "pastors." Prior to the nineteenth century, a "dominie" was a Scottish schoolmaster.

6. Rappaport, "Ritual," 255; Emile Durkheim, *The Elementary Forms of Religious Life*, trans. Karen E. Fields (New York: Free Press, 1995), 41–42; Benedict Anderson, *Imagined Communities: Reflections on the Origin and Spread of Nationalism* (1983; reprint, London: Verso, 1995).

7. Paul A. W. Wallace, *White Roots of Peace* (Philadelphia: University of Pennsylvania Press, 1946), 48. For cogent summaries of the Great League of Peace and Power, see Daniel K. Richter, *The Ordeal of the Longhouse: The Peoples of the Iroquois League in the Era of European Colonization* (Chapel Hill: University of North Carolina Press, 1992), chap. 2; Matthew Dennis, *Cultivating a Landscape of Peace: Iroquois-European Encounters in Seventeenth-Century America* (Ithaca, NY: Cornell University Press, 1993), 6–10, chap. 3; and Christopher Vecsey, "The Story and Structure of the Iroquois Confederacy," *Journal of the American Academy of Religion* 54, no. 1 (1986): 79–106.

8. Kahente Horn-Miller, "Otiyaner: The 'Women's Path' through Colonialism," *Atlantis* 29, no. 2 (2005): 57–59.

9. Wallace, *White Roots of Peace*, 46.
10. Victor Turner, *Dramas, Fields, and Metaphors: Symbolic Action in Human Society* (Ithaca, NY: Cornell University Press, 1974), 239, 243.
11. Bauman, "Performance," 44.
12. Michael D. McNally, "The Practice of Native American Christianity," *Church History* 69, no. 4 (2000): 851; James Peacock, "Ethnographic Notes on Sacred and Profane Performance," in *By Means of Performance: Intercultural Studies of Theatre and Ritual*, ed. Richard Schechner and Willa Appel (Cambridge: Cambridge University Press, 1990), 208; Joshua Bellin, *Medicine Bundle: Indian Sacred Performance and American Literature, 1824–1932* (Philadelphia: University of Pennsylvania Press, 2008), 16; Elizabeth Elbourne, "Family Politics and Anglo-Mohawk Diplomacy: The Brant Family in Imperial Context," *Journal of Colonialism and Colonial History* 6, no. 3 (2005), 1, Project MUSE, doi:10.1353/cch.2006.0004; Turner, *Dramas, Fields, Metaphors*, 242–43.
13. Paul Rabinow, ed., *The Foucault Reader* (New York: Pantheon Books, 1984), 61, 63; Michel Foucault, *Discipline & Punishment: The Birth of the Prison* (New York: Vintage, 1979), 213; Robert Orsi, "Everyday Miracles: The Study of Lived Religion," in *Lived Religion in America: Toward a History of Practice*, ed. David D. Hall (Princeton, NJ: Princeton University Press, 1997), 8; Linford D. Fisher, "Native Americans, Conversion, and Christian Practice in Colonial New England, 1640–1730," *Harvard Theological Review* 102, no. 1 (2009): 104–5.
14. Peacock, "Ethnographic Notes," 208; Taylor, *Archive and Repertoire*, 21; David Delgado Shorter, *We Will Dance Our Truth: Yaqui History in Yoeme Performances* (Lincoln: University of Nebraska Press, 2009), 18.
15. Rogers Brubaker and Frederick Cooper, "Beyond 'Identity,'" *Theory and Society* 29, no. 1 (2000): 14–17.
16. Scott Richard Lyons, *X-Marks: Native Signatures of Assent* (Minneapolis: University of Minnesota Press, 2010), 40.
17. Richard White, *The Middle Ground: Indians, Empires, and Republics in the Great Lakes Region, 1650–1815* (Cambridge: Cambridge University Press, 1991), 50–60.
18. Taylor, *Archive and Repertoire*, 3, 5.
19. On the benefits of studying performances in colonial encounters, see Kathleen Wilson, "Introduction: Three Theses on Performance and History," *Eighteenth-Century Studies* 48, no. 4 (2015): 375–90. For the usefulness of the theory on "identification" over "identity," see Brubaker and Cooper, "Beyond 'Identity,'" 1–47, especially 14–17. On the value of narrative, or stories, in understanding how people make sense of themselves and their place in the world, see Margaret R. Somers, "Narrativity, Narrative Identity, and Social Action: Rethinking English Working-Class Formation," *Social Science History* 16, no. 4 (1992): 591–630. For the "practice-centered" approach to indigenous Christianity, see Fisher, "Native Americans, Conversion, and Christian Practice," 101–24.
20. David J. Silverman, "Indians, Missionaries, and Religious Translation: Creating Wampanoag Christianity in Seventeenth-Century Martha's Vineyard," *William and Mary Quarterly*, 3rd ser. (hereafter *WMQ*) 62, no. 2 (2005): 146. For religious translations among the Illinois in establishing Illinois Christianity in the seventeenth and eighteenth centuries, see Tracy Neal Leavelle, "'Bad Things' and 'Good Hearts': Mediation, Meaning, and the Language of Illinois Christianity," *Church History* 76, no. 2 (2007): 363–94. For nineteenth-century Ojibwe Christianity, see McNally, "Native American Christianity," 834–59.
21. Tom Driver, *The Magic of Ritual: Our Need for Liberating Rites That Transform Our Lives and Our Communities* (San Francisco: Harper, 1991), 169, 202. See also David Snow and Richard Machalek, "The Sociology of Conversion," *Annual Review of*

*Sociology* 10 (1984): 16–74, for a summary and analysis of the various categories used to explain degrees of conversion in sociological terms.

22. For the flexibility of Haudenosaunee "religion," see Daniel K. Richter, *Facing East from Indian Country: A Native History of Early America* (Cambridge, MA: Harvard University Press, 2001), 83–87. For Christian revelation fixed in scripture, see George W. Forell, *The Protestant Faith* (Englewood Cliffs, NJ: Prentice Hall, 1961), 66–78. For a crystal clear explanation of continuous and discontinuous revelation, see John Thornton, *Africa and Africans in the Making of the Atlantic World, 1400–1680* (Cambridge: Cambridge University Press, 1992), chap. 9.

23. Jasper Danckaerts, *Journal of Jasper Danckaerts, 1679–80* (orig. *Journal of a Voyage to New-York and a Tour in Several of the American Colonies in 1679–80, by Jasper Dankers and Peter Sluyter of Wiewerd in Friesland* [Brooklyn, 1867]), ed. Bartlett Burleigh James and J. Franklin Jameson (New York: Scribners, 1913), 205, 209, 211; Webb Keane, *Christian Moderns: Freedom and Fetish in the Mission Encounter* (Berkeley: University of California Press, 2007), 181.

24. Danckaerts, *Journal of Jasper Danckaerts*, 206–11.

25. Father Joseph Francois Lafitau, *Customs of the American Indians Compared with the Customs of Primitive Times* (1724), ed. William N. Fenton and Elizabeth L. Moore, 2 vols. (Toronto: Champlain Society, 1974, 1977) 1:92–282; 2:187–88; Calvin Martin, *Keepers of the Game: Indian-Animal Relationships and the Fur Trade* (Berkeley: University of California Press, 1978), 79–82. For critiques of Martin, see Shepard Krech III, ed., *Indians, Animals, and the Fur Trade: A Critique of Keepers of the Game* (Athens: University of Georgia Press, 1981). For Wouter as a neophyte Christian, see Eric Hinderaker, *The Two Hendricks: Unraveling a Mohawk Mystery* (Cambridge, MA: Harvard University Press, 2010), 43.

26. Barbara J. Sivertsen, *Turtles, Wolves, and Bears: A Mohawk Family History* (Bowie, MD: Heritage Books, 1996), 24; Hinderaker, *Two Hendricks*, 15–16, 37, 40–49.

27. David L. Preston, *The Texture of Contact: European and Indian Settler Communities on the Frontiers of Haudenosaunee, 1667–1783* (Lincoln: University of Nebraska Press, 2009), 104–5.

28. E. Jennifer Monaghan, "'She Loved to Read in Good Books': Literacy and the Indians of Martha's Vineyard, 1643–1725," *History of Education Quarterly* 30, no. 4 (1990): 500–506.

29. David Avery, "Address to the Indians, and Their Answers (Spring 1772)," in *Letters of Eleazar Wheelock's Indians* (hereafter *Wheelock's Indians*), ed. James Dow McCallum (Hanover, NH: Dartmouth College, 1932), 282, 287–88.

30. Gerald Vizenor, *Manifest Manners: Narratives of Postindian Survivance* (Lincoln: University of Nebraska Press, 1994), 64; Gerald Vizenor, *Native Liberty: Natural Reason and Cultural Survivance* (Lincoln: University of Nebraska Press, 2009), 1, 85, 98–103. See Daniel R. Mandell, *Behind the Frontier: Indians in Eighteenth-Century Eastern Massachusetts* (Lincoln: University of Nebraska Press, 1996), chap. 4, for Native Americans "living more like their Christian neighbors."

31. Gail D. MacLeitch, *Imperial Entanglements: Haudenosaunee Change and Persistence on the Frontiers of Empire* (Philadelphia: University of Pennsylvania Press, 2011), 149; Timothy J. Shannon, *Indians and Colonists at the Crossroads of Empire: The Albany Congress of 1754* (Ithaca, NY: Cornell University Press; Cooperstown: New York State Historical Association, 2000), 26; Hinderaker, *Two Hendricks*, 42–47; Preston, *Texture of Contact*, 97–104.

32. William N. Fenton, "Locality as a Basic Factor in the Development of Haudenosaunee Social Structure," *Bulletin* (Washington, DC: Smithsonian Institution, Bureau of American Ethnology) 149, no. 3 (1951): 40; Jill Lepore, "Historians Who Love

Too Much: Reflections on Microhistory and Biography," *Journal of American History* 88, no. 1 (2001): 133, 141–42.

33. For a modern-day Mohawk perspective on the long-term deleterious effects of schooling, literacy, and Christianity on Mohawk individuals, see Tom Sakokwenionkwas Porter, *And Grandma Said . . . Iroquois Teachings as Passed Down through Oral Tradition*, ed. Lesley Forrester (Bloomington, IN: Xlibris, 2008), 28–32. For an interpretation by an Osage scholar of the genocidal effects of missions and missionaries on Native Americans, see George Tinker, *Missionary Conquest: The Gospel and Native American Genocide* (Minneapolis: Fortress Press, 2003).

34. MacLeitch, *Imperial Entanglements*; Preston, *Texture of Contact.*

35. Lydekker, *The Faithful Mohawks.*

36. Lydekker, *The Faithful Mohawks;* Frank J. Klingberg, *Anglican Humanitarianism in Colonial New York* (Philadelphia: Church Historical Society, 1940). Lydekker and Klingberg focus explicitly on Church of England missionaries to the Mohawks. More typical of studies of this generation were those that made little or no mention of the Mohawks, including Carl Bridenbaugh, *Mitre and Sceptre: Transatlantic Faiths, Ideas, Personalities, and Politics, 1689–1775* (New York: Oxford University Press, 1962); Carson I. A. Ritchie, *Frontier Parish* (Rutherford, NJ: Farleigh Dickinson University Press, 1976); and John Frederick Woolverton, *Colonial Anglicanism in North America* (Detroit: Wayne State University Press, 1984).

37. Daniel K. Richter, "Iroquois versus Iroquois: Jesuit Missions and Christianity in Village Politics, 1642–1686," *Ethnohistory* 32, no. 1 (1985): 1–16; Rachel Wheeler, "Hendrick Aupaumut: Christian-Mahican Prophet," in *Native Americans, Christianity, and the Reshaping of the American Religious Landscape*, ed. Joel W. Martin and Mark A. Nicholas (Chapel Hill: University of North Carolina Press, 2010), 225–49; Joel Martin, introduction to *Native Americans, Christianity, and Reshaping*, 10–11. Early studies in the field of indigenes-missionary relations include James Axtell, *The Invasion Within: The Contest of Cultures in Colonial North America* (New York: Oxford University Press, 1985); James Axtell, *The European and the Indian: Essays in the Ethnohistory of Colonial North America* (New York : Oxford University Press, 1981); James Axtell, *After Columbus: Essays in the Ethnohistory of Colonial North America* (New York: Oxford University Press, 1988); James P. Ronda, "'We Are Well as We Are': An Indian Critique of Seventeenth-Century Missions," *WMQ* 34, no. 1 (1977): 66–82; Margaret Connell Szasz, *Indian Education in the American Colonies, 1607–1783* (Albuquerque: University of New Mexico Press, 1988); Jean Fittz Hawkins, "Bringing the Good News: Protestant Missionaries to the Indians of New England and New York, 1700–1775" (PhD diss., University of Connecticut, 1993); James S. Pritchard, "For the Glory of God: The Quinte Mission, 1668–1680," *Ontario History* 65 (1973): 133–48; James T. Moore, *Indian and Jesuit: A Seventeenth-Century Encounter* (Chicago: Loyola University Press, 1982); Bruce G. Trigger, *The Children of Aataentsic: A History of the Huron People to 1660*, 2 vols. (Montreal: McGill University Press, 1976); Bruce G. Trigger, *Natives and Newcomers: Canada's "Heroic Age" Reconsidered* (Kingston, ON: McGill-Queen's College University Press, 1985); James P. Ronda, "The Sillery Experiment: A Jesuit-Indian Village in New France, 1637–1663," *American Indian Culture and Research Journal* 3, no. 1 (1979): 1–18. Among the earliest and more influential scholars to offer the interpretation of deleterious change are Robert Berkhofer, *Salvation and the Savage: An Analysis of Protestant Missions and American Indian Response, 1787–1862* (1965; reprint, New York: Athenaeum, 1972); David B. Guldenzopf, "The Colonial Transformation of Mohawk Haudenosaunee Society" (PhD diss., State University of New York at Albany, 1986); Isabel Thompson Kelsay, *Joseph Brant, 1743–1807: Man of Two Worlds* (Syracuse,

NY: Syracuse University Press, 1984). For a cogent definition of ethnohistory, see Axtell, *European and Indian*, 5. For current discussions on the field of ethnohistory, past and present, see John R. Wunder, "Native American History, Ethnohistory, and Context," *Ethnohistory* 54, no. 4 (2007): 591–604; and Michael E. Harkin et al., "American Society for Ethnohistory Roundtable: *Ethnohistory* at Sixty," *Ethnohistory* 66, no. 1 (2019): 141–98.

38. Alyssa Mt. Pleasant, Caroline Wigginton, and Kelly Wisecup, "Materials and Methods in Native American and Indigenous Studies: Completing the Turn," *WMQ* 75, no. 2 (2018): 207–36.

39. Kenneth M. Morrison, "Discourse and the Accommodation of Values: Toward a Revision of Mission History," *Journal of the American Academy of Religion* 53, no. 3 (1985): 365–82; John Webster Grant, *Moon of Wintertime: Missionaries and the Indians of Canada in Encounter since 1534* (Toronto: University of Toronto Press, 1984, 1992); David Blanchard, ". . . To the Other Side of the Sky: Catholicism at Kahnawake, 1667–1700," *Anthropologica* 24 (1982): 77–102; Robert A. Brightman, "Toward a History of Indian Religion: Religious Changes in Native Societies," in *New Directions in American Indian History*, ed. Colin Calloway (Norman: University of Oklahoma Press, 1988), 223–49; Allan Greer, *Mohawk Saint: Catherine Tekakwitha and the Jesuits* (New York: Oxford University Press, 2005); Preston, *Texture of Contact*; David Silverman, *Red Brethren: The Brothertown and Stockbridge Indians and the Problem of Race in America* (Ithaca, NY: Cornell University Press, 2010).

40. Kenneth Mills, *Idolatry and Its Enemies: Colonial Andean Religion and Extirpation, 1640–1750* (Princeton, NJ: Princeton University Press, 1997), 3–11, 243–85.

41. Mark Christensen, *Nahua and Maya Catholicism: Texts and Religion in Colonial Mexico and Yucatan* (Stanford, CA: Stanford University Press, 2013); William F. Hanks, *Converting Words: Maya in the Age of the Cross* (Berkeley: University of California Press, 2010); Louise Burkhart, *Holy Wednesday: A Nahua Drama from Early Mexico* (Philadelphia: University of Pennsylvania Press, 1996); Louise Burkhart, *The Slippery Earth: Nahua Christian Moral Dialogue in Sixteenth-Century Mexico* (Tucson: University of Arizona Press, 1989); Barry Sell and Louise Burkhart, *Nahuatl Theater: Nahua Christianity In Performance* (Norman: University of Oklahoma Press, 2009).

42. Sergei Kan, *Memory Eternal: Tlingit Culture and Russian Orthodox Christianity through Two Centuries* (Seattle: University of Washington Press, 1999); Richard Dauenhauer, "Synchretism, Revival, and Reinvention: Tlingit Religion, Pre- and Postcontact," in *Native Religions and Cultures of North America: Anthropology of the Sacred*, ed. Lawrence E. Sullivan (New York and London: Continuum, 2000), 160–80.

43. Tracy Neal Leavelle, *The Catholic Calumet: Colonial Conversions in French and Indian North America* (Philadelphia: University of Pennsylvania Press, 2012).

44. Abe Takao, *The Jesuit Mission to New France: A New Interpretation in the Light of the Earlier Jesuit Experience in Japan* (Leiden and Boston: Brill, 2011), chap. 5; Greer, *Mohawk Saint*; Nancy Shoemaker, "Kateri Tekakwitha's Tortuous Path to Sainthood," in *Negotiators of Change: Historical Perspectives on Native American Women*, ed. Nancy Shoemaker (New York: Routledge, 1995), 49–71; William B. Hart, "'The Kindness of the Blessed Virgin': Faith, Succour, and the Cult of Mary among Christian Hurons and Iroquois in Seventeenth-Century New France," in *Spiritual Encounters: Interactions between Christianity and Native Religions in Colonial America*, ed. Nicholas Griffiths and Fernando Cervantes (Birmingham: University of Birmingham Press; Lincoln: University of Nebraska Press, 1999), 65–90; Blanchard, "'. . . To the Other Side of the Sky.'"

45. Silverman, "Indians, Missionaries, and Religious Translation"; Silverman, *Red Brethren;* David Silverman, *Faith and Boundaries: Colonists, Christianity, and Community among the Wampanoag Indians of Martha's Vineyard, 1600–1871* (New York:

Cambridge University Press, 2005); Daniel R. Mandell, "Turned Their Minds to Religion," *Early American Studies* 11, no. 2 (2013): 211–42; Rachel Wheeler, *To Live upon Hope: Mohicans and Missionaries in the Eighteenth-Century Northeast* (Ithaca, NY: Cornell University Press, 2008).

46. Rosemary McCombs Maxey, "Who Can Sit at the Lord's Table? The Experience of Indigenous Peoples," in *Native and Christian: Indigenous Voices on Religious Identity in the United States,* ed. James Treat (New York and London: Routledge, 1996), 42, 40, 43.

47. Adrian Jacobs, "The Meeting of the Two Ways," in Treat, *Native and Christian*, 184–90; Lavern Jacobs, "The Native Church: A Search for an Authentic Spirituality," in Treat, *Native and Christian*, 236–40.

48. See, for example, Keane, *Christian Moderns;* Peter Baker, *A Language of Our Own: The Genesis of Michif, the Mixed Cree-French Language of the Canadian Metis* (New York: Oxford University Press, 1997); Hanks, *Converting Words*; Craig Cipolla, *Becoming Brothertown: Native American Ethnogenesis and Endurance in the Modern World* (Tucson: University of Arizona Press, 2013); Burkhart, *Slippery Earth*; and Sell and Burkhart, *Nahuatl Theater.*

49. Joshua David Bellin and Laura L. Mielke, eds., *Native Acts: Indian Performance, 1603–1832* (Lincoln: University of Nebraska Press, 2001). For studies of whites performing Indianness, see Phil Deloria, *Playing Indian* (New Haven: Yale University Press, 1998); Shari M. Huhndorf, *Going Native: Indians in the American Cultural Imagination* (Ithaca: Cornell University Press, 2001).

50. Neal Salisbury, "Embracing Ambiguity: Native Peoples and Christianity in Seventeenth-Century North America," *Ethnohistory* 50, no. 2 (Spring 2003): 247–59; George Jackson, *The Fact of Conversion: The Cole Lectures for 1908* (New York: Revell, 1908), 97, 191.

51. Major John Norton, *The Journal of Major John Norton, 1816,* ed. Carl F. Klinck and James J. Talman (Toronto: Champlain Society, 1970), 91.

52. Brightman, "Toward a History," 245; Marshall Sahlins, *Islands of History* (Chicago: University of Chicago Press, 1985), viii.

53. Lafitau, *Customs of the American Indians,* 1:261–64.

## CHAPTER 1: "DWINDL'D TO NOTHING ALMOST"

1. Lawrence H. Leder, ed., *The Livingston Indian Records, 1666–1723* (Gettysburg: Pennsylvania Historical Association, 1956), 155; Daniel K. Richter, *The Ordeal of the Longhouse: The Peoples of the Haudenosaunee League in the Era of European Colonization* (Chapel Hill: University of North Carolina Press, 1992), 62. For Mohawk warrior deaths from warfare and disease, see Peter Schulyer's "Journal of His Expedition to Canada, 21 June–9 August, 1691," in *Documents Relative to the Colonial History of the State of New York* (hereafter *DRCHNY*), ed. E. B. O'Callaghan, 15 vols. (Albany, NY: Weed, Parsons, 1853–87), 3:800–805; Proposition of the Senecas and Mohawks at Albany, September 4, 1691, *DRCHNY*, 3:805–9; Proposition of the Commander-in-Chief to the Five Nations, June 6, 1692, *DRCHNY*, 3:840–44; Count de Frontenac to Ministers, November 12, 1690, *DRCHNY*, 9:460–61; "Narrative of the Most Remarkable Occurrences in Canada, 1690, 1691," *DRCHNY*, 9:513–14, 520–24. For Haudenosaunee involvement in King William's War, see Cadwallader Colden, *The History of the Five Indian Nations, Depending on the Province of New-York in America* pt. 2, *1747* (1958; reprint, Ithaca, NY: Cornell University Press, 1988), 81–181; and Richter, *Ordeal of the Longhouse*, 162–89.

2. Robert Livingston's Report of Visit to Onondaga, April 1700, *DRCHNY*, 4:652; Governor Bellomont to Lords of Trade, May 25, 1700, *DRCHNY*, 4:644; Livingston's

Commission, September 15, 1696, *DRCHNY*, 4:203–4; Livingston to Board of Trade, December 28, 1696, and May 13, 1701, *DRCHNY*, 4:252; 4:878, 871–72; Governor Bellomont to the Lords of Trade, July 31, 1700, Addendum, *DRCHNY*, 4:689.

3. Livingston's Report of Visit to Onondaga, April 1700, *DRCHNY*, 4:648; Officers at Albany, December 30, 1691, *DRCHNY*, 3:815–16; Reuben Gold Thwaites, ed. *Jesuit Relations and Allied Documents: Travels and Explorations of the Jesuit Missionaries in New France, 1610–1791* (hereafter *JR*), 73 vols. (Cleveland: Burrows, 1896–1901), 64:59–61; Richter, *Ordeal of the Longhouse*, 173, 169.

4. Major Peter Schuyler's Report to Governor Fletcher, March 1692–93, *DRCHNY*, 4:17, 21.

5. Governor Fletcher's Speech to the Indian Sachems, City Hall, Albany, February 25, 1692–93, *DRCHNY*, 4:21.

6. Answer of the Five Nations to Governor Fletcher, February 25, 1692–93, City Hall, Albany, *DRCHNY*, 4:22–23; Richter, *Ordeal of the Longhouse*, 174.

7. Answer of the Five Nations to Governor Fletcher, February 25, 1692–93, City Hall, Albany, *DRCHNY*, 4:24; Fletcher's reply, *DRCHNY*, 4:24.

8. "Comparative Populations of Albany and the Indians in 1689 and 1698," April 19, 1698, *DRCHNY*, 4:337. For figures that capture the decline in the warrior population in other Haudenosaunee nations as well as the decline in Albany County between 1689 and 1698, see A Memorial . . . to Bellomont, June 1698, *DRCHNY*, 4:330; and Lord Bellomont to Lords of Trade, October 4, 1700, *DRCHNY*, 4:701.

9. Robert Livingston to the Lords of Trade, May 13, 1701, *DRCHNY*, 4:872; Intended Letter of Governor Sloughter to Secretary Blathwayt (n.d., circa 1691), *DRCHNY*, 3:790. For both the Haudenosaunees and New York officials expecting mutual support from the other, see Robert Livingston to Lords of Trade, May 13, 1701, *DRCHNY*, 4:870; Memorial from Livingston to the Commissioners for Trade and Foreign Plantations, 1703, *DRCHNY*, 4:1067; Bellomont to Lords of Trade, various letters, 1700, *DRCHNY*, 4:609, 677, 716, 725.

10. Robert Livingston's Report of His Journey to Onondaga, April 1700, *DRCHNY*, 4:648; Robert Livingston to Lords of Trade, May 13, 1701, *DRCHNY*, 4:871. In 1679 the Jesuit priest Bonniface led forty Mohawk men, women, and children from Gandaouage to Kahnawake (*JR* 52:169). On the mass withdrawal from the easternmost Mohawk castles of Gandaouague and Gannagaro, see *JR*, 57:109–11. For the pull factor of Christianity to Kahnawake, see Daniel K. Richter, "Iroquois versus Iroquois: Jesuit Missions and Christianity in Village Politics, 1642–1686," *Ethnohistory* 32, no. 1 (1985): 1–16.

11. Livingston's Report on Onondaga, 1700, *DRCHNY*, 4:649; Schuyler, Livingston, and Hansen to Bellomont, May 3, 1700, *DRCHNY*, 4:661; Addendum to Bellomont to Lords of Trade, July 26, 1700, *DRCHNY*, 4:689; Allen W. Trelease, *Indian Affairs in Colonial New York: The Seventeenth Century* (1960; reprint, Lincoln: University of Nebraska Press, 1997), 304.

12. Father Joseph Francois Lafitau, *Customs of the American Indians Compared with the Customs of Primitive Times* (1724), ed. William N. Fenton and Elizabeth L. Moore, 2 vols. (Toronto: Champlain Society, 1974, 1977), 2:172. Lafitau, who lived among the Mohawks at the Catholic mission at Caughnawaga (Kahnawake) from 1712 to 1717, observed that a Haudenosaunee family's wealth and power were determined by the number of its family members. Lafitau, *Customs of the American Indians*, 2:99.

13. Commissioners of Indian Affairs to Governor Nanfan, July 5, 1700, *DRCHNY*, 4:690. For references to condoling ceremonies, see Horatio Hale, ed., *The Iroquois Book of Rites* (1883; reprint, New York: AMS Press, 1969); Lewis Henry Morgan, *League of the Ho-de-no-sau-nee, or Iroquois* (1851; reprint, New York: Citadel, 1962), 108–26;

Richter, *Ordeal of the Longhouse*, 32–33, 39–42. For scholarship on the Two Row Wampum Belt that addresses controversies over the belt's origin, meaning, and authenticity, see Jon Parmenter, "The Meaning of *Kaswentha* and the Two Row Wampum Belt in Haudenosaunee (Iroquois) History: Can Indigenous Oral Tradition Be Reconciled with the Documentary Record?," *Journal of Early American History* 3, no. 1 (2013): 82–109; Paul Otto, "Wampum, Tawagonshi, and the Two Row Belt," *Journal of Early American History* 3, no. 1 (2013): 110–25; Kathryn Muller, "The Two 'Mystery' Belts of Grand River: A Biography of the Row Wampum and the Friendship Belt," *American Indian Quarterly* 31, no. 1 (2007): 129–64; Elizabeth Tooker, "A Note on the Return of Eleven Wampum Belts to the Six Nations Iroquois Confederacy on Grand River, Canada," *Ethnohistory* 45, no. 2 (1998): 219–36; Howard R. Berman, "Perspectives on American Indian Sovereignty and International Law, 1600–1776," in *Democracy, Indian Nations, and the U.S. Constitution*, ed. Oren Lyons et al. (Santa Fe, NM: Clear Light, 1992), 125–88. For early comprehensive discussions of the Covenant Chain, see Daniel K. Richter and James H. Merrell, eds., *Beyond the Covenant Chain: The Iroquois and Their Neighbors in Indian North America, 1600–1800* (Syracuse, NY: Syracuse University Press, 1987).

14. Richter, *Ordeal of the Longhouse*, 189, 205–6, 106–28, 221–23, 230–34, 254. For analyses of the political consequences following the war, see Richard Aquila, *The Iroquois Restoration: Iroquois Diplomacy on the Colonial Frontier, 1701–1754* (Detroit, MI: Wayne State University Press, 1983), introduction and pt. 2; Anthony F. C. Wallace, "Origins of Iroquois Neutrality: The Grand Settlement of 1701," *Pennsylvania History* 24 (1957): 223–35; Richard Haan, "The Problem of Iroquois Neutrality: Suggestions for Revisions," *Ethnohistory* 27, no. 4 (1980): 317–30; Richard L. Haan, "The Covenant Chain: Iroquois Diplomacy on the Niagara Frontier, 1697–1730" (PhD diss., State University of New York, Albany, 1987); Francis Jennings, *The Ambiguous Iroquois Empire: The Covenant Chain Confederation of Indian Tribes with English Colonies from Its Beginnings to the Lancaster Treaty of 1744* (New York: W. W. Norton, 1984), pt. 3.

15. Richter, *Ordeal of the Longhouse*, 206.

16. Sherry Ortner, "Theory in Anthropology since the Sixties," *Comparative Studies in Society and History* 26, no. 1 (1984): 126–66.

17. Thomas Barclay to Secretary, September 26, 1700, SPG Letters A, 5:176; Barclay to Secretary, June 12, 1711, SPG Letters A, 6:129; *JR*, 53:189.

18. Anthony F. C. Wallace, "Revitalization Movements: Some Theoretical Considerations for Their Comparative Study," *American Anthropologist* 58, no. 2 (1956): 264–81. For studies that approach revitalization differently, see William G. McLoughlin, *Cherokee Renaissance in the New Republic* (Princeton, NJ: Princeton University Press, 1986); Gregory Evans Dowd, *A Spiritual Resistance: The North American Indian Struggle for Unity, 1745–1815* (Baltimore, MD: Johns Hopkins University Press, 1992); Alfred A. Cave, *Prophets of the Great Spirit: Native American Revitalization Movements in Eastern North America* (Lincoln: University of Nebraska Press, 2006); Rachel Wheeler, "Hendrick Aupaumut: Christian-Mahican Prophet," in *Native Americans, Christianity, and the Reshaping of the American Religious Landscape*, ed. Joel W. Martin and Mark A. Nicholas (Chapel Hill: University of North Carolina Press, 2010), 225–49.

19. Anthony F. C. Wallace, "The Dekanawidah Myth Analyzed as the Record of a Revitalization Movement," *Ethnohistory* 5, no. 1 (1958): 118–30; Wallace, "Revitalization Movements," 275–76.

20. Wheeler, "Hendrick Aupaumut," 225–49; Richter, *Ordeal of the Longhouse,* 31; John Talbot to Richard Gillingham, November 24, 1702, SPG, Letters A, 1:no. 56, n.p.; John Wolfe Lydekker, *The Faithful Mohawks* (New York: Macmillan, 1938), 11n4. To

punctuate the sincerity of their request for pastors, Talbot recorded that the headmen insisted that the commissioners send to the new Queen Anne "a Present, 10 Beaver skins to make her fine, & one fur muff to keep her warm."

21. On satisfying the needs of the Haudenosaunee soul, see Pierre de Charlevoix, *Journal of a Voyage to North-America*, 2 vols. (London, 1761), cited in James Axtell, ed., *The Indian Peoples of Eastern America: A Documentary History of the Sexes* (New York: Oxford University Press, 1981), 186–87, 172.

22. James Tuck, "Northern Iroquois Prehistory," in *Handbook of North American Indians: Northeast*, ed. Bruce Trigger (Washington, DC: Smithsonian Institution, 1978), 15:326; James Tuck, *Onondaga Iroquois Prehistory: A Study in Settlement Archaeology* (Syracuse, NY: Syracuse University Press, 1971), 213, 223–24; Matthew Dennis, *Cultivating a Landscape of Peace: Iroquois-European Encounters in Seventeenth-Century America* (Ithaca, NY: Cornell University Press; and Cooperstown: New York Historical Association, 1993), 50. Paul A. W. Wallace provides an efficient summary of the Deganawidah myth, or the founding myth of the League of the Haudenosaunee, drawn from a variety of sources in *White Roots of Peace* (Philadelphia: University of Pennsylvania Press, 1946).

23. Wallace, *White Roots of Peace*, 48, 46.

24. *JR*, 51:187, 201–11, 57:89–91; Benedict Anderson, *Imagined Communities: Reflections of the Origin and Spread of Nationalism* (London: Verso, 1991).

25. Report of Bleeker and Schuyler's Visit to Onondaga, August 27–September 14, 1701, *DRCHNY*, 4:920; Journal of Bleeker and Schuyler, June 2–29, 1701, *DRCHNY*, 4:893.

26. This summary of the Haudenosaunee creation myth is drawn from a number of sources. Each has a different ethnic origin (for example, Mohawk, Onondaga, Seneca) and thus alters slightly different aspects of the myth. See John Norton, *The Journal of Major John Norton* (1816), ed. Carl F. Klinck and James J. Talman (Toronto: Champlain Society, 1970), 88–97, for an Onondaga version; Hazel W. Hertzberg, *The Great Tree and the Longhouse: The Culture of the Iroquois* (New York: Macmillan, 1966), 12–19, for a Cayuga version; and J. N. B. Hewitt, "Iroquoian Cosmology," pt. 1, in *Annual Report, 1899–1900*, by Bureau of American Ethnology (Washington, DC: Smithsonian Institution, 1903), 141–339, for Onondaga, Seneca, and Mohawk versions.

27. Donald P. St. John, "Iroquois Religion," in *The Encyclopedia of Religion*, ed. Mircea Eliade (New York: Macmillan, 1987), 7:284. I thank Ives Goddard for pointing out to me that the term *orenda* is a Huron term that nineteenth-century Tuscarora ethnologist J. N. B. Hewitt used as a synecdoche for all Haudenosaunee people, despite the fact that each nation used a slightly different term. Mohawks and Cayugas used the terms *orrenna* or *karenna*; Oneidas *olenna* or *kalenna*; and Onondagas and Senecas *gaenna* or *oenna*. See Hewitt's essay "Orenda and a Definition of Religion," *American Anthropologist*, n.s., 4 (1902): 33–46.

28. Elisabeth Tooker, *The Iroquois Ceremonial of Midwinter* (Syracuse, NY: Syracuse University Press, 1970), 39–103.

29. Wallace, *Death and Rebirth*, 50–58.

30. William Andrews to SPG, October 11, 1716, SPG Letters A, 12:241; Anthony F. C. Wallace, "Dreams and the Wishes of the Soul: A Type of Psychoanalytic Theory among the Seventeenth Century Haudenosaunee," *American Anthropologist* 60 (1958): 235–47 (Fremin quote on 234); Norton, *Journal*, 107; St. John, "Iroquois Religion," 7:286; Tooker, *Iroquois Ceremonial*, 85–92.

31. Lafitau, *Customs of the American Indians*, 1: 237–43, 2:209–15.

32. *JR*, 58:173.

33. *JR*, 35:292, 41:85–89, 68:197, 231, 302; To D'Hinse, July 28, 1666, *DRCHNY*,

3:132; Nicolls to Arendt Van Curler, January 11, 1666, *DRCHNY*, 3:147; Governor Tracy to Arendt Van Curler, April 30, 1667, *DRCHNY*, 3:151—52; Thomas Burke Jr., "'The Extreemest Part of All': The Dutch Community of Schenectady, New York, 1661—1720" (PhD diss., State University of New York, Albany, 1984), 122—23, 137—38, 231—32; Barbara J. Sivertsen, *Turtles, Wolves, and Bears: A Mohawk Family History* (Bowie, MD: Heritage Books, 1996), 84. For a brief portraiture of the biracial Kryn, who led the 1690 raid on Schenectady and died in a skirmish shortly thereafter, see Thomas Grasman, "Flemish Bastard," in *Dictionary of Canadian Biography* (Toronto: University of Toronto Press, 1966), 1:307—8; and Henri Bechard, "Joseph Togouironi," in *Dictionary of Canadian Biography*, 1:650—51.

34. Lafitau, *Customs of the American Indians*, 2:217—22. On moieties, see William N. Fenton, *The Great Law and the Longhouse: A Political History of the Iroquois Confederacy* (Norman: University of Oklahoma Press, 1998), 25—28. On reciprocity, see Elisabeth Tooker, "Women in Iroquois Society," in *Extending the Rafters: Interdisciplinary Approaches to Iroquoian Studies*, ed. Michael K. Foster, Jack Campisi, and Marianne Mithun (Albany: State University of New York at Albany Press, 1984), 118—20.

35. For divisions at the national level, see Morgan, *League of the Ho-de-en-o-sau-nee*, 96.

36. Tooker, "Women in Iroquois Society," 119. For a study on the role and power of Haudenosaunee women that is rooted firmly in historical methodology, scholarly analysis, and Haudenosaunee epistemology, see Barbara Alice Mann, *Iroquoian Women: The Gantowisas* (New York: Peter Lang, 2000).

37. *JR*, 55:6; Horatio Hale, ed., *The Iroquoius Book of Rites* (1883; reprint, New York: AMS, 1969), 65. For Haudenosaunee factionalism caused by the presence of Jesuits, see Richter, "Iroquois versus Iroquois."

38. *JR*, 13:17—137. Compare this account to that in *JR*, 39:175—237, a hyperbolic account written in Italian by Father Bressani in 1653. Bruce G. Trigger, *The Children of Aataentsic: A History of the Huron People to 1660* (Kingston: McGill—Queen's University Press, 1976), 638, 645—47, 667—68.

39. *JR*, 52:87—89.

40. *JR*, 57:87—89, 51:187, 209—11. For a study of Mohawks ensuring that their baptized brethren had access to Protestant pastors during the turn of the eighteenth century, see Daniel K. Richter, "Some of Them . . . Would Always Have a Minister," *American Indian Quarterly* 16, no. 4 (1992): 471—84.

41. Governor Dongan to Lord President, February 19, 1687—88, *DRCHNY*, 3:511; Hugh Hastings, ed., *Ecclesiastical Records, State of New York* (hereafter *ERSNY*), 6 vols. (Albany: Lyon, 1901), 2:934, 938—39; Governor Dongan to De Denonville, June 20, 1687, *DRCHNY*, 3:465.

42. James Axtell, *Invasion Within: The Contest of Cultures in Colonial North America* (New York: Oxford University Press, 1985), 77—123.

43. *JR*, 57:85, 153; Allan Greer, *Mohawk Saint: Catherine Tekakwitha and the Jesuits* (New York: Oxford University Press, 2005), 51—53, 100—104; John Steckley, "The Warrior and the Lineage: Jesuit Use of Iroquoian Images to Communicate Christianity," *Ethnohistory* 39, no. 4 (1992): 478—509; Axtell, *Invasion Within*, 91—127. For how the Jesuits reified these concepts in print, see Victor Egon Hanzeli, *Missionary Linguistics in New France: A Study of Seventeenth- and Eighteenth-Century Descriptions of American Indian Languages* (The Hague: Mouton, 1969).

44. David Schuyler to Governor Bellomont, August 17, 1700, *DRCHNY*, 4:747—48; Daniel K. Richter, *Facing East from Indian County: A Native History of Early America* (Cambridge, MA: Harvard University Press, 2001), 122—26. For a reference to familial-size mourning wars, see Jon Parmenter, "After the Mourning Wars: The Iroquois as Allies in Colonial North American Campaigns, 1676—1760," *WMQ* 54, no. 1 (2007): 48.

45. *JR*, 57:85, 153; Greer, *Mohawk Saint*, 100–104; Rodney Stark, *The Rise of Christianity: A Sociologist Reconsiders History* (Princeton, NJ: Princeton University Press, 1996), 211.

46. *JR*, 58:171–73; Eric Hinderaker, *The Two Hendricks: Unraveling a Mohawk Mystery* (Cambridge, MA: Harvard University Press, 2010), 29; John Webster Grant, *In the Moon of the Wintertime: Missionaries and the Indians of Canada in Encounter since 1534* (Toronto: University of Toronto Press, 1992), 239–63; James C. Scott, *Weapons of the Weak: Everyday Forms of Peasant Resistance* (New Haven, CT: Yale University Press, 1985), 284–87.

47. Journal of Frontenac . . . 1673, *DRCHNY,* 9:95–114, esp. 101. Frontenac does not mention Assendasé's name, but his rank in Mohawk society, the large number of sachems in attendance, and Bruyas's account suggest that he was there.

48. Journal of Frontenac . . . 1673, *DRCHNY,* 9:106.

49. Journal of Frontenac . . . 1673, *DRCHNY,* 9:95–114.

50. Richter, *Ordeal of the Longhouse,* 95–102, 20, 359n29; Journal of Frontenac . . . 1673, *DRCHNY,* 9:108–9.

51. Journal of Frontenac . . . 1673, *DRCHNY,* 9:107, 108, 104, 105. The original name of the fort built in summer 1673, located at present-day Kingston, Ontario, was Fort Cataraqui but was changed within a few years to Fort Frontenac.

52. Journal of Frontenac . . . 1673, *DRCHNY,* 9:110–11.

53. *JR*, 58:171–75, 59:237, 57:157 (for *oski*); Bishop of Peterborough in John Calam, *Parsons and Pedagogues: The SPG Adventure in American Education* (New York: Columbia University Press, 1971), 160. Garakontie's "conversion" to Catholicism in 1670 enabled the Jesuits to sprinkle holy water more liberally throughout Iroquoia. For Garakontie, see *JR*, 53:53–57, 57:135–41, 60:177–79, 52:21–33, 41–43, 58:171.

54. *JR*, 58:171, 173, 59:237, 58:175, 60:177.

55. *JR*, 59:237.

56. Richter, *Ordeal of the Longhouse,* 126–28. For portraits of Kateri Tekakwitha, whom the Catholic Church canonized in 2012, see Father Pierre Cholenec to Father Augustin Le Blanc, August 27, 1715, in *The Early Jesuit Missions in North America*, ed. William Ingraham Kip (New York: Wiley and Putnam, 1846), 79–116; Daniel Sargent, *Catherine Tekakwitha* (New York: Longmans, Green, 1936); David Blanchard, "'. . . To the Other Side of the Sky': Catholicism at Kahnawake, 1667–1700," *Anthropologica* 24 (1982): 77–102; K. I. Koppedrayer, "The Making of the First Iroquois Virgin: Early Jesuit Biographies of the Blessed Kateri Tekakwitha," *Ethnohistory* 40, no. 2 (1993): 277–306; Nancy Shoemaker, "Kateri Tekakwitha's Tortuous Path to Sainthood," in *Negotiators of Change: Historical Perspectives on Native American Women*, ed. Nancy Shoemaker (New York: Routledge, 1995), 49–71; Greer, *Mohawk Saint*.

57. Cholenec to Le Blanc, August 27, 1715, in Kip, *Early Jesuit Missions*, 82, 85; *JR*, 41:119; Denys Delage, *Bitter Feast: Amerindians and Europeans in Northeastern North America, 1600–64*, trans. Jane Brierley (Vancouver: University of British Columbia Press, 1993), 225–28.

58. *JR*, 41:119; Cholenec to Le Blanc, in Kip, *Early Jesuit Missions*, 85; Delage, *Bitter Feast*, 225–28. For Native women as cultural and political brokers, see Clara Sue Kidwell, "Indian Women as Cultural Mediators," *Ethnohistory* 39, no. 2 (1992): 97–107; and Mann, *Iroquoian Women: The Gantowisas*.

59. *JR*, 51:193–95.

60. Cholenec to Le Blanc, in Kip, *Early Jesuit Missions*, 87–90; Glenda Goodman, "'But They Differ from Us in Sound': Indian Psalmody and the Soundscape of Colonialism, 1651–75," *WMQ* 69, no. 4 (2012): 795–99; Greer, *Mohawk Saint*, 52–53.

61. Cholenec to Le Blanc, in Kip, *Early Jesuit Missions*, 87–92.

62. *JR*, 63:219; Blanchard, "'. . . To the Other Side of the Sky,'" 95; Cholenec to Le Blanc, in Kip, *Early Jesuit Missions*, 95–96.

63. Cholenec to Le Blanc, in Kip, *Early Jesuit Missions*, 106–11.

64. Blanchard, "'. . . To the Other Side of the Sky,'" 97.

65. Shoemaker, "Kateri Tekakwitha's Tortuous Path," 49–71, esp. 60–61. See also William B. Hart, "'The Kindness of the Blessed Virgin': Faith, Succour, and the Cult of Mary among Christian Hurons and Haudenosaunee in Seventeenth-Century New France," in *Spiritual Encounters: Interactions between Christianity and Native Religions in Colonial America,* ed. Nicholas Griffiths and Fernando Cervantes (Birmingham: University of Birmingham Press; Lincoln: University of Nebraska Press, 1999), 65–90.

66. Greer, *Mohawk Saint*, 111–24.

67. Proposition of the Christian Mohawks to Governor Sloughter, May 26, 1691, *DRCHNY*, 3:771–72.

68. Proposition of the Christian Mohawks . . . 1691, *DRCHNY*, 3:771–72. The language in parentheses appears in the original of *New York Colonial Manuscripts*, vol. 37.

69. Proposition of Christian Mohawks . . . 1691, *DRCHNY*, 3:772.

70. Proposition of Christian Mohawks . . . 1691, *DRCHNY*, 3:772. At the conclusion of their remarks, they presented Sloughter a gift of "a Pouch made of Porcupine quills," which warriors carried into battle, and allegedly asked that he accept it as a token "from your Children," an interpretation that the interpreter or scribe may have inserted.

71. Johannes Megapolensis, "A Short Account of the Mohawk Indians, Their Country, Language, Stature, Dress, Religion and Government . . . August 26, 1644," in *Narratives of New Netherland, 1609–1664,* ed. J. Franklin Jameson (New York: Scribners, 1909), 172.

72. Megapolensis, "Short Account of Mohawk Indians," 175, 177–78.

73. Gerald Francis De Jong, "Dominie Johannes Megapolensis: Minister to New Netherland," *New-York Historical Society Quarterly* 52, no. 1 (1968): 6–47; Rev. Charles E. Corwin, "Efforts of the Dutch-American Colonial Pastors for the Conversion of the Indians," *Journal of the Presbyterian Historical Society* 12 (1924–27): 235, 238.

74. Rev. Godfreidus Dellius to Classis of Amsterdam, February 17, 1690–91, *ERSNY*, 2:1010–11.

75. Church of Albany to Classis of Amsterdam, *ERSNY*, 2:1002–3; Corwin, "Efforts of Colonial Pastors," 238–40.

76. Dellius to Classis of Amsterdam, November 1, 1693, *ERSNY*, 2:1087, 1103; Corwin, "Efforts of Colonial Pastors," 239; Bishop of London to Lords of Trade, November 1, 1700, *DRCHNY*, 4:774; John Miller, *New York Considered & Improved, 1695,* ed. Victor Hugo (Cleveland, OH: Burrows, 1903), 70–72; Ronald William Howard, "Education & Ethnicity in Colonial New York, 1664–1763: A Study in the Transmission of Culture in Early America" (PhD diss., University of Tennessee, 1978), 232. The first entry in *Livingston Indian Records*, dated "18 February 1666," cites Hilletie Couwenliche (Cornelissen) as the interpreter. Her name appears throughout these collected documents, last appearing in the citation for "27 October 1702." Leder, *Livingston Indian Records*, 29, 185, and passim. For a brief but informative biography of Hilletie, see Sivertsen, *Turtles, Wolves, and Bears,* 1–10.

77. Jasper Danckaerts, *Journal of Jasper Danckaerts, 1679–80* (orig. *Journal of a Voyage to New York and a Tour in Several of the American Colonies in 1679–80, by Jasper Dankers and Peter Sluyter of Wiewerd in Friesland* [Brooklyn, 1867]), ed. Bartlett Burleigh James and J. Franklin Jameson (New York: Scribners, 1913), 202–3; Burke, "'Extreemest Part of All,'" 229.

78. Danckaerts, *Journal*, 203–4. Hilletie most likely learned of Christianity through

one of the Jesuit priests who resided in her village, just as Hilletie's nephew Wouter claimed.

79. Danckaerts, *Journal*, xx–xxv, 204.

80. It is also possible that Hilletie was simply fat. Most dictionaries cite an archaic use of "sow" to mean a grossly fat person.

81. Danckaerts, *Journal*, 202, 205.

82. Lafitau, *Customs of the American Indians*, 2:19–23; Charles T. Gehring and William A. Starna, trans. and eds., *A Journey into Mohawk and Oneida Country, 1634–1635: The Journal of Harmen Meyndertsz van den Bogaert* (Syracuse, NY: Syracuse University Press, 1988), 4; *Minutes of the Courts of Albany, Rensselaerswyck, and Schenectady* (Albany: State University of New York at Albany), 3:470–71.

83. Dennis, *Cultivating a Landscape of Peace*, chap. 3.

CHAPTER 2: "ORDERING THE LIFE AND MANNERS OF A NUMEROUS PEOPLE"

1. Proposition of Canada Praying Indians, June–July 1700, *DRCHNY*, 4:692; David Schuyler to Lord Bellomont, August 17, 1700, *DRCHNY*, 4:747–48. For how England used Church of England Protestantism to build and expand its empire in the seventeenth and eighteenth centuries, see Carla Gardina Pestana, *Protestant Empire: Religion and the Making of the British Atlantic World* (Philadelphia: University of Pennsylvania Press, 2009); and Travis Glasson, *Mastering Christianity: Missionary Anglicanism and Slavery in the Atlantic World* (New York: Oxford University Press, 2012).

2. Proposition of Canada Praying Indians, June–July 1700, *DRCHNY*, 4:692–93; Report of the Board of Trade, *DRCHNY*, 4:391–93; Eric Hinderaker, *The Two Hendricks: Unraveling a Mohawk Mystery* (Cambridge, MA: Harvard University Press, 2010), 51.

3. Proposition of Canada Praying Indians, June–July 1700, *DRCHNY*, 4:693.

4. Proposition of Canada Praying Indians, June–July 1700, *DRCHNY*, 4:693. Dowaganhae, or Ojibwe country, lay in the Great Lakes region.

5. Citizens of Albany to Earl of Bellomont, *DRCHNY*, 4:753; Hugh Hastings, ed., *ERSNY*, 2:1376; Council Journal, July 29, 1700, *ERSNY*, 2:1367; An Act against Jesuits and Popish Preists [*sic*], August 9, 1700, *ERSNY*, 2:1368–70; Robert Livingston to Lords of Trade, May 13, 1701, *DRCHNY*, 4:870.

6. Commissioners for Trade and Plantation, September 24, 1696, *DRCHNY*, 4:230.

7. William Kellaway, *The New England Company, 1649–1776: Missionary Society to the American Indians* (New York: Barnes & Noble, 1961), 260–64, 17; Charles E. Corwin, "Efforts of the Dutch-American Colonial Pastors for the Conversion of the Indians," *Journal of the Presbyterian Historical Society* 12 (1924–27): 238–40.

8. Conference of the Earl of Bellomont with the Indians, August 28, 1700, *DRCHNY*, 4:734; Bellomont's Instructions to Col. Romer, September 3, 1700, *DRCHNY*, 4:750; Bellomont to Lords of Trade, October 17, 1700, *DRCHNY*, 4:717.

9. Bellomont to Lords of Trade, October 24, 1698, *DRCHNY*, 4:410; Robert Livingston's Journey to Onondaga, April 1700, *DRCHNY*, 4:649, 652; Schuyler, Livingston, and Hansen to Earl of Bellomont, May 3, 1700, *DRCHNY*, 4:653; Commissioners at Onondaga, April 27, 1700, *DRCHNY*, 4:660–61. Resistance from Dekanissore and other Onondagans and from Colonel Peter Schuyler, who, with Albany merchants, feared forts to the west would draw off trade from Albany, convinced Livingston to shift his position on forts throughout Iroquoia, which angered Bellomont, who desired to harvest the untapped natural resources there. Bellomont to Lords of Trade, November 28, 1700, *DRCHNY*, 4:783–86; Livingston to Lords of Trade, May 13, 1701, *DRCHNY*, 4: 870–79.

10. Jean M. O'Brien, *Dispossession by Degrees: Indian Land and Identity in Natick, Massachusetts, 1650–1790* (Cambridge: Cambridge University Press, 1997), 29–64; Edward E. Andrews, *Native Apostles: Black and Indian Missionaries in the British Atlantic* (Cambridge, MA: Harvard University Press, 2013), 25–53; Kristina Bross and Hilary Wyss, eds., *Early Native Literacies in New England: A Documentary and Critical Anthology* (Amherst: University of Massachusetts, Press, 2008), 105–29; Edward G. Gray, *New World Babel: Languages and Nations in Early America* (Princeton, NJ: Princeton University Press, 1999), chap. 3; Francis Jennings, *The Invasion of America: Indians, Colonialism, and the Cant of Conquest* (New York: W. W. Norton, 1976), 233–53; Neil E. Salisbury, "'Red Puritans': The 'Praying Indians' of Massachusetts Bay and John Eliot," *WMQ* 31, no. 1 (1974): 27–54; Kenneth M. Morrison, "'That Art of Coyning Christians': John Eliot and the Praying Indians of Massachusetts," *Ethnohistory* 21, no. 1 (1974): 77–92. For a discussion of "reduce to civility," see James Axtell, *Invasion Within: The Contest of Cultures in Colonial North America* (New York: Oxford University Press, 1985), 131–78; for Eliot at Natick, see 220–41.

11. George Pigot, *A Vindication of the Practice of the Ancient Christian . . .* (Boston: T. Fleet, 1731), 16, cited in John Calam, *Parsons and Pedagogues: The SPG Adventure in American Education* (New York: Columbia University Press, 1971), 78; Jack Goody, "Oral Culture," in *Folklore, Cultural Performances, and Popular Entertainments: A Communications-Based Handbook*, ed. Richard Bauman (New York: Oxford University Press, 1992), 18; Reverend Gilbert Burnet, Bishop of Sarum, *A Sermon Preach'd at St. Mary-le-Bow, February 18, 1703/04* (London: D. Brown and R. Symson, 1704), 17–18, in *Sermons and Abstracts, 1701–10,* by Society for the Propagation of the Gospel in Foreign Parts (London: SPG, n.d.); Reverend Richard Willis, Dean of Lincoln, *A Sermon Preached before the SPG . . . February 20, 1701/02* (London: M. Wotton, 1702), 17–18, in *Sermons and Abstracts.*

12. Burnet, *Sermon Preach'd*, 14–16.

13. David Humphreys, *An Historical Account of the Incorporated Society for the Propagation of the Gospel in Foreign Parts* (London: Joseph Downey, 1730), iv; Laura M. Stevens, *The Poor Indians: British Missionaries, Native Americans, and Colonial Sensibility* (Philadelphia: University of Pennsylvania Press, 2004), 85–87, 4, 3, 111–37.

14. John Spurr, *The Restoration Church of England, 1646–1689,* (New Haven, CT: Yale University Press, 1991), 2–3, 9, 34–36. Parliament passed several other acts to signal the reestablishment of the Church of England and to punish dissenting churches. Spurr, *Restoration Church*, 34, 51–52.

15. Spurr, *Restoration Church*, 239, 245, 61–68, 103–4, 248.

16. Spurr, *Restoration Church*, 89–95.

17. Gordon Rupp, *Religion in England, 1688–1791* (Oxford, U.K.: Clarendon Press, 1986), 5.

18. Spurr, *Restoration Church*, 277; Rupp, *Religion in England*, 290–96; H. P. Thompson, *Into All Lands: The History of the Society for the Propagation of the Gospel in Foreign Parts, 1701–1950* (London: Society for the Propagation of Christian Knowledge, 1951), 5–8.

19. Rupp, *Religion in England,* 298–99, 303; John Frederick Woolverton, *Colonial Anglicanism in North America* (Detroit: Wayne State University Press, 1986), 84–85. For a mention of charity schools in England, Ireland, the West Indies, and in the colonies as a tool of "reduction," see Lord Primate of Ireland to Secretary, March 20, 1711, SPG Letters A, 6:no. 54, n.p. The SPG would eventually introduce a version of these schools in Mohawk country.

20. Rupp, *Religion in America,* 300. For Bray's brief stay in Maryland, see Thompson, *Into All Lands,* 9–16.

21. Charter of the Society, June 16, 1701, in C. F. Pascoe, *Two Hundred Years of the SPG:*

*An Historical Account of the Propagation of the Gospel in Foreign Parts, 1701–1900* (London: Society for the Propagation of the Gospel, 1901), 932; Thompson, *Into All Lands*, 17; Humphreys, *Historical Account*, xvi, 21–22.

22. Thanks to John Richards for corroborating the Latin translation.

23. Willis, *Sermon Preach'd*, 17 (emphases in the original); Frank J. Klingberg, *Anglican Humanitarianism in New York* (Philadelphia: Church Historical Society, 1940), 14; Sermon of Dr. J. Williams, February 1706, in Klingberg, *Anglican Humanitarianism*, 15; Minutes of SPG Meeting, April 28, 1710, SPG Journals, 1:479; Humphreys, *Historical Account*, 23–24.

24. Charles Smith to Secretary, October 8, 1703, SPG Letters A, 1:no. 102, n.p.

25. Kellaway, *New England Company*, 206. Ironically, Jonathan Edwards, Stoddard's grandson, became the pastor to the Native community at Stockbridge, Massachusetts, in 1749 after he was dismissed by his congregation, formerly his grandfather's, at Northampton.

26. Governor Dongan's Report, February 22, 1687–88, *Documentary History of the State of New York* (hereafter *DHNY*), ed. E. B. O'Callaghan, 4 vols. (Albany, NY: Weed, Parsons, 1851), 1:186–87.

27. Eneas MacKenzie to Secretary, July 28, 1710, SPG Letters A, 5:no. 148, n.p.; John Talbot to Secretary, July 5, 1710, SPG Letters A, 5:no. 139, n.p.; John Thomas to Secretary, June 12, 1709, SPG Letters A, 5:no. 4, n.p.; same, 1712, SPG Letters A, 7:no. 8, n.p.; Ronald William Howard, "Education and Ethnicity in Colonial New York, 1664–1763: A Study in the Transmission of Culture in Early America" (PhD diss., University of Tennessee, 1978), 285; Calam, *Parsons and Pedagogues*, 123.

28. Joyce D. Goodfriend, *Before the Melting Pot: Society and Culture in Colonial New York City, 1664–1730* (Princeton, NJ: Princeton University Press, 1992), 16, 97–110, 113–14; Jacobus van Cortland, "Letter Book, 1698–1700," New-York Historical Society, folio 4; Translation of Elias Neau to Secretary, April 13, 1704, SPG Letters A, 1:no. 178, n.p.; Translation of Elias Neau to Mr. Chamberlayne, February 27, 1708–9, SPG Letters A, 4:no. 121A, 409; Kenneth Scott, "The Slave Insurrection in New York in 1712," *New York Journal of American History* 66, no. 2 (2005): 76–88; Leon A. Higginbotham, *In the Matter of Color: Race and the American Legal Process: The Colonial Period* (New York: Oxford University Press, 1987), 116; Gov. Hunter to Lords of Trade, June 23, 1712, *DRCHNY*, 5:342; Thelma Wills Foote, *Black and White Manhattan: The History of Racial Formation in Colonial New York City* (New York: Oxford University Press, 2004); Leslie M. Harris, *African Americans in New York City, 1626–1863* (Chicago: University of Chicago Press, 2003).

29. Caleb Heathcote to Secretary, "The State of this Country in Relation to the Church," April 10, 1704, SPG Letters A 1:no. 182; Humphreys, *Historical Account*, 33.

30. John Miller, *New York Considered and Improved, 1695*, ed. Victor Hugo (Cleveland: Burrows, 1903), 40–92; Howard, "Education and Ethnicity in Colonial New York," 228–34.

31. Heathcote to Secretary of SPG, November 9, 1705, *DHNY*, 3:117–29.

32. William Stanley, Dean of St. Asoph, February 20, 1707–8 sermon, quoted in Klingberg, *Anglican Humanitarianism*, 29n60, quoting Matt. 9:37.

33. Pascoe, *Two Hundred Years*, 837; Humphreys, *Historical Account*, 66–67; Alfred W. Newcombe, "The Appointment and Instruction of SPG Missionaries," *Church History*, eds. Matthew Spinka et al. (New York: AMS, 1936), 5:342–44, 347; Calam, *Parsons and Pedagogues*, 23–24, 31. Col. Morris of New Jersey preferred that men of age and experience preach to the Haudenosaunees. See Col. Morris to Secretary, 1704, SPG Letters A, 1:no. 171, n.p.

34. Newcombe, "Appointment and Instruction of SPG Missionaries," 347–49.

35. Newcombe, "Appointment and Instruction of SPG Missionaries," 347–49; Humphreys,

*Historical Account,* 72; John Bartow to Secretary, August 8, 1706, SPG Letters A, 3:no. 43, n.p.; John Bartow to Lord Bishop of London, August 16, 1706, SPG Letters A, 3:no. 50, n.p.

36. Thomas Barclay to Lords of Trade, July 5, 1709, SPG Letters A, 5:no. 1, n.p. Common laborers earned about fifty pounds annually, carpenters and masons nearly 100 pounds. See Howard, "Education and Ethnicity in Colonial New York," 318. SPG schoolmasters received very low pay, between ten and thirty pounds annually. See Calam, *Parsons and Pedagogues,* 31.

37. Pascoe, *Two Hundred Years,* 840; Newcombe, "Appointment and Instruction of SPG Missionaries," 346, esp. note 41. Ten out of fifty-one ministers who crossed from the colonies to England to be ordained during the eighteenth century lost their lives at sea.

38. Humphreys, *Historical Account,* 69–71; Pascoe, *Two Hundred Years,* 837–38; Newcombe, "Appointment and Instruction of SPG Missionaries," 353–54; Edward Vaughan to Secretary, December 4, 1710, SPG Letters A, 6:no. 2, n.p.

39. Humphreys, *Historical Account,* 70–71; Pascoe, *Two Hundred Years,* 839; Newcombe, "Appointment and Instruction of SPG Missionaries," 355.

40. Humphreys, *Historical Account,* 71; Pascoe, *Two Hundred Years,* 840; Newcombe, "Appointment and Instruction of SPG Missionaries," 355–56; Col. Heathcote to Secretary, April 10, 1704, SPG Letters A, 1:no. 182, n.p.; same, June 1, 1704, SPG Letters A, 1:no. 174, n.p.

41. Pascoe, *Two Hundred Years,* 844; Calam, *Parsons and Pedagogues,* 108; Pestana, *Protestant Empire,* 7, 61, 63; Hilary E. Wyss, *Writing Indians: Literacy, Christianity, and Native Community in Early America* (Amherst: University of Massachusetts Press, 2000), 7.

42. Pascoe, *Two Hundred Years,* 844.

43. Pascoe, *Two Hundred Years,* 63–64, 845; Translation of Elias Neau to Secretary, July 4, 1704, SPG Letters A, 1:no. 177, n.p.; Translation of Elias Neau to Mr. Chamberlayne, August 29, 1704, SPG, Letters A, 2:no. 19, n.p.

44. Translation of Elias Neau to Secretary, July 10, 1703, SPG Letters A, 1:no. 106, n.p.

45. Translation of Elias Neau to Secretary, July 4, 1704, SPG Letters A, 1:no. 177, n.p.; Translation of Elias Neau to Mr. Chamberlayne, August 29, 1704, SPG Letters A, 2:no. 19, n.p.

46. Geo. Muirson to Secretary, January 9, 1707–8, SPG Letters A, 3:no. 168, 460; Wm. Vesey to Secretary, October 26, 1705, SPG Letters A, 2:no. 26, n.p.; Dr. Sharp's Proposal, March 11, 1712–13, SPG Letters A, 10:no. 9, 241. William Vesey, the rector at Trinity Church, opposed Neau's appointment, noting Neau's difficulty with English, his activities as a merchant, and the fact that he was not ordained. Bottom line, Vesey wanted George Muirson, a schoolmaster in the city, to be appointed catechist and his personal assistant. See various correspondence: Wm. Urquhart to Mr. Stubs, July 4, 1704, SPG Letters A, 2:no. 54, n.p.; Translation of Elias Neau to Secretary, August 29, 1704, SPG Letters A, 2:no. 19, n.p.; Wm. Vesey to Secretary, October 26, 1704, SPG Letters A, 2:no. 26, n.p.; Wm. Vesey to Lord Bishop of London, October 26, 1704, SPG Letters A, 2:no. 40, n.p.; Wm. Urquhart to Mr. Stubs, November 1, 1704, SPG Letters A, 2:no. 41, n.p.

47. Translation of Elias Neau to Dr. Woodward, September 5, 1704, SPG Letters A, 2:no. 48, n.p.; Translation of Elias Neau to Mr. John Hodges, June 22, 1704, SPG Letters A, 2:no. 1, n.p.; Dr. Sharp's Proposal, July 11, 1713, SPG Letters A, 10:no. 9, 250; Translation of Elias Neau to Secretary, November 6, 1704, SPG Letters A, 2:no. 21, n.p.; same, December 20, 1704, SPG Letters A, 2:no. 67, n.p. For Neau's imprisonment, see Sheldon S. Cohen, "Elias Neau, Instructor to New York's Slaves," *New-York Historical Society Quarterly* 55, no. 1 (1971): 8–16.

48. Dr. Sharp's Proposal, July 11, 1713, SPG Letters A, 10:no. 9, 248; Translation of Elias Neau Secretary, July 22, 1707, SPG Letters A, 3:no. 80, 192; same, July 24, 1707, SPG Letters A, 3:no. 128, 301.

49. Elias Neau to Chamberlayne, June 9, 1709, SPG Letters A, 4:no. 155, n.p.

50. According to a census taken in 1698, New York City's total population was 4,937, of which 14 percent, or just under 700, were free and enslaved blacks and indigenes. By 1712, the free black and enslaved population equaled 970, representing 17 percent of the city's total population. See Goodfriend, *Before the Melting Pot,* 61, 63, 112–13.

51. Christopher Bridge to Secretary, November 12, 1710, SPG Letters A, 6:no. 5, n.p.; William Andrews to Secretary, September 7, 1713, SPG Letters A, 8:187; Minutes of SPG Meeting, November 23, 1713, and February 12, 1713–14, SPG Journals, 1:no. 153, n.p., 2:353; An Account for Printing the Prayers etc. in the Indian Language, July 12, 1715, SPG Letters A, 10:239; *Portions of the Prayer Book with Family Prayers and Several Chapters of the Old and New Testaments,* trans. Lawrence Claessen (New York: Bradford, 1715); William Andrews to Secretary, April 20, 1716, SPG Letters A, 11:317; Calam, *Parsons and Pedagogues,* 43–44, 92–93; C. F. Pascoe and H. W. Tucker, eds., *Classified Digest of the Records of the Society for the Propagation of the Gospel in Foreign Parts, 1701–1892* (London: SPG, 1895), 800.

52. Richard Allestree, *The Whole Duty of Man, Laid Down in a Plain and Familiar Way for the Use of All, but Especially the Meanest Reader* (London: R. Norton for R. Pawlet, 1677); Calam, *Parsons and Pedagogues,* 97–98.

53. For survival goods, see Minutes of SPG Meeting, June 17, 1715, and January 11, 1716–17, SPG Journals, 3:65, 3:196; William Andrews to Secretary, September 9, 1717, SPG Letters A, 12:327.

54. Robert Livingston to Lords of Trade, May 13, 1701, *DRCHNY,* 4:872; Conference: Nanfan and the Five Nations, July 10–21, 1701, *DRCHNY,* 4:905–7, 896; Nanfan to Lords of Trade, August 21, 1701, *DRCHNY,* 4:11.

55. Church of Albany to the Classis of Amsterdam, June 5, 1699, *ERSNY,* 2:1316–17; Bellomont to Lords of Trade, July 1, 1698, *DRCHNY,* 4:334; Fraudulent Purchase of Land from Mohawk Indians, *DRCHNY,* 4:345–47, 391–93. For additional evidence on Joseph and Hendrick, see Hinderaker, *Two Hendricks,* 50, 55, 308.

56. Conference of the Earl of Bellomont with the Indians, August 31, 1700, *DRCHNY,* 4:727, 742–43; Rev. John Lydius to the Classis of Amsterdam, August 15, 1700, *ERSNY,* 2:1373–74.

57. Call of the Church of Albany, March 5, 1700, *ERSNY,* 2:1340–45; Rev. John Lydius to the Classis of Amsterdam, August 15, 1700, *ERSNY,* 2:1371–73; Classis of Amsterdam to the Rev. John Peter Nucella, July 18, 1701, *ERSNY,* 2:1471–72.

58. Rev. John Lydius to the Classis of Amsterdam, August 15, 1700, *ERSNY,* 2:1373; Bernardus Freeman to Secretary, May 28, 1712, SPG Letters A, 7:no. 28, 203; Minutes of SPG Meeting, October 10, 1712, SPG Journals, 2:240–41.

59. Richter, *Ordeal of Longhouse,* 222–23, 178; Thomas Burke Jr., "'The Extreemest Part of All': The Dutch Community of Schenectady, New York, 1661–1720" (PhD diss., State University of New York, Albany, 1984), 239. For Dellius's rate of baptism—fourteen a year versus Freeman's twenty-two—see Dellius to Classis of Amsterdam, *ERSNY,* 2:1065.

60. Freeman to Secretary, May 28, 1712, SPG Letters A, 7:no. 28, 203.

61. Bernardus Freeman to Secretary, May 28, 1712, SPG Letters A, 7:no. 28, 203.

62. *ERSNY,* 2:1507, 1532–43, 1607, 1623–35, 1639–41, 1762–67.

63. Conference of Governor Cornbury with the Five Nations, July 15, 1702, *DRCHNY,* 4:983; same, July 18, 1702, *DRCHNY,* 4:986–88.

64. Journal of Bleeker and Schuyler at Onondaga, June 2–19, 1701, *DRCHNY,* 4:890, 893; Richter, *Ordeal of the Longhouse,* 198–99, 210.

65. Report of Bleeker and Schuyler at Onondaga, September 13, 1701, *DRCHNY,* 4: 919–20; Journal of Schuyler and Bleeker, June 2–29, 1701, *DRCHNY,* 4:893.
66. Report of Bleeker and Schuyler at Onondaga, September 13, 1701, *DRCHNY,* 4: 919–20; Journal of Bleeker and Schuyler, June 2–19, 1701, *DRCHNY,* 4:893.
67. Report of Bleeker and Schuyler, August 27–September 14, 1701, *DRCHNY,* 4:920; Journal of Bleeker and Schuyler, June 2–29, 1701, *DRCHNY,* 4:893.
68. Thorogood (Thoroughgood) Moor's Account of His Mission Among Mohawks, March 8, 1704–5, SPG Letters A, 2:no. 75, n.p.
69. Moor's Account, March 8, 1704–5, SPG Letters A, 2:no. 75, n.p.
70. Moor's Account, March 8, 1704–5, SPG Letters A, 2:no. 75, n.p.
71. Moor's Account, March 8, 1704–5, SPG Letters A, 2:no. 75, n.p.
72. Moor to Secretary, November 13, 1705, SPG Letters A, 2:no. 122, n.p.
73. Moor's Account, March 8, 1704–5, SPG Letters A, 2:no. 75; Robert Livingston to Lords of Trade, December 18, 1703, *DRCHNY,* 4:1074–75; John Chamberlayne to Lords of Trade, February 1, 1703–4, *DRCHNY,* 4:1077. The "other castle" Moor refers to was probably Schoharie (Eskare), which lay twelve miles away.
74. Moor's Account, March 8, 1704–5, SPG Letters A, 2:no. 75, n.p.
75. Moor's Account, March 8, 1704–5, SPG Letters A, 2:no. 75, n.p.
76. Moor's Account, March 8, 1704–5, SPG Letters A, 2:no. 75, n.p.
77. Moor's Account, March 8, 1704–5, SPG Letters A, 2:no. 75, n.p.
78. Moor to Secretary, November 13, 1705, SPG Letters A, 2:no. 122, n.p.
79. Moor to Secretary, November 13, 1705, SPG Letters A, 2:no. 122, n.p.
80. Moor to Secretary, November 13, 1705, SPG Letters A, 2:no. 122, n.p.
81. Moor to Secretary, November 13, 1705, SPG Letters A, 2:no. 122, n.p.; Lord Cornbury to Secretary, September 22, 1705, SPG Letters A, 2:no. 131, n.p.; Miller, *New York Considered,* 86.
82. Moor to Secretary, November 13, 1705, SPG Letters A, 2:no. 122, n.p.
83. Moor to Secretary, November 13, 1705, SPG Letters A, 2:no. 122, n.p.
84. Bishop Fleetwood's Sermon (1711), as cited in Klingberg, *Anglican Humanitarianism,* 203.
85. Presents to Five Nations, November 10, 1694, *DRCHNY,* 4:126; Meeting of Gov. Fletcher with Five Nations, September 29, 1696, *DRCHNY,* 4:236; Robert Livingston to the Lords of Trade, May 13, 1701, *DRCHNY,* 4:876.

CHAPTER 3: "LAYING A GOOD AND LASTING FOUNDATION OF RELIGION"

1. Andrews to Rev. Mr. Sharp, November 25, 1712, SPG Letters A, 8:no. 23, 250.
2. Thomas Barclay to Secretary, December 17, 1712, SPG Letters A, 8:no. 16, 125; Andrews to Secretary, March 9, 1712–13, SPG Letters A, 8:no. 24, 143; Meeting of the Commissioners of the Indian Affairs, November 15, 1712, SPG Letters A, 8:no. 25, 254–55; Eric Hinderaker, *The Two Hendricks: Unraveling a Mohawk Mystery* (Cambridge, MA: Harvard University Press, 2010), 109; Timothy J. Shannon, *Iroquois Diplomacy on the Early American Frontier* (New York: Viking Penguin, 2008), 116.
3. Andrews to Rev. Sharp, November 25, 1712, SPG Letters A, 8:no. 23, 250–51; Thomas Barclay to Secretary, December 17, 1712, SPG Letters A, 8:no. 16, 126–27; Meeting of Commissioners of Indian Affairs, November 15, 1712, SPG Letters A, 8:no. 25, 255–56.
4. Extract, Rev. Barclay to Gov. Hunter, January 26, 1712–13, SPG Letters A, 8:no. 24, 251; Hinderaker, *Two Hendricks,* 113–14; Barbara J. Sivertsen, *Turtles, Wolves, and Bears: A Mohawk Family History* (Bowie, MD: Heritage Books, 1996), 75, 92; Austin A. Yates, *Schenectady County, New York: Its History to the Close of the Nineteenth Century*

(New York: New York History, 1902), 237—38; J. H. French, "Schoharie County, NY," *Historical and Statistical Gazetteer of New York State* (1859; reprint, Interlaken, NY: Heart of the Lakes, 1986), 601—2; Daniel Richter, *The Ordeal of the Longhouse: The Peoples of the Iroquois League in the Era of European Colonization* (Chapel Hill: University of North Carolina Press, 1992), 228—31. I am following Barbara Sivertsen's spelling of Taquayanont's name. Other historians have used various spellings, including "Tagnaynaut."

5. Barclay to Secretary, December 12, 1712, SPG Letters A, 8:no. 16, 125; Richmond P. Bond, *Queen Anne's American Kings* (Oxford: Clarendon Press, 1952), 59.

6. Andrews to Rev. Mr. Sharp, November 25, 1712, SPG Letters A, 8:no. 23, 250; Andrews to Secretary, March 9, 1712—13, SPG Letters A, 8:no. 24, 143; John Wolfe Lydekker, *The Faithful Mohawks* (New York: Macmillan, 1938), 36.

7. Barclay to Secretary, December 12, 1712, SPG Letters A, 8:no. 16, 125; Andrews to Secretary, September 1, 1717, SPG Letters A, 13:334.

8. Andrews to Secretary, March 9, 1712—13, SPG Letters A, 8:no. 24, 143; same to Secretary, October 17, 1715, SPG Letters A, 11:269; same, September 7, 1713, SPG Letters A, 8:no. 50, 182—83; Minutes of SPG meeting, November 23, 1713, SPG Journals, 1:no. 153, 548; Lydekker, *Faithful Mohawks*, 43—46.

9. Andrews to Secretary, October 11, 1716, SPG Letters A, 12:239; Minutes of SPG Meeting, October 18, 1717, SPG Journals, 3:312; Secretary of SPG to Governor Hunter, November 11, 1717, SPG Letters A, 12:429; Governor Hunter to Secretary, June 3, 1718, SPG Letters A, 13:331; Minutes of SPG Meeting, February 13, 1718—19, SPG Journals, 4: 26; Andrews to Secretary, October 11, 1716, SPG Letters A, 12:241; Minutes of SPG Meeting, September 20, 1717, SPG Journals, 3:292—93; Andrews to Secretary, April 23, 1717, SPG Letters A, 12:310—11; same, September 26, 1717, SPG Letters A, 12:338; same, April 17, 1718, SPG Letters A, 13:319.

10. James Axtell, *The Invasion Within: The Contest of Cultures in Colonial North America* (New York: Oxford University Press, 1985), 262; Richter, *Ordeal of the Longhouse*, 232—33.

11. Michael Taussig, *Shamanism, Colonialism, and the Wild Man: A Study in Terror and Healing* (Chicago: University of Chicago Press, 1986), 121.

12. Thomas Barclay to Secretary, September, 26, 1710, SPG Letters A, 5:176; same, *DRCHNY*, 9:983; Bond, *Queen Anne's Kings*, 1, 39—40n116. The spelling of the names of the "four kings" appears variously. I have used the spelling that appears by their totems on a letter that each man signed, dated July 21, 1710, and mailed from Boston.

13. Eric Hinderaker, "The 'Four Indian Kings' and the Imaginative Construction of the First British Empire," *WMQ* 53, no. 3 (1996): 497—526; Bond, *Queen Anne's Kings*, 1—16, 94; *The Four Kings of Canada, Being a Succinct Account of the Four Indian Princes Lately Arriv'd from North America* (London: John Baker, 1710; reprint, London: Garratt, 1891); Hinderaker, "'Four Indian Kings,'" 491. An exception to the turban representing elite Muslim status is its representation of holiness and valor for Sikhs. For a study on the rise of the "Persian fashion" look among elite white men in the colonies and the new republic—which also included wearing banyans (robes or gowns)—see Brandon Brame Fortune, "'Studious Men Are Always Painted in Gowns': Charles Wilson Peale's Benjamin Rush and the Question of Banyans in Eighteenth-Century Anglo-American Portraiture," *Dress* 29, no. 1 (2002): 27—40.

14. Bond, *Queen Anne's Kings*, 1—16, 94; *Four Kings*; Hinderaker, "'Four Indian Kings,'" 505—22.

15. The failed 1709 expedition was plagued with many difficulties, beginning with the unexpected death of New York governor Lovelace (1708—9), who was to carry out orders to subdue Canada as part of England's war with France in Europe. Lieutenant

Governor Richard Ingoldsby, former lieutenant general Francis Nicholson, and Colonels Pieter Schuyler and Samuel Vetch assumed responsibility for the plan, which included recruiting Haudenosaunee warriors. The English fleet assembled in Boston harbor ready to sail for Quebec City was ordered to cross the Atlantic to fight in Europe. See Lawrence H. Leder, ed., *The Livingston Indian Records, 1666–1723* (Gettysburg: Pennsylvania Historical Association, 1956), 203–14.

16. *Four Kings,* 4–6; Bond, *Queen Anne's Kings,* 40.
17. Hinderaker, "'Four Indian Kings,'" 519; Hinderaker, *Two Hendricks,* 104–8; Richter, *Ordeal of the Longhouse,* 227–29, 369n32; Francis Parkman, *A Half-Century of Conflict,* 2 vols. (Boston: Little, Brown, 1892), 1:150–75. The Haudenosaunees did not speak with a unified voice on the invasion of Canada. The league's forces included nearly all Mohawk warriors, more than half of the Oneida and Cayuga warriors, but only one quarter of the Onondagas, and no Senecas. *Livingston Indian Records,* 203–14; Richter, *Ordeal of the Longhouse,* 225–26.
18. Minutes of SPG Meeting, April 28, 1710, SPG Journals, 1:479–80.
19. Minutes of SPG Meeting, April 28, 1710, SPG Journals, 1:480.
20. Minutes of SPG Meeting, April 28, 1710, SPG Journals, 1:482.
21. Bond, *Queen Anne's Kings,* 43; Hinderaker, "'Four Indian Kings,'" 492–95.
22. *Four Kings,* 4–6.
23. *Four Kings,* 4–5; Hilary E. Wyss, *Writing Indians: Literacy, Christianity, and Native Community in Early America* (Amherst: University of Massachusetts Press, 2000), 5.
24. Yasuhide Kawashima, "Forest Diplomats: The Role of Interpreters in Indian-White Relations on the Early American Frontier," *American Indian Quarterly* 13, no. 1 (1989): 1–14; Nancy Hagedorn, "'A Friend to Go between Them': The Interpreter as Culture Broker during Anglo-Iroquois Councils, 1740–70," *Ethnohistory* 35, no. 1 (1988): 60–81.
25. Minutes of SPG Meeting, July 21, 1710, SPG Journals, 1:491; same, February 8, 1710–11, SPG Journals, 1:571; Col. Schuyler to Secretary, n.d., SPG Letters A, 6:no. 7, n.p.; Minutes of SPG, March 22, 1710–11, SPG Journals, 1:11; same, January 25, 1711–12, SPG Journals, 2:163; same, November 29, 1711, SPG Journals, 2:126.
26. Four Kings to Lord Bishop of Canterbury, May 22, 1710, SPG Letters A, 6:no. 93, n.p.; Conference of Gov. Hunter with the Indians, August 7–21, 1710, *DRCHNY,* 5:221, 224, 227. Curiously, the 1710 letter refers to "six nations" constituting the league rather than five. The bulk of the Tuscaroras would not arrive to Iroquoia until 1713.
27. Rev. Sharpe to Secretary, November 1712, SPG Letters A, 7:no. 33, n.p.; Contract to Build Forts, *DRCHNY,* 5:279–281.
28. Minutes of SPG Meeting, October 21, 1709, SPG Journals, 1:407; Barclay to Lord Bishop of London, 1709, SPG Letters A, 5:no. 1, n.p.; Elias Neau to Secretary, July 5, 1710, SPG Letters A, 5:no. 134, n.p.; Meeting of SPG, May 18, 1711, SPG Journals, 1:41, and Barclay to Secretary, June 12, 1711, SPG Letters A, 6:no. 129, n.p.; same, December 7, 1710, SPG Letters A, 6 no. 50, n.p.; same, November 21, 1711, SPG Letters A, 7:no. 2, n.p.
29. Barclay to Secretary. December 7, 1710, SPG Letters A, 6:no. 50, n.p.
30. Barclay to Secretary, September 26, 1710, SPG Letters A, 5:no. 176, n.p.; Papers Relating to Albany and Adjacent Places, 1710, *DHNY,* 3:898; Barclay to Secretary, December 7, 1710, SPG Letters A, 6:no. 50, n.p.; same, September 26, 1710, SPG Letter A, 5:no. 176, n.p.
31. Barclay to Secretary, June 12, 1711, SPG Letters A, 6:no. 129, n.p.; same, September 26, 1710, SPG Letter A, 5:no. 176, n.p.; Papers Relating to Albany and Adjacent Places, *DHNY,* 4:899; Barclay to Secretary, June 29, 1714, SPG Letters A, 9:no. 30, 144; same, May 31, 1712, SPG Letters A, 7:no. 29, n.p.; Gov. Hunter to Lords of

Trade, July 11, 1712, *DRCHNY*, 5:344. Barclay may have resented Van Driessen's quick success among the Dutch because the dominie was better connected than he. The Dutch congregation contributed about a hundred pounds sterling per year to support Van Driessen. Barclay's Dutch congregants contributed not a single shilling toward his support. See Barclay to Secretary, April 17, 1713, SPG Letters A, 8:no. 36, 167; same, September 26, 1710, SPG Letter A, 5:no. 176, n.p.

32. Barclay to Secretary, November 21, 1711, SPG Letters A, 7:no. 2, 130; same, September 26, 1710, SPG Letter A, 5:no. 176, n.p.; Papers Relating to Albany and Adjacent Places, *DHNY*, 3:899. Barclay also used gifts to entice Dutch children to catechism school. See Barclay to SPG, September 26, 1710, SPG Letter A, 5:no. 176, n.p.; William Webb Kemp, *The Support of Schools in Colonial New York by the Society for the Propagation of the Gospel in Foreign Parts* (New York: Columbia University, 1913), 198.

33. Minutes of SPG Meeting, April 3, 1712, SPG Journals, 2:182; Barclay to Secretary, April 17, 1713, SPG Letters A, 8:no. 36, 166; Minutes of SPG Meeting, December 4, 1713, SPG Journals, 2:340; Barclay's *Notitia Parochialis*, June 29, 1714, SPG Letters A, 9:no. 25, 233; Barclay to Secretary, October 22, 1714, SPG Letters A, 9:no. 36, 159.

34. Minutes of SPG Meeting, February 22, 1711–12, SPG Journals, 2:173; Certifications, SPG Letters A, 7:no. 3, 51; no. 4, 51–52, and no. 5, 52; Minutes of SPG Meeting, March 20, 1711–12, SPG Journals, 2:178; Andrews's Testimonial, April 1712, SPG Letters A, 7:no. 59, 102–4; Frederick Lewis Weis, "The Colonial Clergy of the Middle Colonies, New York, New Jersey, and Pennsylvania, 1628–1776," *American Antiquarian Society* 66, no. 2 (1956): 170.

35. Secretary of SPG to Gov. Hunter, July 26, 1712, SPG Letters A, 7:no. 13, 267; Bond, *Queen Anne's Kings,* 59–60. On the significance of state seals, see Nancy Shoemaker, *A Strange Likeness: Becoming Red and White in Eighteenth-Century North America* (New York: Oxford University Press, 2004), 75.

36. Andrews to Secretary, March 9, 1712–13, SPG Letters A, 8:no. 24, 145.

37. James Axtell, "The Power of Print in the Eastern Woodlands," in *After Columbus: Essays in the Ethnohistory of Colonial North America* (New York: Oxford University Press, 1988), 86–99; Phillip H. Round, *Removable Type: Histories of the Book in Indian Country, 1663–1880* (Chapel Hill: University of North Carolina Press, 2010), 10–14; Scott Richard Lyons, *X-marks: Native Signatures of Assent* (Minneapolis: University of Minnesota Press, 2010); Shoemaker, *Strange Likeness,* 61–81; Lisa Brooks, *The Common Pot: The Recovery of Native Space in the Northeast* (Minneapolis: University of Minnesota Press, 2006), 12.

38. For older studies on how literacy reorients the minds of oral-based indigenes, see Walter J. Ong, *Orality and Literacy: The Technologizing of the World* (London and New York: Methuen, 1982); Eric Havelock, *The Muse Learns to Write: Reflections on Orality and Literacy from Antiquity to the Present* (New Haven, CT: Yale University Press, 1986); Jack Goody, *The Interface between the Written and the Oral* (Cambridge: Cambridge University Press, 1987).

39. Axtell, "Power of Print," 86–99.

40. I share Lamin Sanneh's contention that empowerment lies in one's own language in print. Lamin Sanneh, *Encountering the West: Christianity and the Global Cultural Process: The African Dimension* (Maryknoll, NY: Orbis Books, 1993). See chapter 4 for a more complete discussion of Mohawk literacy.

41. Andrews to Secretary, October 11, 1716, SPG Letters A, 12:239–40.

42. Andrews to Secretary, September 7, 1713, SPG Letters A, 8:no. 50, 184–85; same, March 9, 1712–13, SPG Letters A, 8:no. 24, 143–46; Minutes of SPG Meeting, October 9, 1713, SPG Journals 2:322; Minutes of SPG meeting, November 23, 1713, SPG Journals, 1:no. 153, 548; SPG to Andrews, February 1, 1713–14, SPG Letters

A, 8:no. 22, 329–330; Andrews to Secretary, October 17, 1714, SPG Letters A, 10:no. 1, 155; Lydekker, *Faithful Mohawks*, 43–46.

43. Andrews to Secretary, September 7, 1713, SPG Letters A, 8:no. 50, 182–83; same, October 15, 1714, SPG Letters A, 10:186. The evidence is unclear as to whether the school building was built in the fashion of a longhouse or of framed construction, or even whether it was built in or near the fort or in the village of Tiononderoge.

44. Barclay to Secretary, December 17, 1712, SPG Letters A, 8:no. 16, 127–28; Andrews to Secretary, September 7, 1713, SPG Letters A, 8:no. 50, 183.

45. Andrews to Secretary, May 25, 1714, SPG Letters A, 9:no. 18, 123; same, September 7, 1713, SPG Letters A, 8:no. 50, 183; R. Bruce W. Anderson, "Perspectives on the Role of the Interpreter," in *The Interpreting Studies Reader*, ed. Franz Pochhacker and Miriam Shlesinger (London and New York: Routledge, 2002), 211. Claessen paid Oliver as much as fifteen pounds per year out of his own annual salary of sixty pounds to have the schoolmaster explain to him what Barclay and now Andrews said so that he might communicate it to the Mohawks. Minutes of SPG Meeting, March 4, 1713–14, SPG Journals, 2:362.

46. Andrews to Secretary, March 9, 1712–13, SPG Letters A, 8:no. 24, 143; same, October 17, 1714, SPG Letters A, 10:no. 1, 155; same, May 25, 1714, SPG Letters A, 9:no. 13, 123; Minutes of SPG Meeting, October 15, 1714, SPG Journals, 13:7; Andrews to Secretary, April 20, 1716, SPG Letters A, 11:317; Jean M. O'Brien, *Dispossession by Degrees: Indian Land and Identity in Natick, Massachusetts, 1650–1790* (Cambridge: Cambridge University Press, 1997), 57–58, 119–20.

47. Andrews to Secretary, addendum, September 7, 1713, SPG Letters A, 8:no. 51, 187; same, November 23, 1713, SPG Journals, 1:no. 153, 548; Minutes of SPG, February 12, 1713–14, SPG Journals, 2:352–53; Andrews to Secretary, May 25, 1714, SPG Letters A, 9:no. 18, 123; Invoice of Goods to Andrews, June 20, 1714, SPG Letters A, 9:no. 33, 71–72; Andrews to Secretary, October 15, 1714, SPG Letters A, 10:185; same, July 1715, SPG Letters A, 10:184, 239. For a description of the eighteenth-century penknife and quill, see Joyce Irene Whalley, *Writing Instruments and Accessories* (Detroit: Gale, 1975), 28, 35–36.

48. Andrews to Secretary, October 15, 1714, SPG Letters A, 10:186; same, May 25, 1714, SPG Letters A, 9:no. 18, 123. The lame youth may have been one of two Mohawk boys that Andrews took into his house to speed along their acquisition of English and perhaps provided him with servant's help. This experiment did not last long, for in October 1714 Andrews reported that the boys "soon grew weary of it," which forced him to teach them to read Mohawk. Andrews to Secretary, May 25, 1714, SPG Letters A, 9:no. 18, 124; same, October 17, 1714, SPG Letters A, 10:no. 1, 160; same, April 20, 1716, SPG Letters A, 11:317–18.

49. Andrews to Secretary, May 25, 1714, SPG Letters A, 9:no. 18, 123; Minutes of SPG Meeting, October 14, 1714, SPG Journals, 12:6.

50. Andrews to Secretary, October 15, 1714, SPG Letters A, 10:186; same, March 9, 1712–13, SPG Letters A, 8:no. 24, 145, 147; SPG to Andrews, February 1, 1713–14, SPG Letters A, 8:no. 22, 329.

51. Invoice and Bill to Andrews, n.d., SPG Letters A, 8:no. 44, 306; Andrews to Secretary, October 17, 1714, Letters A, 10:no. 1, 160.

52. Andrews to Secretary, April 20, 1716, SPG Letters A, 11:319; same, April 17, 1718, SPG Letters A, 13:319; Minutes of SPG Meeting, October 18, 1717, SPG Journals, 3:312; Secretary of SPG to Gov. Hunter, November 11, 1717, SPG Letters A, 12:429; Andrews to Secretary, September 1, 1717, SPG Letters A, 12:335–36; same, July 2, 1719, SPG Letters A, 13:465; same, October 17, 1718, SPG Letters A, 13:321.

53. Andrews to Secretary, October 17, 1714, SPG Letters A, 10:no. 1, 155.

54. Andrews to Secretary, October 17, 1714, SPG Letters A, 10:no. 1, 155; same, September 26, 1717, SPG Letters A, 12:338.
55. Andrews to Secretary, April 23, 1717, SPG Letters A, 12:311. For a study of the role of white women in Protestant churches from the colonial period to the nineteenth century, see Patricia U. Bonomi, *Under the Cope of Heaven: Religion, Society, and Politics in Colonial America* (New York: Oxford University Press, 1988), 111–15.
56. Susan Sleeper-Smith, *Indian Women and French Men: Rethinking Cultural Encounter in the Western Great Lakes* (Amherst: University of Massachusetts Press, 2001); Kathleen Bragdon, "Gender as a Social Category in Native Southern New England," *Ethnohistory* 43, no. 4 (1996): 573–79; William B. Hart, "'The Kindness of the Blessed Virgin': Faith, Succour, and the Cult of Mary among Christian Hurons and Iroquois in Seventeenth-Century New France," in *Spiritual Encounters: Interactions Between Christianity and Native Religions in Colonial America*, ed. Nicholas Griffiths and Fernando Cervantes (Birmingham: University of Birmingham Press, 1999), 65–90; Nancy Shoemaker, "Kateri Tekakwitha's Tortuous Path to Sainthood," in *Negotiators of Change: Historical Perspectives on Native American Women*, ed. Nancy Shoemaker (New York: Routledge, 1995), 49–71; Michael Harkin and Sergei Kan, "Introduction: Native American Women's Responses to Christianity," *Ethnohistory* 43, no. 4 (1996): 566.
57. Andrews to Secretary, October 15, 1715, SPG Letters A, 11:270–71.
58. Andrews to Secretary, October 17, 1718, SPG Letters A, 13:332; Minutes of SPG Meeting, December 5, 1718, SPG Journals, 4:3–4; Axtell, *Invasion Within*, 261.
59. Andrews to Secretary, October 17, 1718, SPG Letters A, 13:334–35.
60. Andrews to Secretary, October 15, 1714, SPG Letters A, 10:188; same, April 16, 1716, SPG Letters A, 11:319.
61. Andrews to Secretary, September 26, 1717, SPG Letters A, 12:338; same, September 1, 1717, SPG Letters A, 12:328–29.
62. Andrews to Secretary, September 1, 1717, SPG Letters A, 12:328–29.
63. Andrews to Secretary, September 1, 1717, SPG Letters A, 12:334; same, September 26, 1717, SPG Letters A, 12:339–40.
64. Andrews to Secretary, July 2, 1719, SPG Letters A, 13:467; same, October 17, 1718, SPG Letters A, 13:335.
65. Andrews to Secretary, March 9, 1712–13, SPG Letters A, 8:no. 24, 147; same, October 17, 1714, SPG Letters A, 10:no. 1, 156.
66. Andrews to Secretary, May 25, 1714, SPG Letters A, 9:no. 18, 124; Minutes of SPG Meeting, October 15, 1714, SPG Journals, 3:7; Andrews to Secretary, March 9, 1712–13, SPG Letters A, 8:no. 24, 144.
67. Andrews to Secretary, October 17, 1714, SPG Letters A, 10:no. 1, 156; same, April 23, 1717, SPG Letters A, 12:311; Representation to His Majesty to prevent Selling Rum to the Indians," n.d., SPG Letters A, 10:no. 10, 31–32.
68. Andrews to Secretary, September 7, 1713, SPG Letters A, 8:no. 50, 185; same, April 20, 1716, SPG Letters A, 11:319; same, April 23, 1717, SPG Letters A, 12:310–11.
69. Andrews to Secretary, September 1, 1717, SPG Letters A, 12:327–28.
70. Andrews to Secretary, October 11, 1716, SPG Letters A, 12:214.
71. Andrews to SPG, April 17, 1718, SPG Letters A, 13:320–21; same, September 1, 1717, SPG Letters A, 12:331; same, April 17, 1718, SPG Letters A, 13:326, 321, 319; same, September 26, 1717, SPG Letters A, 12:338; same, July 2, 1719, SPG Letters A, 13:467.
72. Andrews to Secretary, April 17, 1718, SPG Letters A, 131:319–21, 323; same, October 17, 1718, SPG Letters A, 13:336.
73. Andrews to Secretary, April 17, 1718, SPG Letters A, 13:323, 319–21; same, October 17, 1718, SPG Letters A, 13:331–33; same, July 2, 1719, SPG Letters A, 13:469; An Account . . . left by Mr. Andrews, July 11, 1719, SPG Letters A, 13:487.

74. Andrews to SPG, September 1, 1717, SPG Letters A, 12:336; same, September 26, 1717, SPG Letters A, 12:340; Minutes of SPG Meeting, December 5, 1718, SPG Journals, 4:3; Andrews to Secretary, July 2, 1719, SPG Letters A, 13:469; Minutes of SPG Meeting, December 18, 1719, SPG Journals, 4:80; same, December 15, 1721, SPG Journals, 4:190.

75. Throughout his mission's decline, Andrews continued to baptize Mohawks, mainly young children and infants. See his baptismal lists for April 20, 1716, SPG Letters A, 11:356; October 17, 1716, SPG Letters A, 11:355; April 23, 1717, SPG Letters A, 12:411; April 17, 1718, SPG Letters A, 13:327; October 17, 1718, SPG Letters A, 13:337; and July 17, 1719, SPG Letters A, 13:487.

76. Andrews to Secretary, October 11, 1716, SPG Letters A, 12:241; Andrews to Secretary, September 1, 1717, SPG Letters A, 12:329; same, October 11, 1716, SPG Letters A, 12:241.

77. Andrews to Secretary, October 1717, SPG Letters A, 12:320; Gov. Hunter to Secretary, 1717, SPG Letters A, 12, in Frank J. Klingberg, *Anglican Humanitarianism in Colonial New York* (Philadelphia: Church Historical Society, 1940), 69; Andrews to Secretary, October 17, 1714, SPG Letters A, 10:no. 1, 158.

78. Andrews to Secretary, October 17, 1714, SPG Letters A, 10:no. 1, 158; Gov. Hunter to Secretary, October 2, 1716, SPG Letters A, 12:238.

CHAPTER 4: MOHAWK SCHOOLMASTERS AND CATECHISTS

1. Henry Barclay to Secretary, October 15, 1740, Records of the Society for the Propagation of the Gospel in Foreign Parts, The Letter Books, Series B, 1701–86 (microfilm) (hereafter SPG Letters B), 25 vols. (London, 1964), 7:part 2, 143; Minutes of SPG Meeting, January 17, 1734–35, SPG Journals, 6:204; same, April 18, 1735, SPG Journals, 6:235; Barbara J. Sivertsen, *Turtles, Wolves, and Bears: A Mohawk Family History* (Bowie, MD: Heritage Books, 1996), 125–26.

2. Lord Bishop of London, Subscription toward the Maintenance of a Minister at Albany, n.d., SPG Letters A, 19:435; Miln to Secretary, June 20, 1728, SPG Letters A, 21:412, 414; Miln to Secretary, November 3, 1729, SPG Letters A, 22:357; Miln to Vesey, November 14, 1734, SPG Letters A, 24:164; Minutes of SPG Meeting, January 17, 1734–35, SPG Journals, 6:204; same, April 18, 1735, SPG Journals, 6:235; Walter Butler et al. to Secretary, October 15, 1735, SPG Letters A, 26:73–74; Walter Butler, "Certificate of Mr. Miln's Services among the Mohawk Indians," SPG Letters A, 26:4. Albany's enslaved population in 1710 numbered a little over 100 out of a total town population of nearly 1,150.

3. William Andrews to Secretary, October 17, 1714, SPG Letters A, 10:158; Miln to Secretary, November 4, 1730, SPG Letters A, 23:85; same, November 3, 1729, SPG Letters A, 22:358; Miln to Vesey, November 14, 1734, SPG Letters A, 25:42; Miln to Secretary, November 20, 1734, SPG Letters A, 24:45.

4. Minutes of SPG Meeting, January 17, 1734–35, SPG Journals, 6:204; same, April 18, 1735, SPG Journals, 6:235–36; same, March 20, 1740–41, SPG Journals, 8:233; Barclay to Secretary, November 9, 1741, SPG Letters B, 9:81. For examples of Native schoolmasters, exhorters, and pastors in seventeenth- and early-eighteenth-century New England praying towns, see Daniel R. Mandell, *Behind the Frontier: Indian in Eighteenth-Century Eastern Massachusetts* (Lincoln: University of Nebraska Press, 1996), 56; Jeanne M. O'Brien, *Dispossession by Degrees: Indian Land and Identity in Natick, Massachusetts, 1650–1790* (New York: Cambridge University Press, 1997), 30; David J. Silverman, *Faith and Boundaries: Colonists, Christianity, and Community among the Wampanoag Indians of Martha's Vineyard, 1600–1871* (New York: Cambridge University Press, 2005), 62, 158, 170.

5. Miln to Secretary, June 20, 1728, SPG Letters A, 21:414; Sivertsen, *Turtles, Wolves, and Bears,* 118, 120–21, 143, 152; J. H. French, "Schoharie County, NY," *Historical and Statistical Gazetteer of New York State* (1859; reprint, Interlaken, NY: Heart of the Lakes, 1986), 416.

6. Journal of Indian Affairs, Meeting at Fort Johnson, March 15, 1761, *The Papers of Sir William Johnson* (hereafter *Johnson Papers*), ed. James Sullivan, Alexander C. Flick, and Milton Hamilton, 14 vols. (Albany: University of the State of New York, 1921–62), 10:241–42.

7. Henry Barclay to Secretary, October 15, 1740, SPG Letters B, 7:part II, 143; Minutes of SPG Meeting, March 20, 1740–41, SPG Journals, 8:233; James Axtell, *The Invasion Within: The Contest of Cultures in Colonial North America* (New York: Oxford University Press, 1985), 125.

8. Henry Barclay to Secretary, November 17, 1742, SPG Letters B, 10:112; Minutes of SPG Meeting, October 21, 1743, SPG Journals, 9:199; same, February 17, 1743–44, SPG Journals, 9:234.

9. Henry Barclay to Secretary, October 15, 1740, SPG Letters B, 7:part 2, 143; Minutes of SPG Meeting, March 20, 1741, SPG Journals, 8:233; same, SPG Journals, 11:259, 300. On pay rates, see John Calam, *Parsons and Pedagogues: The SPG Adventure in American Education* (New York: Columbia University Press, 1971), 103–4.

10. For a clear (although regrettably, not error free) introduction to the discourse, or rhetoric, of religion, see Lawrence A. Palinkas, *Rhetoric and Religious Experience: The Discourse of Immigration Chinese Churches* (Fairfax, VA: George Mason University Press, 1989),

11. David J. Silverman, "Indians, Missionaries, and Religious Translation: Creating Wampanoag Christianity in Seventeenth-Century Martha's Vineyard," *WMQ* 62, no. 2 (2005): 146. For an interpretation of the translatability of the scriptures into local vernaculars, see Lamin Sanneh, *Translating the Message: The Missionary Impact on Culture,* 2nd ed. (Maryknoll, NY: Orbis Books, 2009), 7–11.

12. For two foundational studies by Anthony F. C. Wallace on the role of Native prophets, see "Revitalization Movements: Some Theoretical Considerations for Their Comparative Study," *American Anthropologist* 58, no. 2 (1956): 264–81; and *The Death and Rebirth of the Seneca* (New York: Alfred A. Knopf, 1970). On the Huron prophet, Deganawidah, and the founding of the League of the Haudenosaunee, see Paul A. W. Wallace, *The White Roots of Peace* (Philadelphia: University of Pennsylvania Press, 1946), 46; Anthony F. C. Wallace, "The Dekanawidah Myth Analyzed as the Record of a Revitalization Movement," *Ethnohistory* 5, no. 1 (1958): 118–30; and Matthew Dennis, *Cultivating a Landscape of Peace: Iroquois-European Encounters in Seventeenth-Century America* (Ithaca, NY: Cornell University Press; Cooperstown, NY: New York Historical Association, 1993), chap. 3.

13. Frances Karttunen, *Between Worlds: Interpreters, Guides, and Survivors* (New Brunswick, NJ: Rutgers University Press, 1994).

14. Memoir of John Stuart, n.d., *DHNY,* 4:314. On roles played by war chiefs, see Jose Antonio Brandao, *"Your Fire Shall Burn No More": Iroquois Policy toward New France and Its Native Allies to 1701* (Lincoln: University of Nebraska Press, 1997), 32–33.

15. On duties of Iroquois "headman," see Daniel K. Richter, *The Ordeal of the Longhouse: The Peoples of the Iroquois League in the Era of European Colonization* (Chapel Hill: University of North Carolina Press, 1992), 40, 42–46.

16. Richter, *Ordeal of the Longhouse,* 45–47, 6, 40; Cadwallader Colden, *The History of the Five Nations of Canada, Which Are Dependent on the Province of New-York in America . . .* (London, 1747), 14.

17. C. F. Pascoe, *Two Hundred Years of the SPG: An Historical Account of the Propagation of the Gospel in Foreign Parts, 1701–1900* (London: Society for the Propagation of

the Gospel, 1901), 63–64, 845, 837–38; Minutes of SPG Meeting, SPG Journals, 13:184.

18. Sivertsen, *Turtles, Wolves, and Bears*, 33–34, 118, 120.

19. Sivertsen, *Turtles, Wolves, and Bears*, 54, 74, 84, 86. Although Kryn followed the increasing trend of taking his father's name—Kryn (Dutch for Quirine) Onihoen-houndi—he would have identified with his mother's clan.

20. Sivertsen, *Turtles, Wolves, and Bears*, 121, 136–37, 148–49, 173.

21. Sivertsen, *Turtles, Wolves, and Bears*, 147–48, 159.

22. Sivertsen, *Turtles, Wolves, and Bears*, 130, 170, 304n25.

23. Minutes of SPG Meeting, October 21, 1743, SPG Journals, 9:199; same, February 17, 1743–44, SPG Journals, 9:234; Henry Barclay to Secretary, November 4, 1743, SPG Letters B, 11:no. 155, n.p.

24. Minutes of SPG Meeting, December 15, 1749, SPG Journals, 11:176; same, July 20, 1750, SPG Journals, 11:246–47; same, September 21, 1750, SPG Journals, 11:258–59.

25. Minutes of SPG Meeting, 1756, SPG Journals, 13:182–83, in John Wolfe Lydekker, *The Faithful Mohawks* (New York: Macmillan, 1938), 83.

26. Journal of Indian Affairs, Meeting at Fort Johnson, March 15, 1761, *Johnson Papers*, 10:241–42; Ogilvie to Rev. Sir, July 27, 1750, SPG Letters B, 18:no. 102, n.p.; Lydekker, *ERSNY*, 5:77–78; *DRCHNY*, 6:876–77; Minutes of SPG Meeting, September 21, 1750, SPG Journals, 11:258–59.

27. Jonathan Edwards to Jaspar Mauduit, March 10, 1752, Correspondence, Andover Newton Theological Miscellaneous Personal Papers Collection (RG295), Special Collections, Yale Divinity School Library, Seminary (hereafter ANTMPPC), folio 2.

28. Henry Barclay to Secretary, May 31, 1743, SPG Letters B, 11:no. 153, n.p.

29. Minutes of SPG Meeting, September 21, 1750, SPG Journals, 11:259; same, January 18, 1750, SPG Journals, 11:300; William Webb Kemp, *The Support of Schools in Colonial New York by the Society for the Propagation of the Gospel in Foreign Parts* (New York: Teachers College, Columbia University, 1913), 220.

30. Nancy Shoemaker, *A Strange Likeness: Becoming Red and White in Eighteenth-Century North America* (New York: Oxford University Press, 2004), 64–81.

31. Lamin Sanneh, *Encountering the West: Christianity and the Global Cultural Process: The African Dimension* (Maryknoll, NY: Orbis, 1993), 17.

32. Claude Lévi-Strauss, "A World on the Wane," trans. J. Russell (New York: Criterion Books, 1961), 292, cited in Gary Urton, "Numeral Graphic Pluralism in the Colonial Andes," *Ethnohistory* 57, no. 1 (2010): 159; Margaret Bender, "Reflections on What Writing Means, beyond What It 'Says': The Political Economy and Semiotics of Graphic Pluralism in the Americas," *Ethnohistory* 57, no. 1 (2010): 176–79. This entire issue of *Ethnohistory* is devoted to analyzing Native American systems of inscription.

33. Desiderius Erasmus, *Christian Humanism and the Reformation*, ed. John C. Olin (New York: Harper Torchbooks, 1965), 96–97, cited in Sanneh, *Encountering the West*, 73.

34. My thinking on orality, literacy, and the consequences of translating Christian texts into local languages has been influenced most notably by Lamin Sanneh, *Encountering the West*; Jack Goody, *The Interface between the Written and the Oral* (Cambridge: Cambridge University Press, 1987); and Robin Lane Fox, "Literacy and Power in Early Christianity," in *Literacy and Power in the Ancient World*, ed. Alan K. Bowman and Greg Woolf (Cambridge: Cambridge University Press, 1994), 126–48.

35. On power through prayer to God, see Fox, "Literacy and Power," 130. On literacy displacing the authority of elders, see Goody, *Between the Written and Oral*, 164.

36. Thomas Wilson, (bishop of Sodor and Man), *An Essay towards an Instruction for the Indians: Explaining the Most Essential Doctrines of Christianity . . .* (London: Osborn and Thirm, 1740), ii, iii, xvi, 12, 69.

37. Wilson, *Essay towards an Instruction*; Minutes of SPG Meeting, September 19, 1740, SPG Journals, 8:178; SPG to Henry Barclay, June 14, 1743, SPG Letters B, 20:no. 196, n.p.

38. James Axtell, ed., *The Indian Peoples of Eastern America: A Documentary History of the Sexes* (New York: Oxford University Press, 1981), 174–79; Axtell, *Invasion Within*, 15–16; Richter, *Ordeal of the Longhouse*, 9–11; St. John, "Iroquois Religion," 284.

39. Wilson, *Essay towards an Instruction*, 120.

40. Church of England, *The Book of Common Prayer and Administration of the Sacraments and Rites . . . to Which Is Added the Gospel according to St. Mark, Translated into the Mohawk Language by Capt. Joseph Brant* (London: Buckton, 1787), 86.

41. Church of England, *Book of Common Prayer*, 14–15.

42. Church of England, *Book of Common Prayer*, 8–10.

43. Tom Porter (Sakokwenionkwas), *And Grandma Said . . . Iroquois Teaching as Passed Down through the Oral Tradition*, ed. Lesley Forrester ([Philadelphia]: Xlibris, 2008), 376.

44. Scott Manning Stevens, "The Path of the King James Version of the Bible in Iroquoia," *Prose Studies: History, Theory, Criticism*, 34, no. 1 (2012): 13.

45. John Norton, *The Journal of Major John Norton (1816)*, ed. Carl F. Klinck and James J. Talman (Toronto: Champlain Society, 1970), 91.

46. Church of England, *Book of Common Prayer*, 461–62; Andrews to Secretary, September 26, 1717, SPG Letters A, 12:339; Allan Greer, *Mohawk Saint: Catherine Tekakwitha and the Jesuits* (New York: Oxford University Press, 2005), 51–53.

47. Wilson, *Essay towards an Instruction*, 96.

48. Minutes of SPG Meeting, February 17, 1747–48, SPG Journals, 11:89; same, May 20, 1748, SPG Journals, 11:22–23; same, December 20, 1754, SPG Journals, 12:406; same, January 21, 1725–26, SPG Journals, 5:76; same, March 19, 1730, SPG Journals, 5:290; same, November 17, 1758, SPG Journals, 14:106; same, March 19, 1762, SPG Journals, 15:203; same, February 19, 1762, SPG Journals, 15:191.

49. Minutes of SPG Meeting, February 19, 1762, SPG Journals, 15:191; same, October 19, 1770, SPG Journals, 18:437–38; Schoolmaster at Canajoharie to Johnson, March 22, 1764, *DHNY*, 4:216–17.

50. Axtell, *Invasion Within*, 196–200; O'Brien, *Dispossession by Degrees*, 23, 28, 33, 51.

51. Jonathan Edwards to Jaspar Mauduit, March 10, 1752, Correspondence, ANTMPP; Jonathan Edwards to Thomas Hubbard, 1751, Correspondence, ANTMPP; Kellogg to Hendrick Petris, June 20, 1750, SPG Letters B, 18:no. 104, n.p.; Axtell, *Invasion Within*, 196–204.

52. Edwards to Joseph Paice, 1752, ANTMPP, 1752B, no. 6a-6b, no. 7. Edwards may have read Wilson's book while at Stockbridge; one observer noted his "very plain and practical" style when preaching to Native families. Gideon Hawley, "Narrative of his Journey to Onohoghgwage, July 1753," *ERSNY*, 5:3399.

53. For Old Abraham's pleas for missionaries, see *ERSNY*, 5:77–78; and *DRCHNY*, 6:876–77. For Little Abraham's pleas, see Journal of Indian Affairs, Meeting at Fort Johnson, March 15, 1761, *Johnson Papers*, 10:241–42, and SPG Journals, 11:258–59. For a discussion of "talking papers" as written documents—deeds, minutes to council meetings, letters, and so on—see Shoemaker, *Strange Likeness*, 68.

54. Henry Barclay to Secretary, March 12, 1744–45, SPG Letters B, 13:no. 314, n.p.; same, October 21, 1745, SPG Letters B, 13:no. 316, n.p.; Minutes of SPG Meeting, November 15, 1745, SPG Journals, 10:83; same, April 18, 1746, SPG Journals, 10:124; Henry Barclay to Secretary, December 9, 1746, SPG Letters B, 14:99.

55. Ogilvie to Rev. Sir, July 27, 1750, SPG Letters B, 18:no. 102, n.p.; Ogilvie to Secretary, April 14, 1751, SPG Letters B, 19:no. 71, n.p.; Lydekker, *The Faithful Mohawks*, 67.

56. Edwards to Jaspar Mauduit, March 10, 1752, ANTMPP; Edwards to Thomas

Hubbard, 1751, ANTMPP. Edwards believed that the SPG made Old Abraham a catechist in order to counter the Stockbridge mission.

57. Ogilvie to Secretary, August 7, 1751, SPG Letters B, 19:no. 72, n.p.; Minutes of SPG Meeting, March 20, 1752, SPG Journals, 12:114; Proposition of the Christian Mohawks to Gov. Sloughter, May 26, 1691, *DRCHNY,* 3:771–72; Axtell, *Invasion Within,* 199.

58. David J. Silverman, *Red Brethren: The Brothertown and Stockbridge Indians and the Problem of Race in Early America* (Ithaca, NY: Cornell University Press, 2010); Axtell, *Invasion Within,* 196–204.

59. Johnson to Arthur Lee, February 28, 1771, *DHNY,* 4:431.

60. Gansevoort to Sullivan, October 8, 1779, Gansevoort Military Papers, Gansevoort-Lansing Collection, New York Public Library (hereafter NYPL), in Barbara Graymont, *The Iroquois in the American Revolution* (Syracuse, NY: Syracuse University Press, 1972), 219; Johnson to Arthur Lee, February 28, 1771, *DHNY,* 4:431.

61. Minutes of SPG Meeting, June 15, 1759, SPG Journals, 14:186. In response to Paulus going AWOL, Ogilvie withheld three and a half pounds—half his salary. When Ogilvie rehired Paulus several years later, he paid him a salary of only five pounds per year rather than his customary seven.

62. Sir William Johnson to Daniel Claus, March 10, 1761, *Johnson Papers,* 3:355; Johnson to Ogilvie, February 1, 1766, *Johnson Papers,* 5:29; John Stuart to Richard Hind, August 9, 1774, *Johnson Papers,* 8:1195–96. For evidence of Johnson, Ogilvie, Stuart, Daniel Claus, and others trying to meet the repeated Mohawk demands for texts printed in their language, see *Johnson Papers,* 3:384, 630, 4:72, 8:1039–40, 10:264, 333, 935.

63. Journal of Indian Affairs, Meeting at Fort Johnson, March 15, 1761, *Johnson Papers,* 10:241; Council at Albany, June 28–July 11, 1754, *DHNY,* 2:345; Minutes of SPG Meeting, March 15, 1765, SPG Journals, 16:329; same, November 15, 1765, SPG Journals, 16:469.

64. Richard Terrick, Bishop of Peterborough, *A Sermon before the SPG . . . February 1764* (London: E. Owen and T. Harrison, 1764), 28, in Calam, *Parsons and Pedagogues,* 160; Minutes of SPG Meeting, SPG Journals, 13:184; Johnson to Lords of Trade, September 3, 1755, *DRCHNY,* 6:994.

65. For the basis of the dispute between Barclay, Cornelius, and Daniel, see Barclay to Secretary, March 12, 1744–45, SPG Letters B, 13:no. 314, n.p.; same, October 21, 1745, SPG Letters B, 13:no. 316, n.p.; Minutes of SPG Meeting, November 15, 1745, SPG Journals, 10:83; same, April 18, 1746, SPG Journals, 10:124; Barclay to Secretary, December 9, 1746, SPG Letters B, 14:99. Jacob Oel, a German minister operating in the German Flats, took over the duties at Canajoharie after Old Abraham's death. For Oel, see Minutes of SPG Meeting, February 17, 1747–48, SPG Journals, 11:89; same, May 20, 1748, SPG Journals, 11:22–23; same, December 20, 1754, SPG Journals, 12:406; same, January 21, 1725–26, SPG Journals, 5:76; same, March 19, 1730, SPG Journals, 5:290; same, November 17, 1758, SPG Journals, 14:106; same, February 19, 1762, SPG Journals, 15:191.

66. Minutes of SPG Meeting, SPG Journals, 12:232; An Indian Council, August 23–29, 1757, *Johnson Papers,* 9:813; Proposition of the Christian Mohawks to Gov. Sloughter, May 26, 1691, *DRCHNY,* 3:771–72; Proposition of Christian Mohawks . . . 1691, *DRCHNY,* 3:772.

CHAPTER 5: "A SINGLE MISSION IN THE OLD, BEATEN WAY MAKES NO NOISE"

1. Nathaniel Whitaker, "A Sermon Preached on the 30th of June, 1763, after the Ordination of the Rev. Mr. Charles Jeffrey Smith, Missionary among the Indians," in Eleazar Wheelock, *A Sermon Preached before the Second Society in Lebanon, June 30,*

*1763, as the Ordination of the Rev. Mr. Charles Jeffrey Smith, with a View to his Going as a Missionary to the Remote Tribes of the Indians in this Land* (Edinburgh: W. Gray, 1767), 42–43; Wheelock to Johnson, January 20, 1763, *DHNY*, 4:207; Smith to Johnson, January 18, 1763, *DHNY*, 4:325–26.

2. Wheelock, *Sermon Preached June 30, 1763*, 7.

3. Whitaker, "A Sermon Preached on the 30th of June, 1763," 43–44.

4. Wheelock, *Sermon Preached, June 30, 1763*, 10, 14.

5. Johnson to Lords of Trade, November 13, 1763, *DRCHNY*, 7:580; Isabel Thompson Kelsay, *Joseph Brant, 1743–1807: Man of Two Worlds* (Syracuse, NY: Syracuse University Press, 1984), 95. Brant's major opus would be *The Book of Common Prayer and Administration of the Sacraments and Rites . . . to Which Is Added the Gospel according to St. Mark, Translated into the Mohawk Language by Capt. Joseph Brant* (London: Buckton, 1787). For detailed biographies of Joseph Brant, see William L. Stone, *Life of Joseph Brant, Thayendanegea*, 2 vols. (New York: Dearboran, 1838; reprint, Albany, NY: Munsell, 1865); and Kelsay, *Joseph Brant.*

6. Wheelock to Johnson, June 27, 1762, *Johnson Papers*, 10:470.

7. Rev. John Sergeant, *A Letter from the Rev'd Mr. Sergeant of Stockbridge, to Dr. Colman of Boston* (Boston: Rogers and Fowle, 1743), 1, 5. For an example of Sergeant, the New Light minister, urging sinners, backsliders, and the irreligious to embrace Protestant Christianity, see his *The Causes and Danger of Delusions in the Affairs of Religion, Consider'd and Caution'd Against, with Particular Reference to the Temper of the Present Time, in a Sermon Preach'd at Springfield, April 4, 1743* (Boston: S. Eliot, 1743).

8. Wheelock, *Sermon Preached, June 30, 1763*, 18; Eleazar Wheelock, *A Plain and Faithful Narrative of the Original Design, Rise, Progress and Present State of the Indian Charity-School at Lebanon in Connecticut* (Boston: Richard and Samuel Draper, 1763), 11; *Wheelock's Indians*, 12. For the expression "make Indians men," see Charles Inglis to Johnson, March 28, 1770, *Johnson Papers*, 7:506.

9. Inglis to Johnson, March 28, 1770, *Johnson Papers*, 7:505; Inglis to Johnson, June 21, 1770, *Johnson Papers*, 7:764; Inglis to Secretary, June 15, 1770, SPG Letters B, 2:65; John Wolfe Lydekker, *The Faithful Mohawks* (New York: Macmillan, 1938), 126. In this chapter, the term "white" stands for Europeans or Euroamericans, for the term was in common usage by the mid-eighteenth century, preferred over national terms of identity, such as "English" and "Dutch."

10. Richard White, *The Middle Ground: Indians, Empires, and Republics in the Great Lakes Region, 1650–1815* (Cambridge: Cambridge University Press, 1991), 50–60.

11. Minutes of SPG Meeting, November 19, 1756, SPG Journals, 13:182; Gansevoort to Sullivan, October 8, 1779, Gansevoort Military Papers, Gansevoort-Lansing Collection, NYPL, 5, in Barbara Graymont, *The Iroquois in the American Revolution* (Syracuse, NY: Syracuse University Press, 1972), 219, 320n53. For a summary of material possessions owned by the Mohawks, see David B. Guldenzopf, "The Colonial Transformation of Mohawk Iroquois Society" (PhD diss., State University of New York at Albany, 1987), 71, 75. For items bought by Haudenosaunees at Jelles Fonda's store, see Jelles Fonda, Indian Trade Account Book, 1768–1778, B. V. Indians, New York Historical Society, throughout. David L. Preston, *The Texture of Contact: European and Indian Settler Communities on the Frontiers of Iroquoia, 1667–1783* (Lincoln: University of Nebraska Press, 2009), 97–111.

12. Journal of Indian Affairs, January 17–31, 1765, *Johnson Papers*, 11:554. For Gov. Bellomont duping the Mohawks into a logging agreement at the turn of the eighteenth century, see John C. Rainbolt, "A 'Great and Usefull Designe': Bellomont's Proposal for New York, 1698–1701," *New-York Historical Society Quarterly* 53 (1969): 333–51. For Mohawks as landlords, see Kelsay, *Joseph Brant*, 78.

13. For references to the various forms of labor performed by Mohawk men, see W. Max

Reid, *The Mohawk Valley: Its Legends and Its History* (New York: Putnam's, 1901), 121–22; Jeptha R. Simms, *Trappers of New York, or A Biography of Nicholas Stoner & Nathaniel Foster* (Albany, NY: Munsell, 1851), 23–24, 281–82; Augustus C. Buell, *Sir William Johnson* (New York: D. Appleton, 1903), 86 (Buell referred to Johnson's butler as his "half-breed orderly"); William Elliot Griffis, *Sir William Johnson and the Six Nations* (New York: Dodd, Mead, 1891), 199–202; and Guldenzopf, "Colonial Transformation of Mohawk Society," 78–79. For evidence of Mohawks employed as slave catchers, see Fonda, Indian Account Book, 1768–78, 88; and William B. Hart, "Black 'Go-Betweens' and the Mutability of 'Race,' Status, and Identity on New York's Pre-revolutionary Frontier," in *Contact Points: American Frontiers from the Mohawk Valley to the Mississippi, 1750–1830*, ed. Andrew R. L. Cayton and Fredrika J. Tuete (Chapel Hill: University of North Carolina Press, 1998), 88–113. For ginseng, see Minutes of the SPG Meeting, December 21, 1753, SPG Journals, 12:308; Gideon Hawley, Narrative of his Journey to Onohoghgwage [Oquaga], July 1753, *ERSNY*, 5:3400; Guldenzopf, "Colonial Transformation of Mohawk Society," 79.

14. Johnson to Samuel Auchmuty, September 14, 1769, *Johnson Papers*, 7:168; Johnson to Lords of Trade, October 8, 1764, *DRCHNY*, 7:659; Johnson to Rev. Smith, January 3, 1769, *DHNY*, 4:401; Johnson to Daniel Burton, November 8, 1766, SPG Journals, 2:no. 87, folio 274; same, *Johnson Papers*, 5:413; same, December 10, 1768, SPG, Journals 2:no. 89, folio 286; Johnson to Samuel Auchmuty, December 21, 1768, *Johnson Papers*, 6:543; Johnson to Burton, December 6, 1769, SPG Journals, 2:no. 90, folio 290; same, *Johnson Papers*, 7:290. Johnson also acquired the contested glebe which the Henry Barclay family said it owned, but which the Mohawks contended they gave to the missionary in the 1730s in usufruct. For the debate over Barclay's claim to property for the episcopate, see *Johnson Papers*, 14:41. For a history of purchases of Mohawk lands, see Meeting of an Albany Committee with the Mohawks, December 21–22, 1773, *Johnson Papers*, 8:955–69.

15. Ogilvie to Secretary, December 25, 1755, cited in Minutes of SPG Meeting, November 19, 1756, SPG Journals, 13:182–83. See Ogilvie's "Diary, 1750–59," *Bulletin of Fort Ticonderoge Museum* 10, no. 5 (1961): 361–63, for brief, excerpted remarks on the Battle at Lake George. For a comprehensive study of the Seven Years' War, see Fred Anderson, *The Crucible of War: The Seven Years' War and the Fate of the Empire in British North America, 1754–1766* (New York: Alfred A. Knopf, 2000).

16. An Indian Council, August 23–29, 1757, *Johnson Papers*, 9:813; Meeting of the Mohocks & Connojoharys [Canajoharies], August 28, 1757, *Johnson Papers*, 9:819; Ogilvie, "Diary," 377, 381; Ogilvie to Secretary, February 1, 1760, SPG Journals, 2:no. 105, 348; Guldenzopf, "Colonial Transformation of Mohawk Society," 69. See also Journal of Warren Johnson, November 1760–February 1761, *Johnson Papers*, 13:187–207, for evidence of sickness among indigenes, whites, and blacks in the Mohawk Valley.

17. Ogilvie to Secretary, June 25, 1752, SPG Letters B, 20:no. 55, n.p.; Council at Albany, June 28–July 11, 1754, *DHNY*, 2:592.

18. Gen. Johnson to Gov. Delancey, June 2, 1755, *DHNY*, 2:656; Johnson to Gov. Clinton, May 14, 1748, *DHNY*, 2:621; Extract from Johnson's Journal, May 24, 1757, *Johnson Papers*, 9:770. Thirty pounds in 1755 equaled about one-fifth, or two months' worth, of an SPG missionary's annual salary, or a little over $7,000 in 2020 dollars, not an inconsiderable sum.

19. Ogilvie to Secretary, June 25, 1752, SPG Letters B, 20:no. 55, n.p.; Ogilvie to Secretary, July 27, 1750, SPG Letters B, 18:no. 102, n.p.

20. Journal of Indian Affairs, Meeting at Fort Johnson, March 15, 1761, *Johnson Papers*, 10:241; Minutes of SPG Meeting, November 21, 1760, SPG Journals, 15:19; same, December 16, 1763, SPG Journals, 16:45–48; Hawley, Journey to Onohoghgwage,

5:3400; Ogilvie, "Diary," *passim*. In 1764, Ogilvie relocated to Trinity Church in New York City, where he served as an assistant pastor. Minutes of SPG Meeting, December 21, 1764, SPG Journals, 16:244.

21. Cadwallader Colden, in Guldenzopf, "Colonial Transformation of Mohawk Society," 55; Sergeant, *Letter from the Rev'd Mr. Sergeant*, 1.

22. For brief summaries of Wheelock's charity school, see James Axtell, "Dr. Wheelock's Little Red School," in *The European and the Indian: Essays in the Ethnohistory of Colonial North America* (Oxford: Oxford University Press, 1982), 87–109; Margaret Connell Szasz, *Indian Education in the American Colonies, 1607–1783* (Albuquerque: University of New Mexico Press, 1988), 218–57; and Kelsay, *Joseph Brant*, 71–91.

23. Eleazar Wheelock, *A Continuation of the Narrative of the Indian-Charity School, etc.* (Hartford, CT: E. Watson, 1773), 13, 12; Wheelock, *A Plain and Faithful Narrative of the Original Design, Rise, Progress & Present State of the Indian Charity-School at Lebanon in Connecticut* (Boston: Richard and Samuel Draper, 1763), 15, 34–36.

24. Wheelock, *Continuation of the Narrative*, 13, 12; Wheelock, *Plain and Faithful Narrative*, 15, 34–36; Wheelock's Address to the Sachems and Chiefs, April 29, 1765, *DHNY*, 4:356–58; Szasz, *Indian Education*, 222–23; Axtell, "Dr. Wheelock's Little Red School," 98–100.

25. Wheelock, *Plain and Faithful Narrative*, 36, 15; Wheelock to Johnson, September 8, 1762, *DHNY*, 4:314–16; John Smith to a Friend, May 18, 1764, *Wheelock's Indians*, 98–100; Szasz, *Indian Education*, 223.

26. Johnson to Wheelock, November 17, 1761, *DHNY*, 4:305–7; Wheelock to Johnson, August 20, 1762, *DHNY*, 4:313; same, September 8, 1762, *DHNY*, 4:314–15; Johnson to Wheelock, October 16, 1762, *DHNY*, 4:320–21; Wheelock to Gen. Amherst, April 2, 1763, *DHNY*, 4:328–29; Council at Johnson Hall, March 25, 1763, *Johnson Papers*, 4:67; Johnson to Wheelock, August 8, 1766, *Johnson Papers*, 5:343.

27. Wheelock, *Plain and Faithful Narrative*, 39–41; Wheelock to Johnson, September 8, 1762, *DHNY*, 4:314–15; Kelsay, *Joseph Brant*, 73–76. For a list of the Native students who attended Moor's Charity School from 1754 to 1779, see *Wheelock's Indians*, Appendix A: 293–94.

28. Wheelock to George Whitefield, July 4, 1761, *Wheelock's Indians*, 17.

29. Wheelock to Johnson, January 20, 1763, *DHNY*, 4:322–23; Wheelock to Andrew Gifford, February 24, 1763, *Wheelock's Indians*, 70; Wheelock to Johnson, May 16, 1763, *DHNY*, 4:330–31.

30. Wheelock to Johnson, May 16, 1763, *DHNY*, 4:33–31; Kelsay, *Joseph Brant*, 62.

31. David Avery's Address to the Indians, and Their Answers, Spring 1772, *Wheelock's Indians*, 282, 287–88.

32. John Daniel to Wheelock, November 30, 1767, *Wheelock's Indians*, 231; Daniel Simon to Wheelock, September 1771, *Wheelock's Indians*, 221; Edward Drake to Wheelock, June 21, 1768, *Wheelock's Indians*, 65; David Avery's Address to the Indians, Spring 1772, *Wheelock's Indians*, 287.

33. Johnson to Henry Barclay, March 30, 1763, *Johnson Papers*, 4:72–73.

34. Johnson to Wheelock, August 8, 1766, *Johnson Papers*, 5:343; A List of the Indians who Attended Moor's Charity School, from 1754–1779, Appendix A, *Wheelock's Indians*, 294–96.

35. Joseph Johnson to Wheelock, February 10, 1768, *Wheelock's Indians*, 129; same, April 20, 1768, *Wheelock's Indians*, 131.

36. Axtell, "Dr. Wheelock's Little Red School," 100–102; Johnson to Daniel Claus, March 10, 1761, *Johnson Papers*, 3:355; Johnson to Ogilvie, February 1, 1766, *Johnson Papers*, 5:29; John Stuart to Richard Hind, August 9, 1774, *Johnson Papers*, 8:1195–96. For further evidence of Johnson, Ogilvie, Stuart, Daniel Claus, and others trying

to meet the repeated demands of baptized Mohawks for texts printed in their language, see *Johnson Papers*, 3:384, 630, 4:72, 8:1039–40, 10:264, 333, 935.

37. Johnson to William Smith, April 10, 1767, *Johnson Papers*, 5:530; Johnson to Charles Inglis, April 26, 1770, *Johnson Papers*, 7:599; Johnson to Barclay, November 24, 1763, *Johnson Papers*, 10:935–36.

38. Deed Executed at Fort Stanwix, November 5, 1768, *DHNY*, 1:587–91; Rev. Jacob Johnson to Commissioners, October 30, 1768, *DHNY*, 4:394; Speech of Rev. Johnson, October 31, 1768, *DHNY*, 4:395; Position of Jacob Johnson, October 20, 1768, *DHNY*, 4:392–93; Rev. Jacob Johnson to William Johnson, October 22, 1768, *DHNY*, 4:393; Johnson to Gen. Gage, November 24, 1768, *DHNY*, 4:397–98; William Johnson to Daniel Burton, December 10, 1768, SPG Journals, 2:no. 89, 285–86; *Wheelock's Indians*, 22, 23–24n30; Kelsay, *Joseph Brant*, 125–28. For a study on the 1768 Treaty at Fort Stanwix, see William J. Campbell, *Speculators in Empire: Iroquoia and the 1768 Treaty of Fort Stanwix* (Norman: University of Oklahoma Press, 2012). White squatters violated the 1768 agreement as early as 1771 and began to build settlements in Ohio country. Kelsay, *Joseph Brant*, 135.

39. Johnson to Daniel Burton, December 23, 1767, SPG Journals, 2:no. 88, folio 281; same, *Johnson Papers*, 6:28; Johnson to Samuel Auchmuty, November 18, 1768, *Johnson Papers*, 6:464; Johnson to John Wetherhead, February 26, 1769, *Johnson Papers*, 6:639; Johnson to Richard Peters, May 5, 1769, *Johnson Papers*, 6:745; John Daniel Muller's Account, May 12, 1770, *Johnson Papers*, 7:666–68; Johnson to Harry Munro, June 8, 1770, *Johnson Papers*, 7:720; Harry Munro to Daniel Burton, September 25, 1770, SPG Letters B, 3:no. 271, n.p.

40. John Ogilvie to Johnson, January 13, 1763, *Johnson Papers*, 4:17; Johnson to Ogilvie, February 18, 1763, *Johnson Papers*, 4:47.

41. Johnson to Samuel Auchmuty, November 20, 1766, *Johnson Papers*, 5:427–28; same, December 1, 1769, *Johnson Papers*, 7:281; Johnson to Thomas Barton, December 2, 1766, *Johnson Papers*, 5:436; Johnson to Samuel Johnson, December 2, 1766, *Johnson Papers*, 5:439–40; Johnson to Auchmuty, December 2, 1767, *Johnson Papers*, 5:843; Johnson to Thomas Barton, January 5, 1768, *Johnson Papers*, 6:67–68.

42. Johnson to Daniel Burton, December 3, 1773, SPG Journals, 2:no. 94, 307; Johnson to Charles Inglis, February 16, 1770, *Johnson Papers*, 7:392; Johnson to Daniel Burton, November 8, 1766, SPG Journals, 2:no. 87, 274; same, *Johnson Papers*, 5:413–14; Minutes of SPG Meeting, March 17, 1775, SPG Journals, 20:325; Johnson to Auchmuty, July 28, 1768, *Johnson Papers*, 6:293.

43. Samuel Auchmuty to Johnson, November 4, 1766, *Johnson Papers*, 5:410; Johnson to Auchmuty, November 20, 1766, *Johnson Papers*, 5:427.

44. William Smith to Johnson, March 16, 1767, *Johnson Papers*, 5:511–13. For studies on the Jesuit *reducciones de indios* in Paraguy, see Barbara Ganson, *The Guarani under Spanish Rule in the Rio Plata* (Stanford, CA: Stanford University Press, 2003); and Frederick J. Reiter, *They Built Utopia: The Jesuit Missions in Paraguay, 1619–1768* (Potomac, MD: Scripta Humanistica, 1995).

45. Johnson to William Smith, April 10, 1767, *Johnson Papers*, 5:528–31; William Smith to Johnson, June 22, 1767, *Johnson Papers*, 5:569.

46. Charles Inglis to Johnson, January 28, 1770, *Johnson Papers*, 7:357–58; Charter of the Society, June 16, 1701, as cited in C. F. Pascoe, *Two Hundred Years of the SPG: An Historical Account of the Propagation of the Gospel in Foreign Parts, 1701–1900* (London: SPG, 1901), 932; David Humphreys, *An Historical Account of the Incorporated Society for the Propagation of the Gospel in Foreign Parts* (London: Joseph Downey, 1730), 21–22; Charles Inglis, "A Memorial Concerning the Iroquois," October 1, 1771, *DHNY*, 4:1091–1117, esp. 1094, 1096; Inglis to Johnson, March 28, 1770, *Johnson Papers*, 7:507.

47. Inglis to Johnson, March 28, 1770, *Johnson Papers*, 7:506; Inglis, "Memorial Concerning the Iroquois," October 1, 1771, *DHNY*, 4:1093,1097; Inglis to Johnson, June 21, 1770, *Johnson Papers*, 7:764.

48. Inglis to Secretary, May 1770, SPG Letters B, 3:no. 339, n.p.; Lydekker, *The Faithful Mohawks*, 121; Inglis, "Memorial Concerning the Iroquois," October 1, 1771, *DHNY*, 4:1098; Johnson to Inglis, November 1770, *DHNY*, 4:526–29. For further evidence of the debate between Johnson and Inglis, see various letters, Johnson to Inglis, July 4, 1771–January 27, 1772, *DHNY*, 4:453–55, 461–62, 472–73; and Inglis to Johnson, August 19, 1771–October 23, 1771, *DHNY*, 4:457–59, 462–65, 467–69.

49. Charles Inglis to Johnson, October 25, 1770, *Johnson Papers*, 7:964; Inglis, "Memorial Concerning the Iroquois," October 1, 1771, *DHNY*, 4:1102–5.

50. Inglis, "Memorial Concerning the Iroquois," October 1, 1771, *DHNY*, 4:1107–9.

51. Minutes of SPG Meeting, February 17, 1747–48, SPG Journals, 11:89; same, May 20, 1748, SPG Journals, 11:22–23; same, December 20, 1754, SPG Journals, 12:406; same, January 21, 1725–26, SPG Journals, 5:76; same, March 19, 1730, SPG Journals, 5:290; same, November 17, 1758, SPG Journals, 14:106; same, March 19, 1762, SPG Journals, 15:203; same, February 19, 1762, SPG Journals, 15:191. For a study of German Palatines in the Mohawk Valley and elsewhere in the colonies, see A. G. Roeber, *Palatines, Liberty, and Property: German Lutherans in Colonial British America* (Baltimore: Johns Hopkins University Press, 1993).

52. Minutes of SPG Meeting, February 19, 1762, SPG Journals, 15:191; same, October 19, 1770, SPG Journals, 18:437–38; Schoolmaster at Canajoharry to Johnson, March 22, 1764, *DHNY*, 4:339–40.

53. Stuart to Rev. Worthy Sir, January 30, 1771, SPG Letters B, 2:no. 196, 678–79; Minutes of SPG Meeting, May 17, 1771, SPG Journals, 19:44–45; Minutes of SPG Meeting, October 19, 1770, SPG Journals, 18:438; Stuart to Rev. Worthy Sir, June 22, 1771, SPG Letters B, 2:no. 197, 681.

54. Stuart to Rev. Worthy Sir, June 22, 1771, SPG Letters B, 2:no. 197, 680; Stuart to Rev. Sir, January 8, 1772, SPG Letters B, 2:no. 198, 685.

55. John Stuart to Rev. Sir, July 20, 1772, SPG Letters B, 2:no. 199, folio 686–87; Minutes of SPG Meeting, November 20, 1772, SPG Journals, 19:313–14; Stuart to Rev. Sir, August 9, 1774, SPG Letters B, 2:no. 201, folio 690; Minutes of SPG Meeting, March 17, 1775, SPG Journals, 20:329; Stuart to Rev. Sir, October 17, 1775, SPG Letters B, 2:no. 202, folio 694; Stuart to Rev. Sir, October 27, 1775, SPG Letters B, 2:no. 203, folio 700; Minutes of SPG Meeting, January 25, 1782, SPG Journals, 22:369; Memoir of Rev. John Stuart, n.d., *DHNY*, 4:506, 508; Minutes of SPG Meeting, October 15, 1773, SPG Journal, 20:9. Stuart to Rev. Sir, August 9, 1774, SPG Letters B, 2:no. 201, folio 691.

56. John Stuart to Rev. Worthy Sir, June 22, 1771, SPG Letters B, 2:no. 197, 680–81; Minutes of SPG Meeting, October 18, 1771, SPG Journals, 19:110–11.

57. Stuart to Rev. Worthy Sir, June 22, 1771, SPG Letters B, 2:no. 197, 680–81; Minutes of SPG Meeting, October 18, 1771, SPG Journals, 19:110–11; Stuart to Rev. Sir, July 20, 1772, SPG Letters B, 2:no. 199, 686–87; Minutes of SPG Meeting, November 20, 1772, SPG Journals, 19:313–14; Stuart to Rev. Sir, January 8, 1772, SPG Letters B, 2:no. 198, 684; Minutes of SPG Meeting, April 10, 1772, SPG Journals, 19:233–34; Minutes of SPG Meeting, April 16, 1773, SPG Journals, 19:407. A London publisher published Brant's major translated text in 1787, *The Book of Common Prayer and Administration of the Sacraments and Rites . . . to Which Is Added the Gospel according to St. Mark, Translated into the Mohawk Language by Capt. Joseph Brant* (London: Buckton, 1787).

58. Schuyler Indian Papers, 1710–1776, May 19, 1776, NYPL.

59. Schuyler Indian Papers, 1710–1776, May 19, 1776, NYPL; James Axtell, "Scholastic Frontier," in *After Columbus: Essays in the Ethnohistory of Colonial North America* (New York: Oxford University Press, 1988), 72; Graymont, *Iroquois in the American Revolution*, 92–93.

60. Inglis, "Memorial Concerning the Iroquois," October 1, 1771, *DHNY*, 4:1111; *The Oxford English Dictionary*, 2nd ed. (Oxford: Clarendon Press, 1989), 4:121.

61. Robin Lane Fox, "Literacy and Power in Early Christianity," in *Literacy and Power in the Ancient World*, ed. Alan K. Bowman and Greg Woolf (Cambridge: Cambridge University Press, 1994), 126–48; Lamin Sanneh, *Encountering the West: Christianity and the Global Cultural Process: The African Dimension* (Maryknoll, NY: Orbis, 1993), 17.

CHAPTER 6: "AS FORMERLY UNDER THEIR RESPECTIVE CHIEFS"

1. Colin G. Calloway, *The American Revolution in Indian Country: Crisis and Diversity in Native American Communities* (Cambridge: Cambridge University Press, 1995), 290–91. For the impact of the American Revolution on the Haudenosaunees, see also Max M. Mintz, *Seeds of Empire: The American Revolutionary Conquest of the Iroquois* (New York: New York University Press, 1999); Barbara Graymont, *The Iroquois in the American Revolution* (Syracuse, NY: Syracuse University Press, 1972); Isabel Thompson Kelsay, *Joseph Brant, 1743–1807: Man of Two Worlds* (Syracuse, NY: Syracuse University Press, 1984), 161–378; and Calloway, *Revolution in Indian Country*, 129–57.

2. John Wolfe Lydekker, *The Faithful Mohawks* (New York: Macmillan, 1938), 166.

3. Claus to Haldimand, December 15, 1783, Daniel Claus Papers, 1785, National Archives of Canada (Ottawa) (hereafter NAC), 3:273–74; same, Charles M. Johnston, ed., *The Valley of the Six Nations: A Collection of Documents on the Indian Lands of the Grand River* (Toronto: University of Toronto Press, 1964), 42–43; Ernest Cruikshank, "The Coming of the Loyalists Mohawks to the Bay of Quinte," *Papers and Records of the Ontario Historical Society*, no. 6 (1930): 391, 398.

4. Reply of the Indians, delivered by Abraham, a Mohawk Sachem, August 31, 1775, *American Archives*, 9 vols., ser. 4, ed. Peter Force (Washington, DC, 1837–53), 3:485–87, in Caitlin A. Fitz, "'Suspected on Both Sides': Little Abraham, Iroquois Neutrality, and the American Revolution," *Journal of the Early Republic* 28, no. 3 (2008): 299; Graymont, *Iroquois in the American Revolution*, 91–92, 225; Kelsay, *Joseph Brant*, 209, 284–85.

5. Council at Niagara, July 23, 24, 1783, Claus Papers, NAC, 4:245–46, in Graymont, *Iroquois in the American Revolution*, 277; [American] Speech to Mohawks, 1776, in Fitz, "'Suspected on Both Sides,'" 311.

6. Fitz, "'Suspected on Both Sides,'" 299–335; Jon Parmenter, "After the Mourning Wars: The Iroquois as Allies in Colonial North American Campaign, 1676–1760," *WMQ*, 64, no. 1 (2007): 39–82.

7. Eleanor M. Herrington, "Captain John Deserontyon and the Mohawk Settlement at Deserontyon," *Bulletin of the Department of History and Political and Economic Science in Queen's University, Kingston, Ontario, Canada* (1921): 1; Haldimand Papers, n.d., Add. MSS 21, 760, NAC, 5:219.

8. Johnson to Dorchester, January 28, 1790, in Johnston, *Valley of the Six Nations*, 54–55.

9. A. H. Young, "The Rev. Robert Addison: Extracts from the Reports and Journals of the SPG," *Papers and Records of the Ontario Historical Society* 19, no. 4 (1922): 171; R. S. Allen, *His Majesty's Indian Allies: British Indian Policy in Defense of Canada, 1774–1815* (Toronto: Dundurn Press, 1992), 58.

10. Johnson to Dorchester, January 28, 1790, in Johnston, *Valley of the Six Nations,* 54.
11. For studies on Neolin, Tenskwatawa, Tecumseh, Handsome Lake, and other charismatic Native leaders, see Alfred A. Cave, *Prophets of the Great Spirit: Native American Revitalization Movements in Eastern North America* (Lincoln: University of Nebraska Press, 2006); Anthony F. C. Wallace, "Revitalization Movements: Some Theoretical Considerations for their Comparative Study," *American Anthropologist,* 58 (1956): 264—81; Wallace, *The Death and the Rebirth of the Seneca* (New York: Vintage Random House, 1972), esp. pt. 3, 239—337.
12. For a summary of the Mohawk diasporic communities in Upper Canada, see Kelsay, *Joseph Brant,* 394—613.
13. For the political perspective on Native American—Canadian relations in the post-Revolution Great Lakes region, see Johnston, *Valley of the Six Nations,* xxxiii—lxix; Alan Taylor, *The Divided Ground: Indians Settlers, and the Northern Borderlands of the American Revolution* (New York: Alfred A. Knopf, 2006), 326—65; John S. Hagopian, "Joseph Brant vs. Peter Russell: A Re-examination of the Six Nations Land Transactions in the Grand River Valley," *Histoire Sociale/Social History* 30, no. 60 (1997): 300—333; and Allen, *Indian Allies.* See Johnston's lengthy introduction to *Valley of the Six Nations,* ed. Johnston, lxxxix—lxxxviii, for evidence on the struggles of the diasporic Mohawk communities to establish Christianity. For rebuilding the Brantford (Grand River) community through culturally and socially symbolic means, see James W. Paxton, "Merrymaking and Militia Musters: Mohawks, Loyalists, and the (Re)Construction of Community and Identity in Upper Canada," *Ontario History* 102, no. 2 (2010): 218—38.
14. John Webster Grant, *Moon of Wintertime: Missionaries and the Indian of Canada in Encounter since 1534* (Toronto: University of Toronto Press, 1984), 75.
15. Kelsay, *Joseph Brant,* 149—55, 211—12; Calloway, *Revolution in Indian Country,* 137; Taylor, *Divided Ground,* 72—73, 78; Graymont, *Iroquois in the American Revolution,* 284.
16. Taylor, *Divided Ground,* 86—89; F. Douglas Reville, *History of the County of Brant* (Brantford: Hurley, 1920), 33.
17. At Council held in the City of Albany, June 28, 1754, *DRCHNY,* 6:687; Timothy J. Shannon, *Indians and Colonists at the Crossroads of Empire: The Albany Congress of 1754* (Ithaca, NY: Cornell University Press; Cooperstown: New York State Historical Association, 2000), 151.
18. Kelsay, *Joseph Brant,* 190—93; Taylor, *Divided Ground,* 90—91; Daniel R. Mandell, "'Turned Their Minds to Religion': Oquaga and the First Iroquois Church, 1748—1776," *Early American Studies* 11, no. 2 (2013): 238.
19. Kelsay, *Joseph Brant,* 192. On the history of white Americans and some indigenes "playing Indian," see Philip J. Deloria, *Playing Indian* (New Haven, CT: Yale University Press, 1998).
20. Taylor, *Divided Ground,* 91—93; Kelsay, *Joseph Brant,* 205—7; Graymont, *Iroquois in the American Revolution,* 134—47.
21. Taylor, *Divided Ground,* 93—94; Kelsay, *Joseph Brant,* 229—34; Graymont, *Iroquois in the American Revolution,* 168—72.
22. Gansevoort to Sullivan, October 8, 1779, Gansevoort Military Papers, Gansevoort-Lansing Collection, NYPL, 5, in Graymont, *Iroquois in the American Revolution,* 218—19; Taylor, *Divided Ground,* 98; Kelsay, *Joseph Brant,* 267.
23. Sir John Johnson to Haldimand, Haldimand Papers, NAC, Add. MSS. 21, 818, 5:209; Kelsay, *Joseph Brant,* 298; Graymont, *Iroquois in the American Revolution,* 238; Mintz, *Seeds of Empire,* 168.
24. Clinton to President of Congress, February 5, 1781, Continental Congress, Item 67, 2:351—52, as cited in Graymont, *Iroquois in the American Revolution,* 240.

25. April 7, 1779, Claus Papers, NAC, 2: 89–90; Kelsay, *Joseph Brant*, 241.

26. Matthews to Ross, Sept. 9, 1782, NAC, B-124:178–80; Haldimand to J. Johnson, September 9, 1782, B115:8, NAC; Taylor, *Divided Ground*, 106; Graymont, *Iroquois in the American Revolution*, 255.

27. Papers of the Continental Congress, Item 151:137–38, 141–43, 145–46, as cited in Graymont, *Iroquois in the American Revolution*, 225; Barbara J. Sivertsen, *Turtles, Wolves, and Bears: A Mohawk Family History* (Bowie, MD: Heritage Books, 1996), 78, 178.

28. Proceedings with Four Rebel Indians, February 12–18, 1780, Haldimand Papers, NAC, H-1450, B-119:104–8; Graymont, *Iroquois in the American Revolution*, 226–27.

29. Proceedings with Four Rebel Indians, Feb. 12–18, 1780, Haldimand Papers, NAC, H-1450, B-119:104–12; Graymont, *Iroquois in the American Revolution*, 225–228, 259; Johnston, *Valley of the Six Nations*, xxxiii–xxxiv; Fitz, "'Suspected on Both Sides,'" 323–33.

30. *The Correspondence of Lieut. Governor John Graves Simcoe*, ed. Brig. Gen. E. A. Johnson, LL.D. (Toronto: Ontario Historical Society, 1924), 42.

31. Brigadier Gen. Allan MacLean to General Haldimand, May 18, 1783, Haldimand Papers, NAC, H-1447, B-103:175–78; Johnston, *Valley of the Six Nations*, 36–37; Graymont, *Iroquois in the American Revolution*, 260.

32. Brigadier Gen. Allan MacLean to General Haldimand, May 18, 1783, Haldimand Papers, NAC, H-1447, B-103:176; MacLean to Captain Matthews, May 13, 1783, Haldimand Papers, NAC, H-1447, B-103:157.

33. MacLean to Captain Matthews, May 13, 1783, Haldimand Papers, NAC, H-1447, B-103:157; Graymont, *Iroquois in the American Revolution*, 260; Brigadier Gen. Allan MacLean to General Haldimand, May 18, 1783, Haldimand Papers, NAC, H-1447, B-103:182; Kelsay, *Joseph Brant*, 341–43.

34. Claus to Blackburn, June 14, 1783, Claus Papers, NAC, 3:225–26, cited in Graymont, *Iroquois in the American Revolution*, 262. Literacy had become such a commonplace weapon now for many Mohawks when negotiating with whites that at the 1783 conference, the Haudneosaunees demanded written copies of Congress's demands so that they could convey them accurately to the Grand Council back home. Congress refused to comply, lecturing the Haudenosaunees that they could do very well with the wampum belts Congress had provided. Here, Congress confirmed Lévi-Strauss's contention that one party uses literacy to enslave another (see chapter 4). Neville B. Craig, ed., *The Olden Times* (Pittsburgh: Wright & Charlton, 1848), 2:424, cited in Graymont, *Iroquois in the American Revolution*, 279.

35. Graymont, *Iroquois in the American Revolution*, 260

36. Maclean to Haldimand, May 18, 1783, in Johnston, *Valley of the Six Nations*, 36–37; Graymont, *Iroquois in the American Revolution*, 260. Graymont shows that few MPs in Parliament—perhaps three—supported Native claims of sovereignty. These few cited early eighteenth-century precedents, when the British made concessions in past treaties for disfranchised indigenes. However, after being humiliated by the Americans and outraged by the ineptitude of the Crown's advisers, few MPs were in any mood to listen to or acknowledge these precedents. See Graymont, *Iroquois in the American Revolution*, 260–62.

37. William Johnson to Lords of Trade, October 8, 1764, *DRCHNY*, 7:659; Kelsay, *Joseph Brant*, 60–70.

38. Graymont, *Iroquois in the American Revolution*, 259–91; Hagopian, "Joseph Brant vs. Peter Russell," 305–7.

39. Council at Niagara, July 23, 24, 1783, Claus Papers, NAC, 4:245–46; Graymont, *Iroquois in the American Revolution*, 277; Hagopian, "Joseph Brant vs. Peter Russell," 305–7.

40. Jeffrey Olster, "'To Extirpate the Indians': An Indigenous Consciousness of Genocide in the Ohio Valley and Lower Great Lakes, 1750s–1810," *WMQ* 72, no. 4 (2015): 587; Kelsay, *Joseph Brant*, 255; Calloway, *Revolution in Indian Country*, 132–33; Mintz, *Seeds of Empire*, 155.

41. John Johnson to Haldimand, May 18, 1783, NAC, B-115:105; Haldimand to J. Johnson, May 26, 1782, NAC, B-115:113–15; Haldimand to North, June 2, 1783, NAC, B-56:66–68; Graymont, *Iroquois in the American Revolution*, 263.

42. MacLean to Haldimand, June 22, 1783, NAC, B-103:216–17; Claus to Haldimand, December 15, 1783, Haldimand Papers, NAC, B-114:300; same, December 15, 1783, Claus Papers, NAC, 3:275; Graymont, *Iroquois in the American Revolution*, 264.

43. Haldimand to Johnson, March 23, 1784, in Johnston, *Valley of the Six Nations*, 43; Joseph Brant to Johnson, December 15, 1797, in Johnston, *Valley of the Six Nations*, 239; Haldimand's Proclamation of October 25, 1784, in Johnston, *Valley of the Six Nations*, 51; Haldimand to Claus, December 17, 1783, Claus Papers, NAC, 3:277; Graymont, *Iroquois in the American Revolution*, 263.

44. Calloway, *Revolution in Indian Country*, 153.

45. Haldimand's Proclamation of October 25, 1784, in Johnston, *Valley of the Six Nations*, 51, xxxviii; Substance of Brant's Wishes Respecting Forming a Settlement of the Grand River, Haldimand's Papers, NAC, H-1655, B-169:131–35; same, in Johnston, *Valley of the Six Nations*, 44; *Correspondence of Simcoe*, 58; Johnson, *Valley of the Six Nations*, xxxviii, 239; Graymont, *Iroquois in the American Revolution*, 284, 293–94.

46. A. S. De Peyster to Haldimand, June 28, 1784, Haldimand Papers, NAC, H-1447, B-103:443; same, in Johnston, *Valley of the Six Nations*, 49; Calloway, *American Revolution in Indian Country*, 153.

47. David T. McNabb, "'The Promise That He Gave to My Grand Father Was Very Sweet': The Gun Shot Treaty of 1792 at the Bay of Quinte," *Canadian Journal of Native Studies* 16, no. 2 (1996): 293–314.

48. Deserontyon to John Johnson, February 15, 1785, Claus Papers, NAC, 4:69; Graymont, *Iroquois in the American Revolution*, 251, 285. Note that other Haudenosaunees and their allies settled along the Grand River. By 1785, 1,843 indigenes lived here, including 448 Mohawks, 174 "council Fire" Onondagas, 50 Onondagas of Bear Foot's party, among others. See Calloway, *Revolution in Indian Country*, 155. A new council fire was established at Ohsweken on the Grand River. Census of the Six Nations, NAC, B-103:457.

49. François Jean de Chastellux, *Travels in North America in the Years 1780, 1781, and 1782*, ed. Howard C. Rice Jr., 2 vols. (Chapel Hill: University of North Carolina Press, 1963), 1:208; Graymont, *Iroquois in the American Revolution*, 242.

50. Chastellux, *Travels in North America*, 1:208. These refugee families also suffered from smallpox, famine, and inadequate clothing. The 185 blankets provided by the New York Legislature were not enough to cover the more than four hundred Native bodies. Graymont, *Iroquois in the American Revolution*, 242–43.

51. "Substance of Brant's Wishes Respecting Forming a Settlement of the Grand River," Haldimand's Papers, NAC, H-1655, B-169:132; same, in Johnston, *Valley of the Six Nations*, 44; E. Reginald Good, "Lost Inheritance: Alienation of Six Nations' Lands In Upper Canada, 1784–1805," *Journal of Mennonite Studies* 19 (2001): 93–95; Kelsay, *Joseph Brant*, 372. Historians disagree over the amount of land Brant received personally. Their figures range from 570,000 acres (Alan Taylor) to one million acres (E. Reginald Good). I believe the amount of acreage was somewhere between 635,000 and 700,000 acres.

52. Castlereagh to Sir James Craig, April 8, 1808, in Johnston, *Valley of the Six Nations*, 280; Daniel J. Boorstin, *The Lost World of Thomas Jefferson* (Chicago: University of Chicago Press, 1981), 87, 101; Thomas Jefferson, *Notes of the State of Virginia* (New

York: Harpers Books, 1964), 133; *The Writings off Thomas Jefferson*, ed. Andrew A. Lipscomb and Albert E. Bergh, 20 vols. (Washington, DC: Thomas Jefferson Memorial Service, 1903), 15:452, cited in Fawn M. Brodie, *Thomas Jefferson: An Intimate History* (New York: W. W. Norton, 1974), 43.

53. Jefferson, *Notes*, 132–39.

54. Kelsay, *Joseph Brant*, 576; William Stone, *The Life of Joseph Brant, Thayendanegea*, 2 vols. (New York: G. Dearborn, 1838; reprint, Albany: Munsell, 1865), 2:455. Brant's third wife, Catherine Croghan, whom he married in 1779, was biracial. Brant to Kirkland, March 8, 1791, in Johnston, *Valley of the Six Nations*, 269.

55. A Visit with Joseph Brant on the Grand River, 1792, Campbell, *Travels in North America*, in Johnston, *Valley of the Six Nations*, 59–65.

56. Paxton, "Merrymaking and Militia Musters," 225.

57. Substance of Brant's Wishes Respecting Forming a Settlement of the Grand River, Haldimand's Papers, NAC, H-1655, B-169:132–34; same, in Johnston, *Valley of the Six Nations*, 44–43; Lord North to Haldimand, August 8, 1783, in Johnston, *Valley of the Six Nations*, 42. Molly Brant, named "Mary" in the records, received a pension of 100 pounds annually. She and Joseph placed their total losses at 1,449 pounds, 14 shillings, and 9 pence, almost $250,000 today. See "Schedule of Losses," NAC, Q24, 2:299–325; Graymont, *Iroquois in the American Revolution*, 285.

58. Lord North to Haldimand, August 8, 1783, in Johnston, *Valley of the Six Nations*, 42.

59. Brant to Joseph Chew, March 5, 1795, NAC, RG8, 48:46; Good, "Lost Inheritance," 93; E. B. Littlehales to Francis Le Maistre, quoting undated letters from Brant, probably March 29, 1795, in Johnston, *Valley of the Six Nations*, 77.

60. Simcoe to Dorchester, December 6, 1793, in Johnston, *Valley of the Six Nations*, 75; John White to Peter Russell, September 26, 1796, *The Correspondence of Peter Russell*, ed. E. A. Cruikshank, 3 vols. (Toronto: Ontario Historical Society, 1932), 1:46; Good, "Lost Inheritance," 94.

61. Brant's Address to William Claus on the Subject of the Indian Lands, November 24, 1796, in Johnston, *Valley of the Six Nations*, 82.

62. Peter Russell to John Graves Simcoe, September 22, 1796, *The Correspondence of Peter Russell*, 1:134–35; Taylor, *Divided Ground*, 335.

63. Peter Russell to Simcoe, September 22, 1796, in Johnston, *Valley of the Six Nations*, 79; Allen, *Indian Allies*, 57.

64. Robert Liston to Robert Prescott, April 8, 1797, in Johnston, *Valley of the Six Nations*, 85; Taylor, *Divided Ground*, 336; Kelsay, *Joseph Brant*, 574–76.

65. Memoir of William Dummer Powell, 1797, in Johnston, *Valley of the Six Nations*, 90; Russell to Prescott, May 30, 1797, in Johnston, *Valley of the Six Nations*, 86; Taylor, *Divided Ground*, 336.

66. Memoir of William Dummer Powell, 1797, in Johnston, *Valley of the Six Nations*, 90–91. Alan Taylor believes the Dummer memoir is an unreliable source. See Taylor, *Divided Ground*, 338, 486n41.

67. E. B. Littlehales to Francis Le Maistre, quoting undated letters from Brant, in Johnston, *Valley of the Six Nations*, 77; Formal Transfer of the Grand River Tracts, February 5, 1798, in Johnston, *Valley of the Six Nations*, 97–98; Good, "Lost Inheritance," 94–95; Taylor, *Divided Ground*, 330, 336, 338. Claus replaced Brant's preferred choice, John Ferguson, the husband of Brant's niece Magdalene Johnson, whom Russell probably presumed was too attached to Brant to act as a disinterested trustee.

68. Castlereagh to Craig, April 8, 1809, in Johnston, *Valley of the Six Nations*, 280–81; Formal Transfer of the Grand River Tracts, February 5, 1798, in Johnston, *Valley of the Six Nations*, 97–98; Good, "Lost Inheritance," 95–99; A. S. De Peyster to Haldimand, June 28, 1784, Haldimand Papers, NAC, H-1447, B-103:443; same, in Johnston, *Valley of the Six Nations*, 49; Calloway, *Revolution in Indian Country*, 153; Deserontyon to

John Johnson, February 15, 1785, Claus Papers, NAC, 4:69; Graymont, *Iroquois in the American Revolution*, 251, 285; Speech by John Deserontyon at Council at the Bay of Quinte, September 2–10, 1800, in Johnston, *Valley of the Six Nations*, 54.

69. Stuart to SPG, February 23, 1792, SPG Journals, 26:22.

70. Joseph Brant to Johnson, December 15, 1797, in Johnston, *Valley of the Six Nations*, 238; William Claus to Peter Hunter, January 19, 1805, in Taylor, *Divided Ground*, 351; William Claus reply, August 17, 1803, in Johnston, *Valley of the Six Nations*, 133; Kelsay, *Joseph Brant*, 633; Taylor, *Divided Ground*, 351–52.

71. John Stuart to Rev. Sir, October 13, 1781, SPG Letters B, 2:no. 204, 702–3; Memoir of John Stuart, n.d., *DHNY*, 4:505–9; Peter W. Walker, "The Church Militant: The American Loyalist Clergy and the Making of the British Counterrevolution, 1701–1792" (PhD diss., Columbia University, 2016), 142–53.

72. John Stuart to Rev. Sir, October 13, 1781, SPG Letters B, 2:no. 204, 702–4; Memoir of John Stuart, n.d., *DHNY*, 4:512.

73. Minutes of SPG Meeting, January 25, 1782, SPG Journals, 22:368–69; same, December 20, 1782, SPG Journals, 23:2, 6–8. The SPG documents spell Paulus's surname "Sahonwadi," which I assume is a variation of "Saghsanowana," the surname of the schoolmaster Paulus Peters of Canajoharie.

74. John Stuart to SPG, May 25, 1784, SPG Journals, 23:379; same, July 17, 1784, SPG Journals, 23:409, 411; same, May 25, 1785, SPG Journals, 24:141; same, September 26, 1786, SPG Journals, 24:362.

75. John Stuart to SPG, May 25, 1784, SPG Journals, 23:379–81; same, Montreal, July 17, 1784, SPG Journals, 33:417; same, June 20 and August 14, 1787, SPG Journals, 25:25. The Book of Matthew is perhaps the most translated and taught book of the Bible, because unlike the book of Mark, on which it is based, it explains the full divinity of Christ as the son of God.

76. Stuart to SPG, July 2, 1788, SPG Journals, 25:123; same, February 23, 1789, SPG Journals, 25:223; same, October 4, 1790, SPG Journals, 25:322; same, July 5, 1791, SPG Journals, 25:393; same, February 3, 1791, SPG Journals, 25:364.

77. Stuart to SPG, February 23, 1789, SPG Journals, 25:223; same, February 3, 1791, SPG Journals, 25:364.

78. Stuart to SPG, October 4, 1790, SPG Journals, 25:321–22.

79. Stuart to SPG, July 5, 1791, SPG Journals, 25:393; Taylor, *Divided Ground*, 359. The society agreed to raise Norton's annual salary from 17 pounds to 30 pounds (about $4,700 today) if he returned to his post. He declined.

80. Stuart to SPG, February 3, 1791, SPG Journals, 25:363, 365; same, February 23, 1792, SPG Journals, 26:22.

81. Stuart to SPG, February 23, 1789, SPG Journals, 25:223; same, October 4, 1790, SPG Journals, 25:321; same, October 5, 1791, SPG Journals, 25:425–26. The Mohawks laid the floor themselves in the chapel, but hired a mason to plaster the interior walls and to do stonework.

82. Eleanor M. Herrington, "Captain John Deserontyon and the Mohawk Settlement at Deserontyon," *Bulletin of the Department of History and Political and Economic Science in Queen's University, Kingston, Ontario, Canada* (1921): 9, 13; Cruikshank, "Loyalists Mohawks," *Papers and Records of the Ontario Historical Society* 6 (1930): 402–3; Charles Johnston, "Joseph Brant, the Grand River Lands, and the Northwest Crisis," *Ontario History* 55, no. 4 (1963): 271; Kelsay, *Joseph Brant*, 541; Taylor, *Divided Ground*, 336.

83. Stuart to SPG, March 19, 1793, SPG Journals, 26:166; same, October 15, 1793, SPG Journals, 26:201; Stuart to SPG, n.d., SPG Journals, 26:300.

84. Stuart to SPG, n.d., SPG Journals, 26:300; same, April 10, 1795, SPG Journals, 26:375–76.

85. Stuart to SPG, n.d., SPG Journals, 26:300; same, October 12, 1795, SPG Journals, 26:421. The disease described by Stuart may have been either tuberculosis, a common chronic and often fatal communicable disease characterized by intermittent fever, or typhus, an often fatal disease caused by a bacteria carried by fleas, ticks, and mites, which were common pests in homes and factories.
86. Stuart to SPG, April 10, 1795, SPG Journals, 26:375–76; same, March 15, 1794, SPG Journals, 26:343.
87. Stuart to SPG, July 27, 1796, SPG Journals, 27:112; same, November 14, 1796, SPG Journals, 27:180; same, November 14, 1796, SPG Journals, 27:181; same, Kingston, August 3, 1797, SPG Journals, 27:235.
88. Gerald Vizenor, *Manifest Manners: Narratives of Postindian Survivance* (Lincoln: University of Nebraska Press, 1994), 64; Gerald Vizenor, *Native Liberty: Natural Reason and Cultural Survivance* (Lincoln: University of Nebraska Press, 2009), 1, 85, 98–103. See Daniel R. Mandel, *Behind the Frontier: Indians in Eighteenth-Century Eastern Massachusetts* (Lincoln: University of Nebraska Press, 1996), chap. 4, for indigenes "living more like their Christian neighbors."
89. Stuart to SPG, August 3, 1797, SPG Journals, 27:235; same, October 9, 1797, SPG Journals, 27:269.
90. Stuart to SPG, July 14, 1784, SPG Journals, 38:410–11; Claus to Haldimand, September 27, 1781, NAC, B-114:200; Claus to William Morice, October 10, 1781, Claus Papers, NAC, 3:49–50.
91. Stuart to SPG, October 1, 1785, SPG Journals, 24:191; same, July 2, 1788, in Johnston, *Valley of the Six Nations*, 236–37. See also series of excerpted letters from Stuart to SPG in which he discusses life and faith on the Grand River, October 4, 1790–August 27, 1795, in Johnston, *Valley of the Six Nations*, 237–38.
92. A Visit with Joseph Brant on the Grand River, 1792, Campbell, *Travels in North America*, in Johnston, *Valley of the Six Nations*, 59–65.
93. Stuart to SPG, July 2, 1788, SPG Journals, 25:121–23. Stuart breaks Brantford down demographically as follows: men, 120; women, 154; children, 125; for a total of 399.
94. Joseph Brant to Johnson, December 15, 1797, in Johnston, *Valley of the Six Nations*, 238; Stuart to SPG, June 20 and August 14, 1787, SPG Journals, 25:26. The Acts of the Apostles recount the first thirty years of the early Christian church, thus a history translatable to the experiences of displaced Mohawks.
95. On Stuart wanting to give up the Grand River mission, see Stuart to SPG, July 5, 1791, SPG Journals, 25:393. On Addison's appointment to Niagara, see SPG Journals, 25:366; Addison to SPG, April 29, 1792, SPG Journals, 26:45; same, October 3, 1792, SPG Journals, 26:80. On Addison and the Mohawks, see Addison to SPG, April 6, 1793, SPG Journals, 26:180–81; Addison to SPG, October 23, 1793, SPG Journals, 26:217; Stuart to SPG, October 10, 1793, SPG Journals, 26:200.
96. Addison to SPG, Niagara, June 27, 1796, SPG Journals, 27:114; same, Niagara, May 3, 1798, SPG Journals, 27:373; Stuart to SPG, Kingston, October 10, 1793, SPG Journals, 26:200.
97. Brant to John Johnson, December 15, 1797, in Stone, *Life of Joseph Brant*, 2:433–44; same, December 15, 1797, in Johnston, *Valley of the Six Nations*, 238; Stuart to SPG, October 11, 1798, in Johnston, *Valley of the Six Nations*, 241; Addison to SPG, December 29, 1799, in Johnston, *Valley of the Six Nations*, 241–42; Kelsay, *Joseph Brant*, 547, 609–11; Taylor, *Divided Ground*, 353–54.
98. Brant's Power of Attorney to Sell the Indian Lands, November 2, 1796, and Russell to Prescott (with enclosures), February 19, 1798, in Johnston, *Valley of the Six Nations*, 98, 101, 102.
99. Johnson to Dorchester, January 28, 1790, in Johnston, *Valley of the Six Nations*, 54–55.
100. Taylor, *Divided Ground*, 352; Kelsay, *Joseph Brant*, 611–13; Elisabeth Tooker,

"The Iroquois White Dog Sacrifice in the Latter Part of the Eighteenth Century," *Ethnohistory* 12, no. 1 (1965): 131–37; Elisabeth Tooker, *The Iroquois Ceremonial of Midwinter* (Syracuse, NY: Syracuse University Press, 1970), vii, 114–18; William Fenton, "Northern Iroquoian Culture Patterns," in *Handbook of North American Indians: Northeast*, ed. Bruce G. Trigger (Washington, DC: Smithsonian Institution, 1978), 15:316. For evidence of other Native cultures that sacrificed dogs, see William C. Sturtevant, "Oklahoma Seneca-Cayuga," and E. S. Rogers, "Southeastern Ojibwa," both in Trigger, *Handbook*, 15:541 and 15:764, respectively.

101. William N. Fenton, "Locality as a Basic Factor in the Development of Iroquois Social Structure," *Bulletin* (Washington, DC: Smithsonian Institution, Bureau of American Ethnology) 149, no. 3 (1951): 40.

102. Haldimand to John Chew, April 22, 1784, in Johnston, *Valley of the Six Nations*, 46.

103. Stuart to SPG, November 14, 1796, SPG Journals, 27:181; same, August 3, 1797, SPG Journals, 27:235; same, October 9, 1797, SPG Journals, 27:269.

104. Grant, *Moon of Wintertime*, 248, 263.

## CONCLUSION

1. John Webster Grant, *Moon of Wintertime: Missionaries and the Indians of Canada in Encounters since 1534* (Toronto: University of Toronto Press, 1984, 1992), 249–50.

2. Daniel K. Richter, *The Ordeal of the Longhouse: The Peoples of the Iroquois League in the Era of European Colonization* (Chapel Hill: University of North Carolina Press, 1992); Daniel K. Richter, "Iroquois versus Iroquois: Jesuit Missions and Christianity in Village Politics, 1642–1686," *Ethnohistory* 32, no. 1 (1985): 1–16.

3. David K. Jordan, "The Glyphomancy Factor: Observations on Chinese Conversion," in *Conversion to Christianity: Historical and Anthropological Perspectives on a Great Transformation*, ed. Robert W. Hefner (Berkeley: University of California Press, 1993), 286. See also David Snow and Richard Machalek, "The Sociology of Conversion," *Annual Review of Sociology* 10 (1984): 169–74, for a summary and analysis of the various categories that sociologists of religion have used to explain conversions.

4. Anthony F. C. Wallace, "Revitalization Movements: Some Theoretical Considerations for their Comparative Study," *American Anthropologist* 58, no. 2 (1956): 264–81; A. F. C. Wallace, "The Dekanawidah Myth Analyzed as the Record of a Revitalization Movement," *Ethnohistory* 5, no. 1 (1958): 118–30.

5. Kenneth Morrison, "Discourse and the Accommodation of Values: Toward A Revision of Mission History," *Journal of the American Academy of Religion* 53, no. 3 (1985): 365–82.

6. "Account of the discriptions [*sic*] given by Mr. Norton Concerning his Country customs & manners," recorded by Headley, Cambridge, March 12, 1805, archives of New York State Library, folio 23, 26.

7. "Ogden Council of July 1819," Letters Received by the Secretary of War Relating to Indian Affairs, 1800–23, microfilm, M-127, reel 2 of 4 (Washington, DC: National Archives), frames 1475–76, in Granville Ganter, "Red Jacket and the Decolonization of Republican Virtue," *American Indian Quarterly* 31, no. 4 (2007): 573.

8. Journals of Rev. Thompson S. Harris, 289, in Mark A. Nicholas, "Practicing Local Faith and Local Politics: Senecas, Presbyterians, and a 'New Indian Mission History,'" *Pennsylvania History* 73, no. 1 (2006): 74.

9. Goldwin French, *Parsons and Politics: The Role of the Wesleyan Methodists in Upper Canada and the Maritimes from 1780 to 1855* (Toronto: Ryerson Press, 1962), 17–72; C. M. Johnston, *Brant County: A History 1784–1945* (Toronto: Oxford University Press, 1967), 10, 89–91.

# INDEX

Page references in *italics* refer to illustrations and photos.